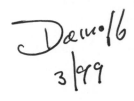

P9-DIW-389

Learning, Remembering, Believing

ENHANCING HUMAN PERFORMANCE

Daniel Druckman and Robert A. Bjork, *Editors*

Committee on Techniques for the Enhancement
of Human Performance

Commission on Behavioral and Social Sciences and Education

National Research Council

NATIONAL ACADEMY PRESS
Washington, D.C. 1994

NATIONAL ACADEMY PRESS • 2101 Constitution Avenue, N.W. • Washington, D.C. 20418

NOTICE: The project that is the subject of this report was approved by the Governing Board of the National Research Council, whose members are drawn from the councils of the National Academy of Sciences, the National Academy of Engineering, and the Institute of Medicine. The members of the committee responsible for the report were chosen for their special competences and with regard for appropriate balance.

This report has been reviewed by a group other than the authors according to procedures approved by a Report Review Committee consisting of members of the National Academy of Sciences, the National Academy of Engineering, and the Institute of Medicine.

The work of the Committee on Techniques for the Enhancement of Human Performance is supported by the U.S. Army Research Institute.

Library of Congress Cataloging-in-Publication Data

Learning, remembering, believing : enhancing human performance /
    Daniel Druckman and Robert A. Bjork, editors.
        p.   cm.
    Includes bibliographical references and index.
    "Committee on Techniques for the Enhancement of Human Performance,
Commission on Behavioral and Social Sciences and Education, National
Research Council."
    ISBN 0-309-04993-8
    1. Performance—Psychological aspects. 2. Learning, Psychology
of. I. Druckman, Daniel, 1939– . II. Bjork, Robert A.
III. National Research Council (U.S.). Committee on Techniques for
the Enhancement of Human Performance.
BF481.L43 1994   94-21350
153.1—dc20   CIP

Copyright 1994 by the National Academy of Sciences. All rights reserved.

Printed in the United States of America

COMMITTEE ON TECHNIQUES FOR THE ENHANCEMENT OF HUMAN PERFORMANCE

ROBERT A. BJORK (*Chair*), Department of Psychology. University of California, Los Angeles

DONALD F. DANSEREAU, Department of Psychology, Texas Christian University

ERIC EICH, Department of Psychology, University of British Columbia

DEBORAH L. FELTZ, School of Health Education, Counseling Psychology, and Human Performance, Michigan State University

LARRY L. JACOBY, Department of Psychology, McMaster University

DAVID W. JOHNSON, Department of Educational Psychology, University of Minnesota

JOHN F. KIHLSTROM, Department of Psychology, University of Arizona

ROBERTA KLATZKY, Department of Psychology, University of California, Santa Barbara

LYNNE M. REDER, Department of Psychology, Carnegie-Mellon University

DANIEL M. WEGNER, Department of Psychology, University of Virginia

ROBERT B. ZAJONC, Department of Psychology, University of Michigan

DANIEL DRUCKMAN, *Study Director*

CINDY S. PRINCE, *Project Assistant*

The National Academy of Sciences is a private, nonprofit, self-perpetuating society of distinguished scholars engaged in scientific and engineering research, dedicated to the further-ance of science and technology and to their use for the general welfare. Upon the authority of the charter granted to it by the Congress in 1863, the Academy has a mandate that requires it to advise the federal government on scientific and technical matters. Dr. Bruce M. Alberts is president of the National Academy of Sciences.

The National Academy of Engineering was established in 1964, under the charter of the National Academy of Sciences, as a parallel organization of outstanding engineers. It is autonomous in its administration and in the selection of its members, sharing with the National Academy of Sciences the responsibility for advising the federal government. The National Academy of Engineering also sponsors engineering programs aimed at meeting national needs, encourages education and research, and recognizes the superior achievements of engineers. Dr. Robert M. White is president of the National Academy of Engineering.

The Institute of Medicine was established in 1970 by the National Academy of Sciences to secure the services of eminent members of appropriate professions in the examination of policy matters pertaining to the health of the public. The Institute acts under the responsibility given to the National Academy of Sciences by its congressional charter to be an adviser to the federal government and, upon its own initiative, to identify issues of medical care, research, and education. Dr. Kenneth I. Shine is president of the Institute of Medicine.

The National Research Council was organized by the National Academy of Sciences in 1916 to associate the broad community of science and technology with the Academy's pur-poses of furthering knowledge and advising the federal government. Functioning in accor-dance with general policies determined by the Academy, the Council has become the principal operating agency of both the National Academy of Sciences and the National Academy of Engineering in providing services to the government, the public, and the scientific and engi-neering communities. The Council is administered jointly by both Academies and the Institute of Medicine. Dr. Bruce M. Alberts and Dr. Robert M. White are chairman and vice chairman, respectively, of the National Research Council.

Contents

PART V NEW DIRECTIONS

APPENDICES

Preface

This is the third report of the Committee on Techniques for the Enhancement of Human Performance (CTEHP). The committee's first two reports, *Enhancing Human Performance: Issues, Theories, and Techniques* and *In the Mind's Eye: Enhancing Human Performance*, issued in 1988 and 1991, respectively, attracted the attention of both researchers and the public. Press conferences for the reports' releases were well attended, the committee's principal conclusions were featured prominently in the media, and reviews of each report appeared in a number of magazines and professional journals. Both books were reprinted in paperback versions.

At the first meeting of the committee in June of 1985, none of its members could have predicted that now, almost 9 years later, the committee would be about to publish its third report, with an agenda for a fourth phase of committee activities mostly in place. The 14 members of the committee, selected for their expertise in relevant basic science areas, were charged with assessing the promise of some "new age" techniques designed to enhance human performance. The Army Research Institute, responding to advocates in the Army as well as in other governmental agencies and in the private sector, had asked the National Research Council of the National Academy of Sciences to convene a committee to evaluate a range of specific techniques, each of which was accompanied by claims of extraordinary effectiveness. Those techniques, developed largely outside the academic research establishment, offered to accelerate learning, foster group cohesion, and—in the parapsychological domain—produce remote viewing and psychokinetic control of electronic devices.

To the charter members of the committee, the committee's task seemed well defined, if somewhat novel. The committee began its work under the assumption that it was embarking on a one-time mission. By the time the first report was released, however, another full agenda for the committee had emerged, partly as a consequence of research developments, both basic and applied, partly as a consequence of the success of certain techniques in the marketplace, and partly as a consequence of changing needs and concerns of the Army. During the committee's second phase (1988–1991), and again in its third phase (1991–1994), the same process occurred.

While the committee continues to live on well past its original life expectancy, it continues to evolve and change as well. In part, that is a matter of changing personnel: of the 12 individuals responsible for the current report, only Daniel Druckman, our study director, and I were involved in the committee's first phase. Beyond changes in personnel, however, the committee has broadened its focus to include potential innovations based on developments in the mainstream of basic research, as well as unusual or controversial techniques developed outside that mainstream. What has stayed largely in place across the committee's phases is its method of operation. Site visits to applied settings, both military and civilian, are an intrinsic aspect of the committee process, as are briefings of the entire committee by advocates, critics, and neutral parties (see Appendix A for a summary of those activities during the committee's current phase). Highly interactive discussions, motivated in part by the need to achieve consensus—every member of the committee must sign off on all of the committee's final conclusions and recommendations—are also an indispensable part of the process.

Veterans of this committee, of which there are now 27, have seemed unanimous in their opinion that serving on the committee was an eye-opening experience. Although each committee member was selected for his or her expertise relevant to some of the issues on the committee's agenda, the give and take of the committee process required that each member become educated, so to speak, about issues and research findings well outside his or her area of expertise. In an era of increased specialization, this kind of challenging and broadening experience has become increasingly rare for scientists in all fields. Serving on the committee also involved interactions with real-world practitioners, who daily face the concrete goal of trying to optimize the performance of individuals or groups in classroom, job, and military settings of various types.

For me, serving on the committee during its first phase and chairing it during phases two and three has been by far the most interesting and rewarding committee assignment of my professional career. It has certainly been an instructive experience, one evidence of which is the discussion of institutional impediments to effective training in the epilogue of this volume. Good things must end, however, and it is time now for a new committee led by a new chair to move on to another set of important issues, and for me to move on to other responsibilities. I will look back on my nine year's involvement with the committee with fondness, and with an appreciation for the extent to which my world view has been altered by the experience: the view from the ivory tower will never be quite the same.

My final duty as outgoing chair is a pleasant one: thanking those who have contributed to the huge effort represented by this report. An appropriate place to start is with the Army Research Institute (ARI), the sponsor of this committee throughout its existence. Edgar M. Johnson, director of ARI, has been a constant source of support, encouragement, and good counsel during the life of the committee. He has managed to avoid even a hint of trying to influence how the committee might carry out its job, while at the same time being a resource to the committee and facilitating activities the committee thought important, such as making site visits to Army locations, gaining access to prior ARI reports, and scheduling briefings of the committee by key ARI personnel. He has our gratitude and respect. We also appreciate the efforts of George Lawton, the ARI liaison to the committee, who was a valuable source of information and advice throughout the current phase of the committee's activities.

A number of individuals gave time and effort to host site visits by the committee. Brigadier General William G. Carter, commanding officer at the Army's National Training Center at Fort Irwin, California, hosted a particularly instructive visit by the entire committee. We appreciate his efforts and those of the staff, whose patience, good humor, and logistical efficiency helped make that visit maximally informative. Other very useful site visits were hosted by Robert Welp, at the National Training Center of the Federal Aviation Administration in Oklahoma City; by John Seely Brown, vice president for advanced research, and Professor James Greeno, senior scientist, at Xerox Palo Alto Research Center; by Michael Brown, director of nuclear training, and Raymond Mulligan, curriculum development coordinator, at the L. F. Sillin, Jr. Nuclear Training Center in Connecticut; by Nels Klyver, Police Training Administrator at the Los Angeles Police Academy; by Barbara Black, director of the ARI field unit and Major Milton Koger of the ARI unit at Fort Knox in Kentucky; and by Elaine Colburn and Julie Crooks, senior simulation analysts at Illusions Engineering in Westlake Village, California. Each of those individuals took time away from their other responsibilities to help the committee; on behalf of the committee I want to express my appreciation to each of them.

Other individuals helped the committee locate certain background materials. We are grateful to Professor Peter Suedfeld at the University of British Columbia for help in locating literature on the REST (restricted environmental stimulation) technique discussed in Chapter 9, to Professor David Orme-Johnson at Marharishi University for making materials on Transcendental Meditation available, and to Norman Freeberg and Judith Orasanu of the Educational Testing Service and the National Aeronautics and Space Administration-Ames, respectively, for providing reports on team performance.

Among the staff at the National Research Council who assisted the committee, several individuals were especially helpful. While our study director worked on an overseas assignment during the summer of 1992, staff officer Anne Mavor kept all work on track. Cindy Prince, Susan Shuttleworth, and Carolyn Sax labored over drafts of the manuscript. The committee is especially indebted to Eugenia Grohman, associate director for reports of the Commission on Behavioral and Social Sciences and Education: this report, like the two before it, benefited from her skillful, if none too gentle, editorial hand. We appreciate her efforts in making technical writing readable. We also appreciate Elaine McGarraugh's thorough and organized job of proofing and copy editing the entire manuscript. Our report also profited greatly from the anonymous reviewers who provided many important criticisms and suggestions.

Finally, I want to thank the members of the committee and certain other individuals who contributed directly to this report. The contributions of professors Daniel McIntosh at the University of Denver and Colleen Kelley at Macalester College to Chapters 10 and 4, respectively, were very substantial and significant. General Paul Gorman (ret.), consultant to the committee, was a remarkable resource. The richness of his knowledge and experience repeatedly helped frame issues in a meaningful way for the committee. Professor Bernie Weiner, a friend and colleague at the University of California at Los Angeles, also provided valuable input and advice to the committee.

To the committee members themslves, I am indebted not only for their cooperation and broad scholarship, but also for their insights and quick humor. The committee's discussions frequently had more the character of an interactive seminar than a committee meeeting; I will miss the unique education afforded by these sessions. To Dan Druckman, our study director, I owe a special debt; it has been a privilege to pull in the same harness with him for almost a decade. He brings to an extraordinarily difficulty job a unique mix of attributes, among which are persistence, patience, and a rare blend of academic and administrative abilities. He has my profound respect, and I treasure the friendship that emerged from our shared mission.

ROBERT A. BJORK, *Chair*
Committee on Techniques for the
Enhancement of Human Performance

Learning, Remembering, Believing

**ENHANCING
HUMAN
PERFORMANCE**

PART I

Overview

The two chapters of this part provide the background and summary of the committee's study. Chapter 1 describes the topics undertaken in this third phase of the committee's work and the relationships between these topics and earlier work done by the committee. It also presents the issues addressed in this book in light of broad questions in human learning and performance.

Chapter 2 summarizes the committee's key findings and conclusions for each chapter. Three types of conclusions are presented: those that summarize implications from completed research on each topic, those that call for needed research, and those that have practical implications for training or performance. The committee's detailed conclusions are presented in the final sections of each chapter.

1

Background

Questions about the "best" way to enhance performance are asked by practitioners in a variety of fields, often in the context of private or public training programs, and large markets exist for techniques to enhance performance. In its first report, the Committee on Techniques for the Enhancement of Human Performance noted that such techniques "have been actively promoted by entrepreneurs who sense a profitable market in self-improvement" (Druckman and Swets, 1988:5); but the committee found that strong claims were seldom accompanied by solid evidence of effectiveness. In its second book, the committee turned from an evaluation of specific techniques to a consideration of more basic issues of performance (Druckman and Bjork, 1991). Many of these issues were addressed in the context of how to train people to acquire and maintain job-related skills, especially the skills needed to accomplish organizational missions.

In continuing its work, the committee in this book examines recent research in learning, memory and cognition, emotions, and social and team processes and their implications for application. The committee pays less attention to the applied research on training and learning in work organizations, including work done in industrial settings on technology issues (e.g., Goldstein, 1993). Parts II and III of this volume examine current issues of learning and performance for individuals and teams. Part IV evaluates techniques for enhancing performance that are accompanied by strong claims of effectiveness. Finally, in Part V, the committee calls attention to some new directions that may have promise for future research and application. Our overall mission is to consider human technologies that are not dependent on major expenditures or high-technology equipment. Similarly, our emphasis on performance enhancement deals primarily with differences between treatments or techniques that apply widely to broadly defined populations, such as an evaluation of effects due to cooperative learning or team-building versus appropriate control conditions; differences among the individuals involved in these treatments or techniques are only occasionally discussed. These emphases may be viewed as complementing the work of other National Research Council committees whose missions are to study high-technology innovations or individual differences. Our findings and conclusions are regarded as being broadly applicable to a wide range of settings and populations, in both private and public organizations.

This book, like the previous volumes produced by the committee, brings basic research to bear on a number of applied issues related to performance. The applied issues drove the selection of topics, but they did not determine the way in which the topics were treated. Each chapter develops the implications for application from the completed research. In some cases, the research provides a basis for making decisions about implementing programs. In some other cases, the research discourages proceeding with certain techniques. And for other topics there is a glimpse of promising avenues for further exploration. Enhancing our perspective on training, the book is framed by two chapters that address very broad issues. The first chapter addresses issues related to situated learning, providing evidence that contributes to the debate over the extent to which training programs ought to be situated in real-world tasks. The final chapter considers the possible effects of organizational factors on decisions to develop training programs and how they are implemented.

CONTINUITIES IN THE STUDY OF ENHANCING PERFORMANCE

In this third phase of the committee's work, we reaffirm our mandate to address broad theoretical principles in an applied context. We attempt to bring the latest scientific evidence to bear on issues of training and performance, recognizing that performance encompasses emotional, cognitive, motor, and social skills. And we continue to subscribe to the philosophy of evaluation enunciated in the committee's first book, *Enhancing Human Performance* (Druckman and Swets, 1988): for basic research, we ask whether inferences made about causation are warranted; for applied research, we ask whether a program has been evaluated in a field setting and, if so, whether it is cost-effective.

The committee's work has evolved from evaluating techniques about which there are optimistic claims for improvement to focusing on the implications of fundamental psychological or social-psychological processes underlying performance. Thus, during its first phase, the committee evaluated such techniques as suggestive accelerative learning and teaching techniques, biofeedback, neurolinguistic programming, Hemi-Sync, and mental practice. Other techniques were evaluated during the committee's second phase, including subliminal self-help tapes, the Myers-Briggs Type Indicator (MBTI), and meditation, but the committee's main focus shifted to implications of research—on long-term retention of skills, modeling expertise, career development, the psychological processes associated with deception, and team performance. Those implications are reported in the committee's second volume, *In the Mind's Eye* (Druckman and Bjork, 1991).

Continuing our emphasis on fundamental processes, this volume examines such topics as cooperative learning, team building, the relation between self-confidence and motivation to perform, the transmission of affect in social situations, and implications of thought suppression. But it also retains its interest in techniques accompanied by strong claims: such "techniques" as hypnosis and restricted environmental stimulation are evaluated, and we revisit issues concerning meditation and sleep learning, topics taken up in earlier phases of the committee's work.

The path taken by the committee—from techniques to processes—has moved the study from the realm of techniques developed by entrepreneurs working outside of academic disciplinary traditions to the realm of research conducted within disciplinary contexts. The change from techniques to processes may be advantageous. In our first report, we argued that techniques should be developed in concert with knowledge generated from research. One problem with many of the techniques examined was that they were largely responses to consumer needs—proposed quick fixes for widely recognized problems. If they had been developed in conjunction with knowledge gained from research and evaluated in a systematic manner, the techniques would have benefited from the latest advances in theory and methodology. Such benefits could well have rendered them more effective for improving performance. The issues and processes examined in this book should contribute to the development of better approaches to enhancing performance in a variety of settings.

Although several new topics are covered in this book, our work has been guided by the familiar themes of learning and mental states. In Parts II and III, we continue to examine issues concerned with transfer of skills from training to work settings: Part II covers individual learning and remembering; Part III considers teams. The issues are discussed in relation to the debate over the extent to which learners should be trained in contexts that closely resemble the work (or other transfer) setting. We also continue our interest in team performance, paying particular attention to issues of team training and team building. This work extends our earlier work on the performance effects of group cohesion (in the first phase) and the effects of performing tasks in teams (in the second phase). Although the social dimensions of learning is recognized in our earlier work, we focus explicitly in this book on cooperative learning, primarily in relation to adult learning.

Added to these topics is the recent work on illusions of comprehension; the committee considers implications of this phenomenon for understanding, noting that self-reports of understanding may not coincide with what has actually been learned. This work relates to our earlier focus on the value of self-report instruments.

In Part IV, on mental states, the committee updates its previous evaluations of sleep learning (in phase one) and meditation (in phase two). The new research we examine on sleep learning was in fact stimulated by our earlier report. In this part we also examine newly available meta-analyses of the effects of transcendental meditation on performance. Our evaluation of that work has implications for the issue of whether meditation produces effects that differ from those induced by other forms of relaxation. In this part we also evaluate the claims made for restricted environmental stimulation as a technique to enhance performance. Another special state of consciousness covered in this part is hypnosis: our review examines when the technique is effective and when it is not. Finally, drawing once again on research from the field of sports psychology, the committee reviews what is known about the role of self-confidence in performance. Two other new topics are addressed in Part V. Our treatment of socially induced affect, which refers to an emotional experience in one person induced by someone else's visible emotions, draws on themes of social influence and nonverbal communication that were explored in our earlier work. Documented by extensive laboratory research, socially induced affect has several practical implications for performance: these implications are illustrated in the chapter; they have not yet been demonstrated in research. In this part we also consider thought suppression, a mental control strategy that has generally been considered in the context of psychological health but that also has implications for performance. The connection between consciousness and performance is a fertile area for investigation. Some ideas for guiding the research are put forth in this chapter.

Lastly, the epilogue addresses a special issue of application. It is often the case that sound advice based on research findings has little impact in an organization. We consider the effects of institutional attitudes and assumptions about the value of training, the issue of selection versus training, and the characteristics of training. The insights in this epilogue are based on the committee's collective experience, from both its previous research and site visits to training facilities, gained during the three phases of work completed to date.

CONCEPTS AND ISSUES

Several concepts cut across all the parts and chapters in this book. Transfer of training issues are considered both with respect to the training of individuals and teams; issues of context are central in our treatments of learning, team training and building, and organizational cultures, and they also affect thought suppression; member interdependence and cohesion play an important role in cooperative learning, team training and building, and socially induced affect; attributional processes contribute to illusions of comprehension and to self-confidence; and, the effects on memory as a mediating process in performance is considered in the chapters on illusions of comprehension, hypnosis and other states of consciousness, and thought suppression. These concepts are at the juncture between individual and social psychology. They will be the foci for research into the next century and, as such, do not represent accumulated knowledge so much as the new ideas that form the basis for future investigations.

This volume reflects the tension between individual and social learning: To what extent should training be situated or "contextualized"? To what extent should learning be cooperative rather than individual? It also reflects tensions between cognitive and affective processes: Do emotional identifications with units hinder or facilitate the process of learning to perform in teams?, and, between scientific research and the organizations that will use the research in the design of training programs: What are the organizational factors that interfere with implementing new training programs? These tensions will remain as issues to be addressed in the years to come; they are the basis for a research agenda put forth by the committee.

Social scientists have not been able to account for performance in terms either of individual or social processes alone. Processes at both levels of analysis are needed for a more complete explanation. Indeed, the committee grapples with the relative emphases to be placed on individual or social learning and performance, focusing our "lens" somewhere between the extreme positions that all learning is, ultimately, an isolated individual process and that all learning is a social process. The interplay between individual and social processes is more explicitly recognized in this book than in our previous work. We recognize some difficulties in operationalizing concepts intended to capture social processes: one example is the idea of "shared mental models"; another is the notion of "meta-cognitions." These are processes that cannot be accounted for solely in terms of individuals. Implications for performance are discussed in some detail in Chapter 6. The issue also has implications regarding how to train soldiers or civilians for work that usually takes place in groups: If social processes are critical for success, as many analysts argue, it would seem evident that training should take place in teams where members interact and coordinate their efforts over relatively long periods of time.

Another theme for our work is the study of consciousness, reflected in the chapters on thought suppression, hypnosis, and special states of consciousness. The phenomenon of consciousness remains a mystery. It is a mystery because we have not been able to explain it without invoking the term "consciousness": According to Dennett (1991:454), "Only a theory that explained conscious events in terms of unconscious events could explain consciousness at all." For many philosophers, the mystery remains because mental events cannot be accounted for solely in terms of physical brain processes. According to the Cartesian dualist view, human brains are unable to accomplish understanding all by themselves; immaterial processes must be invoked to provide a full explanation. For many scientists, the materialist position that human brains are responsible on their own is acceptable; advances in neuroscience and related disciplines are moving some scientists closer to the realization that "understanding is somehow achieved by a process composed of interactions between a host of subsystems none of which understand a thing by themselves" (Dennett, 1991:438-439). Whether a fully satisfactory explanation—based on scientific research or on metaphorical thinking—can ever be achieved is doubtful. Nor does this book contribute in any direct way to this debate. We do, however, develop implications from the results of experiments on the relation between induced mental states and performance.

Those mental states are regarded to reside at a juncture between conscious and subconscious activity. Suppression is a technique for taking unwanted thoughts out of awareness. Avoiding certain conscious thoughts is also accomplished by meditation and restricted stimulation: the altered state may relieve one of the tensions associated with certain mental and physical activities. And, to an extent, sleep serves the same function, although the symbolism of dreams often introduces the same thoughts in different forms. Approached from the other direction, unconscious thoughts may be brought to the surface by hypnosis, an idea central to some schools of psychotherapy. With all these techniques, however, the implications for performance of either confronting or avoiding certain thoughts are unclear. Although much is yet to be learned, we have identified some critical issues that are likely only to be increasingly important and needing the research suggested.

Several of the topics have direct implications for issues raised in the military. Most relevant, perhaps, are the issues surrounding the use of simulated environments for combat training. The hotly debated issue of situated learning, discussed mostly with regard to civilian education, is equally relevant to the acquisition of skills needed for military performance. Included among those skills is performing as members of teams. A focus on a team or unit raises questions about how to promote positive interdependence in task performance. Team learning may be fundamentally different than individual learning, forcing new frameworks for research and practice. Other issues are germane to both individual and unit training. In addition to acquiring and maintaining the needed skills, soldiers must be "ready" to perform. Readiness includes a cluster of motivational processes, which we treat as mental states. With regard to individuals, we examine alternative programs for developing self-confidence, popular methods for inducing those special states of consciousness needed to deal with major challenges or to overcome obstacles to achieving goals, and call attention to some problems associated with a particular mental-control strategy. With regard to teams, we consider the possibility that leaders, by their own facial and bodily expressions, may induce positive emotions in members that contribute to improved team performance.

Although we maintain our focus on performance, the committee "steps back" to examine cognitive, social, and emotional processes that precede and largely account for observed performances. In this book, we address issues that require an understanding of these fundamental processes. While the issues inform the analysis in each of the chapters, we also provide some exposition about the underlying processes involved. In some chapters, we are concerned primarily with the processes and mechanisms responsible for effects. Examples are the chapters on cooperative learning, and on socially induced affect, as well as the section on meditation. In other chapters, the analysis is driven largely by key issues: examples are how much learning should be in context, when to intervene in the team learning process, when best to train people in teams or alone, and how best to build the sort of self-confidence needed for improving performance.

This book, like the previous committee volumes, accomplishes several purposes. Our treatment of some topics—for example, situated learning, hypnosis, restricted environmental stimulation—serves either to confirm or not to confirm common beliefs and practices about techniques, interventions, or approaches to learning and training. The chapters on cooperative learning and team performance provide a structure to a disorganized field of research and theory. The reviews of research on socially induced affect and thought suppression document phenomena largely ignored in previous work. These chapters are presented as new directions for research in the decade ahead. The work on self-confidence draws out clearer conclusions from a body of research than has been previously done. All of the chapters attempt to refine or redefine questions of applications from the implications of the basic research. Finally, in the epilogue, we consider the larger institutional context in which most performance takes place.

2

Summary

This chapter presents the key findings and conclusions of our work, organized into four categories, as is the book: learning and remembering, learning and performing in teams, mental and emotional states, and new directions. Together, the various lines of research covered in this volume reveal both the complexity of the problems involved in enhancing human performance and some approaches that can improve performance of both individuals and teams. For some topics, conclusions follow from a large body of research findings and clearly indicate approaches to enhancing performance: for example, the effect of context on training and hypnosis. For other topics, however, the evidence accumulated to date leads primarily to suggestions for further research: for example, cooperative learning and team development. In some cases, a small body of research has accumulated; for example, thought suppression. In other cases, the research has not made direct connections with issues of performance; for example, the chapter on socially induced affect.

LEARNING AND REMEMBERING

Chapters 3 and 4 deal with issues related to individual learning and remembering. The work reviewed in Chapter 3 has implications for questions about how best to structure learning programs to optimize transfer to other settings and about the value of what is known as situated learning. The work reviewed in Chapter 4 has implications for judgments of performance made during training and on the job. The performance setting of interest is usually a workplace, although implications are also derived for classrooms and sports settings.

Transfer

In many domains, fundamental skills are important to acquire before special skills that are relevant to particular settings are learned. The evidence obtained to date does not support the hypothesis that performance is enhanced to the extent that skills are learned in the setting in which they will be performed. Although concrete experience is very important, the teaching of abstract principles plays a role in acquiring skills over a broad domain of tasks. It is clear that learning need not be situated in the performance context to be effective.

A training approach that provides learners with varied contexts and general procedures allows them to adapt to new situations not encountered during training. In certain settings, training techniques based on the idea of part-to-whole transfer would be useful to develop. Although longer training sessions may improve performance, they can also lead to inflexible performance if the training fails to anticipate the variability that exists in the performance settings.

In its second report the committee concluded that immediate and constant feedback may fail to optimize performance. Delayed and intermittent feedback may produce superior performance because it allows learners to detect and correct errors (Druckman and Bjork, 1991:Ch.3). The evidence reviewed since that report supports this conclusion; it also shows that delayed and intermittent feedback diminishes reliance on extrinsic feedback.

Simulators are frequently used in training. At issue is the extent to which the simulated environment should resemble the performance setting: this is referred to as task fidelity. The research shows that the level of fidelity needed in simulators depends on the results of a task analysis of the specific skill to be taught. Such an analysis can identify the critical elements in the skill that should be identical in the training and performance environments. Advances in understanding the way that skills transfer from training to performance environments depend on a careful analysis of the social characteristics of these settings.

Illusions of Comprehension and Control

Subjective experience is a compelling basis for judgment. It is also an error-prone source for judgment. The paradox suggested by these statements is understood when one realizes that people do not regard their own experience as being error prone. Feelings of knowing and actual comprehension of a topic are often disparate. Reasons for this disparity are people's failure to recall material or solutions presented in the past, confusing the way material is presented with understanding of the material, confusing general knowledge about a domain with the specific knowledge represented in a text, and a confusion of memories for imagined events with events that really happened. Also misleading is people's assumptions about other people's subjective experience: people often fail to realize that any event can have multiple interpretations. Indeed, most sources of knowledge are subject to debate and "resolved" through a better understanding of the reasons for different interpretations.

The committee has found that teachers, trainers, and students can reach a judgment that they are more proficient at a task than they are. Subjective experience can be misleading. Regular challenges are needed to provide learners with experiences that reveal the actual extent of their understanding of the task or material they are learning. In fact, benefits may derive from making the conditions of learning more demanding than the anticipated real-world (performance) conditions.

LEARNING AND PERFORMING IN TEAMS

Chapters 5-7 cover factors that influence performance in team settings. Recognizing that the operating unit in most organizations is the team, the committee considers what factors contribute to improved team performance.

Cooperative Learning

Cooperative learning consists of peers working together to enhance their individual acquisition of knowledge and skills. Although some techniques are tailored to particular content areas and institutional settings, most are general-purpose "packages" with the following characteristics: precooperation activities (specifying the technique, creating goals and incentives, group assignment and, often, training on the cooperative script and roles to be enacted); the cooperation episode, which may include such aids as worksheets, visual displays, and computer assistance; postcooperation activities in which group members examine how they have functioned; and outcome assessments of knowledge and skill acquisition. Little empirical attention has been given to the effect of pretraining in the precooperation stage, to the use of task aids in the cooperative phase, to the effects of self-analysis on subsequent activities, or to transfer to other tasks during the outcome assessment. (The lack of attention to transfer is also characteristic of evaluations of simulated role exercises, discussed in Chapter 6.)

Nowhere in this volume is the interplay between social and individual processes more evident than in work on cooperative learning. The framework developed by the committee combines insights from a social-behavioral perspective that emphasizes task and incentive structure with those derived from a cognitive-developmental perspective that emphasizes cooperative activities. The cooperative experience is an attempt to foster individual learning and social interactions, both of which lead to enhanced performance.

The evidence accumulated to date supports the effectiveness of the approach, at least under some conditions. But there are limitations. One important limitation is that most of the research has been done with children. Adults may not benefit from cooperative approaches in the same manner as do children, and there is a need to take into account the complexity of most adult learning tasks and to augment the cooperative experience with appropriate aids. Unlike many children, adults may be skeptical of attempts to manipulate the learning environment; they need to understand precisely the purpose of the intrusion and to perceive the benefits likely to result from the experience.

Research on cooperative learning with adults is limited, and additional research is needed to validate several tentative conclusions. If implemented appropriately, adult cooperative learning apparently can be more effective than individual learning across a variety of topics and tasks. Participation in well-constructed cooperative learning exercises can result in the acquisition of skills that can be used in a variety of settings. During the early stages of cooperation, participants benefit from such aids as information displays, worksheets, computers, and tutoring. For participants who lack experience with cooperative learning, it is useful to expose them to scripts that encourage productive cognitive and social activities. However, for adults, group rewards are unnecessary and may even hinder script enactment.

Further research is needed to understand why cooperative learning effects occur and the conditions that determine when they will occur. Effects of a number of potentially critical variables have not been explored to date. Examples include effects of pretraining on group skills, the availability of various communication aids, the effects of group processing, and assessment of transfer to other group tasks. Particular attention needs to be paid to the cognitive activities that are salient during the cooperative interactions, many of which are largely unobservable during individual training.

The Performance and Development of Teams

Critical to an understanding of the factors that influence team performance is the idea of "throughputs" or mediating processes. The structural aspects of tasks and team members affect performance *because* they affect such mediating processes as interaction, coordination, and cohesiveness. Although various team-building interventions have been shown to influence these processes, team performance is also affected by the organizational context within which it occurs. Recent findings make clear the key role of the external environment in decisions made by teams.

A broader framework for thinking about teams emphasizes the way they relate to each other across boundaries as a "network" of interacting entities that can contribute in positive or negative ways to organizational effectiveness: for example, team representatives can amass important resources through effective negotiation, and they can also develop "blind spots" and perceptual distortions due to the pressures on them to identify strongly with team products and positions. Yet even expanded perspectives on team performance do not capture the learning process that must be understood by trainers. More useful approaches to team learning come from other directions, including work on developmental phases, metacognitions, and shared mental models.

Particularly compelling is the notion of transition points in a team's development. These are junctures during a team's life history when "a major jump" in progress occurs. It is the time when team-building interventions and related forms of feedback are likely to have significant effects on performance. Knowing just when these turning points are likely to occur is a major challenge to both analysts and organizational consultants.

This work has major implications for training. First, knowing which variables have strong effects on performance suggest where to focus the training effort. Second, being able to distinguish between those variables over which teams members have some control from those over which they have little control further defines a trainer's focus. Third, knowing when important changes in the life cycle of a team may occur helps to identify points of entry into the process. And, fourth, knowing about some consequences of member identification with teams can alert trainers to sources of conflict between teams.

Team Development

Team-building interventions may boost morale and enhance team cohesion, but they have less effect on team performance, which is influenced more by contextual and organizational factors. Although further research is needed, these findings suggest caution be used in claiming that the techniques benefit performance. The research should follow a multimethod approach in which both quantitative and qualitative methods are used.

The enhanced cohesion and morale resulting from team-building activities can increase intra-organizational conflicts between teams. By strengthening the ties between members within teams, the interventions can weaken relationships with members of other teams. This effect is heightened to the extent that team-building exercises include strategy formation as part of the procedure. The impact of team building on interteam relationships requires further examination.

Team-building interventions can be improved in three ways: timing the intervention to occur during transition periods, defined usually at the temporal midpoint of a team's calendar, when a major jump in progress occurs; after team members engage in a self-diagnosis of their problems; and when shared mental models are developed during the team's preparation sessions. The development of shared mental models among team members deserves further study.

Team variables exert stronger influences on the performance of individuals in teams than do member characteristics. However, the social processes of interaction, coordination, and cohesion are critical determinants of the way that team inputs (task characteristics and team resources) influence team outputs (quantity, accuracy, and proficiency of performance). For example, the effects of task fidelity on the accuracy or quantity of a team's output depends on the way that fidelity affects coordination. These findings derive from the path models developed from a meta-analysis of the team performance literature. Models of this type deserve greater attention in the development of theories of team performance.

Interactive Games

Educational games are more effective than other methods in instilling positive attitudes toward a subject and in enhancing interest in the material, but they are not more effective than other methods in teaching subject matter. They may, however, aid in the retention of material already learned.

Further research should be designed to provide answers to questions about the reasons for effects shown to occur in gaming environments. Most evaluations reported to date have been demonstration studies focused on whether the technique works. In fact, both team-building and gaming exercises need to be "unpacked" in order to determine what works. In addition, research is needed to establish the value of games in team training.

Training in Teams

Team training can be distinguished from team-building or cooperative learning. Training in teams can be considered in a four-part framework: inputs, the resources and tasks used for training; the individual processes influenced by the training tasks; mediators, the social processes that must be taken into account for effective team training; and outcomes, the kinds of individual and team changes that result from training. The clear conclusion is that training in teams has many benefits. To realize these benefits, however, entails an understanding of the way that the process works. A framework that recognizes the process provides the ingredients for effective training: what to provide (inputs), what to focus on (processes), how to structure the training (mediators), and what to assess at the end (outcomes). Training effectiveness can be improved at each phase. With regard to inputs, trainee motivation can be enhanced by a supportive atmosphere, by knowing what to expect, by encouraging voluntary participation, and by the realization that what is learned in training will be used on the job. The importance of ensuring that the resources needed for training are provided should not be underestimated. Especially for complex tasks, it is important to give learners a conceptual understanding of the problems, ensure active involvement in learning, provide process feedback from other team members, and strengthen critical attitudes—namely, commitment to quality work and self-efficacy—during training.

Teams have been found to be effective vehicles for enhancing these processes. But they are more likely to be effective if the teams are structured on the basis of positive interdependence and face-to-face promotive interaction. Equally important are the mediating variables of individual accountability for performance, interpersonal skills, and team processing. The idea of a team that monitors its own progress and reacts to feedback provided by observers is central. Such team processing has been shown to contribute to effective performance on tasks that require coordination for success. Results from many studies on team performance can be explained in terms of the development of shared mental models (e.g., Orasanu and Salas, 1993). Team outcomes are multifaceted: they refer to more than proficiency and productivity. Positive relationships, psychological health, self-esteem, and social competencies are important contributors to performance in the workplace. So, too, are the various changes that occur at the level of teams. The relative emphasis to be placed on each of these individual and team outputs depends on how tasks are accomplished on the job.

The committee also concludes that intact work teams are likely to gain more from training than ad hoc assemblies of people assigned to teams only for training sessions. Long-term performance gains for teams are more likely if trainees function in similar team configurations in the workplace and are supported for doing so.

MENTAL AND EMOTIONAL STATES

Chapters 8 and 9 deal with the role of mental states in performance. Of particular interest is the way that altered states may affect performance. We cover processes related to building self-confidence, hypnosis, restricted environmental stimulation, meditation, and sleep learning.

Self-Confidence and Performance

It has become apparent that perceptions of self-confidence play an important role in performance. It is also apparent that these perceptions can be manipulated to enhance performance. However, such manipulation is not a simple matter. Perceived self-confidence involves both cognitive and motivational processes. It is rooted in beliefs about what contributes to performance. It also reflects a desire to perform in the sense of being "psyched" for the challenge. Thus, information about accomplishments and feelings of readiness to perform contribute to people's sense of effectiveness. These findings provide a basis for suggesting programs designed to enhance performance through increasing a person's perception of his or her efficacy.

One suggestion is that the speed and quality of skill acquisition can be improved by emphasizing the learnability of the skill to be taught. Another is to provide opportunities for learners to observe people of widely different backgrounds succeeding at the task. A third suggestion is to help learners to attribute their success to skill improvement or hard work and their sub-par performances to a lack of effort, a lack of sufficient practice time, or the use of inappropriate strategies. And a fourth suggestion is to make rewards contingent on performance rather than given simply for participation or distributed in the context of competitions that heighten social comparisons.

Four kinds of programs provide alternative ways to strengthen perceptions of self-confidence. Programs that emphasize performance accomplishment consist of instructional strategies that use goal setting and feedback to bolster the process-related goals of effort, form, and strategy, all of which are under a performer's control. Programs that focus on modeling techniques use model performers who demonstrate how a task is done, along with coping strategies. Included also in such programs is the use of videotapes to enable a performer to edit out mistakes. The third kind of programs use persuasion techniques, which are especially useful during the early stages of skill acquisition. They consist of "sandwiching" skill instructions between words of encouragement, such as compliments for achievements, and goads to keep trying.

The fourth program type is designed to reduce anxiety in order to increase a performer's perceived coping efficacy. As concluded in the committee's first report (Druckman and Swets, 1988), anxiety is effectively reduced when individuals feel that they have control over an uncertain future and the potential threats or risks that exist in those unknown situations. By concentrating on short-term goals, learners' feelings of uncertainty are likely to be reduced. Participation in simulation exercises can serve to reduce uncertainty, especially when the experience is viewed as being successful. Although those four types of programs are often presented as alternative strategies, they can be used in combination.

Altering States of Consciousness

Chapter 9 discusses some implications of altered states of consciousness for performance: hypnosis, transcendental meditation, restricted environmental stimulation, and sleep learning.

Hypnosis

A long history of research and practice clearly shows that hypnosis is effective in reducing the experience of pain. Therefore, it enhances performance to the extent that performance is impaired by feelings of pain and fatigue. Although not everyone is hypnotizable enough to experience this effect, some people may still receive some benefit from the placebo component of the hypnotic procedure or from training in nonhypnotic stress inoculation. The effectiveness of hypnosis in increasing muscular strength and endurance, sensory thresholds, learning, and remembering has not been demonstrated. Hypnotized subjects may believe that they are doing better, and this belief may have positive motivational implications for performance; however, the subjective experience of performance enhancement due to hypnosis appears to be illusory.

Transcendental Meditation

Transcendental meditation has been promoted as a technique for enhancing performance, largely by reducing the deleterious effects of stress. The evidence to date does not support that claim. The committee's analysis focused on physiological arousal, relaxation and anxiety, and psychological health. Although there is a voluminous body of research on transcendental meditation, the studies reported to date suffer from a variety of methodological flaws that prevent making firm conclusions. For example, it is not clear whether the positive effects reported for transcendental meditation (versus other forms of relaxation) are due to the unique features of the technique, or to the frequency and discipline with which transcendental meditation is practiced.

Restricted Environmental Stimulation

Restricted environmental stimulation (REST) is a set of techniques designed to reduce the level of environmental stimulation to a practicable minimum. It has also been promoted as a technique for enhancing performance. The evidence supporting this claim is based on the therapeutic effects of REST in habit control. Despite examples of the performance-enhancing effects of REST and published reports of demonstration experiments, the evidence to date does not lead to firm conclusions about the effects and their underlying mechanisms.

Sleep Learning

In the committee's first report (Druckman and Swets, 1988), the possibility was raised that sleep learning may be possible, that material learned during light sleep could be expressed as implicit memory in the absence of explicit recollection. Recent evidence, however, does not support this possibility. Although some degree of sleep learning may be possible, it is likely to be inefficient and to have detrimental effects on a person's subsequent waking performance.

NEW DIRECTIONS

Chapters 10 and 11 present new directions for future research and application on two topics that have recently been considered more closely in relation to enhancing human performance: socially induced affect and thought suppression. We cannot draw implications for techniques from the tentative conclusions now possible, but they are a basis for a research agenda proposed by the committee.

Socially Induced Affect

Social influences on performance are evident in many of the chapters of this volume. Communication and influence are central processes in cooperative learning, team training, and motivational programs. The social dimensions of performance were also evident in earlier topics discussed by the committee; for example, influence through mimicry (Druckman and Swets, 1988:Ch. 8), group cohesion (Druckman and Swets, 1988:Ch. 9), and deception detection (Druckman and Bjork, 1991:Ch. 9). In each case, the communication process contains both verbal and nonverbal elements—message content and expressions that convey emotion. Socially induced affect considers the possible effects of emotions transmitted from one person to another during social interactions.

Considerable evidence supports the idea of socially induced affect, that is, that one person's expressed feelings can influence another's feelings. The transmission is especially strong for influencing emotions of the same valence (happy to happy or sad to sad feelings) than for influencing emotions of the opposite valence (happiness to envy or vice versa). Less clear, however, is the role of socially induced affect as a contributor to one's overall emotional experience, the frequency and strength of its occurrence, the way it is manifest in real-life situations, and the variables that influence it. Also unclear are the mechanisms that cause it to occur: some alternative theories concern the role of cognition in attributing intentions to the model, classical conditioning of the association between events and emotions, and mimicry of facial expressions that precede the experienced emotions. It may be that each of these mechanisms plays a role in the transmission process, but that one or another is more important in any particular instance. There are some interesting implications for performance of socially induced affect, but they are still subject to further documentation by research, as are the more basic questions about the fundamental phenomenon.

Thought Suppression

Thought suppression is the intentional avoidance of a thought or category of thoughts. Although everyone has reasons to avoid thoughts about painful experiences or uncertain future events, recent research suggests that the desire to suppress thoughts may not be effective. Paradoxically, when people use suppression to free themselves of unwanted thoughts, they may actually increase the emotional power of the very thoughts they are trying to avoid. This paradox was recognized by Freud and it is now being explored in laboratory experiments. The early research suggests that an attempt not to think about an unwanted thought is likely to fail if it is the only strategy a person adopts for dealing with that thought.

Alternatives to thought suppression exist that are likely to be more effective. In cases of anxiety-producing or obsessive thoughts, successful avoidance of the unwanted thought may occur when one faces the thought and even concentrates on it. Encouraging people to talk about their unwanted thoughts may enhance their ability to cope with the events. It is not known whether this strategy is useful in all cases, and there are important exceptions. For example, encouraging depressed people to dwell on their problems is a technique that has not received enough research attention to allow any evaluation. In the cases of unwanted thoughts about fears, traumas, or worries, however, the approach of confronting them may be more beneficial than the approach of trying to suppress them.

Further research is needed on the circumstances in which dwelling on an uncomfortable thought can be detrimental. Research is also needed on the implications of forgetting old, unneeded, information that may interfere with performing a new task, such as reaching for a control that was in a different location on an old plane. Continued sensitivity to the old information may result from earlier attempts to suppress that information. But if there are new replacements for old information that allows a person to update his or her memory, the person may not suffer from the undesired retrieval of irrelevant old items. The research challenge is to discover ways to forget unneeded information without suffering the troubling effects of thought suppression.

IMPEDIMENTS TO EFFECTIVE TRAINING

In the epilogue the committee discusses institutional impediments to effective training. Many of the conclusions reached in this report, and in the committee's previous two volumes, suggest training procedures for improving performance, but whether organizations actually implement such suggestions is at issue. On the basis of more than two dozen site visits, the committee has observed a number of organizational values, attitudes, and structures that appear to impede effective training.

Training is often not highly valued within organizations. This is due in part to financial constraints, but it is also the result of an attitude that attributes differences in performance not to levels of training, but to "aptitude." This attitude—the innate-ability fallacy—leads organizations to emphasize selection more than training. It ignores the large body of research findings that suggest that practice, not innate ability, is the critical factor in determining performance.

This attitude toward the primacy of selection also leads to a misunderstanding of the training process in several ways. First, the tendency to avoid errors during training contradicts the findings that making mistakes is a necessary part of the training process. Second, the tendency to view tests as assessment devices negates their value as learning devices. And, third, the tendency to use evaluations of performance immediately after training as indicators of success misses the goal of training, which is to transfer learned skills to the settings in which trainees will work. These attitudes create a "catch 22" that impedes progress: training programs are not as effective as they might be because training is not highly valued, and training programs are not highly valued because they are seldom as effective as they might be.

Organizational attitudes and structures also effect the extent to which a trainer can maximize his or her effectiveness. The tendency to view teaching as a talent rather than a learned skill impedes the development of the skills needed to be an effective teacher. Similarly, the failure to view teaching itself as a difficult skill to be learned leads organizations to recruit experts in a given domain without regard to their experience as teachers. In addition, there is the tendency of organizations to design administrative structures that isolate instructors or put them in competition with each other. These structures impede the kind of communication and cooperation needed to share knowledge, innovations, and solutions that enable teachers and trainers to be as effective as possible.

PART II

Learning and Remembering

This part considers a number of issues related to individual training. Chapter 3 focuses primarily on the extent to which training should be situated in environments that resemble the settings in which performance occurs. Chapter 4 addresses the interesting issue of illusions of comprehension that occur when people do not understand the reasons for the "right" answers to problems.

In considering how to design a training environment, in Chapter 3 we consider the gains to be expected from a close match between training and task settings. We also address the distinction between physical and psychological fidelity of training and task situations, as well as the cost-effectiveness of various alternative strategies. In Chapter 4 we call attention to some pitfalls of self-assessments of learning, since subjective experience plays a central role in learning and performance: it is the primary basis for all human judgments of competence. As such, it needs to be taken into account in training, distinguishing when it is accurate and when it may be in error.

3

Transfer: Training for Performance

Probably the most critical issue in any type of learning is how well the learning transfers from one situation to another, particularly to the actual performance of a task. Although there is a broad consensus that transfer is an important aspect of learning, training, and performance, it is not always clear what is meant by transfer or how to achieve it. In this chapter we focus particularly on situations in which there is some period of training prior to on-the-job execution of a task. We focus exclusively on individuals in the training context. That context may or may not be a group setting; Chapters 5-7 consider group learning.

The ability to transfer between the training and application contexts is the crux of the frequently made distinction between learning and performance. One may learn to perform a task quite well during training, according to some criterion, but later find that the acquired knowledge is not sufficient to perform in the day-to-day task environment.

The distinction between learning and performance is critical because most training and task contexts differ in some way. The differences may involve situational characteristics external to the task per se, such as social interaction patterns; stress or ambient noise; explicit or implicit rules that directly govern task performance; the range of variation in the stimulus environment; the nature of available responses; performance schedules; or characteristics of the performer, such as levels of motivation, fatigue, or stress. Indeed, training cannot generally anticipate the full range of circumstances that will be encountered in task performance, and even an anticipated circumstance may be impossible to fully simulate in training. Ideally, a training program should produce the ability to accommodate some degree of variability—both within the task environment and between the training and task environments—as well as establish basic skills required for the task itself.

One principal question underlies this chapter: How much does the training context have to incorporate the performance context in order to produce effective transfer? This question applies to training on mathematics problems at school, flying a plane, training for combat, controlling airplane traffic at an airport, playing a championship tennis match, or operating a nuclear power plant. It is a fundamental issue in the design of simulator-based training devices. How close in fidelity to the performance situation must a device be in order to be effective? Simulating unnecessary aspects of the performance context means that resources have been wasted, but failing to simulate necessary ones means that training will be inadequate. The fundamental issue of specificity of training (fidelity of simulation in training) is determining the factors that produce transfer. Only when those factors are understood can resources be balanced against outcomes to design optimal training programs.

An issue related to training fidelity is the relative importance of training individuals on abstract generalizations, in contrast to specific, contextualized examples. Abstractions may or may not be important, and even if they are, it is arguable whether they are best taught directly (e.g., by the instructor's articulating rules) or whether they are best inferred from examples. This chapter discusses a strong position in regard to this issue, which is called the theory of situated learning.

Implicit in our comparisons between situated learning and other approaches to learning are certain basic constructs concerning transfer. Positive transfer refers to the facilitation, in learning or performance, of a new task based on what has been learned during a previous one. Negative transfer refers to any decline in learning or performance of a second task due to learning a previous one. These types of transfer are often measured as a percent savings or loss, respectively: How fast (or accurately) is the target task acquired after learning a similar (transfer) task in comparison with learning without a prior task? Transfer can be from a component of one task to a more complex task that encompasses that component. This is called part-to-whole or vertical transfer. In contrast, horizontal transfer is between tasks that are similar in complexity and do not have an inclusion relation.

TRANSFER BY IDENTICAL ELEMENTS

As noted above, a major issue in developing training programs is the required similarity between the training and performance contexts. If the training context exactly simulates the performance context, transfer should be perfect, but this situation rarely exists. Theories of transfer have stressed the requirement of learning and performance similarities; in this section we review such theories.

Thorndike and Woodworth's theory of "identical elements," published in 1901, stated that the determinant of transfer was the extent to which two tasks contain identical elements: the more shared elements, the more similar the two tasks, and the more transfer there would be. This position was in stark contrast to the long-standing view that the condition of a person's mental faculties accounted for transfer. Thorndike rejected the view that the mind is a muscle that must be strengthened with good exercises—such as the study of topics like Latin and geometry—and that with such rigorous studies, transfer between any two fields would be straightforward. The problem with Thorndike's approach is that it is unclear exactly what defines identical elements. There was some suggestion that he meant mental elements, although his theory was typically interpreted to mean stimulus-response connections.

Identifying the elements that should be identical, in order to produce transfer, is critically important. If one first observes transfer and subsequently infers what the identical elements must have been to produce it, the reasoning is obviously circular. But advance specification of identical elements is more difficult than it might appear. Some situations that seem to have substantial identical elements produce little or no transfer, and some that do not seem to have similarities produce a substantial amount.

One example of transfer of identical elements comes from Singley and Anderson (1989), who taught people three different computer text editing programs, varying the order of acquisition of the three programs across subjects. They developed a set of 107 rules capable of simulating editing in the three programs. Some of the rules were shared by all three programs, some by two, and some were unique to a specific program. A given editing task using one program might or might not share many rules with the comparable task using a different program. Their expectation was that there would be savings in performance with the second program to the degree that the rules had already been acquired. The data were in strong support of their predictions.

A different example—or transfer between nonidentical elements—comes from MacKay (1982), who reported data from a group of English-German bilingual speakers who were asked to produce the same sentence in the same language 12 times, with a 20-second pause between sentences. They were to produce the sentence as quickly as possible. The production time declined regularly over the 12 repetitions, to an asymptote of about 2 seconds. In the last 20-second pause interval, each subject was asked to produce the same sentence, but in the alternate language. The speed of production for this transfer sentence was found to be identical to that of the trial before. That is, the subjects remained at asymptote, and the new sentence functioned as if it were identical to the previous ones, despite a complete change in the motor movements necessary for output.

An example of very little transfer comes from Logan and Klapp (1992), who had subjects solve alphabetic arithmetic problems (e.g., if A = 1, B = 2, etc., does A + 2 = D?) with one set of 10 letters and the digits 2-5 for 12 sessions of nearly 500 trials each. Initially, the subjects' response times increased markedly with a new digit (e.g., there was a longer time for B + 5 than for B + 2 problems), as if they were moving forward through the alphabet from the given letter for the required number of digits (e.g., for B + 2: B, C, D). The slope of this increasing function was 486 milliseconds (ms) per count in the first session. By the 12th session, however, the slope was only 45 ms, suggesting development of a new strategy. The subjects were then transferred on session 13 to a new set of 10 letters. Although the task remained unchanged, the slope of the function relating response time to new digit increased dramatically—to nearly the value it had had in the initial sessions. That is, there was only a small amount of transfer.

These three examples represent very different degrees of transfer: partial transfer, depending on shared rules; virtually perfect transfer despite apparently substantial differences between the training and transfer contexts; and virtually no transfer from one problem to another. How can these differences be explained? The answer lies in what elements are and are not identical.

Cognitive Abstractions

Singley and Anderson (1989) and Bovair et al. (1990) have developed formal theories that specify the "elements" of cognitive tasks. They show that holding these elements identical across learning situations predicts positive transfer. At the heart of these theories is the idea that transfer is produced when cognitive abstractions that are formed in one context—rules or knowledge chunks—can be used in another. The models from these theories, as well as the model of Polson and Kieras (1985) are similar to Anderson's (1983) ACT (Adoptive Control of Thought) model, so ACT is described as an illustration. (See Gray and Orasanu, 1987, for an excellent review of work on skill transfer explained within this framework.)

The theory assumes that there are two types of memory, a declarative or fact memory and a procedural or skill memory. Many of the tasks that people perform are originally encoded in memory in declarative memory as verbalizable rules. As they become practiced and strengthened, these declarative facts are often compiled into procedural rules that are executed automatically and are not open to inspection. So, for example, when one first learns to drive a stick shift in an automobile, one says implicitly to oneself: "Push in the clutch with the left foot, lift up the right foot to release the gas pedal and use the right hand to move the stick shift to another position." As this skill becomes compiled into an automatic procedure, one might not be aware of exactly what one's feet are doing while shifting (Anderson, 1976).

Declarative facts are stored in a type of semantic network of nodes or chunks that are connected together by associations acquired through experience. These nodes or chunks may vary in strength as will the associations among them, depending on the amount of exposure (practice) they have received. Performance will vary as a function of the amount of activation that any particular memory structure receives. Activation of a structure depends on the number of competing associations linked to a node and the relative strength of the associations and nodes.

Procedural memories are condition-action, or production, rules: condition is the "lefthand side" of the production; action is the "righthand side" of the production. The righthand side of a production specifies an action, and it is executed when all of the elements of the lefthand condition side are met, that is, match the contents of working memory. When the condition side of a production is matched, and thus the action side is executed (the production "fires"), the production is also strengthened. When more than one production could fire, because the condition side of multiple productions could match to the situation, the selection (or conflict resolution, as it is called) of a single production to fire is determined by the specificity and the strength of the competing productions. Specificity refers to the number of condition elements that match on the lefthand side. More specific (or complex) productions are easier to fire than more general productions, all else being equal. A production can vary enormously in complexity. For example, it can set up new goals to be achieved, place new elements in working memory, or initiate a simple motor response.

According to models such as ACT, transfer between tasks is achieved when the tasks share elements, either chunks in declarative memory or productions in procedural memory. Acquiring and strengthening declarative memory chunks and productions for one task will facilitate performance of another task to the extent that memory chunks and productions are shared. Anderson (1993) suggests that there are other means by which one experience can influence another, such as analogy: extending knowledge from one situation to a new situation that is only similar.

MacKay (1982) has also emphasized transfer based on identical elements at abstract levels, focusing particularly on the domain of motor performance. His model makes hierarchical distinctions between high-level structures representing abstract rules for a task and low-level structures representing commands to peripheral mechanisms that will directly produce performance. In the speech domain, for example, the hierarchy comprises

distinct structures for meaning, sound, and control of the speech musculature. In this model transfer occurs between tasks that share mental structures. Practice on one task strengthens linkages that are necessary for the
other.

The MacKay model actually predicts perfect transfer for one situation:
when the unshared structures are so extensively practiced already that their
linkage strengths are at asymptotic levels and could not benefit further.
This model explains the transfer between a sentence in German and its
translation in English. The idea is that the shared structures between these
tasks are conceptual ones that have not been previously practiced (since the
phrase is novel), and the unshared structures are phonological and muscle-
movement ones that are well practiced in both languages and hence would
not benefit from further practice. Transfer at the conceptual level is then all
that is needed. Given that the two languages share a single conceptual
system, perfect transfer will occur because practicing the phrase in one
language is equivalent at the conceptual level to practicing it in the other.

The transfer will not be prefect, however, if the unshared structures
between two tasks are not well practiced, for example, when one attempts to
write with the nondominant hand. Only the abstract level of structure pertaining to the written words is shared in this case; the muscle-movement
structures for the nondominant hand are not well practiced, and being unshared,
they do not benefit from practice with the dominant one. Furthermore, in
this case the shared mental structure—the name—is already well practiced
and cannot benefit further from the commonalities between learning and
performance.

Exemplars

A theory of Logan (1988) makes the fundamental assumptions that people
performing in a task store instances of past performance in memory and that
each instance is stored as an independent copy or "exemplar." On their first
encounter with the task, having no stored instance, people will use whatever
strategic, rule-based tools they have available; this constitutes a task "algorithm." Subsequently, however, they will have available not only the algorithm, but memory of the past instance of performance, or as many instances as the number of times the task has been performed. When the task
recurs, performance is based on the first solution that is retrieved from
memory, the algorithm or a retrieved instance. The time to retrieve each
past instance is assumed to vary stochastically (the probability being a function of previous instances) so that the algorithm competes for retrieval with
that instance having the fastest current retrieval time, that is, the lowest
value drawn from a set with similar distributions, one for each instance that
has been stored. With enough stored instances, the algorithm will tend not

to be retrieved faster than the fastest instance, even if its mean retrieval time is the fastest. Responses will come to rely virtually exclusively on past instances. Automaticity, according to the instance model, corresponds to this shift from algorithmic to instance-based retrieval.

A principal assumption of the instance model is that if a previously solved task is presented, past instances of that same task are retrieved from memory. The emphasis is on "that same task." Under the assumption that the subject comes to rely on specific stored instances, the task here constitutes not only the general type of problem that must be solved, but also the specific parameters that are provided. Learning is item-specific, and retrieval is of the same items that were previously used in the task. It is assumed that transfer between distinct items within the same task does not occur because presentation of a novel item does not lead to retrieval of an item used previously in training. This theory explains why so little transfer was obtained in the Logan and Klapp experiment of letters and numbers when the specific letters changed. What little transfer did occur was attributed to better learning of an algorithmic solution (e.g., with practice, subjects became able to count faster from the new letter).

It should be noted that Logan emphasizes tasks in which conceptual structures are minimally important and instance retrieval provides an effective solution. Without identical elements at the instance level, there is little transfer. Singley and Anderson (1989), and MacKay (1982) as well, emphasize tasks in which conceptual structures are very important and responses are either extremely well practiced or minimally taxing parts of the task. Hence, nonidentical elements at the output level matter little. (We return below to the issue of how transfer may be governed by different principles in different tasks.) Logan's experiment clearly supports Thorndike's view that the mind is not like a muscle. Subjects had ample "exercise" with the mental arithmetic task, but without identical problems, there was virtually no transfer.

The Ease or Difficulty of Transfer

The cases of successful transfer discussed above, along with much of the research discussed below, make clear that transfer is not invariably difficult to achieve. However, there is also a surprising amount of research demonstrating the difficulties of achieving transfer. In the difficult cases, performance often seems to be overembedded in the training context, so that the identical elements across contexts are not perceived and so do not have an effect.

The failure of learners to recognize and capitalize on identical elements between training and task contexts has been well documented (see Patrick, 1992, and as reviewed by Chipman et al., 1985; Segal et al., 1985). Hayes and Simon (1977), for example, showed little transfer between two structurally or formally identical problems that differed in superficial characteristics. Gick and Holyoak (1983) used a task in which a memorized story should help, by analogy, to determine the solution of a subsequent problem. Analogical transfer was rare, however, unless a hint of the similarity of elements was given.

Charney and Reder (1987) proposed that an important component of cognitive skill acquisition, such as learning to use a personal computer operating system or an electronic spreadsheet, is the ability to recognize the situations or conditions under which a particular procedure should be used. If the training context always makes obvious which procedure should be practiced, then an important element of the skill—the ability to recognize when to use each procedure—is not trained.

Theories based on production rules describe lack of transfer as being caused by production rules that are too specific in the condition elements contained in the "if" part of an "if-then" rule. That is, people do not realize that an old rule can be applied in a new context. Anderson's (1983) model of skill acquisition allowed for generalization to occur by reinforcing more general (less specific) productions when there was variable practice. Unfortunately, there was little evidence that people actually generalized from variable practice to novel situations if the new situations were very different from the example or training problems. It seems that generalizations have to be explicitly encoded, either through conscious discovery by the learner who encounters multiple scenarios and notices the similarities or from explicit instruction.

Transfer failure also occurs not only because the context or situation is very different, but also because the task has dramatically changed. For example, Knerr et al. (1987) reported that a group trained to recognize correct flight paths was superior in recognizing correct flight paths, but not in producing them. McKendree and Anderson (1987) and Kessler (1988) found that being trained to evaluate some functions of the programming language LISP facilitated performance on evaluation of other LISP functions (compared to a control), but not on generating LISP functions, and vice versa.

In theory, when productions are initially formed they are very condition- and action-specific. The specificity of the production rules would be unnoticed in everyday situations because one does not usually practice only half of a skill, such as learning to evaluate LISP functions but not to generate them. In order to achieve transfer, a learner must make a conceptual generalization of actions. For example, if a learner is used to using a command-based computer and then moves to one that is menu driven, successful transfer requires that the learner be able to map old actions (such as typing in a string of letters in order to rename a file) into new ones (such as calling up a menu dealing with file manipulation and clicking on a "re-name" option). This type of successful transfer occurs frequently; however, when people accomplish the mapping (the transfer), the success is taken for granted. Only when the attempted transfer fails is it considered remarkable.

Situated Learning

Recently there has been a somewhat different approach to the idea of identical elements, one that emphasizes the context in which learning and performing occur. This general approach is called situated learning (e.g., Lave, 1988; Lave and Wenger, 1991), although closely associated terms are situated cognition and situated action. The situated approach is taken by researchers from several fields, including psychology, anthropology, and philosophy. Its fundamental tenets include an emphasis on contextual determinants of performance, particularly on social interactions in the task environment, and on the importance of situating the learner in the context of application, as in apprenticeship learning (called legitimate peripheral participation by Lave and Wenger, 1991). Part of this view is that learning is fundamentally a social activity.

Although proponents of situated learning do not necessarily agree on all of its details, four general principles characterize the approach:

(1) Action is grounded in the concrete situation in which it occurs. A potential for action cannot fully be described independently of the specific situation, and a person's task-relevant knowledge is specific to the situation in which the task has been performed.

(2) Psychological models of the performer in terms of abstract information structures and processes are inadequate or inappropriate to describe performance. A task is not accomplished by the rule-based manipulation of mediating symbolic representations. Certain task-governing elements are present only in situations, not representations.

(3) Training by abstraction is of little use; learning occurs by doing. Because current performance will be facilitated to the degree that the context more closely matches prior experience, the most effective training is to act in an apprenticeship relation to others in the performance situation.

(4) Performance environments tend to be social in nature. To understand performance, it is necessary to understand the social situation in which it occurs, including the way in which social interactions affect performance.

Situated learning has become a major theoretical framework that is hotly debated by those concerned with education and training. There is little disagreement among cognitive scientists that there exist contextual effects in learning, transfer, and retention. Indeed it is not news that performance is affected by context, as has been amply demonstrated. In verbal

learning, for example, the principle of encoding specificity holds that retrieval of learned information directly depends on similarities between the
retrieval and learning contexts (Tulving and Thomson, 1973). In applied
research based on this principle, Godden and Baddeley (1975) demonstrated
remarkably strong encoding-specificity effects when deep-sea divers learned
material on land or underwater and were tested in matching or nonmatching
situations.

What makes the situated-learning approach different is the degree to which
learning is claimed to be context specific and the implications of this claim for
education and training. For example, Greeno et al. (1993:99) state:

> Knowledge—perhaps better called knowing—is not an invariant property
> of an individual, something that he or she has in any situation. Instead,
> knowing is a property that is relative to situations . . . (just as) motion is
> not a property of an object.

An important implication is the idea that school is just another context and
therefore that what one has learned in school can only be used there. Lave
and others reject the premise that school constitutes a neutral setting in
which things are learned that can later be applied in the real world. Brown
et al. (1988) argue that success with schooling has little bearing on performance elsewhere. So, for example, rather than being taught mathematics as
an abstract skill, a person should learn the mathematical techniques relevant
for his or her trade in the situations in which they will be needed. Some
theorists of situated learning also argue that people tend not to remember
skills or be able to apply them if they are taught in an abstract manner.
Only when they are learned "on the job," embedded in the performance
situation, can the skills be used in those situations.

Another important aspect of the situated learning approach is the view
that cognition cannot be represented symbolically, that people perceive the
environment directly and use that perception to support thought. Stucky (in
press) argues that rather than using contextual clues to represent relevant
aspects of a situation, people use contextual cues directly to calculate their
actions. Following the general approach of ecological psychologists, Greeno
et al. (1993) similarly suggest that performers perceive physical properties
of situations that make certain activities possible. For example, they find it
unlikely that children have symbolic representations of physical properties
of objects, such as the flatness of a surface; rather, they propose, children
directly perceive flatness and the consequences of it, like stacking. Transfer from one environment to another then depends on common properties
that produce invariance of interaction.

It cannot be contested that one of the most important goals of training
is improving teaching techniques so that the application of a skill in new
situations is easily achieved. An implication that might be taken from the

failures of transfer just described is that training must be situated in the performance context in order to be effective. This is of course a fundamental premise of the situated-learning approach. In support of the premise, there are many cases of superior performance with more specific, relevant practice. And because it is difficult to anticipate all of the features of a performance context, it would seem appropriate to train in that context to ensure that training covers all of those features.

However, a strong position that basic training is a waste of time, because learning must be situated, is false. There are many domains in which fundamental skills are critical to acquire before more specific training can occur, such as learning to catch a ball before playing any sport with a ball. Furthermore, there are certainly basic skills acquired in school that transfer easily and are heavily used in situations outside the classroom. Reading and writing are obvious examples.

Conceivably, there are individual differences among learners for their need for concrete, motivating "real-life" contexts. Consider mathematics learning, for example. The view that learning mathematics will necessarily be better if it is learned in real-world contexts is debatable, and there have been no studies that address this complex issue. We suspect that for people with strong mathematics skills, embedding mathematics in real-life contexts takes away valuable time from the acquisition and practice of fundamental concepts and procedures.

The theory that training in the performance context is optimal led the advocates of situated learning to propose that the best form of learning involves an apprenticeship in the real-world context where the training is to be applied. However, in evaluating apprenticeship training, it is important to consider costs external to training per se. To the extent that the presence of an apprentice disrupts performance in the work context, the output of the system as a whole may be diminished. Training in the context of application may be unfeasible for economic reasons as well. The target context may limit the number of trainees that can be handled at one time, or it may involve costly equipment or supplies.

It is also unclear how one graduates from being an apprentice in a real-world task to an actual participant who performs the task competently. If learning is so contextualized that one must serve as an apprentice to learn, how does one actually acquire the skills of the master if one has only been the apprentice? Current theories that emphasize situated learning do not adequately deal with the transition from apprenticeship to mastery. And there are many situations in which one cannot imagine placing a novice directly in the work context: playing in an orchestra, copiloting an airplane, or serving in a tank crew are perhaps obvious examples, but even providing nursing care or fighting a fire do not seem feasible.

Yet another problem with training in the target context is the potential for variability within that context. Because one cannot always anticipate the future contexts that will be required of the learner, a major instructional goal is to devise a training procedure that will optimize performance in various contexts.

For a variety of reasons, then, a training environment that simulates the relevant features of the task might be a more feasible and appropriate technique for many tasks than fully situated learning. Since 1982, for example, soldiers have been trained in simulated battles at the National Training Center at Ft. Irwin in the Mojave Desert, California (see Wiering, 1992). Over the course of a 4-week rotation at the center, trainees become demonstrably better at fighting simulated battles. There is reason to believe that this training, using real armored vehicles, negotiating in real deserts, improved performance in the transfer task of fighting real desert battles in the Middle East. (Simulation is discussed further below.)

One point that can be well taken from situated-learning theorists is the stress on evaluating the role of the performance context of—particularly the social context—when designing a training regimen. The report on the Los Angeles Police Department following the 1991 riots mentions the common statement to police officers newly placed on the beat: "Forget everything you learned at the [Police] Academy" (Independent Commission on the Los Angeles Police Department, 1991:125). The implication is that the social milieu of the working officer has little to do with the training environment. Although this is an extreme example, there are social-interaction characteristics of most workplaces, and the training program may often ignore them. A workplace analysis may reveal such characteristics and lead to their being dealt with during training to the extent that it is possible to do so.

GENERAL PRINCIPLES OF TRANSFER

A general principle of transfer seems to be that identical elements are necessary. But which elements? And how much identity is necessary? Must learning be situated in the transfer context in order to be effective? Or does learning in one context become so situated that it cannot be generalized to other contexts? The rest of this chapter discusses many aspects of these broad questions.

Role of Abstract Concepts and Rules

A position of some advocates of situated learning is that skills to be learned should not be taught in an abstract fashion. One of the influences of this approach was Whitehead's (1929) inert knowledge problem, which points to knowledge that can be recalled when specifically asked for, in something like a school setting, but is not used spontaneously when needed in actual problem solving, where the knowledge could be applied. Lave (1988; Lave and Wenger, 1991) is one of the most outspoken proponents of this position. She has made a distinction between "indoor" research and "outdoor" or real-world research and has claimed that school-learned (indoor) algorithms are not the procedures used in the real world. For example, mathematics training in school is said to be irrelevant to mathematical performance on the job in later life and in other real-world situations. In this view, the educational system provides minimal preparation for real-world problems.

Greeno (1989) has also argued that symbolically represented knowledge does not translate well into useful skills. Moore and Greeno (1991) proposed that symbolic knowledge domains, such as physics and mathematics, should be taught by using physical models rather than using symbolic formulas and algorithms. As noted above, proponents of situated learning emphasize the importance of knowledge embedded in the performance situation and to deemphasize the role of manipulating internal symbols in accomplishing a task. One problem with this view is that it fails to explain cases where the abstract concept is developed before the real-world model. For a classic example, G. F. B. Riemann developed his non-Euclidean geometry as an abstract theory much before Albert Einstein used it to provide an explanation of the universe based on general relativity.

Greeno et al. (1993) propose a more general view that transfer can occur to the extent that the situations share characteristics or similarities for interaction, which can be perceived without there being a symbolic representation of the properties that specify the similarities. In the example given above, children can directly perceive flatness of a surface without having a symbolic representation of flatness. Vera and Simon (1993:22-23) responded:

> Greeno argues that physical models having component objects that correspond closely with those found in real situations are better pedagogical tools than symbolic formulas and algorithms. Does this argument imply that symbolic knowledge does not underlie the central processes of ordinary everyday cognition? We think not.

There are many examples in which abstract instruction has been shown to be superior to concrete instruction when the transfer task is not very similar to the original training situation. Singley and Anderson (1989) showed this type of result in the context of learning to solve algebra word problems. They presented students with either concrete or abstract tabular representations of "mixture" word problems, such as a coin problem in which pennies and nickels are mixed together to yield some total amount. By appropriately labeling a tabular representation, this problem could be treated as specific to coins (using labels of "penny," "nickel," or "total value") or as involving, more abstractly, the combination of parts into wholes (using labels of "part 1," "part 2," and "whole"). The abstract labels could be applied to a wide range of mixture problems, involving mixing two solutions together, selling different kinds of sandwiches at a picnic, gambling with a certain amount of money won or lost with each bet, and so on. Singley and Anderson found that, with the same amount of training (number of problems solved), those students who got concrete labels did better on problems of the same type but did worse on mixture problems of different types.

This near-transfer/far-transfer interaction is reminiscent of much earlier Gestalt research that showed that it is sometimes easier to learn a rote procedure than a principle, but the procedure only applies in very limited contexts. In a classic study, for example, Katona (1940) showed that in problems requiring that matchstick shapes be altered to make new ones, subjects who memorized the required moves outperformed subjects who tried to discover general principles—but only on the originally learned tasks. On transfer to new problems, the discovery group excelled.

Further evidence for the usefulness of teaching abstract concepts to facilitate transfer has been shown in a number of subsequent studies. Mayer and Greeno (1972) found that subjects who were taught to solve binomial probability problems with a formula outperformed those taught to deduce the formula from principles and examples, but only on solving problems similar to those encountered during training. The other group showed better comprehension of the formula and better ability to recognize problems that could not be solved. Similarly, Singley (1986) explicitly taught subjects the abstract goal structure for solving related-rates calculus word problems and found that this led to faster learning and more transfer to new types of problems. Klahr and Carver (1988) found that when children learned how to debug programs in the LOGO computer language, they performed better when the high-level goal structure for debugging was explicitly presented in its abstract form.

A somewhat different example of transfer that was facilitated by abstract instruction concerns learning to throw darts to hit a target under water (Scholckow and Judd, as described by Judd, 1908). If a thrower aims directly at the target under water, the dart will go beyond the actual location of the target, because of the misleading cues from the refraction of light. One group of fifth- and sixth-grade students received an explanation of light refraction, while another group did not. On the initial task, where the depth of water was 12 inches, both groups performed about equally well; however, when the water level was changed to 4 inches, the difference between groups became striking: the students without the abstract instruction were confused and made large and persistent errors, while those who had received the abstract instruction corrected their aim quickly. When the depth of water was changed again, to 8 inches, the abstract-instruction group did better once again. A conceptual replication by Hendrickson and Schroeder (1941) used two levels of abstract explanation as well as a control group and found more transfer with more abstract instruction.

A seemingly visual skill, pattern identification, has also been shown to be aided by abstract instruction. Biederman and Shiffrar (1987) found that novice subjects could be taught to determine the sex of pictured chickens at the level of experts merely by receiving instructions as to the location and qualitative shape (convex, concave, or flat) of a critical feature distinguishing males from females. This skill had previously been thought to require many hours of visual training. (Note, however, that the experimental task involved sextyping photographs of chickens, while an additional part of an expert's skill involves knowing how to pick up a chicken to determine its sex.)

These studies provide strong support for the benefits of abstract instruction, but it is important to emphasize that abstract instruction in the absence of concrete examples rarely results in transfer. It is well understood among educational and cognitive psychologists that concrete examples are important to facilitate appropriate use of acquired knowledge (Simon, 1980). Sandberg and Wielinga (1992) point out that the real problem has always been how to design teaching methods that teach both the declarative subject matter and its use. "Anchored instruction" (Cognition and Technology Group at Vanderbilt, 1990) provides an approach to education that creates learning experiences in a school setting that have some of the properties thought to be important in apprenticeship training.

Environmental Context

The question of whether the environmental context of learning matters—whether task-irrelevant elements have to be duplicated for transfer to occur—has been addressed primarily in research on verbal learning. That research focuses on whether changes in the environmental context from learning to remembering affect the amount that is remembered.

This issue refers to the effects of incidental context, defined as features of the learning environment that are not part of the to-be-learned material itself and that should not directly affect how people deal with that material (Bjork and Richardson-Klavehn, 1989). For example, the presence of posters citing cancer statistics in a room where people receive an anti-smoking lecture would be considered an influential rather than incidental context.

In a prototypical experiment, subjects learn in a room with walls of one color, then recall in a room with walls of the same or a different color. If recall is superior in the same-color environment, a positive effect would be said to occur. Environmental context effects have also been addressed by asking whether experiencing multiple environments during learning helps people to remember (a paradigm that is similar to that used to study variable practice effects; see below).

The literature on environmental context effects in verbal learning has a somewhat checkered history. Sometimes effects have been found, and sometimes they have not. There have also been failures to replicate seemingly robust cases of environmental influences (e.g., Fernandez and Glenberg, 1985). This inconsistency in outcomes can be better understood if one considers two factors that have been suggested to modulate the degree of environmental influence: the availability of memory cues other than the environment, and the extent to which the subject tries to recollect the original context at the time of the memory test.

According to the "outshining hypothesis" (Smith, 1988; Smith and Vela, 1986), environmental influences will be reduced (outshone) when there are strong retrieval cues present at the time of the memory test. This can occur, for example, because the test itself provides strong cues, as in a recognition situation. It can also occur because the original learning situation promoted self-cuing, such as instruction at the time of learning that encouraged subjects to think about items conceptually and relate them to one another (e.g., forming words into a story). Bjork and Richardson-Klavehn (1989) suggested that this hypothesis should be augmented by a "reinstatement hypothesis," that physically reinstating the context of learning will be useful only when subjects cannot mentally do so for themselves. For example, if a person studied in a pink room but is tested in a green one, imagining the green walls to be pink may compensate for the change in environment (see, e.g., Smith, 1979). According to these hypotheses, variations in the nature of the retrieval and learning situations may underlie the inconsistent effects of environmental context that have been observed.

In a meta-analysis of the literature on environmental context, Vela (1989) found support for the outshining hypothesis. Analyzing more than 50 studies and calculating the size of the context effect (defined as the performance difference between no-context-change and context-change groups), Vela found overall a moderate, statistically significant advantage for the same context in learning and test. This result was modulated by both the nature of the retrieval test and the conditions of study, as predicted by the outshining hypotheses.

Extrapolating from these studies to the more general topic of transfer, we infer that changes in seemingly irrelevant aspects of task context between training and performance can be detrimental. The effects are not always robust and can apparently be reduced by providing strong cues to performance in the transfer context and by motivating strong cuing from relevant aspects of the task (as opposed to incidental environmental features) during the training procedure. It would be useful to verify these conclusions in a broad range of performance settings.

Fidelity of Training to Anticipated Experience

It is interesting that the traditional literature on transfer gives many examples in which a situation that does not closely mirror the target task is considered optimal. Two types of data are particularly relevant, dealing with superiority of transfer after variable practice relative to fixed practice and with transfer to the whole after training on parts.

Variable Practice

Almost all tasks are variable in some aspects of their context, and this variability is generally not predictable. This is true for tasks like flying a fighter plane in combat or seemingly invariant tasks like performing the broad jump, what Schmidt (1988) has called open and closed tasks, respectively. This means that it is not possible to train an individual on every task variation that will be encountered. The learner must aspire to be flexible enough to handle the variation that will be encountered.

A potential way to induce flexibility in transfer is by introducing variability in training. Generally, the effects of variability in training are positive (see reviews in Cormier, 1984; Shapiro and Schmidt, 1982; Johnson, 1984; Newell, 1985; Schmidt, 1988; and Shea and Zimny, 1983). Variable practice can facilitate subsequent performance not only in open tasks, where intrinsic variation is high, but also in closed tasks, where variations in the transfer context are relatively minimal (e.g., Kerr and Booth, 1978; see also Chapter 4 for a description of this experiment).

The committee's previous book (Druckman and Bjork, 1991) discussed two effects related to the issue of variable practice: contextual interference and use of variable examples during training. It has been suggested that these are part of a common phenomenon (Schmidt and Young, 1987; Schmidt, 1988), and we treat them together. Contextual interference refers to the addition of task demands during training, which tends to inhibit initial acquisition of task competency but ultimately to facilitate transfer. Demands may be introduced, for example, by randomly varying conditions from trial to trial (Reder et al., 1986; Shea and Morgan, 1979) or by adding a second task requirement (Battig, 1956). Variability of examples refers to training with varied task content but with the same general task requirement; for example, throwing bean bags of several different weights in practice before transferring to a novel weight (Carson and Wiegand, 1979). Again, such variation has been found to facilitate transfer, although not without exception (Van Rossum, 1990, see also Chapter 4 in this volume).

Several theories have been proposed to explain practice variability and contextual interference effects. Battig (1979) proposed that in an effort to overcome contextual interference, learners undertake elaborative and variable, rather than rote and repetitive, encoding of task information. Such a strategy has two consequences. First, the information is more retrievable, so that previously practiced instances will be performed better at transfer. Second, task-relevant information becomes better distinguished from irrelevant context, so that elements central to the task achieve higher strength and adaptation to new instances is promoted. Similar consequences could also arise because variability in task instances leads to distributed rather than massed practice. That is, when training is varied, repetitions of the same instance tend to occur at longer intervals, which again promotes richer and more varied encoding and reduces the contextual elements of the encoded information.

Elaborations of these strengthening and "decontextualizing" mechanisms have been offered in subsequent theories. Shea and Zimny (1983) proposed that variable presentations increase the likelihood that different elements of information will reside concurrently in working memory and hence will be associatively related at encoding. Anderson (1983) has suggested that variable practice leads to more general productions with wider applicability because each specific production (with more contextual elements) is only strengthened when it is practiced, while the more general form of the production is practiced each time any of the variations is practiced. Thus, one develops a stronger version of the general form of the production.

A number of additional accounts of variable-practice effects have been offered. Charney and Reder (1987) have suggested that variable practice facilitates a component of skill acquisition in which the learner becomes able to recognize the appropriate procedure to use in a given context. Variable practice of exercises forces the learner to practice the procedure selection component of the task: figuring out which procedure to use for this situation. This selection makes the task more difficult initially, but target performance is better because the learner now is able to select the procedure that is appropriate in each context. In keeping with this view, Reder et al. (1986) found that when exercises were not grouped (blocked) by type and subjects had to figure out which procedure to use to solve the problem, initial performance was worse, but final performance was better.

Variable-practice effects have also been interpreted in the context of theories that stress the importance of schematic knowledge representations of the elements that must be identical for transfer to occur. In Schmidt's (1975) schema theory for motor learning, it is assumed that performance is guided by schemata that represent movement parameters and movement outcomes, on the basis of past experience. The recall schema represents an abstract motor program, and the recognition schema represents expected feedback consequences of an action—in essence, what it should feel like. The two are used together to plan and generate actions. For example, there might be a generalized schema for throwing a ball, with a force parameter used to adjust the throw so that balls of different weights can be thrown equivalent distances. Formation of these schemata is assumed to be promoted by presentation of varying instances because it provides more data about the underlying rules that relate movement parameters and sensory consequences (including observed outcomes). Transfer to new instances is then facilitated because the existing schema can be applied, allowing the performer to generate appropriate parameters and expected consequences. One can see why this would help in open tasks, when variability is high and new instances of the task are frequently introduced. Under the assumption that a schema is more stable or retrievable in memory than are isolated instances, this approach might also explain why performance in a closed task benefits from variations in training (see Shapiro and Schmidt, 1982).

The idea of schema abstraction has been similarly proposed in theories of analogical transfer, where solution of an initial "source" problem (e.g., an algebra "word problem") is intended to facilitate later solution of a "target" problem that is structurally similar but different in surface description. It has been suggested that successful analogical transfer leads to the induction of a general schema for the solved problems that can then be applied to subsequent problems (Holyoak, 1984; Novick and Holyoak, 1991; Ross, 1989). If a schema is used in this way, one would expect to find that practice with a greater number of instances facilitates analogical problem solving. Consistent with this idea, analogical transfer has been found to be facilitated by the provision of multiple analogous source problems, along with instructions to compare them (Catrambone and Holyoak, 1989; Gick and Holyoak, 1983).

Yet another possibility is that the set of component processes that is trained under a variable practice regimen is more inclusive than one trained under specific practice. This explanation is suggested by studies using a variant on a contextual-interference paradigm (Carnahan and Lee, 1989; Langley and Zelaznik, 1984; after Shea and Morgan, 1979). Subjects were trained to knock down three wooden barriers placed an equal distance apart. Some subjects were trained to produce a target total time (duration training), and others were trained on different component times for each barrier that added to the same total time (phase training). When the subjects transferred to a task requiring a new total duration, duration-trained subjects performed no better than those given prior phase training, but the phase training group was superior on transfer to a new phase-control task. Langley and Zelaznik (1984) suggested that this might occur because control of phasing is a higher order skill that incorporates control of duration. Thus phase-trained subjects had learned skills applicable to both tasks, but duration-trained subjects had not.

An alternative hypothesis is that of contextual interference, since the phase-trained group had three different movement components to learn while the duration-trained group had only one. However, evidence against this hypothesis was provided by Carnahan and Lee (1989), who contrasted phase-trained groups that were trained either on three distinct intervals, one for each submovement, or on the same duration for each submovement. Although the variable phasing group performed with more error during learning (as would be expected if they had higher contextual interference), the two phase-trained groups performed equally at transfer, and both outperformed a duration-trained group. Thus, the higher level skill requirements of the phasing task, rather than interference during training, appeared to be responsible for more effective transfer.

It is interesting to consider the issue of practice variability in the context of a distinction between the content of a task and the task requirements for processing that content (Smith, 1990). Initial training may lead to both content-specific learning and mastery of the process. When variable instances are introduced in training, but the task itself remains the same, learners are faced with varying content but a constant set of task processes, and the positive effects of variable training on transfer to new instances can then be viewed in two ways: first, variability could have a greater strengthening effect on task processes than constant practice (e.g., by eliminating strategies that work only for limited content). Second, exposure to varying previous content could improve accessibility to new content (e.g., by associative priming or by precluding perseveration in retrieval routes). It seems likely that the extent of these effects varies with the task. For example, if process learning is a small part of a task, and if there is little interaction between old instances and new ones, there should be little advantage for variable training. This might be the case with alphabet arithmetic, for which transfer is minimal even after extended training with multiple instances (Logan and Klapp, 1992). In contrast, Smith et al. (1988) had people make judgments of the form, Is behavior X trait Y? (e.g., Is hitting friendly?). When subjects were given 200 trials with one trait, but using different behaviors, there was substantial transfer to a new trait. (This study did not address the effects of practice variability, since all subjects were given varied instances in training.)

Part-Task Training

There are many everyday situations in which one learns a task in parts, then transfers to a whole situation. This is called part-to-whole (or vertical) transfer, or in applied contexts, part-task training. Learning to drive a car is an example; novices are typically trained separately on shifting gears and steering. There has been interest in the efficacy of this approach since the inception of formal studies of learning (for reviews see Knerr et al., 1987; McGeoch and Irion, 1952; Naylor, 1962; Wightman and Lintern, 1985). A general issue is whether part-task training is superior to training that uses the whole task from the outset, which would violate the general claim that training should simulate the transfer context as closely as possible. Even lacking an overall advantage, one can still ask to what extent part-task training produces positive transfer to the task as a whole.

Knerr et al. (1987) reviewed part-task training in the context of airplane flight skills and pointed to practical reasons for developing such training methods. One is the level of complexity of flight tasks. When tasks are complex enough to comprise multiple distinct components, part-task training seems both natural and imperative. There is also substantial potential for saving money by training in parts, especially when some task components can be trained by simulation. Training transitions, such as updating techniques in response to new equipment, may also be facilitated by part-task retraining. In addition, many applied tasks involve working in teams, and training of individuals outside of the team constitutes a form of part-task training (Salas et al., 1993). These practical considerations could justify a part-task training program as long as it produced a reasonable degree of positive transfer, even if there was no overall advantage over whole-task training.

Does part-task training produce positive transfer, and if so, is it as effective as or even more effective than whole-task training? Like many issues related to transfer of training, the answer to this question is complex. The efficacy of part-task training depends in large part on the nature of the task that is to be learned. Two task variables that have received particular emphasis are the difficulty or complexity of the task and the degree to which it is structurally integrated or organized. Naylor (1962) hypothesized that these variables interact: when a task is highly organized, the usefulness of whole-task training will increase with task complexity; when a task is easily decomposed into parts, the usefulness of part-task training will increase with task complexity. Naylor's hypothesis has received substantial support, but there have also been opposite outcomes (see Knerr et al., 1987).

In the domain of motor performance, Schmidt and Young (1987) suggested that when a task constitutes a sequence of distinct components or "programs" and has a relatively long duration (e.g., longer than 10 seconds), practicing subcomponents will produce positive transfer. One could potentially identify boundaries between such subcomponents by looking for points at which temporal aspects of the task vary the most from one performance to another. But when the task is continuous and its subcomponents do not form a clear sequence, there is often little transfer from part-task training. This is likely to be the case for example, for rapid, ballistic tasks (Schmidt, 1991). In this case, negative transfer from part-task training may actually occur, because the neuromuscular structure of a component may be fundamentally different when it is practiced in isolation from its structure in the whole-task context.

Tasks may be divided into parts not only sequentially, but on the basis of the cognitive or perceptual processes involved. A successful part-task training program based on task division into cognitively distinct components was devised by Mane et al. (1989). They devised a space fortress video game in which the objective was to destroy a space fortress by firing missiles from a spaceship. The part-task training prior to whole-task training was cost-effective in that the savings in later training was greater than the amount spent in the part-task training. Patrick (1992) suggested that task components might be distinguished on the basis of required processes, such as perceptual detection, concept learning, problem solving, motor coordination, and rule following. Christina and Corcos (1988) pointed to another cognitive factor, the attention span of the learner, that may limit the ability of an individual to deal with the whole-task situation.

The success of part-task training also depends on training procedures, such as how the task is decomposed during training and how it is reconstructed at transfer. Three general methods for decomposing a task are simplifying, fractionating, and segmenting. Simplifying is done by modifying or eliminating task demands, for example, reducing dimensions of control or eliminating time constraints. Fractionating refers to separate practice on components of tasks that in the whole-task form would overlap in time: an example is dividing control of a plane into separate pitch, roll, and yaw components. Each practice condition is simplified, but no task component is eliminated from consideration. Segmenting refers to division of a task into temporal or spatial components.

The effectiveness of these various methods depends in part on how they are recombined. Methods for recombination include pure part (practice each part in isolation, then combine all), progressive part (incrementally add parts to a combination, practicing each separately before adding it), and repetitive part (incrementally add parts to a combination, but without separate part practice). Incremental additions may be further varied by whether parts are added in the order of whole-task execution or the reverse order. There are also variations in how much the combined group of subtasks is practiced between new additions.

The aviation training literature suggests that segmentation is highly effective when tasks are recombined by a reverse repetitive-part technique; that is, successively adding task components in reverse order, from those performed latest to those performed earliest. This technique, called "backward chaining," was used successfully by Bailey et al. (1980) in training a dive-bomb maneuver as a four-segment event. Pilots trained with segmentation and backward chaining tended to learn faster and, when transferred to the whole sequence, they outperformed pilots given whole-task training.

The evidence for fractionation and simplification is somewhat mixed. By its very nature, fractionation eliminates training on how to integrate and share components of the task over time. Not surprisingly, then, it appears to be particularly deficient, relative to whole-task training, when tasks have interdependent, time-shared components. On the other hand, fractionation does generally produce some positive transfer and may become more effective at higher levels of practice (Knerr et al., 1987).

With simplification, there is some danger of negative transfer, since the more complex version of the task may call for new responses to the same stimulus conditions used previously (Lintern and Roscoe, 1980). Wightman (1983) suggested that simplification will be most effective if the simplified task focuses on those components that potentially produce the greatest error. In landing on an aircraft carrier, one such task is controlling the glideslope to the landing. He found that a manipulation designed to simplify this component—shortening the lag between the throttle input and the visual glideslope indicator—had little effect on training or transfer. Again, the problem appeared to be negative transfer: the progressive lengthening of lag over training called for new responses, but there was no corresponding change in the stimulus display.

A general message from the part-task training literature is that careful analysis of the task is called for. There is a clear need for a task taxonomy that identifies the variables that predict the potential success of a part-task training program and, for a given task, suggests techniques for decomposition and recombination that optimize part-task training. It seems clear that at least some tasks are aided by part-task training, and given the practical considerations mentioned above, there is strong motivation for the development of these training techniques.

Length of Training

The relationship between level of initial learning and transfer is complex. Although higher levels of initial learning lead to longer retention, they do not necessarily produce greater benefits in a transfer situation. This result reflects the fact that differences between the training and transfer contexts may be more difficult to accommodate after higher levels of initial learning.

Early studies of transfer in a verbal learning context attempted to experimentally isolate the basic underlying stimulus-response processes. They typically used paired associate paradigms, in which subjects learned a list of A-B pairs (e.g., A terms are words; B terms are digits) and then were given new lists to learn. Performance of the experimental subjects were compared with subjects who learned the second list without prior training on another list. Learning in this task can be subdivided into (at least) four components: learning the stimulus terms, learning the response terms, learning the stimulus-response associations, and learning the response-stimulus associations. The transfer context can retain any of these component processes while placing demands on others. For example, transfer from pairs like sweet-7 to sour-7 and happy-8 to sad-8 should take advantage of learning on all prior components (assuming mediation between antonyms like sweet and sour), whereas transfer from pairs like sweet-7 and happy-8 to sweet-8 and happy-7 should benefit from initial learning of the individual stimuli and responses, but suffer from interference due to remapping of associations. Not surprisingly, these procedures did produce positive and negative transfer, respectively.

The effect of the amount of prior learning depends in part on the rate of learning of the various components. For example, in a transfer situation in which old stimulus and response items are retained but are associated in new ways, there will be positive effects from prior item learning but negative effects from prior associative learning. If the items (positive effects) are learned faster than the associations (negative effects), it would be better to transfer early in learning, when positive benefits have been attained without too much cost on the negative side. But one cannot be sure that items are learned faster than associations; indeed, it depends greatly on the nature of the paired associates themselves. Thus, it is not surprising that in a review of the verbal transfer literature, Kausler (1974:232) termed amount of learning to be an "enigmatic variable."

Similar principles can be applied outside of the relatively simple context of paired verbal associates. Mastery of a task requires learning the pool of relevant stimulus cues, learning to perform the response repertoire, and learning the relationship between the cue context and the responses. Longer training periods should produce greater learning of all of these components, but some of that learning may not be productive in the transfer context.

The picture is further complicated when one considers that the nature of processing can change qualitatively over the course of learning and so affect transfer. Such changes include modification of the stimulus cues that control responses, for example, changes from visual control to proprioceptive (internal muscle sensations) control in tracking tasks (see Cormier, 1984). Stimuli may also be redefined: for example, they may become responded to as category members rather than instances (Cheng, 1985). Another idea is that people learn to extract the "invariants" (Gibson, 1979) that are the predictors of response requirements and to ignore uncorrelated cues that accompany them (Lintern, 1991). Still another assumption is that attentional demands of tasks are reduced, that is, that individuals become automatic responders over the course of skill acquisition (e.g., Ackerman, 1988; Schneider and Shiffrin, 1977). All of these changes over the course of learning have effects on transfer that interact with the relationship between the training and transfer contexts.

Automatic processing, in particular, has been suggested to produce potentially negative effects because of the specificity of learning that results (see Cormier, 1984). It is difficult to change automatic responses given a change in task conditions. Fisk et al. (1991) demonstrated these effects in a category search task, in which people indicated the position of an exemplar of some target taxonomic category among a vertical array of three items (e.g., looking for a bird name in an array: robin, arm, hand). Under consistent mapping conditions, a given taxonomic category was always used for targets and never for distractors: for example, a subject might search for a bird name among body parts but never search for a building name among birds. Under variable mapping conditions, a given taxonomic category provided targets on some trials and distractors on others. Consistent mapping from stimulus to response has been shown to be critical for developing the characteristics of automatic processing: low response times and errors and null effects of increasing workload (e.g., increasing the number of targets to be sought on any one trial). After 10 training sessions, subjects showed positive transfer from consistently mapped tasks to new tasks using the same targets with novel distractors or the same distractors with novel targets, relative to performance with entirely new sets of targets and distractors. In contrast, pronounced negative transfer resulted from reversing responses to consistently mapped targets or distractors, so that previous targets became distractors, or vice versa. This negative transfer occurred even when a subset of the original consistently mapped items was maintained unchanged, that is, when old targets were sought among items that had previously been consistent targets, or when previously consistent distractors became new targets that were sought among old distractors. The cost of remapping targets was greater than that for remapping distractors.

These results were interpreted in terms of a strength theory that is reminiscent of earlier theories of transfer in paired-associate learning tasks. Automaticity is assumed to result in a high strength in memory for consistent targets and a low strength for consistent distractors. Negative transfer results when target and distractor roles are reversed either because the low-strength items have relatively weak signals and form poor targets or because the high-strength items have relatively strong signals and cannot be easily rejected. These changes in strength resulting from consistent training, particularly of target items, are not easily overcome.

An important conclusion from this research is that once automatic responses are attained to a stimulus set, changes in even part of that set will substantially disrupt performance. If lengthy training leads to automatic responses to task-irrelevant stimuli, which are not similarly linked to those responses in the transfer context, transfer performance will be impaired. But against the potentially negative effects of automaticity, with concomitant overspecificity of the stimulus representation, must be balanced the positive effects of extended learning in the form of mastering the repertoire of responses, integrating and strengthening the representation of relevant stimuli, and learning the rules that associate them.

The Role of Feedback

A surprising general finding from research on the importance of feedback to ultimate performance is that it rarely helps and sometimes actually hurts long-term learning (for reviews, see, e.g., Salmoni et al., 1984; Wheaton et al., 1976). This finding holds for both motoric and cognitive tasks in nature.

Although the overall finding is clear, it is important to distinguish between intrinsic and extrinsic feedback, concurrent and terminal feedback, immediate and delayed feedback, and separate and accumulated feedback. Intrinsic feedback refers to the knowledge one gets immediately and automatically simply by attempting to perform a task. It is obvious when one hits the tennis ball out of the court or when one misses when swinging a baseball bat at a ball. Extrinsic feedback comes from outside the learner, provided either by an individual or a training device. If the feedback is received while the activity is being performed, such as while riding a bicycle, the feedback is concurrent; in contrast, the outcome of a tennis stroke is terminal when one sees where the ball lands. Extrinsic feedback that is provided after the execution of the task (terminal) can be further classified by whether the feedback is immediate or delayed, and if not delayed whether it is given for each attempt (separate) or is accumulated across trials and only a summary of performance is given. A final distinction that can be made is between knowledge of results and knowledge of performance: the former refers to how well one did at executing a task in terms of the outcome of the action; the latter refers to the action or movement pattern involved in the skill (e.g., "your elbow was bent when you tried to hit the ball").

Most research on feedback has looked at the effectiveness of knowledge of results. Schmidt (1988) provides a thorough review of much of the literature pertaining to motor learning. An interesting finding from his laboratory is that if the feedback on results is provided after each trial, immediate performance is better than when only summary performance is given every 15 trials; however, long-term or ultimate learning is facilitated by giving only summary feedback intermittently such as after 15 trials.

Anderson et al. (1989) examined feedback in the context of learning the programming language LISP. They taught the language using a computer-based tutor and varied whether or not they provided feedback and when it was provided. Like Schmidt, they also found an immediate benefit of feedback but no long-term benefit. In contrast to some of the results that Schmidt reports, however, Anderson et al. did not find a long-term deficit of feedback.

An explanation for the lack of long-term benefit from error feedback was suggested by Miller (1953), who realized that offering feedback concurrent with doing a task might serve as a crutch. When the feedback is removed during performance, those trained with the feedback are at a disadvantage. Goldstein and Rittenhouse (1954) provided some of the first evidence that concurrent feedback (as opposed to summary information at a delay) produces short-term gains but no long-term benefits. One should not conclude that it is optimal to deprive the learner of any knowledge of results; rather, feedback should not provide too much information too soon.

This conclusion may seem at odds with literature from the tradition of verbal learning and concept formation, in which subjects learn to assign multi-attribute items to classes according to some experimenter-designated rule (e.g., Restle, 1962; Bower and Trabasso, 1964). In these tasks, there is usually an arbitrary stimulus-to-response mapping, and no intrinsic feedback about the correctness of a response is available. Feedback then apparently enables subjects to prune the set of possible hypotheses about the correct rule (Levine, 1966; Trabasso and Bower, 1966), and its delay only imposes the load of holding previous stimulus-response pairings in memory. In contrast, this section has emphasized task situations in which intrinsic feedback is typically available and the stimulus-response mapping is not arbitrary.

Predicting Transfer

Transfer is a problem of high dimensionality. Much of the controversy over transfer may result from different theorists and experimenters working within different areas of a high-dimensional transfer "space," in which transfer is predicted by a host of variables, some of which have not yet been studied.

The notion of a transfer space was suggested for the learning of lists of verbal stimulus-response associates by Osgood (1949). He constructed a theoretical three-dimensional transfer surface, where two of the dimensions were the similarity between the original and transfer lists with respect to the stimulus and response terms, and the third dimension was the amount (and direction) of transfer. For example, having learned the pair dog-basket, transfer to canine-basket would involve a semantically similar stimulus term, while transfer to dog-bucket would involve a semantically similar response term. Positive transfer was predicted in situations with semantically similar stimuli and responses; considerable negative transfer was predicted when the same stimulus items were trained with one set of response terms and then paired with new ones at transfer. Predictions of the Osgood model were not always accurate, particularly with respect to negative transfer (Bugelski and Cadwallader, 1956). Negative transfer was found to be anomalously strong when old stimuli were paired with responses that were new but similar to the old ones (an effect sometimes called the Skaggs-Robinson paradox; Robinson, 1927). In addition, particularly in the domain of motor-skills learning, negative transfer effects were often small and vanished with practice (Bilodeau and Bilodeau, 1961).

Holding (1976) proposed a modification of Osgood's transfer surface that, while admittedly imperfect, was consistent with general findings regarding similarity effects in motor learning. These findings include a decrease of positive transfer as the stimulus similarity between training and transfer tasks decreases, no transfer when entirely new stimuli and responses are used in the transfer task, large positive transfer when the previously trained responses are used with different stimuli, and negative transfer when the same stimuli are used at transfer but with responses that are different from, but similar to, the originals. Holding suggested that most practical transfer is positive and that negative transfer is most likely when there is a failure to discriminate between distinct training and transfer stimuli that are intended to elicit distinct responses, or when the responses themselves cannot be well discriminated.

At the same time, Holding (1976:8) noted: "There are, in fact, good reasons for viewing all transfer surfaces with mistrust." A major problem is their low dimensionality; many important influences on transfer have been ignored by the research on transfer surfaces. That work stresses the similarity of the training and task environment, but there are also influences from the nature of the training, such as training schedules and the availability of feedback. Situated learning theorists stress social variables; one could also consider motivational variables.

Efforts to understand transfer would clearly be helped by greater efforts to characterize the nature of relevant variables. A valuable addition would be a task taxonomy, stressing distinctions such as those between cognitive and motor tasks, between tasks performed in isolation and those performed in groups, or between tasks limited by perceptual, memory, or response factors. All of these (and more) are likely to modulate the effects of other variables on the nature and degree of transfer. Efforts to make relevant distinctions can be seen, for example, in the literature on part-whole training, which focuses on the intrinsic integration (or lack thereof) of task components as a determinant of training outcomes.

The Role of Fidelity in Simulation

The fundamental tenet of situated learning, that learning should occur in the same context as eventual execution, has been evaluated particularly carefully in the context of simulator devices. Training devices that simulate the actual situations in which learners will ultimately find themselves vary in terms of the fidelity or realism of the device, in relation to the actual performance environment. The size and complexity of the task that is simulated can also vary, for example, from a hand grenade that has its explosive charge replaced with sand to teach the skill of activating and throwing a grenade to a full-scale flight simulator. The latter can use computer-generated imagery of the landing field, a full motion platform, complete cockpit instrumentation, etc. The common feature to all simulations is that they provide practice on aspects of the task environment.

There are several reasons for simulating a performance situation rather than actual training in it: the real environment may be too dangerous, too costly, too time consuming, or too rare to find. For example, the National Training Center at Ft. Irwin provides soldiers with tough, realistic training, using air-land battle exercises in the Mojave Desert involving "infantry, armor, artillery, aviation, chemical, logistics, air defense, engineering, military police, electronic warfare, and special operations units" (Wiering, 1992:18). There is a very high priority placed on realism: if a commander wants a ditch dug, he sends his soldiers out and they dig that ditch. If a soldier is "injured" in a battle, he must be evacuated, and if he "dies," a replacement soldier must be requisitioned. The simulated enemy forces were actually American troops trained to fight according to Soviet military doctrine. There are key differences between this simulation and real warfare that make the Ft. Irwin training an effective teaching device, including observer controllers who monitor performance during each simulated battle. An important learning component is intense after-action review, in which strategic mistakes are discussed and soldiers are encouraged to discover their own correct actions and mistakes. Soldiers who are "killed" (tagged by a laser weapon) in a simulated battle have a chance to learn from their mistakes. Historically, it is the first major battle of any war that creates the most casualties. With experience, soldiers make fewer mistakes.

Another obvious task for which simulators are important is for training airplane pilots. Not only is it considerably safer to use training devices, it is often cheaper than flying a real plane, which requires fuel and maintenance. Errors can be corrected during training in a simulator that might cost a life in a real airplane. Furthermore, specific types of errors can be identified and enable a learner to practice those subcomponents of the task that need most attention. Another advantage of simulators is that difficult or emergency situations (e.g., failure of an indicator) can be simulated at will to see whether or not the learner responds correctly.

Others suggest that high levels of fidelity are not cost-effective and may even be detrimental (e.g., Andrews, 1988; Patrick, 1992). Too much fidelity to an actual complex system can sometimes be worse than a simpler representation of the environment. As Andrews (1988:49) states:

> Trainees who are new to a particular piece of equipment such as an aircraft, a sonar system, or a nuclear control panel often have a difficult time in learning the proper operation or maintenance techniques. This is so because the cues of the real equipment to which the trainees must respond are too subtle, fast, transitory or complex for the novice to fully comprehend.

On the basis of ideas of Miller (1954) and Gagne (1954), Patrick (1992:503) suggested that different types of simulation be used for different levels of proficiency of the same skill. During the initial stages of skill acquisition, learners would do better to be familiarized with very simple representations of the equipment if the task and equipment are quite complex:

> In the first stage of skill acquisition . . . simple simulations (pictures, diagrams, mock-ups) could be used to familiarize the trainee with the no-menclature and location of the displays, and with the controls involved in the perceptual-motor tasks . . . In the second stage of skill acquisition . . . the trainee should be able to practice coordinating movements and also making anticipations in the same manner as that required by the operation-al task. In the final stage . . . simulation should support high levels of practice of the task at high speeds and under heavy workloads or in low signal-to-noise ratios.

Although developers of simulation devices are often concerned with how many real-world phenomena can be mimicked, the important question is: Which perceptual cues should be reproduced in the training cycle. Miller (1954) has made an important distinction between engineering fidelity and psychological fidelity. The former is the degree to which the training device duplicates the physical characteristics of equipment or the surrounding environment in which the learner will ultimately be required to perform. Miller argued that there is a point of diminishing returns in terms of cost savings of training per degree of increased engineering fidelity. That is, beyond certain levels, increasing the fidelity of the simulation device will yield only small improvements in perfor-mance over a simpler device. Patrick (1992) has suggested that engineering fidelity is not the issue at all, that the critical determinant of transfer is the psychological fidelity of the simulation device. He notes that when training for cognitive tasks and procedures, high transfer can be achieved with simula-tions of low physical fidelity. The key issue is what are the necessary factors that produce psychological fidelity in a simulation. Research on transfer of training is critical to addressing this issue.

There have been a number of studies that have shown no advantage for real equipment or realistic simulators as compared with very inexpensive cardboard mock-ups or simple drawings when teaching various types of procedural tasks (e.g., Caro et al., 1984; Cox et al., 1965; Crawford and Crawford, 1978; Grimsley, 1969; Johnson, 1981; Prophet and Boyd, 1970; Trollip, 1979; see Valverde, 1973, for a review of early studies). For example, Cox et al. (1965) trained Army personnel to operate a 92-step procedure on a control panel. They compared training using real equipment (costing $11,000) with training using a realistic simulator (costing $1,000) and with cheap cardboard mock-ups and photographs. There were no ob-served differences in training time or in long-term performance or retention. Prophet and Boyd compared acquisition of the start-up and shut-down procedures for a Mohawk aircraft when trained with the real thing or a cheap mock-up, and there was no difference.

The degree to which simulations must incorporate specific features of the real-world environment can be thought of in terms of a given feature's "cuing potential" (Cormier, 1987). In order to execute the appropriate actions, a person needs to be able to recognize the cue in the target task as the same cue that was used for training. This view is similar to the notion of identical elements, but emphasizes that the recognition of a cue may fail if the surrounding context is different. Instead of merely including the surrounding context as other elements that must match, one can speak of the similarity of the context and how easily it affords recognition of the cuing elements. If the simulation or training elements are not recognized as cues for response, the simulation will not be effective for later performance.

In principle, one can analyze the correspondence between cues of the learning task or simulation and those of the transfer task, thereby determining the level of fidelity required. Salvendy and Pilitsis (1980) compared training programs for teaching suturing techniques to medical students and found that the best performing groups were those groups that used an electromechanical device, allowing them to puncture simulated tissue and providing auditory and visual feedback on correctness of technique. Those that merely heard lectures about suturing or watched a movie of the techniques did not perform as well.

Certainly, there are tasks where added simulation fidelity helps training; this has been heavily documented with respect to aircraft simulators. But one must be cautious in making general statements about the degree of fidelity required for optimal training because seemingly minor differences in transfer contexts may produce substantial differences in simulator effectiveness. For example, motion cues in flight simulators sometimes improve training; at other times, they do not. Ince et al. (1975) found that different kinds of motion (rough-air simulation or cockpit motion during turns) have different effects. Furthermore, whether motion cues are important during training also depends on the nature of the task required of the pilot during transfer. That is, transfer from the training environment to the performance environment is not a simple function of the overlap in identical elements. Some are more important to be represented in the training task, and which ones are more important depend on what performance features had to be recalled.

CONCLUSIONS

There is broad consensus that positive transfer is typically very specific to the contexts in which training has occurred, but this result is not invariant. Failures of transfer, being more noticeable, tend to overshadow many successes.

Identical Elements

As a general principle, having identical elements between training and performance contexts facilitates transfer. However, it is impossible in most cases to fully anticipate the performance contexts, rendering fully situated learning impossible. Furthermore, many factors may reduce the effectiveness of situated learning, including, for example, high costs of achieving training fidelity, reduction of time spent on acquisition and practice of underlying procedures, and disruption of other performers from the presence of novices.

Mismatches between task-irrelevant elements of the training and performance context can produce slight decrements in transfer; however, this can be ameliorated by varying the training context with respect to these elements.

The principle that training and transfer should have identical elements suggests training should mimic the experiences that are anticipated. The positive outcomes of variable practice and part-whole training suggest strong constraints on this conclusion.

The level of fidelity that is required in simulators in training depends on the nature of the elements that must be preserved. In many cases, a high degree of fidelity is not required and may be detrimental.

Type and Length of Training

Although concrete experience is critically important, the teaching of abstract principles has been shown to play a role in acquiring skills over a broad domain of tasks.

Somewhat surprisingly, giving immediate and constant feedback may fail to optimize training; delayed and intermittent feedback may produce superior results because it allows learners to detect and self-correct errors and it diminishes reliance on extrinsic sources.

The relation between length of training and performance is not a simple one. Clearly, longer training has facilitatory effects, but it can also lead to inflexibility when the training fails to anticipate variability in the performance context.

In summary, few generalizations can be made about transfer as a whole; what is needed is a task taxonomy that characterizes the nature of the critical elements that should be held identical between the training and performance contexts. For example, conceptually based tasks may be very different from rote motor tasks with respect to the need to maintain superficial, physical elements of the performance context.

4

Illusions of Comprehension, Competence, and Remembering

People's performances as individuals, and their contributions as members of groups, depend not only on their actual competence, but also on their assessment of that competence. The reading people take of their own state of knowledge or level of skill determines how they allocate their time and energy and the influence they have on others. Many things depend on people's subjective assessment of what they know and do not know: whether they volunteer for certain roles or tasks, whether they seek further practice or instruction, and whether they instill confidence in others, as well as the answers they give to questions from superiors and subordinates and the affect they induce in others by facial expressions and body language (see Chapter 10). Recent evidence suggests, however, that under certain conditions, people's assessments of what they know or remember can be seriously flawed, particularly when they use one index, such as familiarity, recognition, or fluency, to predict something else, such as unaided recall or production.

There are a variety of ways in which people can be fooled. Consider some of the assessments college students typically make in a course. They must decide if they are prepared for an upcoming test. In order to allocate study time, they must monitor the state of their own learning and comprehension across the topics for which they are responsible. If they end up doing poorly on the test, they may take a reading of their memories for how much time they spent studying. At the end of the course, they may also monitor their learning and comprehension in the course—when asked to judge the effectiveness of the instructor, for example, or deciding whether to recommend the course to a friend.

For each of these situations, the students must make a judgment on the basis of subjective experience: the subjective experience of comprehending a text, the subjective experience of remembering studying, or the subjective experience of learning during the course.

For each situation, there can be discrepancies between answers based on subjective experience and answers based on a more objective measure. Students may be confident that they understood a chapter yet do poorly on a test of the material in it; they may have confidence in their memories of studying much of the weekend, while a more objective record showed otherwise; and they may have confidence in their judgment that a given instructor is a great teacher, while a more objective measure revealed that students are learning little in that instructor's course. Even in the face of such discrepancies between subjective experience and objective measures, however, people find subjective experience a compelling basis for judgment. The subjective experience of understanding material might be less reliable as a measure of comprehension than is a more objective test, for example, but it is critical nonetheless—because it is the basis on which people guide their own behavior and make judgments, such as whether further study is necessary.

People are reluctant to give up subjective experience as a basis for judgments. Imagine a student who feels he or she has understood the material but obtains a low score on a test. The student may well question the fairness of the test before questioning his or her own feeling of comprehension. And a high score on an objective test is not always a satisfactory substitute for a feeling of comprehension. In addition, an objective record of a past event does not substitute for the subjective experience of remembering that event. While researchers have concentrated on objective measures of performance on cognitive tasks, it is the subjective experience of cognitive activities—such as comprehension, memory, and learning—that seems most important to the person engaging in those tasks.

The reason that the subjective experience of comprehending, knowing, or remembering is so compelling to people may stem from their intuitive theories of memory and knowledge. People seem to be naive realists about cognitive functions. The student who receives a bad grade on a test may wail "but I knew the material!" Similarly, a subject in a recent memory experiment who was asked to recall an event—and then asked "How do you know this event really happened?"—said: "How else could it be in memory [if it didn't really happen?]" (Johnson et al., 1988:374).

People believe that the feeling of remembering directly reflects access to something in memory. Similarly, people may think that their feelings of comprehension directly reflect how much they know. But there is growing evidence that in a variety of situations a person's subjective experience is actually an inference or an attribution, rather than a direct reading of cognitive functioning. From that perspective, it is understandable that illusions of knowing, comprehending, or remembering occur, and that illusion can be as compelling a basis for action as a real measure of knowing, comprehending, or remembering.

In this chapter we summarize recent research findings that demonstrate that the subjective experience of remembering can be produced even though the "remembered" event never occurred. We also address people's confidence in their own subjective experience as an objectively accurate characterization of the world. That is, people engage in a form of egocentrism when they fail to realize that their subjective experience of the difficulty of a problem, the comprehensibility of a text, or the ease of learning a task may not generalize to other people's experience of the problem, text, or task. Subjective experience can also fail as a basis for judging for others because of the effects of specific past experiences on one's performance. People sometimes show effects of prior experience on their objective performance even though they do not remember the prior experience that led to those effects.

SUBJECTIVE EXPERIENCE AND JUDGMENT

Subjective experience of an event is a function not only of the objective qualities of that event, but also of what a person brings to the event. Past experience, privileged knowledge, or the products of one's imagination can alter how one perceives an event or experiences a situation, and people are surprisingly insensitive to the ways their particular construal of a situation is idiosyncratic. Emphasis on such effects has been the hallmark of the subjectivist tradition, including the "new look" at perception initiated by Bruner and Postman (1949). The results of an overwhelming number of experiments support the idea that subjective experience does not reliably reflect some fixed, objective reality, but, rather, is often constructed. We describe only a few of those experiments to illustrate ways that reliance on subjective experience can produce errors in understanding and predicting the performance of others.

Errors resulting from reliance on subjective experience provide convincing support for a subjectivist tradition. Cognitive illusions that reflect effects of past experience on current subjective experience are analogous to perceptual illusions. Illusions of both types can be used to reveal mechanisms underlying subjective experience. However, emphasis on errors runs the risk of giving the mistaken impression that subjective experience is always an inferior basis for judgments. But people have little choice—it is nearly impossible to avoid basing judgments on subjective experience. In addition, subjective experience is sometimes superior to a more objective basis for judgments. We first describe the research that demonstrates this phenomena and then examine the role of subjective experience in the self-monitoring of learning.

Cognitive Illusions

Newton (1990) provides a powerful demonstration of how imagination can color subjective experience. She asked half of her student subjects to be "tappers" and half to be "listeners." The tappers were asked to select songs from a list of 25 common titles and tap out the rhythm to listeners sitting near them. Listeners did not know the list of potential songs. Then the tappers were asked to estimate the probability that their listeners could correctly identify the song from the taps and to estimate the numbers of students in general who could identify the song from the taps. To appreciate the study, you might want to pause and tap out a song and reflect on your subjective experience. Tappers do not hear merely a series of taps on the table, but a whole imagined rendition of the tune, with orchestration and voices. The imaginative additions apparently also transform one's experience of the taps: tappers estimated the likelihood that listeners could correctly identify the songs at 50 percent; the actual rate of correct identification was a mere 2.5 percent. Griffin and Ross (1991) make the point that to correctly estimate the likelihood that listeners would identify the song, tappers needed to recognize the extent to which their subjective experience of the taps differed from the subjective experience of the listeners, and they needed to make allowance for the difference in experience when making their estimates. Tappers may have failed to grasp the degree of difference their privileged information made in their experience of the taps, or they may have been unable to adequately judge how much they needed to adjust their estimates.

It is not difficult to imagine how such processes probably color many interactions in the workplace. Inefficient communication from superiors to subordinates, and vice versa, and among coworkers in general, is no doubt frequently the product of people's inability to make allowances for the difference between their subjective experience and the likely subjective experience of their listener.

Griffin and Ross (1991) argue that a variety of anomalies in social judgment and prediction stems from variations in how particular people construe a situation, and their failure to appreciate that their construal is only one of many possibilities. The "false consensus effect" in social judgment refers to people's tendency to overestimate the commonness of their own beliefs and choices (Ross et al., 1977). For example, subjects might be asked the question: "Which kind of music do you like better, music from the 1960s or music from the 1980s?" and then asked to estimate the proportion of college students who would make the same choices. The subject has to make a particular interpretation of what is meant by "1960s music" and what is meant by "1980s music" and then choose between the two. But as was the case for the tappers in Newton's study, subjects who interpret such questions may not realize the degree to which their particular construal of the elements of the choice is idiosyncratic. That is, they might think of five or six really good bands from the 1960s and several bad bands from the 1980s, choose "1960s music," and assume that most people would make a similar choice. In contrast, someone else might quickly think of a number of good bands from the 1980s, and several lousy bands from the 1960s, choose "1980s music" and assume that their preference would be widely shared. Gilovich (1990) argued that the false consensus effect occurs because the phrasing of the options only partially specifies their meaning. Dawes (1990) questioned the false consensus effect, showing that errors are often people's overestimating the extent to which they are unique, rather than the opposite.

The important point for present purposes is that reliance on subjective experience as a basis for judgments is prone to error because of failure to take individual differences into account. Griffin and Ross (1991) point out that much human misunderstanding may stem from people's failure to appreciate the degree to which their construal of a situation differs from that of other people. Disagreements often arise because of what Asch (1969) called different objects of judgments (different construals), rather than different judgments of the same object. Conflicts are exacerbated by people's resistance to accepting the possibility of multiple construals. It is common for partisans in a disagreement to feel that their own beliefs follow from an unbiased consideration of facts and arguments, while the other side's beliefs are affected by biased interpretation of facts and arguments. That is, others are open to the effects of beliefs on construal, but not oneself.

One source of variation in people's interpretation or construal of a situation is past experience. In one study, people who walked down a hallway that contained a poster of a missing child were more likely to interpret an ambiguous interaction between a child and an adult as a possible kidnapping (James, 1986). That effect could be an instance of memory without remembering: recent experience with one event made particular construals of a later event more available. Impressions of others are also influenced by "priming" effects of this sort. People's judgments about another person are influenced by what categories are made most easily accessible by recent prior experience (see e.g., Higgins, 1989; Srull and Wyer, 1979). The same behavior, for example, can be judged as "assertive" or as "aggressive," depending on which category has been primed. These effects occur even though subjects cannot "remember" or are unaware of the relevance of the priming stimulus.

Construal of a current situation is often determined by small details that make the current situation analogous to a particular past experience. Gilovich (1981) has shown that subjects' recommendations of how to resolve a hypothetical international crisis were influenced by irrelevant similarities between the hypothetical crisis and historical analogies. Politicians know that by describing a conflict as analogous to Vietnam they can very effectively color the interpretation of that conflict. Such effects on interpretation of an ambiguous stimulus can depend on specific details that recruit memory for one particular prior event rather than another. For example, Smith and Zarate (1992) showed that the likelihood of interpreting someone in terms of a stereotype depends on the similarity of the current situation to a prior situation in which the stereotype was invoked. Ross (1977) demonstrated similar specificity in the likelihood of solving a problem that is analogous to a prior problem: even irrelevant details in the current situation can change the probability of recruiting and using memory for a prior problem. This work shows that past experience influences people's interpretation or what comes to mind in a current situation and, thereby, their judgments.

Past experience can also alter social judgments by making cognition more fluent. In a series of experiments, subjects were asked to solve anagrams (e.g., fscar) and then rate the difficulty of the anagrams for others (Jacoby and Kelley, 1987). Subjects tended to use their own experiences in solving the anagrams as a basis for judging the difficulty of the anagrams for others—the correlations between speed of solving the anagrams and difficulty ratings were quite high. Before attempting to solve and rate the difficulty of the anagrams, subjects in some conditions read a list of words that were the solutions to half of the anagrams they were later asked to solve. Prior reading of those words led to faster solution of those anagrams. However, subjects continued to use their subjective experience of difficulty as a basis for judging difficulty for others, even though their experience had been affected by the effects of prior reading of the solution words. They rated anagrams of the studied words as easier for others to solve than anagrams of equal difficulty constructed from words not presented earlier.

People in the anagram experiments may have failed to recognize that half of the solution words they produced had been on the list they studied earlier. Or, even if they recognized the solution words from the list, they may have failed to appreciate that reading the solution words led them to solve those anagrams more quickly. In follow-up experiments, subjects were informed of the effect of prior reading of solution words on later anagram difficulty or informed of the effect and asked to attempt to recognize each solution word before judging the anagram difficulty. In the first case, subjects who were informed of the effect nonetheless rated old anagrams as easier for others than new anagrams. However, subjects who were informed of the effect and asked whether they recognized the solution words as from the list they had studied did not rate the old anagrams as easier to solve than new anagrams: those subjects avoided the biasing effects of memory by switching from subjective experience to a more objective basis for judgments (see below). That switch was necessary because there is no sure way to correct subjective experience. That is, the question "How easy would this anagram seem had I not read the solution?" is impossible to answer.

Subjects in the anagram experiments were extremely reluctant to give up subjective experience as a basis for predicting the performance of others. As described in the next section, there is good reason for that reluctance: even spoiled subjective experience can provide a more accurate basis for predicting the performance of others than do alternative, more objective bases for judgment.

Subjective experience has a bad reputation as a basis for judgments. Treating one's own experience as a mirror of objective reality can lead to egocentric errors as extreme as those made by children (Piaget and Inhelder, 1956). Olson (1986) argued that children fail to distinguish between what they see and what they know and therefore mistakenly extend their privileged interpretation to others. The examples given in the preceding sections show that such egocentrism is not restricted to children; adults make similar errors. Apparently, people do not develop a general ability to distinguish what is given in a stimulus and what is an interpretation. Instead, they continue to rely on their subjective experience—even though that experience may be spoiled by factors such as memory.

People do come to realize that in certain situations they must give up subjective experience and rely on a more analytic, objective basis for judgments. Good teachers must be mindful that their understanding of material is not an appropriate basis for judging their students' understanding. As Piaget (1962:5) pointed out:

> every beginning instructor discovers sooner or later that his first lectures were incomprehensible because he was talking to himself, so to say, mindful only of his own point of view. He realizes only gradually and with difficulty that it is not easy to place oneself in the shoes of students who do not yet know what he knows about the subject matter of his course.

Goranson (1976) created a series of demonstrations of the problems of hindsight in judging the difficulty of problems for others. When people were given the answers to puzzles and problems and asked to "go through the motions of solving the puzzle just as if you didn't already know the solution," he found that they vastly underestimated the time it would take to solve the problem in comparison with a group that actually attempted to solve it. This hindsight effect could lead teachers who rely on their own subjective experience of understanding as a basis for judging the difficulty of problems to judge their students as dull and slow. Goranson suggested a number of strategies for teachers to use to more accurately assess students' understanding: frequent tests, checking students' lecture notes, and individual tutorials.

The ability to know that subjective experience is a bad basis for predicting for others may be situation specific. To avoid egocentrism, one must have an objective basis for judgment that can replace subjective experience. One objective basis for judgments is a theory. In the case of the anagram experiments described above, subjects who had read the solutions to anagrams in the first phase and then realized that their subjective experience of difficulty was a poor basis for judging difficulty for others, could have switched over to analytic judgments based on some theory of what makes an anagram easy or difficult. Judgments could be based on rules such as "low frequency words are difficult to solve," or "anagrams with many vowels are more difficult to solve." To see how effective those rule or theory-based judgments were, subjects in one condition in the anagram experiment were shown the solution word to the anagram immediately before seeing the anagram, for example, "scarf" then "fscar." Reading the solution word prevented subjects from having any experience of the difficulty of the anagram and forced them to rely on rules as a basis for judgments. Those rules turned out to be inadequate: the correlation between judged difficulty for anagrams presented with solutions and the actual time to solve those anagrams in the control condition was quite low. Furthermore, the rule-based judgments were even worse than judgments based on subjective experience that had been altered by prior reading of the solution words. Unless people have a well-specified theory, they may be better off relying on their subjective experience as a basis for judgments.

Analysis and reason may actually lead to worse judgments than unanalyzed feelings or intuitions when one is predicting preferences or other personal judgments. Wilson and Schooler (1991) found that translating affect into reasons may be disruptive. They asked subjects to taste and rate the quality of five different brands of strawberry jam. Their criterion measure of "goodness of ratings" was the rank-ordering of the jams by a panel of experts who had rated the jams on 16 dimensions for *Consumer Reports*. When subjects were asked simply to taste the jams and rank them, their rankings correlated fairly well with the experts' rankings (average correlation, .55). However, when another group of subjects was asked to provide reasons for their judgments, their rankings of the quality of the jams was less like that of the experts (average correlation, .11). Wilson and Schooler argued that forcing their subjects to think about why they liked or disliked each jam turned an affective response into a more cognitive one, and in this case the cognitive judgments appeared to be less correct.

In another study by Wilson et al. (1984), couples in steady dating relationships were asked how well adjusted they thought their relationship was. In the "control condition," that's all they were asked. In the "reasons condition," they were also asked to list all the reasons they felt the way they did about their dating partners. Several months later, it appeared that asking subjects for reasons undermined the accuracy of their assessment of their relationships: the correlation between ratings of the relationship and whether they were still dating their partner several months later was only .10 in the reasons condition; it was .62 in the control condition. (It is safe to assume, the researchers hope, that there was no causal relationship between having subjects list their reasons and their reduced likelihood of continuing to date the rated partner.) People's analysis of what makes a jam good or what makes a relationship good may simply be bad theories. Perhaps an unanalyzed affective response captures more important dimensions or weights the dimensions more appropriately, about a relationship than any theory of what makes a couple compatible.

Self-Monitoring of Learning: Illusions of Comprehending and Knowing

An important determinant of learning is a learner's ability to self-monitor knowledge and learning. Among the consequences of self-monitoring are effects on judgments of one's self-efficacy, which is important for motivation and performance (see Chapter 8). An attribution process clearly underlies people's evaluation of their own abilities, as shown in a classic series of experiments done by Jones et al. (1968), who investigated the effects of varying distributions of success and failure on attributions of intellectual ability.

Jones et al. (1968) arranged conditions such that success rate in solving problems either increased or decreased across a series of problems; the total number of successful solutions was the same for the two conditions. Subjects were asked to estimate their future performance. Subjects in the "ascending success" condition were more confident about their own ability than were those in the "descending success" condition. However, results were the opposite when subjects were given the same patterns of successes and failures of others and asked to evaluate their abilities. In that case, a performer with a descending success rate was judged as more intelligent and expected to outperform a performer with an ascending success rate. Jones et al. explain their results in a way that is reminiscent of Heider's (1958:157) proposition that perceivers are prone to attribute the reactions of another person to characteristics of the person (e.g., intelligence), while one's own reactions are attributed to the objective world (e.g., the difficulty of problems). The early failures of others in the ascending success condition give rise to a first impression of low intelligence and that first impression is not reversed even in the face of others' future successes. For oneself, in contrast, the early failures in the same ascending series is attributed to the greater difficulty of early problems, settling into the task, and so forth.

Jones et. al. (1968) considered the practical implications of their research. They ask one to imagine a situation in which A is observed by B to show systematic improvement in performance, for example, an improving player (A) observed by a coach (B). Results of their experiments suggest that A will feel very confident about his or her future performance, while B will predict that A's future performance will be relatively low. The improving player is outraged and does not understand why he or she was kicked off the team just as his or her true ability was beginning to show. Examples of this sort underline the importance of considering attribution processes in educational settings.

As is true when predicting the performance of others, monitoring one's own performance can rely on subjective experience and, consequently, is subject to errors that reflect cognitive illusions. For example, the ease or fluency of identifying a briefly presented word is often used as a basis for judging the visual duration of the word. Similarly, the ease of generating an answer to a question may be one basis for confidence that the answer is correct. To illustrate, what was Buffalo Bill's last name? If an answer comes quickly to mind, how do you know it was correct?

Kelley and Lindsay (1993) found negative correlations between the latency to think of an answer and confidence in that answer (see also Nelson and Narens, 1990). They then manipulated the speed with which correct and incorrect answers came to subjects' minds by having subjects first read a list of answers to general knowledge questions and then attempt to answer those questions. Prior exposure to correct answers (e.g., Cody) increased the speed and frequency with which correct answers were given on the general knowledge test and also increased subjects' confidence in those answers. Even stronger evidence for the claim that the speed with which an answer comes to mind is a basis for confidence was gained by changing what answers came to mind. Illusions of knowing occurred when subjects studied closely related but incorrect answers (e.g., Hickock). The studied but incorrect answers were more likely to be confidently given as answers to the general knowledge questions. Kelley and Lindsay (1993) argued that those effects could occur without conscious memory for the list of words.

Nelson and his colleagues (for a review, see Nelson and Narens, 1990) point out the importance of monitoring one's own learning for the control of study time in self-paced learning. Unfortunately, judgments of learning are surprisingly inaccurate under certain conditions. For example, subjects might study a list of unrelated paired associates, such as *ocean-tree*, and then be asked to predict the probability of their being able to recall *tree* to the cue *ocean* on a memory test a short time later. On some judgment-of-learning trials, the pair studied earlier was shown intact; other trials consisted of the cue *ocean* being shown alone. Judgments of learning have little predictive value if the judgments are made immediately after one has studied the item. However, the predictive accuracy soars to almost perfect if the judgments of learning are delayed for several minutes after studying the item and if the cue word is shown without the target word (Dunlosky and Nelson, 1992; Nelson and Dunlosky, 1991). Nelson and Dunlosky argued that people make judgments of learning by using the cue *ocean* to retrieve information from memory. If the judgment is made immediately after studying an item, such as *ocean-tree*, the response term *tree* is still available from short-term memory, and the subject may be unable to assess how readily available *tree* would be from long-term memory. Delaying the judgment for more than 30 seconds means that it is then based on information in long-term memory, which appears to be a much better source of information for the later memory test. When the to-be-recalled target word was shown to subjects, they, like the subjects who were presented the answer to an anagram along with the anagram, could apparently no longer judge the likelihood that they would have been able to come up with the answer on their own. Giving the target word paired with the cue word at a delay appears to ruin subjects' subjective experience in a fashion analogous to that experienced by subjects in the anagram experiments. Spellman and Bjork (1992) have argued that with the target word present subjects are denied the opportunity to exercise and benefit from the retrieval processes that will be later required on the final cued test.

Evaluation of Instruction

During training and education, learners monitor changes in their performance or understanding and use those changes to evaluate the instruction. However, changes in ease of performance or increased understanding can be attributed to a variety of sources and so give rise to different judgments. The new understanding can be mistakenly interpreted as something "obvious" that the student knew all along.

One "knew it all along" effect of this sort has been documented in laboratory investigations (e.g., Fischhoff, 1975; Hasher et al., 1981). People were unable to remember their original knowledge state—that Aladdin, of the magic lamp story, originated in Persia—after the experimenter has provided them with outcome information—it was really China. The effect is an example of hindsight bias: people are prone, with hindsight, to treat an observed outcome as inevitable even though the outcome may have objectively been an unlikely one (Fischhoff, 1975). Errors of this sort are pervasive. However, Hasher et al. (1981) showed that the "knew it all along" effect can be avoided. Under the proper test conditions, people can recover their original state of knowledge and realize the difference between that original state and outcome information. That is, the later outcome information does not erase or "overwrite" original knowledge. These findings are important for questions about recall processes, especially those involved in eyewitness testimony (considered below).

The "knew it all along" effect can be understood as another example of fluency being misattributed to produce a cognitive illusion. The effect is quite similar to the effect of the ease of generating an answer to a question on confidence in the correctness of the answer (Kelley and Lindsay, 1993). When a question is answered easily, the subjective experience may be that the answer came from one's general knowledge held prior to the experiment—one "knew it all along" even when the "it" was misleading new information gained in the experimental setting (e.g., Buffalo Bill's last name was Hickock). Similar misattributions can produce errors in self-monitoring of knowledge and learning.

The opposite effect can also occur in instruction: students can misattribute their improved performance or understanding to a quality of the task or material. For example, across a series of lectures, students may think their instructor's style is improving—that the instructor is speaking more slowly, perhaps, or making more organized presentations. The students' subjective experience of greater clarity may be a misattribution of effects due to their improved understanding of the subject; the speech habits of the lecturer may be completely unchanged. The subjective experience of greater clarity of speech may depend on increased ease of comprehension, analogous to the influence of memory on noise judgments, as discussed below.

Speculatively, it might be possible to intentionally arrange conditions to create an illusion of effective instruction. This devious possibility was suggested by an acquaintance of the authors who became suspicious about a book he bought to help him prepare for the Law School Admissions Test (LSAT). The book provided sample questions and discussion of strategies to use, followed by repeated tests that were scored in ways that supposedly paralleled the actual LSAT. The person worked through the first few tests and was horrified when he obtained low scores. He had scored well on standardized tests in the past, and after calming down, he wondered if there was something peculiar about the book. He turned to the end of the book and took the last test, and scored very well. After closer inspection of the questions, he became convinced that the sample questions on the earlier tests were objectively more difficult than those on the later tests. He argues that the book was written in a way to intentionally create an illusion of improvement so as to increase sales of the book. This case history is not cited to suggest applications to how one should structure training to give an illusion of improvement, but to illustrate the ambiguity in interpreting changes in one's performance.

Knowing and Learning

Although people may be unable to remember the answer to a knowledge question, they sometimes have a feeling of knowing the answer (a "feeling of knowing"), and in that state they can predict with considerable accuracy the likelihood that they will be able to pick out the correct alternative on a subsequent recognition test (e.g., Blake, 1973; Hart, 1967). The "calibration" of judgments refers to the correlation of people's self-predicted performance and their actual performance. People are usually overconfident: their predicted level of performance is higher than their actual performance. Such overconfidence resembles that of people's confidence in their responses to inquiries concerning matters of fact (e.g., Fischhoff et al., 1977). Despite such overconfidence, feeling-of-knowing judgments are reasonably well calibrated (see Nelson, 1988). People might rely on feeling of knowing as an indication of what question answering strategy should be used: given a positive feeling of knowing, people attempt to answer a question rather than simply to give up (e.g., Reder, 1987). This use of feeling-of-knowing judgments requires that they be made rapidly. In fact, Reder (1988) found faster reaction times for making feeling-of-knowing judgments than for answering questions.

What mechanisms underlie feeling-of-knowing judgments? Studies show that prior exposure of the target item, which would aid its later retrieval, is less important for feeling-of-knowing judgments than is prior exposure to the question or cue. For example, Reder and Ritter (1992) found that when exposure to parts of problems requiring arithmetical calculation were manipulated along with prior exposure to answers for the problems, it was frequency of exposure to parts that increased the feeling of knowing (see also Schwartz and Metcalfe, 1992, who obtained analogous results in subjects' memory for cue-target word pairs). Reder and Ritter (1992) concluded that assessing familiarity of questions allows one to make fast decisions without retrieving the target information. To the extent that feeling-of-knowing judgments reflect familiarity of the cue rather than partial retrieval of the target, feeling-of-knowing judgments will not accurately predict performance on subsequent tests of memory for the target. That is, illusory feeling of knowing can be produced by misattributing the familiarity of a question to knowledge of the answer to that question.

A similar misattribution underlies illusions of comprehension. Self-assessment of comprehension of expository text is often a poor predictor of objectively assessed comprehension, as shown in a series of studies by Epstein et al. (1984) and by Glenberg et al. (1982). High confidence in understanding of text was often coupled with failure to detect contradictions within the text. That is, people claimed to fully comprehend a text even though it could be shown that they failed to note that sentences embedded in the text were contradictory. Methodological problems in those early experiments led to the underestimation of the correlation between self-assessment and objectively assessed comprehension (Weaver, 1990); however, even when those methodological problems were corrected, the correlation is still low. More recent investigations have used measures that are akin to those used in feeling-of-knowing experiments to reveal illusions of comprehension. For example, Glenberg and Epstein (1985) required subjects to rate their confidence in their ability to verify inferences derived from a text they had read. The calibration of subjects' judgments was assessed by computing the correlation between their predicted and actual performance: the correlation was typically near zero!

One cause of illusions of comprehension is confusion between knowledge of the domain that a text represents and knowledge gained from the text—misattribution of familiarity. Glenberg and Epstein (1987) had students with expertise in physics or music theory read expository texts from both domains and predict their ability to verify inferences based on the central premises of the texts. Results showed that subjects were well calibrated across domains; physics students, for example, were more likely to correctly predict that they could verify inferences from a physics text than were music students. More interesting, within a domain, expertise was inversely related to calibration, that is, experts were more confident than they should have been. Confidence judgments were apparently based on self-classification as expert or nonexpert in the domain, rather than on comprehension of the particular text that was read. Familiarity with the domain was misattributed to comprehension of the text. Because of reliance on prior knowledge when judging comprehension, an expert is even more subject to illusions of comprehension than is a novice.

Similarly, Begg et al. (1989) point to the importance of the form of questions posed to subjects when they are asked to predict the likelihood that they will remember an item on a future memory test. They argue that memory predictions are based on implicit judgments of how easily the item is processed while answering the predictive question. If items are processed easily for reasons that also contribute to successful memory performance, predictions are accurate; otherwise, predictions are less accurate. An interesting implication of their view is that "well-polished" lectures contribute to an illusion of comprehension. The danger is that students mistakenly attribute the fluency of their understanding to actual comprehension of the substantive aspects of the lecture rather than to the lecturer's easily accessible language and sentence construction. (The "Feynman effect" is the supposed evidence that the students of the famous lecturer and physicist, Richard Feynman, did poorer on standard physics exams than did students in other sections—owing presumably to Feynman's making difficult content seem easy to understand, which in turn gave students a false reading of their own knowledge—and their need to study.) The problem is that the criterion of "easy to listen to" that the student uses to judge comprehension is radically different from the later test used by the lecturer as a measure of comprehension and memory. Good speakers may pay the price of being accused of giving unfair tests.

Ability to judge one's reading comprehension is important for budgeting study time, as well as many other purposes, and there is no easy substitute for subjective experience as a basis for monitoring comprehension. This being the case, are there means by which illusions of comprehension can be avoided? The most promising way of helping people to avoid illusions of comprehension is by giving them experience with the type of test that will be used to measure comprehension. Glenberg et al. (1987) provide evidence that calibration is enhanced when the processes and knowledge tapped by a pretest are closely related to those required by the criterion test. Familiarity with the form of comprehension test is critical. Drum et al. (1981) looked at predictors of performance on standardized, multiple-choice tests of reading comprehension. These predictors included passage difficulty, characteristics of the question, characteristics of the correct choice, and characteristics of the distractors incorrect choices. The major explanation of the variance was characteristics of the distractors: distractor plausibility alone accounted for about 25 percent of the variance. Given that the distractors are not known until a person takes a test, it is virtually impossible for a person to accurately predict test performance without some good foreknowledge of the test.

In light of the importance of foreknowledge of a test, illusions of comprehension can be understood as reflecting a problem that is similar to that of construal problems (described above). The problem is that of misconstruing the form of test. But as in the examples of construal, such as the "tappers" judgment of the likelihood that a listener will identify the tune, the illusion of comprehension does not feel like a particular "construal" of what the test will be, but, rather, like some sort of absolute comprehension of the text. The problem is a general one: it is often the case that present performance is misleading.

Druckman and Bjork (1991:Chapter 3) and Schmidt and Bjork (1992) have argued that individuals responsible for the design of training programs can be seriously misled by assuming, explicitly or implicitly, that the conditions that enhance performance during training are also the conditions that enhance the posttraining or transfer performance. What one sees during training is current performance, which is an unreliable indicator of the learning that can support the longer-term performance that is the goal of training. There are many manipulations that speed the rate of improvement in performance during training—such as massing practice, providing very frequent feedback, and keeping the conditions of practice constant—that are among the very worst training conditions in terms of long-term retention and the ability to transfer or generalize training to altered conditions and tasks. Conversely, certain manipulations that appear to introduce difficulties for the learner, slowing the apparent acquisition of the skills and knowledge to be learned— such as spacing practice sessions on a given subtask, providing only intermittent summary feedback, and inducing variability in the conditions of practice—can enhance long-term performance and the ability to transfer or generalize. (Examples of the many studies demonstrating the differing short-term and long-term consequences of the spacing of practice, the scheduling of feedback, and the variation of conditions of practice are, respectively, Bahrick, 1979; Schmidt et al., 1989; and Catalano and Kleiner, 1984.)

The important point for present purposes, as argued by Bjork (1994), is that not only teachers, trainers, and instructors can be fooled by performance during training, but also learners themselves can be fooled. As discussed throughout this chapter, is very difficult to assess one's true state of knowledge and skill. In the absence of being able to take a "pure" subjective reading of the current level of learning achieved during training, a learner is susceptible to making the same inferential error to which trainers are susceptible: if I am performing well and appearing to improve rapidly, I am learning; if I am making errors and struggling, I am not. Such inferential errors can result in learners' being enthusiastic about training and instruction that are far from optimal, while being displeased with an excellent training regimen.

In short, learners do not necessarily know what is best for them. An experiment by Baddeley and Longman (1978) nicely illustrates this point. They had postal workers in Britain learn keyboard skills under varying conditions of the spacing of practice sessions. Consistent with the results of laboratory studies going back decades, they found that the more distributed in time were the practice sessions, the more efficient the learning per session. When, however, subjects were asked at the end of training to rate how pleased or displeased they were with their own particular training schedule, their reactions were negatively correlated with the efficiency of their training. Those with the most massed (and inefficient) schedule of practice were the most pleased; those with the most distributed (and efficient) schedule were the least pleased.

In general, people learn by making and correcting mistakes. In that sense, making errors during training can be viewed as an important part of subjective experience. Conditions during training that serve as crutches for performance—massing practice by subtask, for example, or keeping multiple aspects of the task environment fixed and predictable—are conditions that, in effect, deny learners the opportunity to learn what they don't know. Rather than learning from errors in the training context, those errors are deferred to some posttraining real-world environment in which performance matters. This is a particularly critical consideration for individuals in occupations for which society, and the individuals themselves, cannot afford on-the-job learning: police officers, air-traffic controllers, nuclear-plant operators, and so forth.

It is important, then, that training routines simulate the types of demands and variability of task conditions that can be expected in the transfer or real-world environment (see Chapter 3). As Bjork (1994) has argued, however, attempting to simulate the exact posttraining environment during training may not be optimal. There are experimental results that suggest that training programs should introduce variability and other demands that go beyond that expected in the real-world environment. A good example is an experiment by Kerr and Booth (1978), in which 8-year-old children were given practice in a task that required throwing small beanbags underhanded at a 4-inch by 4-inch target on the floor. During a series of training trials, each child was permitted to view the target, then asked to throw with his or her vision of the target blocked, and then shown the outcome to that throw. For half the children, the target distance was fixed at 3 feet; for the other children, the distance trial by trial was either 2 feet or 4 feet, but never 3 feet. On a final criterion test, during which all children were tested at 3 feet, the children who had practiced at 2 and 4 feet, but never at 3 feet, were significantly more accurate than the children who had been trained exclusively at the criterion distance. The same pattern was obtained with 12-year-old children, where the criterion distance was 4 feet and the training trials were either at that distance or were alternated between 3 feet and 5 feet.

Using adult subjects, Shea and Morgan (1979) found a strikingly analogous result in the transfer of blocked and random conditions of training. Subjects were given training on three different movement patterns, each of which involved knocking over several of a set of hinged barriers in a prescribed sequence as rapidly as possible. All subjects received 51 training trials, 17 on each movement pattern. For half the subjects, the trials were in blocks by movement pattern: they received all 17 trials on a given pattern before moving on to practice the next pattern. For the other half of the subjects, the patterns to be practiced on successive trials were determined by a random schedule, so the trials on the differing patterns were interleaved and unpredictable from the subject's standpoint. Not surprisingly, during training, the subjects in the blocked practice trials had better performance results across the trials on a given pattern than did the subjects in the intermixed trials. On a final retention test, however, carried out under either blocked or random conditions, the picture was dramatically different. Not only did the subjects who received random practice perform much better than blocked-practice subjects when tested under random conditions, they also performed better when the final criterion test was carried out under blocked conditions! Recently, Hall et al. (1992) have found the same pattern of results when players on the baseball team at California Polytechnic State University, San Luis Obispo, were given two sessions of extra batting practice a week for 6 weeks. Each such sessions consisted of 45 pitches (15 curve balls, 15 fast balls, and 15 change-ups): some players received those pitches blocked by type; for other players the pitch on a given trial was determined by a random schedule. The percentage of solid hits during practice, and during the two posttraining criterion sessions—the first carried out under random conditions, the second under blocked conditions—were judged by assistant coaches who were blind to the purpose of the experiment. As in the Shea and Morgan (1979) study, random practice not only yielded better performance on a retention test carried out under random conditions, it also yielded better performance on the blocked criterion test.

ILLUSIONS OF REMEMBERING

Memory Without Remembering

It is logically possible that the feeling of remembering reflects faithfully the process of having access to a memory trace, and that such access is necessary and sufficient to produce a subjective experience of remembering. It is easy to demonstrate, however, that the link between subjective experience and the actual changes that have or have not taken place in one's memory is weak—in both directions. In a subsequent section we illustrate that people can experience illusory remembering. In this section we discuss the opposite case, that is, unconscious effects of past experience.

Cases of unconscious plagiarism illustrate how the past can unconsciously affect people. One famous case of plagiarism involved Helen Keller (Bowers and Hilgard, 1988). When Helen was 11 years old, she wrote a short story that was published as part of a newsletter by Helen's school. Readers of the story identified it as remarkably similar to a story published years earlier by an author named Margaret Canby. Helen was accused of plagiarism, but vigorously denied ever having read Canby's story. Eventually, however, a family friend came forward and said that she had signed the story to Helen during a visit 3 years earlier. Helen apparently used memory for the story when writing her own, without consciously remembering having previously heard it. That is, the story came to mind without an accompanying feeling of familiarity and was mistakenly accepted as her own invention. (For further discussion of unconscious plagiarism, see Brown and Murphy, 1989; Reed, 1974.)

The most dramatic examples of such memory without remembering come from amnesic patients. Amnesic patients, who totally lack the subjective experience of remembering, still show specific effects of prior experience on performance as measured by indirect tests of memory. On an indirect test, people are not asked to report directly on memory for an event, as would be the case on a direct test of memory, such as recall or recognition. Rather, a person performs some task that can indirectly reflect the effects of prior experience. For example, an amnesic patient might first be asked to read a list of words and then later asked to complete words based on only some of the constituent letters in those words. Amnesiacs, who perform very poorly on direct tests of memory, such as recall and recognition, nonetheless perform better on the identification of fragmented words that have been presented earlier than they do on other words not presented earlier (see, e.g., Warrington and Weiskrantz, 1974). People with normally functioning memories also show dissociations between performance on indirect and direct tests. They, too, for example, show effects of memory on fragment-completion tasks that are not accompanied by the subjective experience of remembering (for reviews, see Richardson-Klavehn and Bjork, 1988; Roediger and McDermott, 1993).

Prior experience may increase the ease or efficiency of later perception and thought: reading a list of words makes them easier to identify later from a fragmented or degraded form, and Helen Keller's experience of Margaret Canby's story may have made "creation" of a similar story easier 3 years later. One may either correctly interpret that ease or fluency of perception or thought as due to past experience or may misattribute those effects to qualities of the current situation.

Jacoby and Dallas (1981) examined the effects of prior study of words on people's ability to identify the words when they were presented briefly on a computer screen. In comparison with words not studied earlier, words that had been previously read in the experimental setting were more likely to be correctly identified when flashed for 35 milliseconds. The subjects in the experiment commented that some words were easier to read than others, but rather than correctly attributing that difference to the effects of having read the words in the first phase of the experiment, they said they thought some words were presented for a longer duration than other words. That is, the ease of perception due to memory was misattributed to a difference in presentation duration. Witherspoon and Allan (1985) then changed the subjects' task in the perceptual-identification part of the experiment by asking them to identify the duration of the words: they found that a single prior presentation was sufficient to lengthen the apparent duration of a word's presentation. Similarly, Jacoby et al. (1988) had subjects read a list of sentences and then listen to those sentences and analogous new sentences presented one at a time against a background of noise. Subjects misattributed their ease of hearing the old sentences to a lowering of the intensity of the background noise.

Past experiences may be a pervasive source of unconscious influences on subjective experience, and, in turn, on judgments based on subjective experience. For example, people judge a problem as easy if they can solve it easily, a paper as well written if they can read it fluently, and an argument as well reasoned if they can follow it easily. In each case, however, prior experience may have affected the subjective experience. The apparent difficulty of a problem might decrease if one had solved it previously, the apparent quality of a paper might increase if one had read it (or written it!) previously, and the apparent force of an argument might increase if one had heard it before. As noted above, subjective experiences are important because people tend to assume their own experiences will be shared by others and so base judgments for others on the basis of their own experiences.

False Memories

Just as a past experience can change subjective experience of the present, without conscious awareness that one has been influenced by the past, the opposite attributional error can occur and produce illusions of remembering. The subjective experience of remembering partially depends on an inference or an interpretation of various cues. One cue that may lead one to experience remembering is the ease or fluency of current perception and cognition. Because past experience commonly enhances later perception and cognition, the fluency of perception and thinking is a valid indicator that one has seen a face before or read a text before. In particular, fluent perception may be one basis for the feeling of familiarity in recognition. We noted above that perceptual identification of briefly presented words is enhanced if the words have been studied previously (Jacoby and Dallas, 1981), and that if subjects are directed to make visual-duration judgments, they will misattribute the easy perception of old words to a change in duration of presentation. Can that same perceptual fluency be correctly interpreted as familiarity due to having read the words previously? Johnston et al. (1985) found a correlation between ease of perception and recognition memory judgments for pseudo words. Pseudo words that were easily identified perceptually were more likely to be recognized as "old."

If ease of perceptual processing is a cue that can serve as the basis for the feeling of remembering, then it should be possible in subtle ways to manipulate ease of perceptual processing and to create illusions of remembering. In an attempt to create memory illusions, Jacoby and Whitehouse (1989) varied the ease with which words on a recognition memory test were perceived. Subjects studied a list of words and then took a recognition test. Immediately prior to the presentation of each word on the recognition test, the same word (match) or a different word (mismatch) was briefly flashed on the screen, so briefly that subjects were unaware that any character string had been presented. For both old and new words on the recognition memory test, a matching context word increased the probability of judging an item old, while a mismatching word decreased the probability of judging the item old. The matching word facilitated perceptual processing of the following test word and so increased subjects' feeling of familiarity. In the case of new words, the brief presentation of a matching context word created an illusion of memory. An important control condition in the Jacoby and Whitehouse experiment illustrates how these illusions of memory depend on an inference or an attribution about the source of easy perceptual processing. In a second condition, the matching or mismatching context words were presented for much longer so that subjects were fully aware of them. When subjects were aware of the context words, they were actually less likely to call either an old or a new recognition test word old when the context word matched the test word than when no context word or a mismatch context word was presented. When they were unaware of the context word, people mistakenly attributed their enhanced processing of the test word to having studied it and so judged it old. In contrast, when aware of the context word, people correctly attributed their enhanced processing of the test word to having just read it as a matching context word. In fact, subjects in the aware condition tended to overcorrect for the effect of the matching word and so were less likely to judge the test word old than if no context word had been presented.

Whittlesea et al. (1990) manipulated the fluency of perceiving the test words shown on a recognition test by masking those words with greater or lesser amounts of visual noise. Words made relatively easy to perceive because of less visual noise were more likely to be judged as having appeared in a studied list of words, whether or not the target words were actually old or new. When subjects were made aware that fluency of perception was being manipulated by the experimenter, they no longer interpreted variations in perceptual fluency as familiarity, but instead correctly interpreted those variations as due to changes in visual clarity.

These experiments illustrate how ease of perception can be manipulated to produce illusions of familiarity. Similarly, variations in the ease of more conceptual analyses may be interpreted as familiarity. Whittlesea (1993) tested this possibility by manipulating the conceptual analysis of recognition test words. Each trial in the experiment began by having subjects read a rapidly presented list of seven words (66 milliseconds per word). Following the last word, there was a brief pause, and then a recognition test word was presented as the last word in a sentence. The sentences were constructed to make the last word more or less predictable: "The stormy seas tossed the BOAT" or "He saved up his money and bought a BOAT." (Previous experiments in the series confirmed that subjects could generate the last word of the sentence more rapidly for the more predictable sentence contexts.) Subjects were more likely to judge the target word as from the list of seven briefly presented words when it was the last word in a more predictable sentence context, whether or not the target word actually had been presented in the list of seven words. That is, subjects mistakenly attributed the ease of reading the word due to the predictable sentence context as familiarity due to having read the word in the seven-item study list: they experienced illusions of familiarity.

In addition to perceptual and conceptual ease of processing as a basis for the feeling of familiarity, other qualities of current experience can lead to the inference that one is remembering rather than imagining. For example, events are embedded in a train of events, so the ability to remember what happened before and after a particular memory bolsters a feeling that it is a real memory (Johnson, 1988). The vividness of an image can also be a cue that one is remembering rather than imagining. Brewer (1988) studied students' ability to remember events up to 55 days later. Subjects were most confident that they were remembering when they had vivid visual imagery for the event. However, just as perceptual and conceptual fluency on a memory test can be manipulated to produce illusions of memory, the vividness of images and the ease of elaborating on a "memory" can be manipulated and so create illusions of remembering.

Hypnosis appears to create the experience of enhanced imagery (e.g., Crawford and Allen, 1983) and a feeling of effortless imagining. Thus people attempting to remember while hypnotized may be prone to interpret the images that come to mind as memories because they have the qualities of memories: vivid, detailed, and effortlessly generated. Dywan and Bowers (1983) found that people who had been hypnotized and attempted to recall pictures they had studied a week earlier were more confident in their memories, and that they did remember more pictures than their nonhypnotized counterparts. However, they also confidently recalled a number of items they had never studied (see also Laurence and Perry, 1983).

If memory is indeed an interpretation of current perception or imagination, then the social context of the rememberer can also contribute to the creation of illusions of memory. When one is attempting to remember something and other people, perhaps with some authority, treat the ideas produced as memories, then one might be more likely to also treat those ideas as memories. Loftus (1992) described a series of demonstrations that memories can be created through suggestion. Subjects were younger relatives of the experimenters. The experimenters essentially reminisced with the subject about shared childhood events over several days. However, one of the reminiscences that was introduced was a false memory of the subject getting lost on a shopping trip. Chris, the younger brother of one experimenter was told the following story:

> It was 1981 or 1982. I remember that Chris was 5. We had gone shopping at the University City shopping mall in Spokane. After some panic, we found Chris being led down the mall by a tall, oldish man (I think he was wearing a flannel shirt). Chris was crying and holding the man's hand. The man explained that he had found Chris walking around crying his eyes out just a few moments before and was trying to help him find his parents.

Initially, Chris said he didn't remember getting lost at the mall. But after several days of working to recall the real memories and this false memory, he began to add in details to the "lost in the mall" event and to feel that he was remembering.

Loftus notes that children and their parents share a fear that the child will get lost—there are even children's books on the topic, such as one in which the Sesame Street character Ernie gets lost in the mall. If people are attempting to recall details of an event that someone else seems to remember clearly, they may have a ready source of details from books, movies, or other people's lives that allow them to generate details. In a social context that biases one to interpret those details as remembered, they may take on a feeling of familiarity.

Loftus points out how similar social dynamics could occur in therapy sessions when a therapist believes that a client has been sexually or physically abused as a child and sets out to assist that client in uncovering repressed memories of that abuse. Some therapists assess their clients' symptoms and inform the clients that the symptoms are suggestive of childhood abuse or trauma of some sort. Popular books on recovering repressed memory of abuse also suggest that people give up their normal criteria for judging whether a memory really happened, suggesting that the memories recovered will not feel like normal memories. The combination of certainty from an expert that "you have the kind of symptoms I've seen in people who have been abused as children" and the suggestion that any image of abuse that comes to mind should be accepted as a memory may produce a potential for the creation of false memories.

There is increasing evidence against a "naive realist" view of memory as an objective record of the past. Instead, the feeling of remembering depends on a particular interpretation of evidence, such as the ease of generating images, the vividness of those images, and the social support for the "memory." People can mistake memories of imagined events or fictional events for events that really happened to them, and they can mistake current imagining for remembering.

CONCLUSIONS

In our previous book, we concluded (Druckman and Bjork, 1991:47):

> The effectiveness of a training program should be measured not by the speed of acquisition of a task during training or by the level of performance reached at the end of training, but, rather, by learner's performance in the posttraining tasks and real-world settings that are the target of training.

We amend that conclusion by noting that it is as important to educate learners about subjective experience as about performance. Subjective experience is of obvious relevance to motivation, and is also important as a basis for self-monitoring learning and performance. It is important that the conditions of practice be structured to reveal when understanding has not yet been achieved or when a procedure cannot yet be executed in conditions that differ from those experienced thus far in training. Experience in the setting that is the target of training serves to educate subjective experience of the learner as well as providing a measure of the effectiveness of training. In fact, it may be optimal to make the conditions of practice be more demanding, and, hence, more revealing to the learner, than are the anticipated real-world conditions.

Subjective experience does not faithfully reflect "situation-free" knowledge. Rather, subjective experience relies on an unconscious attribution or inference process and, consequently, can be misleading. The effects of memory can be misattributed to the characteristics of a present situation and give rise to unconscious plagiarism, mistakes in evaluating the level of comprehension of one's students, and so forth. The effects of factors that influence fluency, in turn, can be misattributed and experienced as remembering, such as the false recovery of a "memory." Much like the person who taps a song, everyone lives in a world that is, in part, of his or her own making, not realizing that subjective experience might rest on a misconstrual of the current situation.

That subjective experience is error prone might be taken as a good reason for banishing it as a concern, and for concentrating only on objective performance. However, subjective experience does not appear to its holder as being error prone. Although the instructor might attempt to banish the student's subjective experience, the student does not do so nor does the instructor banish his or her own subjective experience, and, rightfully, they should not. More "objective" bases for evaluation may not exist and some, such as a theory, are sometimes inferior to subjective experience as a basis for judgments.

More research is needed to better specify the cues that are used and the processes that are involved in the creation of subjective experience. Doing so is important to allow people to avoid the deleterious effects of misleading subjective experience. Of more immediate utility, people can be aware that subjective experience is largely unavoidable and serves important functions, but it cannot be fully trusted.

PART III

Learning and Performing in Teams

This part considers several aspects of learning and performing in teams. In Chapter 5 we review and evaluate the research on cooperative learning, with an emphasis on adult learning. We also discuss some implications of the cooperative experience for performance in nonclassroom settings.

Chapters 6 and 7 focus on team performance and team training, respectively. Chapter 6 examines the effects of task variables explored in laboratory settings, reviews the effects of team-building interventions, and evaluates the effects of interactive game experiences on learning and retention. Chapter 7 provides a framework for organizing the many parts of the team training process: we expand on simple models by including mediating variables that account for the way inputs influence outputs. The chapter also highlights the importance of implementation goals—holding trainees accountable for what they have learned—and providing social support.

Skill acquisition through formal training is one contributor to job performance. Performance is also influenced by the way that tasks are designed, by the way teams are structured, and by organizational factors. It is important to take account of the way that teams learn, as well as the way that attitudes toward teams evolve and change. These issues are discussed in Chapter 6.

5

Cooperative Learning

Cooperative learning involves people of equal status working together to enhance their individual acquisition of knowledge and skills. It can be contrasted with two of its close relatives: tutoring and team training. Tutoring involves a clear distinction in status (expertise) among the participants; team training focuses on the enhancement of team (group) rather than individual outcomes.

Cooperative learning has a rich empirical and pragmatic history, although most of the systematic work has focused on children. Consequently, the general reviews and theoretical articles are heavily weighted by outcomes from experiments with learners in grades 2-9. (For reviews, see D.W. Johnson and R.T. Johnson, 1989; Nastasi and Clements, 1991; Totten et al., 1991 provide an annotated bibliography of 818 studies.) Studies with adults—college students and technical trainees—are included in the research, but they are not generally given special status. The assumption seems to be that cooperative learning principles, methodologies, and findings are applicable across ages and learning contexts.

This chapter explores some of the boundaries of that assumption by examining adult cooperative learning in light of the general literature. We begin with a description of the prototypical elements of cooperative learning and then use that description to guide our review of the theories and research and their limitations. We then consider in detail the research on cooperative learning in adult populations and its implications for future research and implementation.

In general, this chapter focuses on studies that compare cooperative and individual learning on the basis of dependent measures of individual achievement or performance. It is concerned with the factors that make cooperative learning more effective so that it can produce results that are superior to some central condition of individual learning.[1] This focus excludes an extensive body of research that compares group products (outcomes) with individual outcomes (for a review see D.W. Johnson and R.T. Johnson, 1989). It also excludes cooperative learning effects on nonperformance variables, such as intrinsic motivation (see, e.g., D.W. Johnson et al., 1985), self-esteem (see, e.g., D.W. Johnson and R.T. Johnson, 1985a), and attitudes toward minorities (see, e.g., Bossert, 1988). Positive gains on these variables may have indirect influences on subsequent individual achievement, but we did not find any published research on this connection.

KEY ELEMENTS OF COOPERATIVE LEARNING

Many different types of cooperative scenarios have been developed and explored; most can be characterized in either of two ways.

One is team learning, in which students are directed to assist each other in learning a body of material (e.g., DeVries and Edwards' teams-games-tournaments techniques, 1974; Slavin's student teams-achievement division, 1983). The other is expert groups, in which students become experts in a content area and then teach groupmates (e.g., Aronson's [1978] jigsaw approach). Although there are tutoring episodes within this format, equal status is maintained across members of the learning groups over time.

The implementation and evaluation of most team learning and expert groups involve as many as four phases (see Figure 5-1): (A) precooperation instructions and activities; (B) the cooperation episode; (C) postcooperation activities (often not included); and (D) outcome assessment. Figure 5-1 also shows information about the general cooperative learning literature: the elements in the unshaded boxes labeled 1 in phases A, B, and D have been the focus of prior research; the elements in the shaded boxes labeled 2 and in phase C have been largely neglected.

Precooperation instructions and activities (phase A1) have received the most attention in cooperative learning research. Most of the work considers the establishment of positive interdependence among the group members as the critical step in promoting successful cooperative learning (e.g., D.W. Johnson and R.T. Johnson, 1989; Slavin, 1992). This interdependence is presumably heavily influenced by prescribed goals, incentives, tasks, cooperative instructions, and group assignments. The general objective of this phase is to cultivate a belief among group members that their individual success is positively linked to the success of the other group members. This positive interdependence presumably leads to productive activities during the cooperative episode and subsequently to positive outcomes on individual achievement measures.

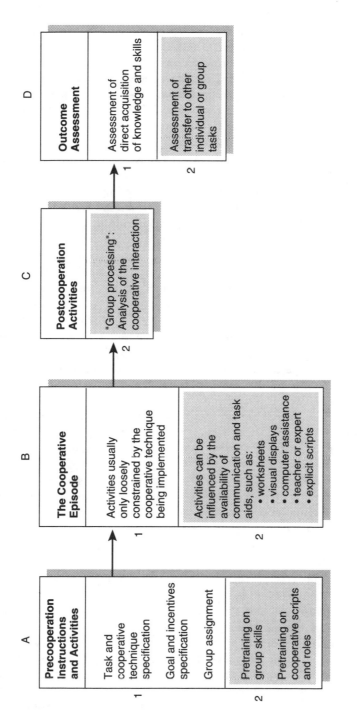

FIGURE 5-1 Phases of cooperative learning. Topics in unshaded areas (1) have been focus of research; topics in shaded areas (2) have been largely unstudied.

It has been recognized that positive interdependence may not be sufficient if the participants do not possess the appropriate skills and strategies for interacting with one another (e.g., D.W. Johnson et al., 1990). To remedy this situation, pretraining for the cooperative episode (phase A2) involving social skills training (e.g., Mesch et al., 1988) or more specific training on enacting a cooperative script (e.g., O'Donnell et al., 1987) has been used. Unfortunately, there is very little empirical work on the effectiveness of these types of pretraining.

During the cooperative episode itself (phase B), the participants typically direct their own specific activities and interactions under the loose guidance of whatever cooperative format they are implementing. The general expectation is that the participants will engage in "face-to-face promotive interactions" (R.T. Johnson et al., 1990) during this episode. For example, in some cooperative scenarios, learners are expected to promote each other's success by giving and receiving assistance, exchanging information, giving and receiving feedback about performance, challenging each other's ideas, building trust, mutually influencing each other, and reducing each other's anxiety about failure. Although this phase is considered to be the heart of cooperative learning, there have been relatively few efforts to directly examine, measure, or influence these interactions (phase B2) except for informal instructor monitoring. The use of explicit, detailed roles and scripts to guide the participants during the cooperation episode has received only limited attention (for a review, see O'Donnell and Dansereau, 1992). Also, there have been only scattered studies examining the effects on cooperative learning outcomes of visual aids (e.g., Patterson et al., 1992, 1993; Rewey et al., 1992), computer assistance (Hythecker et al., 1985; R.T. Johnson et al., 1986; Rocklin et al., 1985), and expert facilitators (e.g., teachers; Brown and Palinscar, 1989).

Closely related to pretraining is the postcooperation activity of "group processing" (phase C). In this activity, group members (often guided by an instructor) examine how well they are functioning in the group and how this functioning might be improved prior to engaging in another cooperative episode. In essence, group processing acts as pretraining for future episodes. As indicated by the shading, only a few studies have explicitly examined the impact of group processing on subsequent outcomes (e.g., R.T. Johnson et al., 1990; Yager et al., 1985).

The final phase, outcome assessment (phase D1), has typically involved the evaluation of the direct acquisition of knowledge and skills from the tasks and materials provided by the instructor. An exemplary study by Fantuzzo et al. (1989a) compared four groups of college students on a comprehensive final exam in an abnormal psychology course. Students were assigned to one of four conditions: (1) in the dyadic structured format (DS), students intermittently developed and answered test questions during a structured series of reciprocal tutoring sessions with a randomly assigned partner; (2) in the dyadic unstructured format (DU), students intermittently prepared for and discussed general course topics with a randomly assigned partner (no specific structure for these discussions was provided); (3) in the independent structured format (IS), students developed test questions and answers in the same manner as the DS group, but they did not interact with a partner; and (4) in the independent unstructured format (IU), students prepared discussions on general topics in the same manner as the DU group but did not interact with a partner. The means and standard deviations on the comprehensive course exam: DS, $M = 84.8$, $SD = 10.1$; DU, $M = 70.1$, $SD = 15.5$; IS $M = 69.0$, $SD = 17.5$; IU $M = 66.3$, $SD = 18.8$. The results showed significant main effects for the dyadic formats versus the independent ones and for the structured formats versus the unstructured ones.

This study is exemplary in its use of a collection of appropriate comparison groups: both individual learners and partners implementing an alternative cooperative strategy. Many of the studies reported in the literature use only an individual comparison group without strategy instructions.

To summarize, cooperative learning as studied typically involves the specification of a task, a cooperative technique, the goals and incentives for the cooperative episode, and the assessment of knowledge and skills directly acquired from the learning episode. Pretraining, direct support and scripting of the cooperative episode, postcooperation activities, and assessment of transfer to new individual learning tasks are only rarely included.

GENERAL THEORETICAL PERSPECTIVES AND FINDINGS

Overview

Two Theoretical Perspectives

Two general theoretical perspectives appear to have guided research on cooperative learning. The first one, social-behavioral, emerges primarily from social psychology and, to a lesser extent, from behaviorism. Investigators who emphasize this approach tend to focus on establishing conditions that promote effective cooperative learning (the elements in phase A1 of Figure 5-1). Within this perspective are two distinct viewpoints that emphasize different types of preconditions: *social interdependence*, which emerges directly from group research in social psychology and focuses on the impact of different types of cooperative, competitive, and individualistic goal structures; *incentive structuring*, which is based on behaviorism and focuses on the use of group rewards to promote cooperation. These social-behavioral approaches tend not to focus directly on the activities occurring during the cooperative activity itself (phase B of Figure 5-1). The second general theoretical perspective, cognitive-developmental, focuses less on the establishment of conditions and much more on the activities taking place within the cooperative episode and of the individual learners. This two-category scheme certainly simplifies the work to date, but it is useful in presenting the findings in this chapter. The two theoretical perspectives are also not mutually exclusive; they have served primarily to guide the selection of experimental variables.

A framework for viewing these theoretical perspectives, presented in Figure 5-2, incorporates some of the terminology developed by D.W. Johnson and R.T. Johnson (1989). The top strand of this figure represents social-behavioral perspectives. Group cohesion (positive outcome interdependence) is fostered by appropriate goals, tasks, and, under some conditions, incentives or reward structures. This cohesion leads to increased motivation to achieve individually and to help other group members achieve. This increased motivation may lead directly to positive outcomes by enhancing individual efforts or indirectly by increasing promotive (positive) interactions among group members. The bottom strand of Figure 5-2 illustrates the cognitive-developmental perspectives. In this case, the specification of information processing activities and the provision of processing supports creates explicit process interdependence (e.g., depending on others for feedback), which, in turn, increases the promotive interactions among group members. The increase in promotive interactions may lead to enhanced outcomes directly by increasing learning, indirectly by increasing general motivation due to the occurrence of successful and rewarding interactions, or both.

General Findings

With a few exceptions (see D.W. Johnson and R.T. Johnson, 1987; D.W. Johnson et al., 1991a, 1991b), all the books and articles on cooperative learning tend *not* to draw sharp distinctions between findings based on children and adults. Because studies done with children represent the bulk of the research, the adult findings tend to be relegated to the background in examinations of the general literature. (For excellent recent reviews, analyses, and annotated bibliographies of the general cooperative learning literature, see D.W. Johnson and R.T. Johnson, 1989; Knight and Bohlmeyer, 1990; Nastasi and Clements, 1991; Slavin, 1987, 1990, 1992; Totten et al., 1991).

As noted above, evaluations of the effects of cooperative learning on performance variables require an examination of individual rather than group outcomes. The most extensive review of cooperation is reported in D.W. Johnson and R.T. Johnson (1989). In examining over 575 experimental research studies since 1898, they identified 104 studies that compared coop-

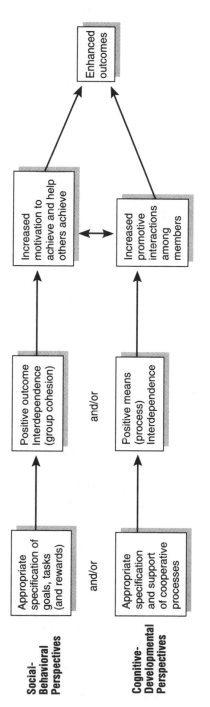

FIGURE 5-2 Theoretical perspectives on dynamics of positive outcomes in cooperative learning.

erative and individualistic efforts on individual achievement (D.W. Johnson and R.T. Johnson, 1989:Table 3.5). The mean effect size for cooperation was 0.51 with a standard deviation of 0.60. However, in an analysis of 32 cooperative learning studies involving durations of at least 4 weeks, Slavin (1990) found a median effect size of only 0.30.

Although positive effects for cooperation continue to be reported (e.g., Nastasi and Clements, 1991; O'Donnell and Dansereau, 1992), there has been a substantial number of reports of no differences (e.g., Slavin, 1990). Unfortunately, the huge number of practitioner-oriented articles about cooperative learning (see bibliography in Totten et al., 1991) tend to ignore these findings of no differences. In order to clarify this situation, many researchers have attempted to determine what elements are necessary and sufficient for effective cooperative learning.

Social-Behavioral Perspectives and Findings

Social-behavioral perspectives, which emphasize the establishment of appropriate cooperative conditions (phase A1 in Figure 5-1), have dominated the cooperative learning literature. Within these perspectives, there has been controversy over which conditions or combinations of conditions are critical for productive learning. Social interdependence theory, which is derived from the early work of Lewin (1935, 1948) and Deutsch (1949, 1962), is based on the premise that the type of social interdependence, created by goal specification, determines how individuals act and interact within the situation, which, in turn, determines outcomes (D.W. Johnson and R.T. Johnson, 1989). According to this theory, positive goal interdependence results in enhanced motivation to engage in promotive interaction: participants focus on both increasing their own achievement and increasing the achievements of their groupmates. Conversely, negative goal interdependence results in oppositional interaction: participants focus on increasing their own achievement but also on discouraging and obstructing others' efforts to achieve. In the absence of goal interdependence, there is no interaction: participants work independently, focusing on increasing their own achievement while ignoring as irrelevant the efforts of others. In the context of this chapter, social interdependence theory assumes that positive cooperative efforts are based on motivation that is generated by joint aspirations to achieve a significant goal, and by interpersonal factors such as being part of a mutual effort, a joint sense of purpose and meaning, social support, and positive relationships among group members.

This focus on goal interdependence conflicts somewhat with a behaviorally oriented, incentive viewpoint, which emphasizes the importance of providing group incentives or rewards to promote cooperation. The research findings are mixed. Some earlier work (Slavin, 1983) concluded that both cooperative task structure (i.e., goal or resource interdependence) and a cooperative (group) incentive structure (e.g., certificates to be given to groups whose members achieve a prescribed level of individual achievement) were necessary for significant gains in achievement in comparison to individual learning. There is also evidence that positive goal interdependence alone is sufficient to increase individual achievement (D.W. Johnson and R.T. Johnson, 1983, 1987; Mesch et al., 1988). More recently, Slavin (1992) found that, under some circumstances (e.g., intrinsically interesting learning tasks), group incentives may not be necessary. Other work (e.g., Mesch et al., 1986) concludes that, while positive goal interdependence is sufficient to produce higher achievement, the combination of goal and reward interdependence is more effective.

Both Slavin and the Johnsons believe that the motivation that results from positive interdependence is the primary cause of the promotive interactions that eventually lead to positive outcomes. Except for a few studies examining social skills pretraining, postcooperative group processing, and the effects of controversy (e.g., D.W. Johnson et al., 1985), the social-behavioral theorists have not attempted to systematically examine or directly manipulate the information processing within and between cooperating group members. The general assumption apparently has been that if the cooperative conditions (e.g., goals, incentives, resources) are appropriately established, the participants will naturally engage in effective information processing. This view may be overly optimistic under some circumstances. Research with individual learners suggest that they typically do not use optimum cognitive (e.g., Dansereau, 1985) or metacognitive (Palinscar and Brown, 1989) strategies and that their learning outcomes can be improved substantially by strategy training (see O'Neil, 1978; Segal et al., 1985; and Weinstein et al., 1988, for reviews of this work).

Slavin (1990) reviewed 68 studies of cooperative learning in elementary and secondary schools; each involved durations of at least 4 weeks and compared individual achievement gains due to cooperative learning with those of control groups. Slavin reports that of 43 studies of cooperative learning methods that provided group rewards based on the sum of group members' individual learning outcomes, nearly all found positive effects on achievement. Studies of methods that used group goals based on a single group product or provided no group reward found few positive effects. This pattern of results is partially congruent with D.W. Johnson and R.T. Johnson's (1989:60) observations that studies that do not include positive interdependence through group rewards tend not to find cooperative effects on individual outcomes. However, other researchers within the social-behavioral perspective have found that positive cooperative effects can occur without group incentives. Under some circumstances, clearly specifying group goals and appropriately dividing the learning tasks to create social cohesion appears to be sufficient to generate positive outcomes (e.g., Sharan and Shachar, 1988; Yager et al., 1985). As an attempt at resolution of differences with regard to critical elements, Slavin (1992) suggests that group rewards may be necessary for less interesting and lower-level tasks, such as fact memorization, while other methods of establishing interdependence may be sufficient with more interesting, and somewhat more complex, conceptual tasks.

Cognitive-Developmental Perspectives and Findings

In contrast to the social-behavioral researchers, cognitive and developmentally oriented researchers have made the task-oriented cooperative interactions the focus of their inquiries. For example, Webb (1980, 1982, 1985, 1989, 1992) has conducted extensive analyses on the internal dynamics of small-group learning with particular emphasis on the activities of asking for, receiving, and giving help. She has outlined the complex relationships between the success and failure of these activities and learning outcomes (for details, see Webb, 1992). Recent research by Meloth and Deering (1992) and Ross and Raphael (1990) have validated and extended Webb's findings to more structured interactions.

From a developmental perspective, the theories of Vygotsky (1978) and Piaget (1926) both have implications for the processing mechanisms underlying successful cooperative learning. Vygotsky (1978:86) suggests that effective instruction falls within a zone of proximal development: "the distance between the actual developmental level as determined by independent problem-solving and the level of potential development as determined through problem-solving under adult guidance or in collaboration with more capable peers." Since cooperating peers are likely to have some compensatory strengths and weaknesses, they would be likely to help each other, moving within their respective zones by modeling and feedback processes.

Piaget has strongly implicated confrontation and conflict as major catalysts for change and cognitive growth. Many modern Piagetians (e.g., Damon, 1984; Dimant and Bearison, 1991; Murray, 1982) have argued that cooperative interactions among students on learning tasks will lead directly to improved outcomes because, in their discussions, cognitive conflicts between students occur and are resolved and inadequate reasoning is exposed and modified.

Although there clearly needs to be some incentive for individuals to engage in cooperation, the cognitive-developmental perspective would suggest that, once engaged, the cooperative activities themselves are motivating and, to some extent, self-sustaining. Consequently, group rewards based on subsequent individual achievements are considered to be largely unnecessary.

Researchers viewing cooperative learning from cognitive-developmental perspectives focus on manipulating and measuring the actual interactions occurring within the cooperative episode (see Figure 5-2). In general, they appear to believe that the direct manipulation of cooperative activities (e.g., by altering the make-up of the group to ensure heterogeneity of cognitive styles and by promoting intellectual controversies) should supersede the manipulation of conditions surrounding cooperation (i.e., the development of positive goal interdependence, as advocated by social-behavioral theorists).

Researchers operating within cognitive-developmental perspectives have found the following manipulations to be effective in enhancing individual achievement in cooperative learning scenarios:

• the use of explicit, instructor-provided, interaction scripts to orchestrate the cooperative activities (e.g., Fantuzzo et al., 1990; Fantuzzo et al., 1989a; D.W. Johnson and R.T. Johnson, 1979; O'Donnell and Dansereau, 1992; Smith et al., 1984; Tjosvold, 1991);

• the use of an instructor to monitor and guide the peer interactions (e.g., Brown and Palinscar, 1989; Rosenshine and Meister, 1991);

• the use of computer software support to direct and enhance the cooperative activities (e.g., Hythecker et al., 1985; Swallow et al., 1988);

• the use of pretraining and post-cooperation group processing to improve critical interaction skills and patterns (e.g., Mesch et al., 1988).

These direct methods of scripting, teacher and computer guidance, and training, as well as in-depth examinations of process (e.g., Webb, 1992), have received substantially less attention than have the indirect methods of social structure and reward.

Conclusions

Given that methods developed from both the social-behavioral and cognitive-developmental perspectives appear to have the potential for promoting cooperative effects under some conditions, it is tempting to conclude that combining elements of all of these approaches would produce the ultimate cooperative scenario. Obviously, however, the development of any combinatorial approach must proceed with caution. Not only may some of the components be in conflict with one another, but even a set of synergistic components can quickly overload participants during cooperative learning (see Dansereau, 1988). Rather than building the ultimate cooperative scenario, a more reasonable goal, following the suggestions of Slavin (1992), would be to examine which elements are necessary and sufficient in particular learning contexts.

Overall, the research on cooperative learning provides sufficient evidence to establish the efficacy of this approach for enhancing individual achievement under some conditions. This literature also provides some initial ideas about the mechanisms underlying successful cooperation. What is now needed is more systematic examinations of the processes by which cooperation leads to achievement, development of theories to reflect these processes and mechanisms as they operate in specific educational environments, and development and evaluation of new cooperative learning methods that incorporate these theoretical advances (see Knight and Bohlmeyer, 1990).

Limitations of the Research

Although some limitations of the research and development efforts are implicit in the previous sections, in this section we make them more explicit. The identified limitations are divided into three categories: quality and precision of the research, scope and neglected issues, and context dependency.

Quality and Precision

As with many domains, the quality of cooperative learning research is highly variable. The laboratory studies in this area are typically in the tradition of experimental social psychology, and, consequently, have tended to use artificial tasks. Although these types of experiments can be useful for theory construction, they have often been inappropriately used to establish the validity of cooperative learning. But the field studies of cooperative learning have frequently not been well controlled (e.g., nonrandom assignments to treatments, uncontrolled "teacher" and treatment effects). With few exceptions (e.g., Webb, 1989; D.W. Johnson and R.T. Johnson, 1989; King, 1990; Meloth and Deering, 1992; Ross and Raphael, 1990), there has been virtually no examination of the relationship between the characteristics of cooperative processing and subsequent outcomes, either through direct observation or diagnostic questionnaires and tests. Generally, cooperative manipulations are not carefully controlled, making the interpretation of findings difficult.

Most of the dependent measures used in cooperative experiments are omnibus, nondiagnostic measures of learning, rather than the more specialized sets of measures typically used in individual learning and cognition experiments (e.g., recognition versus recall). Consequently, it is not clear what kinds of information are being learned or not learned during cooperation. Furthermore, the lack of focus on individual differences in cooperative learning has limited the use of more powerful statistical methods for finding between-group differences and has precluded the examination of interaction effects. In general, as cooperative learning research moves beyond the effect demonstration stage, it behooves researchers to incorporate more of the precise methodologies used in research on individual learning and cognition in their experiments.

Another major problem with research and development in cooperative learning has been the lack of communication among researchers. There have been numerous conceptually overlapping cooperative techniques and approaches developed independently by individuals from diverse backgrounds. Part of the difficulty has stemmed from the variety of journals in which researchers in this field publish. Only very recently have integrated reviews (e.g., D.W. Johnson and R.T. Johnson, 1989; Nastasi and Clements, 1991; Slavin, 1992) begun to bring this field together.

Scope and Neglected Issues

As Slavin (1992) indicates, a large number of the studies often included under the rubric of cooperative learning compare team or group performance directly to individual performance. Not surprisingly, there is a clear-cut advantage for groups in these cases (see D.W. Johnson and R.T. Johnson, 1989). However, most researchers would agree that one of the primary criteria for effective cooperative learning is the facilitation of individual achievement and performance. In this regard, there are far fewer studies that have successfully demonstrated advantages for cooperative versus individual learning. It is clear that many additional, well-controlled studies are needed to understand the parameters and boundary conditions relevant to cooperative enhancement of individual outcomes.

We believe four issues deserve particular attention. First, researchers should examine methods for directly promoting and supporting effective interactions between cooperating individuals. Such methods include pretraining; guidance during cooperation with scripts, instructors, and computers; the use of visual aids and worksheets; and the use of postcooperation group processing. These approaches stem from the cognitive-developmental perspective, which has been underrepresented in the cooperative learning literature.

Second, assessment and diagnosis of cooperative failures and potentially negative cooperative outcomes (e.g., overdependence on social support for task performance) are needed. Although a number of detrimental effects arising from cooperation have been identified—the "free rider," the "sucker," the "status differential," and "ganging up" effects (see e.g., Salomon and Globerson, 1989)—there has been little formal experimentation on what promotes these effects and how they can be ameliorated. Furthermore, there appears to be no research on potential long-term negative effects of cooperation, such as dependency on social support for effective learning.

Third, researchers need to examine skill transfer. In addition to learners' direct acquisition of content-related knowledge and skills, there is some limited evidence that, under certain conditions, cooperative experiences can indirectly foster learning, thinking, and communication skills that can be transferred to other group and individual tasks (see O'Donnell and Dansereau,

1992). Further research is needed to identify principles governing this type of transfer.

Fourth, there has been very little work on the relationship between individual difference variables and cooperative performance indices and subsequent outcomes. The research that has been conducted (e.g., Hall et al., 1988; Wiegmann et al., 1992) is likely to be of limited value due to the idiosyncratic nature of the cooperative techniques and dependent measures used.

Context Dependency

Although some cooperative learning techniques have been specialized for specific content domains (e.g., small-group learning and teaching in mathematics, Davidson, 1990; team-assisted individualization, Slavin, 1985), most of the highly publicized techniques (circles of learning, Johnson and Johnson, 1975; student teams-achievement divisions, Slavin, 1980) are considered to be general purpose ones, useful in a large number of content areas, with a variety of different types of learners. Furthermore, the underlying principles guiding the development and implementation of cooperative scenarios (e.g., goal, task, and reward interdependence) are often described as being context-independent. As a result, cooperative learning approaches are being implemented in a wide range of instructional settings with only minimal evaluation and tailoring. Given the limited arenas in which they have been developed, primarily grades 2-9, it seems likely that these approaches and the principles that they are built on will not always match specific contextual constraints and learner characteristics. Unfortunately, at present these mismatches may be generally undetected because of "placebo" and "bandwagon" effects.

More specifically, techniques developed primarily for young children are typically applied with little modification to college and adult instructional contexts without systematic evaluation and experimentation (see Cooper and Mueck, 1990; Cooper et al., 1990). If nothing else, the dramatic differences between children and adults in cognitive and social developmental stages warrant a close look at the general applicability of cooperative principles across these age groups.

ADULT COOPERATIVE LEARNING

Although the research and development work with children should inform the study of adult cooperative learning, there are three strong age- and situation-related differences that need to be considered. First is context. In comparison with grade school and middle school, adult courses in colleges and technical settings are usually shorter duration and faster paced, leaving much less instructional time for cooperative activities. Consequently, adult cooperative episodes typically need to be highly focused and intense.

The second set of differences concern materials and tasks. Adult materials (particularly in college courses) are usually at a high level of complexity, and typically require a greater emphasis on comprehension than memorization. In technical training and laboratory courses, the focus is often on learning to perform difficult procedures. Because of the difficulty and complexity of the tasks and materials, adult cooperation may require joint effort and outside support for all learning phases, rather than divided efforts on portions of the material as occurs with some of the techniques used with children.

The third difference is learner characteristics. Adults are typically at higher cognitive developmental stages than children and are more socially sophisticated and skilled. These characteristics may reduce the need for token group rewards (especially token rewards) to promote productive cooperation among adults. Most adults can see the intrinsic cognitive and social value of engaging in cooperative learning.

In addition, adults are often defensive about their learning, thinking, and communication skills, and frequently have well-established, though often inadequate, strategies for dealing with complex materials and tasks (Dansereau, 1985). These cognitive and communication characteristics and deficits suggest that adult cooperative episodes may need to be carefully scripted in order to encourage participants to engage in the type of cognitive activities necessary for enhanced learning.

In general, this analysis of differences between adults and children suggests that the cognitive-developmental and social interdependence perspectives may be more potent than the social-behavioral, incentive-structuring perspective in examining and structuring adult learning. In this next section we examine the research on adult cooperative learning with these issues and perspectives in mind. We consider general findings, nature of adult cooperative techniques, role of communication aids and cooperative support, transfer to new learning tasks, and individual differences.

General Findings

The research on adult cooperative learning can be conveniently divided into two categories: implementation studies in ecologically valid settings and controlled laboratory studies. In general, the effect sizes tend to be in approximately the same range as found in the research with children (0.30 to 0.50; see, e.g., D.W. Johnson and R.T. Johnson, 1989).

Implementation studies in adult courses have usually compared cooperative learning with individual learning on typical achievement measures. The reported results indicate positive effects for cooperation over a variety of topics and courses, including: abnormal psychology (Fantuzzo et al., 1989a, 1989b), engineering (Smith et al., 1984, 1986), social psychology (Fraser et al., 1977), multicultural education (Jacobs and Icola, 1990), chemistry (Marks, 1991), statistics (Bansangue, 1991), physical education (R.T. Johnson et al., 1983), introductory physics (Heller et al., 1992), methods of teaching music (Hwong et al., 1993), military history in college reserve officers training corps (ROTC) (D.W. Johnson et al., 1991), educational methods (King, 1990), preparation for nursing boards (Frierson, 1986), the charts and publication unit from an air-traffic control course (Holubec et al., 1993; Vasquez et al., 1993), Army communications electronics operating instructions (Shlechter, 1988), Army equipment records and parts specialist training (Brooks et al., 1987; Hagman and Hayes, 1986), and an Air Force communication center specialist course (Hungerland et al., 1976).

But a number of adult implementation studies have failed to find differences on achievement measures between cooperative learning and control groups (e.g., Carpenter, 1986; Lewis, 1991; Palmer and Johnson, 1989; Sherman, 1986). Since most of the significant and nonsignificant implementation evaluations are published in journals that do not require detailed reporting of methods and results, it is very difficult to assess the validity of these studies and to determine a pattern of differences between successful and unsuccessful implementations. Although the weight of the evidence suggests that cooperative learning can be effective in adult settings, the few published findings of no differences and the fact that such findings are generally underreported suggest that positive conclusions be drawn cautiously.

There have been relatively few controlled laboratory studies of the effects of cooperative learning on individual achievement with adult subjects. The most systematic program of laboratory research in this area has focused on the examination of scripted cooperation with pairs of college students (e.g., Hall et al., 1988; Hythecker et al., 1988; Larson et al. 1985b, 1986; Larson and Dansereau, 1986; O'Donnell and Dansereau, 1992). Typically, these student dyads are instructed to follow a cognitively based interaction script in the studying of excerpts from introductory science textbooks or in the learning of concrete procedures (e.g., administration of intravenous therapy). Figure 5-3 shows versions of two sample scripts. The stated learning goal is for the students to help each other acquire the presented information; no group rewards are given. Performances on tests taken individually over the material are compared with individual study control groups and with other scripted and unscripted cooperative groups. On some occasions, transfer to subsequent individual study tasks is assessed. The specific objective of this research has been to determine the critical elements in cognitively based scripts. In this regard, the results of these laboratory studies have indicated that certain types of explicit cooperative scripts lead to better performance than unscripted cooperation and individual study (see below).

Learning Script	Teaching Script
1. Randomly designate Partner A and Partner B.	1. Randomly designate Partner A and Partner B.
2. Both partners read Passage 1.	2. Partner A reads Passage 1. Partner B reads Passage 2.
3. When both are finished, put the passage out of sight.	3. When both are finished, put the passage out of sight.
4. Partner A then orally summarizes the contents of Passage 1.	4. Partner A then orally summarizes (teaches) the contents of Passage 1.
5. Partner B detects and corrects any errors in Partner A's summary (metacognition step).	5. Partner B asks clarifying questions (metacognition step).
6. Both partners work together to develop analogies, images, etc., to help make the information memorable (elaboration step).	6. Both partners work together to develop analogies, images, etc., to help make the information memorable (elaboration step).
7. Both partners read Passage 2.	7. Steps 4–6 are repeated for Passage 2 with Partners A and B reversing roles.
8. Repeat steps 4–6 with Partners A and B reversing roles.	8. Both partners read the passage that they did not read originally.

FIGURE 5-3 Sample cooperative scripts.

Adult Cooperative Techniques: Group Rewards and Scripts

As noted above, the primary goal of cooperative techniques is to increase task motivation or promotive interactions between group members in order to enhance learning. From the social-behavioral perspective, the goal is typically accomplished by promoting outcome interdependence through extrinsic group rewards contingent on the performance of the individual members. From the cognitive-developmental perspective, this enhanced learning is produced by promoting process interdependence through the provision of a cognitively based script for the members to follow. Of these methods, the use of group rewards has generated the greatest amount of controversy. With children involved in relatively low-level learning (as defined by Bloom's 1956 taxonomy), group rewards appear to be important in maximizing the effects of cooperative learning (Slavin, 1992). Even in this case, however, Kohn (1991) has warned against the potential long-term negative effects on intrinsic motivation of such an incentive system. However, there is some evidence that, with higher-order learning (e.g., Sharan, 1990) and with scripted and supported cooperation (e.g., Brown and Palinscar, 1989), group reward may be unnecessary even for children.

In the adult literature, the importance of explicit outcome interdependence promoted by group incentives is diminished even further. Numerous implementation studies (Fantuzzo et al., 1989a, 1989b; King, 1990; Riggio et al., 1991) and laboratory studies (Dansereau, 1985, 1987, 1988) have shown cooperative effects without the use of group rewards. These findings are echoed strongly by James Cooper (editor of the *Cooperative Learning and College Teaching* newsletter) and his colleagues (Cooper et al., 1990:13):

> At the collegiate level, participation in [the] cooperative learning groups appears to be sufficiently self-motivating that extrinsic reinforcers such as grades may not be critical to motivate students in groups. The group work is intrinsically reinforcing as long as criterion-referenced grading and individual accountability are components of the cooperative learning system and the tasks performed in the groups are perceived as meaningful to the students, not just busy work . . . .

This conclusion concerning the relative unimportance of group reward presumably would be true of adult learning in military and industrial settings as well. However, there is a notable exception: two well-controlled experiments by Hagman and Hayes (1986) with Army trainees showed that cooperative learning promoted significant gains in individual achievement only when a group reward was used and that the effect of the reward was to increase within-group communication. One difference between these two experiments and those that showed cooperative effects without rewards is in the degree of interactive scripting. The studies without rewards provided strong guidance as to the roles and activities of the participants; in the Hagman and Hayes experiments, no guidance was provided. Hagman and Hayes (1986:20) acknowledged and elaborated on this issue:

> Although the present experiment used group rewards to encourage within-group communication, any cooperative procedure that ensures meaningful communication among group members should also promote individual achievement. Thus, group reward may not be necessary when communication is brought about by other means. Recent research supports this notion (Dansereau, 1983; Yager et al., 1985). Dansereau (1983) for example, has shown that structuring interaction within cooperative groups by giving members specific assignments to orally summarize and elaborate upon to-be-learned materials can effectively promote individual achievement in the absence of group reward. The present research suggests that if group interaction is left unstructured, then group reward can be used to encourage the interaction among group members necessary for promoting individual achievement gains when trainees work cooperatively.

We note, however, that underlying this conclusion is the assumption that unscripted group members know beforehand how to best learn the material and how to help one another and that the major issue is motivating the participants to communicate. In the Hagman and Hayes (1986) experiments, the learning material was highly structured information on maintaining a prescribed load list (a portion of the Army's equipment records and parts specialist training sequence). This material was relatively straightforward and primarily required memorization; consequently, it is likely that participants knew effective methods for learning it. With more complicated material that requires substantial comprehension and organization skills, however, it is less likely that participants will have optimal learning and communication strategies in their existing repertoire (Dansereau, 1985, 1988). Under these conditions, merely increasing motivation by providing group incentives may not be sufficient to enhance performance; the provision of a coherent cooperative script is likely to be much more effective.

Although it may be tempting to combine cooperative group rewards (based on achievement scores) with cooperative scripts, recent research by O'Donnell (1992) suggests these two components may not be synergistic. Explicit incentives appear to cause the participants to deviate from the script and to engage in their typical, often nonproductive, learning behaviors, such as rote rehearsal (see also King, 1990; and Pressley et al., 1988). One promising combination that does not seem to have been formally examined is the use of process rewards in conjunction with explicit scripts: that is, group members are rewarded on the basis of effective implementation of the cooperative activities rather than their outcome scores.

The interactions among cooperative group members can be scripted indirectly by dividing up the task or materials and by pretraining on social skills or, it can be done directly by providing explicit scripts that prescribe specific cognitive or social roles and activities. Task division approaches to influencing interactions and interdependence require students to master different parts of the material and teach it to the other members of their groups. These approaches are likely to be effective with material that is easy to understand and organize, but they appear to be relatively ineffective with larger bodies of complex information for which collaboration over the entire set of material may be important (see Lambiotte et al., 1987; and Palmer and Johnson, 1989).

Some of the most promising research with adult learners encourages all members of the group to focus on all aspects of the material with explicit scripting, including structured controversy (D.W. Johnson et al., 1986); reciprocal peer tutoring (Fantuzzo et al., 1989a); reciprocal questioning (King, 1990); and scripted cooperation (O'Donnell and Dansereau, 1992). These methods presumably enhance the possibility that cooperating individuals will share perspectives, insights, and elaborations and will challenge and correct each others' misconceptions. Engaging in cooperative information processing is also believed to increase an individual's motivation and activity level. Two of the most thoroughly researched approaches to scripting are scripted cooperation and structured controversy.

Scripted Cooperation

O'Donnell and Dansereau (1992) have articulated a general conceptual framework for examining and structuring cooperative interactions. This framework is based loosely on Webb's analyses of children's cooperative interactions (e.g., Webb, 1989, 1992), King's analysis of college students' interactions (e.g., King, 1990), and a series of experiments on manipulating cognitive scripts (e.g., Lambiotte et al., 1987; Larson et al., 1985b; McDonald et al., 1985; Wiegmann et al., 1992). In this framework, group interactions are considered to involve complex combinations of learners' cognitive/motor, affective, metacognitive, and social activities, referred to as CAMS. Cognitive/motor activities include comprehension, elaboration, organization, retrieval, and skilled performance. Affective activities include motivation, anxiety, and concentration. Metacognitive activities include monitoring of comprehension and performance, detection and correction of errors, and awareness of performance levels. Social activities include awareness of and effective communication with others in the cooperative situation. In this framework the effectiveness of a cooperative learning situation is believed to depend on the combination of CAMS activities of participating members: an overemphasis on any one activity may disrupt the synergistic balance and inhibit performance. If, for example, a participant places too much emphasis on the metacognitive system, the participant's ability to generate information may be impaired.

The CAMS framework has been used to guide the design of dyadic cooperative scripts. One example is a simple text-processing script, cooperative *murder* (Dansereau, 1985); mobilize, understand, recall, detect, elaborate and review. Participants first mobilize their resources for learning by establishing an appropriate mood and by surveying the text to establish cooperative action points (asterisks in the margin to indicate where they will stop reading and engage in cooperative information processing). Both partners then read for understanding until they reach the first action point. One partner then (recalls or recites) what has been learned to that point while the other partner detects and corrects errors and omissions. Both partners then collaboratively elaborate on the material by forming images, analogies, and direct connections to other information. They then continue reading for understanding until they reach the next action point where they reverse roles and repeat the recall, detect, and elaboration steps. The partners proceed through the material, alternating roles until they have completed the assignment. They then cooperatively review and organize the entire body of information, once again alternating presentation and monitoring roles.

This script, which has been generalized to writing and concrete performance tasks, was designed to facilitate a number of potentially effective activities that have emerged from research findings in cognitive and educational psychology, such as oral summarization during the recall and recite stage (Ross and DiVesta, 1976; Yager et al., 1985), metacognitive activities during the detect and correct stage (Baker and Brown, 1984), elaborative activities during the elaboration stage (Reder, 1980), cross-modeling and imitation of personal strategies and perspectives throughout the stages (Bandura, 1971), and the use of multiple passes through the material (Dansereau, 1985).

Research with college students enacting versions of the *murder* script without group rewards have shown that it leads to better individual outcomes than unscripted cooperative scenarios in which the participants determine their own cooperative activities. This outcome is not surprising given the adult learner characteristics described above. Since adults often have not developed optimum strategies for handling complex information and many are defensive about their own thinking, learning, and communication skills, they are likely to gravitate toward familiar and comfortable roles and activities that minimize productive interactions with their learning partners.

Structured Controversy

A natural occurrence in cooperative learning groups is for members to disagree and argue with each other. Such intellectual conflicts can have powerful influences on learning when they are managed constructively. D.W. Johnson and R.T. Johnson (1979) described such conflicts as controversies and proposed both a theoretical explanation of why they are so powerful and an operational procedure for instructors to use in structuring or scripting controversies among students.

Controversy exists when one student's ideas, information, conclusions, theories, and opinions are incompatible with those of another, and the two seek to reach an agreement. Controversies are an inherent aspect of virtually all decision making, problem solving, reasoned judgment, and critical thinking. If students get intellectually and emotionally involved in cooperative efforts, controversies will inevitably occur. In a structured controversy, students make an initial judgment, present their conclusions to other group members, are challenged with opposing views, become uncertain about the correctness of their views, actively search for new information and understanding, incorporate others' perspective and reasoning into their thinking, and reach a new set of conclusions.

The process through which controversy works can be described in more detail. When individuals are presented with a problem or decision, they have an initial conclusion based on categorizing and organizing incomplete information, their limited experiences, and their specific perspective. When individuals present their conclusions and rationales to others, they engage in cognitive rehearsal, deepen their understanding of their position, and use higher-level reasoning strategies. The presenters are then confronted by other people with different conclusions based on other people's information, experiences, and perspectives. They become uncertain as to the correctness of their views. A state of conceptual conflict or disequilibrium is aroused.

Uncertainty, conceptual conflict, and disequilibrium motivate an active search for more information, new experiences, and a more adequate cognitive perspective and reasoning process in hopes of resolving the uncertainty. This active search is called epistemic curiosity (Berlyne, 1960). Divergent attention and thought are stimulated. By adapting their cognitive perspective and reasoning through understanding and accommodating the perspective and reasoning of others, individuals develop a new, reconceptualized, and reorganized conclusion. Novel solutions and decisions are detected. Individuals working alone in competitive and individualistic situations obviously do not have the opportunity for such a process.

Using this process, D.W. Johnson and R.T. Johnson (1992a) have developed a procedure for structuring experimental controversies in cooperative learning:

1. Students are assigned to a cooperative learning group of four, divided into two pairs. Each pair is assigned the task of researching and preparing the best case possible for either the pro or con position on the issue being considered. In an engineering class, for example, pairs may be assigned two different ways of disposing of hazardous waste or the need to be concerned about acid rain in their design of power plants.

2. Each side presents its position to the other. The pair's task is to present the best case possible for the position they have been assigned with the goal of persuading the opposing pair to agree with them. This task requires students to rehearse orally the relevant information, advocate a position and point of view, and teach their knowledge to peers.

3. Both sides participate in an open discussion characterized by refutation and rebuttal. Students are given two major tasks. The first is to analyze, critically evaluate, and then refute the rationale underlying the opposing position. To do so, students must reason both deductively and inductively. Intensive criticism of ideas and logic is encouraged. The second task is to rebut the attacks made on their position and its rationale by the opposing pair.

4. Each side engages in a perspective-reversal in which they present the perspective, position, and rationale of the opposing pair. Students are

to ensure that they completely understand the opposing position and its rationale.

5. All advocacy is ended, students view the issue from both perspectives simultaneously, and a common position is agreed on through synthesis and integration. To arrive at their best reasoned judgment about the issue, students synthesize and integrate information into factual and judgmental conclusions that are summarized in a joint position that both sides support.

Research on structured controversy with adults has been conducted primarily in engineering schools (Smith et al., 1984, 1986) and in business settings (Tjosvold, 1991). The results of this research indicate that controversy, compared with concurrence-seeking, debate, and individualistic efforts results in greater achievement and retention (Smith et al., 1981), higher quality problem-solving (Maier and Hoffman, 1964; Nemeth and Wachtler, 1983; Tjosvold, in press), greater creativity (Hall and Williams, 1966, 1970; Torrance, 1970, 1971, 1973), and more accurate exchange of expertise (Lowry and Johnson, 1981).

Other Factors: Communication Supports, Transfer, and Individual Differences

Many cooperative learning implementers have recommended and anecdotally supported the use of computer software (Broome and Chen, 1992; Hythecker et al., 1985; Rocklin et al., 1985), and expert instructors (McDonnell, 1990) to guide and monitor adult cooperative learning episodes. Although these supports may have initial value in getting the cooperative interactions on track, it is not clear that they offer any advantages over a detailed script for most adult tasks. Furthermore, since they usually require additional resources, extensive use of such supports may not be cost-effective in many settings. However, in the case of cooperation between individuals who are not in physical proximity, computers may provide a useful communication vehicle. Computer-mediated approaches have been used effectively in collaborative writing (see Duin, 1991 for a review), and, more generally, in education (e.g., O'Malley and Scanlon, 1990).

With regard to communication aids, a few studies have indicated that providing cooperative groups with spatial-verbal displays of the to-be-learned information—such as diagrams and flowcharts—rather than purely verbal textual presentations leads to better individual outcomes (e.g., Patterson et al., 1992, 1993; Rewey et al., 1992). Presumably the spatial and graphic signaling provides for easier reference during group discussion. On the basis of these findings, it would be expected that any visual aid that enhances the availability and accessibility of information during cooperative interactions could lead to more productive cooperative information processing and thus more positive individual outcomes.

There is evidence that adults given scripted cooperative experiences perform better than control subjects on subsequent individual learning tasks (see Dansereau, 1987; and O'Donnell and Dansereau, 1992). Apparently, individuals acquire content-independent knowledge and skills from a cooperative episode that can be used to improve individual learning of new information. This type of content-independent transfer seems to occur only when the cooperative interactions are well scripted (McDonald et al., 1985), and especially when the scripting emphasizes cognitive elaboration activities (Larson et al., 1985b). In the studies cited above, content-independent transfer was an incidental outcome from the cooperative experience. During cooperative learning, the participants in these studies were directed to learn a particular body of information; they were not informed about the subsequent individual transfer task. In essence, they appeared to acquire transferrable knowledge and skills as a by-product of engaging in a task-oriented cooperative episode. The implementation of new learning strategies with a detailed script and the opportunity for cross-modeling between partners may be responsible for this incidental acquisition.

There has been very little research examining the effects of individual differences on adult cooperative learning outcomes. In one study, it was found that college students with relatively high scores on a measure of social orientation gain more from cooperative interactions than from individual study sessions, but the reverse is true for students with low scores on that measure (Hall et al., 1988). In terms of matching cooperative partners, Larson et al. (1984, 1985a) looked at the effects of verbal skills and field dependence/independence (the skill of separating target information from a complex background) on gains achieved in adult cooperative learning dyads and found that students with lower verbal skills performed best when paired with students with higher verbal skills. Importantly, the students with higher verbal skills were not adversely affected by these pairings. Similar patterns of results were found for the field dependence/independence variable. These results are congruent with the recommendations of heterogeneous groupings from various cooperative learning researchers (e.g., D.W. Johnson et al., 1991b).

Conclusions and Future Directions

Although there has been substantially less cooperative learning research conducted with adults than with children, there is sufficient information to draw a few tentative conclusions:

• Adult cooperative learning can be more effective than individual learning across a variety of topics and tasks. However, because of the complexity of adult learning tasks, explicit cooperative scripts that encourage promotive interactions may be necessary to reap the benefits of cooperation, at least with participants who lack previous experience with cooperative learning.

• Because most adults are able to see the potential value of collaboration, group rewards appear to be generally unnecessary and may even hinder following a script.

• Cooperative supports, such as worksheets, computers, and instructors, may be useful in the early stages of cooperation and with potentially difficult materials.

• Information displays (e.g., maps, charts, diagrams, and pictures) that increase the availability and accessibility of material during cooperative processing appear to enhance individual outcomes.

• Transferrable individual learning skills can be acquired as a by-product of well-scripted cooperative episodes.

Needed Research

These conclusions about adult cooperation are attenuated by many of the same factors discussed above as limitations of the general field of cooperative learning. Certain components of cooperative scenarios (see Figure 5-1) have been underresearched. In particular, very little is known about the nature of adult cooperative interactions. Analyses of the type conducted by Webb on children (e.g., Webb, 1992) are needed at the adult level in order to provide a foundation for further theoretical developments. At the same time, the more precise experimental methodologies used in the areas of individual cognition and learning need to be modified and implemented in the study of cooperative learning and cognition. This approach may, in return, also facilitate the understanding of individual processing. Cooperative learning episodes tend to make public the participants' thinking in a relatively naturalistic way, thus providing processing data that is less artificial than that typically collected through asking individuals to describe their thinking. It is also possible that certain cognitive processes may be more highly activated during socially driven cognition than during individual cognition: if so, these processes may be more available for examination during cooperation.

Group processing to improve subsequent cooperative episodes does not seem to have received experimental attention in the adult literature (see phase C in Figure 5-1). Such research would be useful not only in guiding further implementation, but in allowing participants to elaborate on their thinking during the cooperative episode. This research would provide converging information on expert, Webb-like analyses of the interactions. Expert and participant analyses of cooperative episodes could also be used as the basis for assigning group rewards. Such work would permit a comparison of the effectiveness of process-based and outcome-based rewards.

There is also a need for additional studies on the role of individual differences in adult cooperative learning and on the potential of cooperative learning as a training ground for individual learning and thinking skills.

Implementation

Approaches to implementing cooperative learning can be placed on a continuum from conceptual applications to direct applications. In conceptual applications, instructors are taught a general conceptual model of cooperative learning, which they use to tailor cooperative learning specifically for their circumstances and trainees. Direct applications are packaged lessons, curricula, and scripts that are used in a prescribed manner.

There are a number of advantages of both approaches. The direct approach requires very little instructor training and, therefore, is quick and cheap. Initial instructor success rates in using cooperative learning are high. In a way, direct approaches tend to train instructors to be technicians who use the cooperative learning curriculum or strategy without a theoretical understanding of how it works. In contrast, the conceptual approach trains instructors to be engineers who adapt cooperative techniques to their specific circumstances, students, and needs. The specific planning and adaptation required of instructors by the conceptual approach may promote more personal commitment to and ownership of cooperative learning than the direct approach (D.W. Johnson and R.T. Johnson, 1985b, 1992b).

Training may proceed best when both the conceptual and direct approaches are used. Simply presenting a theoretical framework makes it too difficult for most instructors to create their own cooperative learning lessons. Simply teaching instructors how to use a lock-step cooperative procedure that they do not understand, however, allows them to use it immediately but leaves them without the conceptual tools required to adapt it to their students and situation and without the skills to solve implementation problems. A carefully crafted training program may require both a clear conceptual understanding of the nature of cooperative learning, its essential elements, and the instructor's role, and concrete examples of scripts, structures, and lessons.

There are two recent guidebooks for implementing cooperative learning in college settings. A 51-page book by Cooper et al. (1990) discusses principles that can be used to guide implementation and provides examples of a few cooperative learning exercises. A comprehensive report by D.W. Johnson et al. (1991b) describes underlying principles, supporting research, and an extensive collection of specific guidelines for implementing cooperative learning in college courses.

One of the most thoroughly developed approaches presented by D.W. Johnson et al. (1991b) is the use of formal, informal, and base cooperative groups in the context of an ongoing course. In formal cooperative learning groups, participants work together, for one class period to several weeks, to achieve shared learning goals and complete specific tasks and assignments. Informal cooperative learning consists of having students work together to achieve a joint learning goal in temporary, ad hoc groups that last from a few minutes to one class period. Cooperative base groups are long-term, heterogeneous cooperative learning groups with stable membership that last for a semester, a year, or even longer.

According to these authors, formal cooperative learning groups can be used for almost any learning assignment. In formal cooperative learning groups, teachers (1) specify the objectives for the lesson; (2) make a number of preinstructional decisions (e.g., size of groups, assignment to groups, materials needed, room arrangement); (3) explain the task and the positive interdependence; (4) monitor the interaction among learners and intervene to provide task assistance, assistance in using an assigned script, or assistance in using social skills appropriately; and (5) evaluate trainees' learning and ensure that group members process how effectively they are working together.

However, there are times when instructors have to make an extended presentation of factual information in an organized and logically sequenced way. In such situations, informal cooperative learning groups can be used to ensure that learners actively process the information being presented. In such informal cooperative learning groups, learners engage in (1) an introductory focused discussion aimed at promoting advance organizing of what the trainees know about the topic to be presented and establishing expectations about what the lecture will cover; (2) a discussion in pairs every 10-15 minutes to summarize what has just been presented; and (3) a focused discussion at the end of the lecture to provide an overall summary of its content and intellectual closure to the lecture session. There are many important advantages to having students discuss what they are learning with a partner before, during, and after a lecture, film, or demonstration. In the traditional lecture and whole-class discussion, most students stay uninvolved (Barnes, 1980), a very small minority of students tends to dominate (Karp and Yoels, 1987), and many students are inhibited from participating (Stones, 1970). Informal cooperative learning groups can positively alter this pattern.

Cooperative base groups are long-term settings that provide a permanent set of relationships with other trainees. The purposes of the base group are to give the support, help, encouragement, and assistance each learner needs to progress successfully through the training program. Base groups may meet at the beginning and ending of each day (or at least twice a week) to discuss current assignments and the progress of each member and to plan how members can give each other assistance and encouragement. Base groups build relationships among learners to motivate them academically and ensure successful completion of the training program. In this regard, it is important to note that the major reason given for dropping out of training programs and colleges is the failure to establish a social network of friends and classmates. Tinto (1975, 1987) concluded that the social networking processes—social involvement, integration, and bonding with classmates—are strongly related to higher rates of student retention. Astin (1985), on the basis of 10 years of research on colleges, concluded that involvement with peers and instructors was the "cornerstone" of persistence and achievement, especially for "withdrawal-prone" participants (such as disadvantaged minorities) who are generally passive in academic settings. Cooperative learning experiences have been found to lead to lower rates of attrition and higher achievement (Wales and Stager, 1978), especially for black students majoring in math and science (Treisman, 1985).

The formal, informal, and base-group approach developed by D.W. Johnson et al. (1991b) has been used primarily in college settings. The needs and structures of technical training courses may require a somewhat different approach. Along this line, Brooks (1987) has developed an instructor's guide for implementing cooperative learning in an Army Quartermaster course. This document is based on the reward-driven cooperative strategy investigated by Hagman and Hayes (1986; discussed above). Although often specialized, some aspects of this guide are generally applicable to implementation of cooperative learning in technical training settings.

Although the various implementation guides provide useful general approaches, it is important to keep in mind that they are based on very little adult research. Most of the recommendations are derived directly from techniques developed for children; development of more precise guidance for cooperative learning awaits further research.

Cooperative learning typically does not require more instructional resources than those provided in most academic and technical courses. In fact, except for cooperative training materials (which are typically only one or two pages in length), cooperative approaches may actually require less resources than individual learning approaches since cooperative group members can often share computers and laboratory materials. However, greater classroom space may be needed to accommodate increased noise levels during cooperative activity.

Start-up costs include instructor and student training. This training typically requires no more than a one-day workshop for instructors and approximately two class periods for students. Of course, these times are dependent on the cooperative technique being taught and on the nature of the implementation setting.

In comparison with other emerging instructional technologies—such as computer tutoring systems—cooperative learning is extremely low cost. This low cost, in conjunction with its apparent effectiveness, makes it very attractive as a potential instructional alternative. The fact that it can be used in conjunction with a variety of educational approaches further enhances its attractiveness.

NOTE

[1] It is important to note that one could ask the symmetric question: What factors control the effectiveness of individual learning that make it superior to some central condition of cooperative learning? This is not the focus of this chapter, but it is surely a topic that deserves attention.

6

The Performance and
Development of Teams

The focus of this (and the next) chapter is on teams, which can be regarded as a type of small group. Although the terms "team" and "group" are often used interchangeably (even within the same study), it is useful to distinguish between these concepts to provide the boundaries for the review in this chapter. Our implicit working definition of teams is not so broad as to encompass all kinds of small groups, nor so narrow as to exclude important insights from the literature on groups.

In distinguishing between groups and teams, Hare (1992) notes that "group" is the more general term and refers to a set of individuals who have some common characteristic—without actually interacting with one another. "Team" is more specific term: joint action is implied, with sports teams being a very visible example. Dyer (1987:24-25) defines a team as "a collection of people who must collaborate, *to some degree*, to achieve common goals."

Hare suggests that teams can be placed along a continuum according to the amount of collaboration—integration and role differentiation—required. In sports, golf would be considered low in both integration and differentiation, football high in both, with track (high differentiation, low integration) and synchronized swimming (low differentiation, high integration) high in one and low in the other (Hare, 1992:Fig. 2.2). Concluding that a team is more than a collection of individuals, Francis and Young (1979:6-7) describe an effective team as one that "combines high morale, effective task performance, and clear relevance to the organization. Bassin's (1988) requirements for high performance teams include vision (a shared purpose), perceived dependent needs, leadership, coordination, and the skillful use of feedback to adjust and adapt to changes. These criteria are similar to those suggested in other writings on team building (see review in Hare, 1992). Bassin

113

classifies teams by such functional characteristics as discovery driven (research and development teams), rule driven (sports teams), product driven (business teams), and technology driven (plane crews).

Freeberg and Rock (1987) define a team in terms of such distinct features as a goal or mission orientation, formality of structure, a requirement for member interaction stemming from task interdependence, and the assignment of special roles to members. Citing work done by Hall and Rizzo (1975), Freeberg and Rock (1987:5) conclude that the "hallmarks of team interaction processes appear to draw upon the behavioral dimensions of collaboration, coordination, and communication" (see also Rizzo, 1980). Within these broad features, there are variations in emphasis from one study to another. One important difference is whether the team interacts with machines or people. Another is the extent of task interdependence in problem-solving situations. Teams also vary in terms of the rigidity of their structures. Contrast, for example, mission-oriented military teams with research teams: the former are likely to exhibit a higher degree of member specialization and coordination in task performance, as well as a clearer designation of positions or assignments, than the latter. Concentrating on work teams, Sundstrom et al. (1990:120) offer the definition as "small groups of interdependent individuals who share responsibility for outcomes of their organizations." Their analysis examines teams that function in the context of organizations.

Team performance is defined usually in terms of outcomes, although process measures are sometimes included. In addition, most of the experimental investigations have construed team performance in linear ("input-output") terms, although some recent work, largely case studies, provides a basis for reconceptualizing the process in nonlinear terms. Furthermore, the production process may be more complex. For example, Hackman (1987) suggested that teams evaluate their collective performance as they work, and evaluations affect team processes, which influence subsequent performance—as self-reinforcing spirals of increasing or decreasing effectiveness (see also Hall and Watson, 1971; Steiner, 1972).

This chapter reviews the work from both linear and nonlinear views of team performance. We cover both the internal interactive processes emphasized by Freeberg and Rock (1987), and the external (contextual and boundary variables) influences highlighted by the Sundstrom et al. (1990) framework. We begin with what is known about team performance from laboratory research, then turn to the broader frameworks for understanding performance, including contextual influences. In the main part of the chapter, we examine team developmental processes, addressing issues about how teams learn and the effectiveness of team-building interventions. Finally, issues of performance and development are considered in relation to the use of games as vehicles for training. (Related issues of team training are treated in the next chapter.)

DETERMINANTS OF TEAM PERFORMANCE

A Meta-Analysis of Laboratory Studies

Freeberg and Rock (1987) conducted a meta-analysis of many studies dealing with input, mediating (throughput), and output (performance outcome) variables in team research. Emphasizing internal team processes, they organized their meta-analysis in terms of 12 dependent outcome and process categories:

Outcomes

1. team accuracy
2. time required to achieve a solution
3. amount of product produced
4. extent of task transfer
5. solution agreement among members
6. originality of solutions
7. perceived satisfaction
8. trials to acquisition
9. performance proficiency

Process measures

10. team cohesiveness
11. coordination among members
12. suitability of interaction or communication among members.

There were 25 independent variables used in the meta-analysis, grouped in the broad categories of team member characteristics (e.g., sex, prior experience with task, time worked together), team task characteristics (e.g., complexity, task fidelity, feedback of results), and team organization variables (e.g., communications structure, assigned roles and role stratification, coordination of member functions). Studies chosen for the analysis were those that dealt exclusively with task-interacting groups in which "team" was a unitary entity (also referred to as an ad hoc laboratory team). Most were laboratory studies (79 percent) conducted with college student populations; the average team size was 3.2 members, the average sample size (number of teams in the analysis) was 39. However, due to the strict statistical requirements that must be met to perform the analysis, only 21 percent of the available literature (117 of 547 papers) could be used in the meta-analysis. The strongest effect sizes[1] were obtained for studies of highly rated laboratory (rather than field) studies, studies with smaller team sizes, and those rated highest in data reporting.

The strongest relationships were obtained for three outcome measures: accuracy of team task performance, time required to achieve a solution to the task, and quantity of the team product. The seven strongest independent variables, by rank, were task complexity, task structure, performance over time (practice), interaction/communication, task load, cooperation /competition, and coordination. (These relationships are depicted in Figure 6-1.) Negligible effect sizes were obtained for prior task experience, team members' individual skills, feedback, and cohesiveness. With regard to those variables most relevant to training—prior task experience, practice, and feedback—practice showed the strongest effect sizes in relationships with quantity of output and accuracy of product. Moderate effect sizes were obtained for feedback with solution time and interaction/communication.

A major contribution of this analysis is the development of three "minimodels" in which the authors connect input to output variables through each of three mediating variables, interaction/communication, coordination, and cohesiveness. Each model highlights one of these mediating variables, showing how relationships between particular inputs and outputs may depend on the way they influence that process. Model 1 indicates that the mediating influence of communication results from the effects of three heavily task-dependent team conditions: load, feedback, and practice. These inputs influence the outputs of time, proficiency, and accuracy through a communication process. Of the various relationships specified by this model, the relationship between feedback and performance accuracy has received the least attention in the research literature. Model 2 highlights the importance of cooperation/competition as an influence on team output, both in terms of their direct effects on team accuracy and their indirect effects through the mediating variable of coordination. The model also calls attention to the

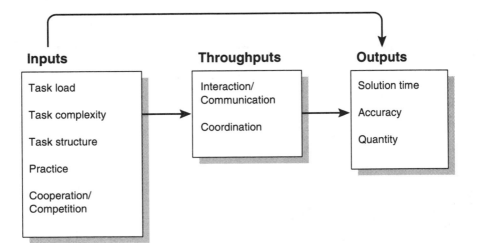

Inputs	Throughputs	Outputs
Task load	Interaction/ Communication	Solution time
Task complexity		Accuracy
Task structure	Coordination	Quantity
Practice		
Cooperation/ Competition		

FIGURE 6-1 Input, throughput, and output variables in team performance.

importance of task fidelity (comparability to real-world tasks) as an influence on outputs. Both cooperation/competition and fidelity affect team coordination which, in turn, affects the accuracy and quantity of team output. Both are central to the committee's appraisal of the team literature. Model 3 further underscores the importance of cooperation/competition: in this model they operate through team cohesiveness to produce effects on the outcome variables of quantity and proficiency. These results suggest that intrateam conflict has a strong effect on team performance. They provide a basis for recommending research into the way that conflict is manifest in the team process, for example, by probing relationships between types of intrateam conflict and modes of settlement or resolution. More generally, the analysis shows that team variables exert stronger effects on outputs than do member characteristics.

The Freeberg and Rock (1987) meta-analysis provides an important cumulation function for research on team performance. Similar to meta-analyses performed on other topics, this work distinguishes among variables that have relatively strong and weak influences on team outputs across many studies. The authors also distinguished among variables that had direct versus indirect effects on outputs. For example, in one model, feedback was found to relate to interaction or communication which, in turn, was linked to several performance outcomes. In other words, knowledge of results is likely to exercise some of its effects through the patterns of member communication established within a team. Further specification is achieved when the same variables—for example, task load and practice—are shown to have strong indirect effects on such output variables as time and direct effects on such other measures of team performance as quality of product. Identifying possible causal paths through which variables operate to produce effects is a major addition to the direct bivariate (two-variable) relationships uncovered in the meta-analysis. They highlight the importance of team process and, by so doing, uncover effects of some input variables shown to have relatively weak direct effects on team output (e.g., feedback, cooperation and competition, task fidelity). They also make research gaps evident and, therefore, provide an analytical basis for further research on the topic. One direction for further research is to trace the linkages suggested by the models over time in different group tasks.

The Freeberg and Rock (1987) analysis is limited by the nature of the sample of studies included. Those studies may not be representative of the universe of studies on team performance. The sample is small and biased toward laboratory experiments, although it is of high quality in terms of methodological criteria. It may well be that these studies represent the only body of work that merits the sort of cumulative analysis performed by the authors. Related to the issue of biased sampling is the problem of overlooking certain variables rarely included in laboratory exercises. One set of variables, referred to as "context," consists of aspects of larger organizations within which teams function, including relations among different teams operating within the same or different organizational environments. Another set of variables are those that refer to team-building and identification processes that occur over a longer period of time than is available for laboratory experiments. These processes have been examined primarily in field studies of particular cases. Both types of variables are discussed in the sections to follow.

Contextual Variables

Broader frameworks for analyzing factors that influence team performance include contextual variables. Emphasizing the context within which teams perform, Sundstrom et al. (1990:122) define performance as the "acceptability of output to customers within or outside the organization who receive team products, services, information, decisions, or performance events (such as presentations or competitions)." This customer-driven definition is complemented by more specific criteria of effectiveness, which include "quality, quantity, downtime, satisfaction, group stability over time" (from Goodman, 1986:145).

Sundstrom et al. (1990) distinguish between context and process in their attempt to organize the literature of work teams. For them, factors external to the group may have stronger effects on performance than internal processes. By context, they refer to the culture of the larger organization within which the group operates and its physical environment. But they also include such factors as technology, mission clarity, autonomy, performance feedback, rewards and recognition, and training and consultation. Process is referred to as team development and consists of interpersonal processes—Freeberg and Rock's communication and interaction—norms, cohesion, and roles. Between context and process are boundaries that differentiate a work unit from others, as well as the barriers that prevent access to information, goods, or people, and serve as points of external exchange with other teams, customers, competitors, and so on. Sundstrom et al. are vague about causal and temporal dynamics, preferring to treat these factors as interrelated processes, but "output" is team effectiveness, which they define as performance (acceptability of output to customers) and viability (members' satisfaction, participation, and willingness to continue working together).

Particularly notable in the Sundstrom et al. list are those factors that have received little attention in the experimental literature reviewed by Freeberg and Rock. These factors include organizational cultures, the physical environment, and the integration and differentiation aspects of group-organization boundaries. This set of variables defines the relation of a work team to its organization and determines what constitutes effectiveness in its particular context. The key point is that teams vary in the extent to which their performance is affected by the larger organization in which they are a part.

The more that team performance depends on synchronizing with counterpart units, the less that performance is a function of internal group processes. Externally oriented teams are probably less differentiated, less autonomous, and more integrated into the larger system "through coordination and synchronization with suppliers, managers, peers, and customers" (Sundstrom et al., 1990:124). They are also more influenced by the culture of the organization than more differentiated or autonomous units and arrange the physical environment in ways that foster external exchanges. Whether externally oriented teams pass through the same developmental sequences as the more autonomous "inward-looking" teams remains an issue. The intertwining of process and context, suggested by the Sundstrom et al. framework, suggests that team development varies with differences in organizational contexts. Experimental research has done little to elucidate this issue since laboratory teams are largely without context and interact over short periods of time. Field research may, however, provide the needed clarification.

Support for the central role of contextual variables in team performance is provided by Gladstein (1984). Data from members of 100 sales teams in the communications industry were used to test a comprehensive model of group effectiveness, defined as satisfaction, self-reported effectiveness, and sales performance. Interestingly, the satisfaction and effectiveness ratings did not correspond to actual performance. Team members attributed sales to their internal interactions and experience rather than to the key contextual variable of market growth. Intragroup processes, leadership behavior, training, and experience influenced self-reported effectiveness and satisfaction, but actual performance was related to the way teams managed their interactions with outside groups and other aspects of their organizational context. One implication of these findings is that attempts to foster internal processes such as cohesiveness may not improve team performance as much as negotiating favorable objectives or by promoting group products to top management. It may even lower performance, as when cohesive groups enforce group standards that restrict output (Schachter et al., 1951; Berkowitz, 1954). Another implication is that process changes alone are unlikely to improve performance when structural (contextual) factors are not also taken into account. Interventions may encourage members to attribute the source of problems to their own behavior—e.g., lack of skill in conflict management—and prevent them from considering the source as organization-level phenomena. For example, team building is unlikely to boost sales in a stagnant market over which the team has little control. However, it may boost morale, which sustains the team through a downward cycle, keeping it intact to take advantage of an upturn in the market.

When context is taken into account, teams are seen as part of larger structures. The connections between team and organizational performance may be quite complex. Successful interventions at the level of teams may not translate into improved organizational performance: structures and processes that may serve as facilitators or inhibitors of change from one level to another. To date, methods have not been developed to follow changes through a system—from individual to group to organization. Nor is there a framework that can guide research on linkages between levels of analysis—for example, the effect of team productivity on organizational productivity or other types of performance—although progress toward developing such a framework is being made (see Harris, 1994).

Context also refers to organizational culture. Cultural analysis is common when one thinks of ethnic or national entities but it has recently been applied to the study of groups and organizations within a society. Although "culture" is still an elusive concept, the rapid development of a literature on the subject attests to the likelihood of cultural influences on the way that people in organizations think, feel, and act. Put another way, the need for a concept of culture reflects the judgment that behavior cannot be accounted for only in terms of structure and processes.

Less consensus exists on a formal definition. Schein argues (1985:6):

> the term culture should be reserved for the deeper level of *basic assumptions* and *beliefs* that are shared by members of an organization, that operate unconsciously, and that define in a basic 'taken-for-granted' fashion an organization's view of itself and its environment.

Others have included in their definition observed behavioral regularities, norms that evolve in working groups, dominant values espoused, a guiding philosophy, the rules of the game, and a feeling or climate conveyed in an organization. For Schein, these various meanings are reflected in leader behavior and are, in fact, regarded as the primary functions of leadership. Just how cultures are conveyed to group members and the effect of those cultures on behavior are demonstrated in case material used by Schein and others. (Relying also on case material, in Chapter 12 we illustrate the role played by organizational cultures in affecting decisions about training programs.)

Another contextual variable is the relationship between organizations during times of change (see Gladstein, 1984). Restructuring in response to market changes consists both of internal changes in structure and mode of operation and external changes in relations with other organizations. Critical to this process are the decision makers in boundary roles—those who negotiate relationships between departments within an organization or between autonomous organizations. A substantial literature on boundary roles provides many insights into the constraints, opportunities, and tactics used by negotiators in these roles (for a recent review, see Kahn, 1991). The management of interdependence, joint ventures, and the establishment of new "regimes" are responses to change that can be orchestrated through a negotiation process (see Kremenyuk, 1991). The research literature on organizations contributes to the understanding of these processes.

TEAM DEVELOPMENT

Teams are dynamic entities. According to Tannenbaum et al. (1992:2): "roles and norms evolve, members develop new skills and attitudes, tasks are modified, communication patterns unfold, goals are revised, personnel may change and hopefully, progress occurs." The inevitability of change makes it useful to focus on developmental phases, transition points, and team building. These concepts are discussed in this section in three parts: team learning processes in which cognitive variables are emphasized; team building, which highlights the role played by motivation in performance; and, third, the implications of team building for interteam relations. Each of these parts focuses on process (throughput) variables rather than outcome or output measures.

Team Learning, Developmental Phases, and Metacognition

Recent conceptual work has concentrated less on the determinants of team performance—construed in input-process-output terms—than on the way teams learn through time and repeated interactions among their members. These investigators examine the details of group processes and ask questions about the way that teams learn or acquire new insights that contribute to performance. By merging cognitive and social phenomena, these studies explore the "mechanisms by which people actively shape each other's knowledge and reasoning processes" (Resnick, 1991:2). Rather than viewing context as an exogenous influence on performance (as does Sundstrom et al., 1990), this view argues either that the social context in which cognitive activity takes place is an integral part of that activity or that context and process are intertwined, with effects occurring in both directions.

Shared perspectives, reframing, shared meaning, changed schemas, and metacognition are some of the concepts used to describe team learning. The process is often conceived in terms of a sequence of developmental stages. Whether teams follow a fixed sequence or show different temporal patterns in varied organizational contexts has not yet been determined. For Dechant and Marsick (1992), team learning evolves through four phases. In the first phase, "contained learning," the individuals in a group become aware that they are part of team, but there is little exchange of perspectives or reframing based on the perspectives of others. In the second phase, "collected learning," members share their understandings of the problem, but there is no collective reframing. In the third phase, "constructed learning," members develop a language of shared meaning, including a lexicon containing models and metaphors. A consensus begins to develop through a process of exchange, criticism, and role reversing. In the fourth phase, "continuous learning," the group extends its consensual understanding to other parts of the organization—referred to as "boundary crossing"—and, by so doing, broadens its own perspective. Proceeding in a linear fashion, members become, over time, more like a team in the sense of acquiring shared meaning around language, roles, mission, and purpose. This conception takes on added significance when the phases are construed by the authors as intervening processes between influences and learning results at each of three levels of analysis—individual, group, and organization. Although developed largely on the basis of observations made in one company, and therefore subject to bias, the authors have developed a "Team Learning Survey" used for data collection in other large companies.

In a study of the lifespans of eight naturally occurring teams, Garsick (1988) challenges the view of a stage-like process through which groups develop. Her concept of "punctuated equilibrium," borrowed from evolutionary biology (Gould and Eldredge, 1977), refers to "progress through an alternation of stasis and sudden appearance—long periods of inertia, punctuated by concentrated revolutionary periods of quantum change" (Garsick, 1988:16). She is less interested in slow evolutionary learning processes, as depicted by Dechant and Marsick and elsewhere (see, e.g., Tuckman and Jensen, 1977), preferring to concentrate on the *transitions* that occur, usually at the temporal midpoint of a team's calendar, when a "major jump in progress" takes place. Parallel concepts from other areas of research include midlife transitions in adult development (Levinson, 1986), framebreaking changes in career development (London, 1985), and turning points in negotiation (Druckman et al., 1991; Druckman, 1986). This work directs attention to periods of stability and change, noting the importance of situational contingencies that can influence significantly the path a team takes. More important, perhaps, are implications for intervention activities—activities that affect a team's development. Knowing when these transitions are likely to occur can facilitate the timing of interventions: interventions that occur either "too early" or "too late" can prevent a team from turning a crisis into an opportunity for growth and development. Interventions or feedback that help members reframe their problems during transition periods can make the difference between effective and ineffective teams. Garsick provides a useful description of the process. Further work is needed to develop indicators of transitions and to distinguish between effective and ineffective interventions.

Transitions or turning points are not imposed on teams. They typically result from activities in which members monitor their own progress and use resources to accomplish objectives. This process can be aided by feedback provided by observers. Recent work by Klein et al. (1992) highlights the strategic role of feedback in facilitating the way that teams handle information. Although the authors are less concerned about assessing the effect of the feedback on team performance, they provide categories that define what to look for. Referred to as "behavioral markers," the categories are based on a theory about the ways in which teams change and improve—by developing a sense of identity, by moving toward goals, by learning how to perceive the world, by achieving a higher level of cognitive complexity, and by learning to monitor themselves, "metacognition." Examples of the categories are anticipate/confirm, clarify/compensate, detect and fill information gaps, and share mental and time management activities. Incidents are translated into these categories as observers learn "to use specific conversations and behaviors as the basis for feedback delivery, rather than global ratings or general evaluations of team effectiveness" (Klein et al., 1992:21). This framework appears to be useful for observing, and then correcting, performance at a microlevel of specific interactions among team members. However, it does have shortcomings. The strong emphasis on cognitive factors may leave out important motivational variables likely to affect a team's performance. An exclusive focus on internal group processes omits attention to context and boundary processes (discussed above). Moreover, their preoccupation with usefulness apparently leads them to overlook the role of research in documenting the impact of different kinds of feedback.

Taken together, the studies reviewed in this section underscore the relevance of social and cognitive processes that can only be understood at the level of groups. Group-level explanations for behavior have been a conceptual and methodological challenge for social psychologists since the founding of the field. The team-development perspective advanced by Dechant and Marsick (1992), Garsick (1988), and others (e.g., Glickman et al., 1987; McGrath et al., 1986) describes a process in which members become increasingly self-conscious of their team identification. They acquire shared perspectives that transcend, and differ from, the meanings brought to the group by its members. As such, cognition becomes metacognition as this term is used by Klein et al. It is a property of teams in the sense that social processes are internalized in a manner similar to Mead's (1934) idea of "conversations with the generalized other" (see also Vygotsky, 1978). These studies seem to be struggling with concepts that situate group processes between the earlier "collectivist" notions of a "group mind" (e.g., see Allport, 1969) and the modern-day cognitive social psychologists' emphasis on individual thinking that is influenced by others with whom he or she interacts (e.g., Nisbett and Ross, 1980). The middle ground may well be found in a focus on the characteristics and products of the interaction process (Sherif and Sherif, 1956:342), including "developing reciprocities among individuals, organizational structures, and group products, like social norms." It is also found in Wegner's (1986) recent work on transactive memory, which takes into account both the diversity and uniformity of group members' thought patterns. But, even at this middle level, the phenomena have eluded measurement because of uncertainties about how to combine performances of team members: Are they to be combined by using linear (additive or multiplicative) or nonlinear algorithms?

The usefulness of emergent concepts is illustrated by Orasanu and Salas' (1993) attempt to organize the literature on team decision making. Their concept of "shared mental models" seems to account for research findings on the distinguishing features of effective and ineffective teams operating in field (not laboratory) settings. It refers to organized knowledge shared by team members who work together over relatively long periods of time. According to Orasanu and Salas (1993:7): "such knowledge enables each person to carry out his or her role in a timely and coordinated fashion, helping the team to function as a single unit with little negotiation of what to do and when to do it." In many of the studies they reviewed, effective teams were those that developed "shared models of the game and their roles in it so that much of their teamwork was habitual and that minimal language served a guiding or correcting role" (p. 10). When asked to account for a team's success, coaches will often say that they play well together or that they anticipate each other's moves. What the coaches may be observing is the effect on performance of having shared mental models or of developing a "team mind" (see Klein and Thordsen, 1989).

Central to this process, according to Orasanu and Salas, is the role played by team leaders. For example, in a study of cockpit simulations, Orasanu (1990) found that leaders of high-performing crews explicitly stated more plans, considered more options, provided more explanations, and sounded more warnings or predictions. Supported by results obtained in other studies (e.g., Chidester and Foushee, 1988), the Orasanu finding suggests that future research should focus on the role of leader communication in team performance. The research should also distinguish between decisions and performance: better decisions made by leaders may not translate into improved performance by members or a leader's poor decisions may be well implemented by the team. In stratified teams, such as in the military, decision making may be a different process than team performance or operation. Overall, however, the link between team decisions and performance has received little attention. This lack of attention may be due, at least in part, to separate traditions of research: one tradition focuses on decision processes, the other on measuring performance outcomes.

The literature on teams illustrates considerable breadth in terms of the variety of concepts, methods, and settings used. The meta-analysis performed by Freeberg and Rock (1987) call attention to the large number of laboratory studies using quantitative methods to evaluate influences on performance. Field studies have been both quantitative (e.g., Gladstein, 1984) and qualitative (e.g., Garsick, 1988; Argyris et al., 1985). Each of these types of studies has contributed in important ways to an understanding of team performance. The contributions can be regarded as being complementary. The quantitative research has been useful in modeling the sequence of influences on performance. The qualitative studies have made evident some advantages of regarding teams as entities for study in their own right. Dechant and Marsick's (1992) work illustrates an attempt to merge the approaches. Their qualitative work, performed in the context of one company, produced a theory of team development. Their quantitative work, using large samples of teams in the field, serves to test hypotheses derived from the theory. The advantage of combining the approaches is that concepts developed from the qualitative work become the variables that are evaluated for their effects in the quantitative studies. The committee endorses this multimethod strategy for further research on team learning and development.

Team Building and Performance

Many of the investigations of team learning overlook the role played by motivation in performance. Focusing primarily on cognitive processes, the studies have described team development in terms of the acquisition of new concepts that contribute to problem solving or task products. But team development can also be described in terms of acquiring an identification or enhancing cohesion. These processes are heavily influenced by motivational variables. Insights into those processes derive largely from the literature on organizational development and team building. There are different approaches to team building, but all accept the assumption by Tannenbaum et al. (1992:3):

> a team's active involvement in planning change is more likely to result in favorable consequences than imposing change and that the people closest to the task situation can solve their own problem if provided with an appropriate structure and process for doing so.

Four general approaches to team-building interventions emphasize goal setting, interpersonal relations, role clarification, and problem solving. There is much enthusiasm for these approaches among practitioners and consultants, but it is not matched by strong empirical support for their effect on team performance.

Results from reviews of studies that evaluated effects of team-building interventions (DeMeuse and Liebowitz, 1981; Woodman and Sherwood, 1980; and Buller, 1986) do not find strong effects. Although positive results for team building were found in many of the early studies—for example, 80 percent of the studies reviewed by DeMeuse and Liebowitz (1981) and 63 percent of the studies examined by Woodman and Sherwood (1980)— few of the effects were obtained on performance variables. Rather, effects were obtained primarily on perceptions and attitudes. It may well be that the interventions exert a stronger influence on perceptions and attitudes than on performance, but it is also possible that methodological problems prevented the detection of effects. One problem is that many studies did not measure performance or effectiveness: of the 52 team-building studies identified by Buller (1986), only 9 used performance criteria. Another problem is that the team-building interventions were weak or obscure. A third problem is that the study designs were flawed by confounding variables contained in the intervention package. Of the nine studies that measured performance, only five used experimental or quasi-experimental designs with some control over extraneous variables. Interestingly, an inverse relationship was found between degree of rigor and outcome success for the team-building intervention: the more rigorous the design, the weaker the outcomes.

These evaluation studies highlight a discrepancy between the generally accepted assertion that the way a team interacts influences its effectiveness and the weak relationships obtained in the studies. Three interpretations are possible: the assertion is incorrect; the interventions did not improve team interactions; or the studies did not detect relationships that exist because of inadequate designs.

More recent reviews of studies designed to avoid some of the methodological problems have clarified some of the effects. In a review of 17 empirical team-building studies reported since 1980, Tannenbaum et al. (1992) found many improvements in methodology in comparison with the earlier work. Eleven of the 17 studies used a quasi-experimental design—in particular, a pretest, posttest, nonequivalent control group design. However, the sample size of teams examined remained small, although the incidence of single team studies decreased.

Improvements in team members' perceptions or attitudes were shown more consistently than behavioral changes. Four of the ten studies that assessed behavioral change reported mixed or nonsignificant results. A similar pattern was obtained for the studies that used the strongest research designs: most of these studies showed positive results for perceptual or attitudinal change; only one study found a significant behavioral change. Other changes in team-building interventions are a trend toward using multiple approaches and the inclusion of more than self-report indicators. Over 75 percent of the more recent studies evaluated interventions targeted at more than one obstacle to team development. It is not clear, however, why any particular approaches are used: specific team concerns are not coupled in a clear way with particular interventions. Team building may not be an appropriate intervention in some circumstances: a mix of types of interventions—team building, counseling, training—may work better. Such a mix is captured in the problem-solving approach to team building. This consists of a self-diagnosis followed by interventions designed to focus on the diagnosed problems. Most studies do not include a thorough diagnosis prior to the treatment. Those that do report more effective problem solving for the groups that diagnose the problem before beginning solutions (e.g., Hirokawa, 1983). By withholding proposed solutions until after a diagnosis, a group is more likely to suggest several alternatives for consideration (Maier and Maier, 1957). They are also less likely to become enamored of particular solutions leading to decisions based more on persuasiveness than on solution quality (Maier and Hoffman, 1960). These findings have implications for practice. Following Tannenbaum et al. (1992), we believe that team building should be considered part of a larger improvement strategy that includes multiple interventions.

The preference of most investigators is to assess team processes rather than performance. Yet as the studies reviewed above found, improved process may not translate to improved team performance. Effects of team building interventions may differ for different dependent variables: they appear to have a stronger effect on perceptions and attitudes than on behavioral changes. Although process measures are valuable in explaining why an intervention succeeds or fails, changes in process do not mean that the intervention influenced performance (see Gladstein, 1984). The relationship between process and performance is likely to be complex. Insufficient time lags used in most of the studies may have masked the relationship: process changes may be manifest in performance only after a period of time has passed; conversely they may dissipate through time. Long-term effects are rarely studied; most interventions are essentially one-time events. Further work should use causal modeling techniques to detect reciprocal relationships between process and performance over time. It should also investigate effects of task and developmental stage as variables that may moderate the process-performance relationship. The type of assessment also matters. Tannebaum et al. (1992:26) concluded that "the further removed the dependent variable is from the immediate control of the team . . . the less likely that the team building intervention will demonstrate improvements." Team building is most likely to improve those aspects of performance that are in control of the team and less likely to affect aspects of performance determined by external factors. Needed are more precise connections between the specific procedures used in an intervention and the particular variables affected by those procedures, with proper control for assessments of casual paths.

Some progress toward better designed evaluations is reflected in two studies reported by Buller and Bell (1986) and Wolfe et al. (1989). Buller and Bell (1986) designed a field experiment to examine the effects of two interventions, team building and goal setting, on the performance of hard-rock miners working in an underground metal mine. Using a quasi-experimental design, the study assessed the independent and interactive effects of these variables (before and after the interventions) on several measures of productivity over a period of 3-1/2 months' quantity of production (tons per man-shift) and quality of production (grade of silver). Although care was taken to ensure a relatively unambiguous interpretation of the results, limitations still existed. The slight improvements that occurred for the team-building intervention are inconclusive due to a lack of control over several factors in the field setting.

The limitations in the mine study may be symptomatic of field research on this topic. One limitation is that team-building interventions are diffuse. The intervention "packages" contain many elements that, together, can produce either strong or weak effects on performance. For example, some aspects of the package that enhance performance may be offset by other aspects that interfere with performance. Due to their complexity, team-building interventions do not focus specifically on the performance variables (which, in this study, were tons per man-shift and quality of ore). In this sense, team-building packages are similar to the packages designed for accelerated learning, stress reduction, or influence as described in the committee's first report (Druckman and Swets, 1988): although it may be possible to demonstrate effects, it is difficult to ascertain which part of the package accounts for those effects. Another limitation is that relatively short-term evaluations may not capture the full effects of the intervention. French and Bell (1984) noted that team building may be a relatively slow process of developmental change that is manifest only over the long term. The Buller and Bell (1986) evaluation period (3-1/2 months following the intervention) may not have allowed for detection of a slow process.

Two other problems characteristic of field research are referred to as selectivity biases and reactive effects of the experiment. Pre-experimental differences between the treatment groups (intervention and control) make it difficult to compare effects on performance. In many field settings these differences are unavoidable. Although it is often possible to adjust these differences statistically (correcting for different baseline performances), the problem is not entirely solved in this way. More informative data on performance would be those on changes over time *within* treatment groups. But there are problems with this measure, too: changes may be a result of the increased attention given to those employees in the experiment. The increased motivation that may result from such attention, "Hawthorne effects," could account for improvements. Many packages intended to improve performance may well be capitalizing on these effects (Druckman and Swets, 1988). In fact, Buller and Bell (1986:325) argue "that the objective of (team-building) interventions is a sustained Hawthorne effect." If this is the case, then team-building effects on performance, when they occur, are due primarily to the increased attention to employees and their work.

More recently, Wolfe et al. (1989) evaluated effects of team building on the performance of a simulated company. Following Buller and Bell, these authors comment on the weakness of the team-building interventions used in earlier experiments. Their experiment was an attempt to strengthen the effect of team building on performance by having "a practiced interventionist implement a team development effort within an intensive format" (Wolfe et al., 1989:393). The strongest effects occurred on team cohesion. Cohesion was measured on an index consisting of three correlated parts emphasizing belongingness and commitment to the team (Seashore, 1954): extent of perception of self as a member of the team; extent of preference to remain on the team; and extent of perception that the team is better than other teams with regard to the way members get along, the way they help each other, and the way they stick together (see also Norris and Niebuhr, 1980). Teams exposed to the intervention were more cohesive in this sense than control groups throughout the simulation; they also expressed higher levels of self-disclosure during the interactions. However, the intervention produced only marginally better economic performance during the early stages of the simulation, due largely to the increased cohesiveness. They were able to maintain their advantage but not increase it through the course of the simulation. Nor did the "treated" teams indicate that they learned more or express higher levels of satisfaction with the experience than the "untreated" teams.[2] They also underestimated their performance during the early phases of the experiment, but by the end they overestimated their team's performance. These results support findings obtained in earlier studies (e.g., McKenney and Dill, 1966; Deep et al., 1967; Hand et al., 1975) showing that the major contribution of team building is its effects on morale, cohesion, cooperation, and mutual trust. These effects do not translate into improved team performance in a simple or direct way. For example, a cohesive team may not improve its performance due to a lack of resources, poor intergroup relations, technical problems, or adverse conditions in the environment. The effects on team process, however, do have implications for relations between teams, a topic to which we now turn our attention.

Team Building and Interteam Relations

Team-building interventions not only foster positive intrateam relations, but also produce negative interteam relations. The enhanced cohesion resulting from team-building exercises may be a source of biased images and negative attitudes toward other teams. The well-known hypothesized relationship between ingroup amity and outgroup enmity (see, e.g., LeVine and Campbell, 1972), has been supported by results obtained in numerous laboratory and field studies on intergroup relations (for reviews Stein, 1976; Tajfel, 1982). Less clear, however, is the direction of causality: Does internal cohesion cause external conflict or is the cohesion a reaction to conflict? The cohesion produced by team-building interventions is due largely to such internal group processes as cooperative problem solving and conflict management within the team. External competition is rarely included as part of the package. At issue is whether this source of team identification, developed in the absence of interteam competition, leads to conflict.

With regard to biased perceptions, results from many experiments show that the bias can be aroused by mere categorization; results from other experiments link the bias to competitive situations. Together, the studies suggest that competition is not a necessary condition for ingroup bias, although it can result from competition and is probably stronger in competitive situations (see reviews by Tajfel, 1982; Brewer and Kramer, 1985). Focusing on mechanisms, Messick and Mackie (1989) discuss alternative theories intended to explain the results of these studies. Most promising perhaps is Turner's (1987) self-categorization theory, which posits that evaluative bias ("our group is better than yours") is a function of perceptual bias (categories that distinguish among groups in terms of similarities and dissimilarities). Without perceptual distortions, the evaluative biases would not occur. Implications for team building turn on whether the "treatment" produces the sorts of categorical distinctions that lead to biased evaluations.

More relevant, perhaps, are the studies that examined behavior in intergroup settings. Most of these studies showed that groups play games more competitively than individuals and that people who are representatives of groups are more competitive bargainers than those who are not (Messick and Mackie, 1989). At issue in these studies is whether the observed competitiveness is a function of group identification per se or other factors in the situation. Results obtained by Insko et al. (1988) suggest the other factors explanation for competitive behavior. They showed that the increased competitiveness of groups was due to intragroup consensus about the group's strategy; when groups acted in lock step, enhanced competition occurred. A similar finding was previously obtained by Druckman (1968): the most competitive groups in his study were those that agreed in prenegotiation sessions on the relative importance of the issues under discussion. Thus, it may be that a consensual strategy, rather than group identification per se, is responsible for the observed increase in competitive behavior.[3]

Further support for the importance of strategy development comes from the results of a recent meta-analysis of findings on compromise behavior in bargaining situations (Druckman, 1994). The analysis addressed the issue of the relative importance of variables that are hypothesized to influence interteam bargaining. By including the variables of strategy preparation and group representation in the analysis, it was also possible to address the specific issue of the relative importance of group identification and strategy development on bargaining behavior. The results showed that group representation or accountability was not a strong influence on compromise behavior; representatives compromised only somewhat less than nonrepresentatives. Stronger effects were obtained for the way teams prepare for negotiation, their orientation toward the negotiation, and the size of the conflict defined in terms of initial position distance. Specifically, Druckman (1994) found the following effect sizes[4] for the nine variables: bargainer's orientation as competitive or cooperative (.42), prenegotiation experience as strategy versus study (.37), time pressure as deadline or no deadline (.37), initial distance between positions (.35), opponent's strategy as tough or soft (.32), team representation as bargaining for a team or for self (.30), accountability to the team (.27), visibility of the negotiation as audience present or not present (.21), and whether the issue was large or small (.18). An implication of these findings is that bargaining competitiveness is more likely to be increased or decreased by "affecting" the way team representatives prepare for the discussions or their orientation toward the negotiation than by the extent of their "loyalty" or their accountability to the team.

These results highlight the importance of strategy development as an influence on the extent of conflict between teams; it may also be a positive influence on team performance. The Buller and Bell (1986) study found that strategy development was a key variable that intervened between the team-building interventions and performance. According to Buller and Bell (1986:326): "team building may have influenced the development of strategies which in turn may have improved quality of grade." This is consistent with earlier models of factors that influence the behavior of individuals in organizations (e.g., Hackman, 1976). While serving to focus the team effort, careful planning sets in motion processes that heighten team identity, which, in turn, may hinder relations with other teams. The intrateam dynamics would seem to foster the kinds of perceptual distinctions that lead to evaluative biases, consistent with Turner's (1987) theory (discussed above). One sequence of events is as follows:

> within-team strategy formation → intrateam consensus on goals → enhanced sense of member identity with the unit → perceptual distinctions between "us" and "them" → evaluative biases and related distortions → heightened competitiveness, win-lose dynamics → reduced willingness to collaborate, compromise, and so on.

Although this sequence captures some of the implications of the research completed to date, it is presented primarily as a set of hypothesized relationships that should be subject to further research. It calls attention to linkages between internal, intrateam development and external, interteam relations. Those connections provide a conceptual bridge between developmental sequences and boundary-role processes (discussed above). The committee endorses attempts to design new studies that explore these relationships.

The Freeberg and Rock (1987) meta-analysis makes evident the importance of such training variables as prior task experience, practice, and feedback or knowledge of results. The case studies of team development emphasize the importance of the active learner who controls the pace and content of his or her own learning. Neither tradition of team research deals with the issue of transfer of skills from learning to performance settings. That issue is addressed with regard to simulations in Chapter 3.

INTERACTIVE GAMES

The terms simulation and games are often used interchangeably. In this section, we focus primarily on games that are role-playing exercises involving groups. This is considered to be a type of simulation although it differs from the kind of mechanical simulators or training simulations discussed in Chapter 3. Most of the games discussed in this section are concerned less with the training of specific mission-oriented operational skills and the transfer of those skills than with learning general and social skills in educational settings. Because of its popularity as a training and research device, particularly in the military, the "technology" of game design and evaluation has been the subject of considerable research and conceptual work.[5] In this section, we discuss issues related to the use of games and provide a summary of the evidence obtained to date on their effectiveness.

Games are frequently used as exercises in team development packages designed by organizational consultants. One of the more popular games is "Pumping the Colors" created by Gary Shirts for facilitating team building. Rarely, however, are the exercises evaluated in terms of whether they accomplish their objectives. Even when used as tasks in studies that are comparing different team-building interventions, the game exercises are not evaluated (e.g., Wolfe et al., 1989; Miesing and Preble, 1985; Hsu, 1984; Norris and Niebuhr, 1980). Thus, implications for the effectiveness of games used for team development must be derived from more general research on educational games. That research has addressed both cognitive and motivational effects of games; by so doing, it has implications for their effect on team-learning and team-building processes. However, measures of individual learning and motivation, used in most of these studies, may not translate into team outcomes. At issue are the effects of team members' development for a team's performance, and few studies to date have addressed this relationship (see Druckman and Bjork, 1991:Ch.12).[6]

The kinds of exercises used most often for training take the form of games played by students or trainees to discover new concepts or to develop new skills. At issue is whether the intended learning—defined either as acquiring concepts or skills—occurs. This issue has been addressed by research designed to evaluate outcomes of the learning experience. A second issue is whether the new knowledge or skills can be used effectively in other environments. Beginning in the early 1960s, an active network of gaming researchers devoted their careers to finding answers to these questions. Many of these studies have been reported in the journal, *Simulation & Gaming*, as well as in a number of edited books that cover a variety of types of uses and applications; see also Crookall and Oxford (1990) for an extensive bibliography of general and specialized sources. Our review draws on this literature, emphasizing, in particular, work reported during the past 15 years. We concentrate on gaming technology in general, rather than specific simulations intended to develop particular operational skills (see Chapter 3).

Games have a number of features that should facilitate learning. Among the features highlighted in the literature are involving students in an active learning situation (Glenn et al., 1982), enhancing their control over the learning environment (Boocock and Schild, 1968), focusing on learning principles and referents for concepts (Greenblat, 1975), rapid feedback and the learning of strategies (Schild, 1968), enhancing motivation to learn (Bredemeier and Greenblat, 1981), and providing an opportunity to encounter problems in ways analogous to the way they are encountered in real-world contexts (Van Sickle, 1978). The key question is whether these features contribute to better learning.

Cherryholmes (1966) is often credited with the earliest evaluation of learning through game playing. On the basis of only a few studies completed to that date, he concluded that only interest in the material being learned improved significantly; negligible changes occurred on cognitive and attitudinal variables. Somewhat more optimistic conclusions were reached 10 years later. Pierfy (1977) reviewed studies, reported during the 1960s and 1970s, that compared learning through games versus other educational experiences. With regard to learning, 15 of 21 studies showed no significant difference between experimental and control groups, indicating that the games were not more effective than conventional instructional techniques: of the other 6, 3 studies showed games to be better, 3 showed conventional methods to be better. With regard to retention, 8 of 11 studies reported significant differences in favor of games, indicating that students retained information longer than those trained with more conventional approaches. With regard to attitude change, 8 of 11 studies showed that games had a greater effect on attitudes—in terms of increased realism and approval of real-life persons—than conventional methods. For interest, 7 of 8 studies reported significantly more interest in the simulation activities than in the more conventional classroom activities, a finding that supports Cherryholmes' earlier conclusion.

Pierfy goes on to indicate that deficiencies in research design render these conclusions tentative. He lists a number of sources of possible confounding factors in many of the studies, including:

- unintended biases from game designers who also conduct the studies;
- unintended effects of instructor variables when matched classes are taught by different instructors;
- "Hawthorne effects" due to the difference between one group receiving a new method (game) while the other group is exposed to a familiar, conventional method;
- for some studies, administration of the posttest after a debriefing, allowing for the possibility that the posttest responses were influenced by the debriefing discussion;
- the techniques used in control classes may be regarded by students as vague, dull, and incomplete, so that any gains shown for the simulation classes are not strongly biased;
- use of only a pretest-posttest design—not adding groups without the pretest—allowing for the possibility that the pretest interacted in different ways with one or another method of instruction.

These flaws are not limited to game evaluations, but also characterize much of the evaluation literature in general; many of them can be remedied.

Stronger studies have appeared in more recent years due, in part, to attempts by designers and users to routinely incorporate evaluations in their packages. In addition, comparability from one study to another can be increased if the same categories of learning are used in constructing dependent variables, including knowledge of facts, analogies, game structure, skills needed for playing the game, knowledge of outcomes of various strategies used in the game, perceptions of the game, and attitudes toward the game (see also Fletcher, 1971). A variety of methods can be used to measure any particular learning objective, as Anderson and Lawton (1992) illustrate with respect to the objectives of basic knowledge, comprehension, application, analysis, synthesis, and evaluation. Furthermore, replication of studies in a variety of settings would help to distinguish between findings that hold across situations from those that are specific to particular situations. Such replication can reduce the impact of confounding variables; see, especially, Campbell and Stanley's (1963) discussion of a "heterogeneity of irrelevancies."

Another methodological concern is that even the best evaluations may not uncover causal mechanisms. Most of the studies reviewed by Pierfy were demonstration experiments that simply show effects of the instructional packages: Does it work? Few attempts are made to "unpack" the parts in order to determine what may account for the observed effects on learning or motivation: How does it work? This distinction was recognized in early appraisals of learning in simulation and games. In their wide-ranging survey of the issues, Boocock and Schild (1968) distinguish between the "engineering" and the "science" approaches to understanding: the former consists of demonstrating that a social technology produces gains; the latter is the identification of the mechanisms responsible for the gains. Few of the studies they examined searched for mechanisms; nor has there been any trend toward explanatory studies in more recent years. Investigators seem to have largely ignored the Boocock and Schild distinction.

Also missing in the research on simulations and games are issues raised by Bredemeier and Greenblat (1981) in their update of the Pierfy review. Bredemeier and Greenblat (1981) divide learning into three parts: subject matter, attitudes, and learning about oneself. With regard to subject matter, the available evidence suggests that games are at least as effective as other methods and are more effective aids to retention. With regard to attitudes, the evidence suggests that games can be more effective than traditional methods of instruction in facilitating positive attitude change toward the subject and its purposes. With regard to learning about oneself, they cite the results obtained by Johnson and Nelson (1978) showing that subjects who played games (versus those who did not) showed greater positive change on willingness to communicate. The positive effects on self-awareness may, however, depend on the extent to which the game was experienced in a positive way. Many of these conclusions support those reached in the earlier review by Pierfy. They do not illuminate reasons for why the effects do or do not occur and, therefore, make only small contributions to the development of theory in this area.

More recently, Randel et al. (1992) updated the earlier reviews in an examination of 69 studies that had been conducted over a 28-year period. Overall, they found that 56 percent of the comparisons between simulation games and conventional instruction showed no difference, 32 percent found differences favoring games, 7 percent favored games but their controls were questionable, and 5 percent found differences favoring conventional instruction. Dividing the studies into six subject-matter areas, the authors found that the greatest percentage of results favoring games were in mathematics (seven of eight studies) and language arts (five of six studies). Although the largest number of gaming evaluations have been in the area of social science, the majority of these studies (33 of 46) showed no differences in performance between games and conventional instruction. A meta-analysis of social science simulations (Van Sickle, 1986) reported a small effect size.

On the basis of these findings, Randel et al. (1992:269) concluded that games are likely to be more beneficial for topics "where very specific content can be targeted and objectives precisely defined." They also reaffirmed conclusions reached in earlier reviews that games show greater retention for students over time and elicit more student interest than more conventional instruction. As did the earlier reviews, Randel et al. (1992) call attention to many of the design and measurement problems typical of the studies. They add to the earlier lists the possible confusion between effects produced by the game and those produced by the debriefing sessions. They also emphasize the importance of distinguishing between preferences expressed by players and what it is that they learn from the games.

The reviews make evident that there is much yet to be understood about the effects on learners of participation in games or simulations. Progress toward richer theory and application may depend on providing answers to the following questions:

• What accounts for the discrepancy between learners' impressions and subjective reports, and the weak evidence on performance?
• What is the relationship between motivational and learning variables? How does involvement in the game affect learning?
• Why are motivation and interest stimulated by games?
• To what extent are effects due to instructor variables? For example, those instructors who are amenable to using games may be people who stimulate relaxed classrooms as well as facilitate later changes in classroom atmosphere.
• What aspects of games are expected to have what sorts of distinct effects on what sorts of participants?
• Does what one learns in a particular game transfer to other situations? To what range of situations do the lessons learned in a particular game apply?

The promise of interesting games as vehicles for learning skills and concepts have been largely unrealized to date. That promise is based on the assumption that role-playing activities may do more than stimulate interest; they "may also involve students in an active learning situation that may teach them specific skills" (Glenn et al., 1982:209). Although the evidence to date is inconclusive, the problems may rest not with the technology but with the way it is implemented and evaluated. A clearer definition of what is to be accomplished by the experience, how to accomplish it, and, then, how to evaluate effects would help. So too would a theoretically based taxonomy of games that distinguishes among games used for different purposes (see Bredemeier and Greenblat, 1981). Game designers need to be guided by conceptual frameworks. Game evaluators need to increase their sensitivity to relevant methodological issues. Advances along both these lines will, almost certainly, strengthen the state of the art. They will also clarify the distinction between cognitive and motivational effects on participants in gaming exercises used for team development.

CONCLUSIONS

The research to date on teams provides a base of knowledge for improving team performance. A variety of input variables—such as task complexity, structure, and task load—have been shown to relate to the output variables of quantity, accuracy, and efficiency. These relationships depend on the way that the inputs influence such mediating processes as interaction, coordination, and cohesiveness. For example, effects of intrateam cooperation or conflict on the quantity and proficiency of team output depend on the way that cooperation or conflict affects cohesion. These findings derive from the path models developed by Freeberg and Rock (1987), which deserve greater attention in the development of theories of team performance.

Claims have been made for the performance-enhancing effects of team-building interventions. However, such interventions appear to have limited effects on performance. Further research is needed to determine if consultant and practitioner enthusiasm is warranted. The research should follow the multimethod approach of Dechant and Marsick (1992) in examining teams both qualitatively and qualitatively.

Recent studies have identified certain processes or activities that could enhance the effect of team-building interventions. One of these is timing: interventions are likely to be most effective during transition periods. Another is to elicit from a team a self-diagnosis of its problems before proceeding with an intervention. A third consists of developing shared mental models among members during periods when teams prepare to perform. The development of shared models among team members deserves further study.

One format for implementing these interventions is through gaming exercises. Games are popular training vehicles used widely in the military. Their popularity is based mostly on judgments made by participants, rather than on carefully designed evaluation studies. Although the literature on games is large, much of it consists of demonstration experiments or poorly-designed studies. The few well-designed studies suggest that while they are effective in instilling positive attitudes toward and interest in the subject matter, they are not more effective than other methods as aids to learning. By producing stronger effects on motivational variables, games may be more useful for team-building than team-learning exercises. Further research is needed to establish the value of games in team training. In fact, both team building and gaming interactions need to be "unpacked" in order to determine what works.

Improved team performance may not translate into improved organizational performance. Factors external to the organization and largely out of its control—such as market growth—may account for its performance (Gladstein, 1984). Internal factors also influence organizational performance. The enhanced cohesion and morale resulting from team-building activities may increase intraorganizational conflicts between teams. By strengthening the ties between members within teams, interventions can weaken relationships with members of other teams. This effect is heightened to the extent that team-building programs include strategy formation as part of the procedure. The effect of team building on interteam relationships requires further examination.

Interteam relations involve negotiation and other boundary-spanning processes that require harmonious relations for coordination to occur. They also call attention to the concept of linkages between levels of an organization. Research is just beginning about the way that improvements at one level of an organization affect performance at other levels. Integration of the literature on organizations with the literature on team effectiveness would help clarify relationships between micro- and macrolevel processes and organizational effectiveness.

NOTES

[1]The effect sizes used in the Freeberg and Rock analysis are correlation coefficients calculated from reported t or F ratios, according to conversion formulas given by Wolf (1986).

[2]Evaluations of educational or training simulations focus on learning gains and satisfaction with the experience. Different results often occur: while expressing high levels of satisfaction with the experience, players do not usually show the expected gains in learning (see below).

[3]Whether strategy formation also produces evaluative biases that favor one's own group in noncompetitive situations is not known. It is possible that intragroup consensus contributes to the perceptual discrimination that seems to precede evaluative biases; this, too, remains to be explored.

[4]The effect sizes are averages, expressed as correlation coefficients. Each coefficient is highly significant based on the Stouffer method of adding Zs (see Wolf, 1986).

[5]A detailed survey of uses of simulations and games in the military is reported by Shubik and Brewer (1972). They identified approximately 135 active military simulations in use at the Department of Defense. To our knowledge, this survey has not been updated, nor have we been able to locate a similar survey of games developed for other uses. However, it is possible to get a rough estimate of popularity from various published sources. In the section on "Newly Available Simulations," appearing in each issue of the journal, *Simulation & Gaming* (formerly *Simulation and Games*), a wide variety of packaged games are made available. The games are distributed directly by the designers, by the institutes or councils that sponsored the gaming activity, by small companies formed to market particular games, or by book publishers. Sales for most games number in the thousands, but a few, such as the well-known cross-cultural game BAFA BAFA, have sold well over 100,000 worldwide. However, sales may not be a good indicator of use for at least three reasons. First, the same packaged materials are used by many people: Gary Shirts, the designer of BAFA, estimates that players of his games number in the millions (private communication). Second, many games are designed and used for relatively idiosyncratic purposes, such as classroom adjuncts to other teaching techniques, experimentation in specialized areas, or training of highly specialized skills. Third, many games are distributed for free or are available in texts that contain role-playing exercises.

[6]Highly technical simulations have also been designed for military training. Combat exercises have been simulated in the form of board games, computerized virtual realities, and field exercises that provide soldiers with broad experiences of many facets of combat over relatively long periods of time; see Oswalt (1993) for a review of current military applications. Unfortunately, few of these exercises have been evaluated systematically in terms of their effect on training goals. Most evaluations reported in the published literature have concentrated on games designed to improve skills in such areas as business management, language learning, negotiation, medical education and hospital administration, environmental management, and social science concepts. Thus, implications for the effectiveness of military simulations must be derived from a literature on nonmilitary applications.

7

Training in Teams

Training is instruction aimed at procedural knowledge and proficiency, at knowing how to execute the procedures necessary to do a job. It can be distinguished from declarative knowledge, which is knowledge of facts or static information. Training programs have three general goals: successful training, transfer to the work situation (generalization), and long-term use on the job of what was learned (maintenance). Training can be structured for trainees to learn individually (either in competition with peers or on their own) or in teams. Training can focus on individuals who are selected from their job situations (or from a general population of potential job applicants), assigned to training teams and given training, and then returned to their job situations (where the trainees work alone or as part of a team, which may be nested in a network of teams). Or training can focus on cohort, intact teams that are given training as a team at a training site and then returned to the job site. Team training can be defined as training in which teams are used to increase individual procedural knowledge and proficiency in doing a job (taskwork), individual procedural knowledge and proficiency in functioning as part of a team (teamwork), and overall team performance. Team training can be differentiated from team building, which takes place at the job site and focuses on analyzing a work team's procedures and activities to improve the team's productivity (see Chapter 6). Team training can also be differentiated from cooperative learning, which usually takes place in schools and is focused primarily on declarative knowledge, rather than procedural knowledge and proficiency (see Chapter 5).

When team training takes place at a training site, it has four elements (see Figure 7-1): inputs (individual trainees or cohort teams, resources, task characteristics, preparatory activities); training processes (training for taskwork, teamwork, and team performance); mediating variables (positive interdependence, promotive interaction, individual accountability, and team processing); and outcomes (individual and team proficiency on the job; improved relationships; individual psychological health; changes in a team's norms, roles, mental models, and communication patterns; and team activities after training). This chapter discusses each of these elements in turn, which are presented in terms of a framework that serves to organize the available research. The discussion results in a set of guidelines for research and practice, but the guidelines must be tempered by awareness of some limitations of the research.

The research on team training covers two interrelated literatures—a professional literature and a scientific literature. The professional literature tends to emphasize applied studies that have demonstrated that team training works in specific settings. This literature consists primarily of case studies that present descriptions of the effects of using specific training programs in specific situations. In contrast, the scientific literature consists of carefully controlled research studies conducted to validate or disconfirm theory. Most of them have been conducted in either laboratory or field experimental settings. They often lack external validity—that is, they are not conducted in workplace settings—which reduces their credibility among practitioners. The professional and scientific studies, however, complement each other and strengthen each other's findings.

There are a number of problems with the professional literature on team training, some of which spill over into the scientific literature. First, the definitions of teams and team training are not unambiguous. It is difficult to differentiate between what is a team, a small group, a working group, an organization, or even a family. Without a clear conceptualization of what is and is not a team, it is difficult to build a coherent program of research. A related second problem is that it is difficult to summarize what is known about the use of teams for training purposes because of the many different kinds of teams. Some researchers have even studied "teams" made up of coacting individuals who never see or interact with each other. Often the units that have been studied are not described very clearly.

Third, much of the literature on team training lacks a theoretical base. This leaves research on team training without a direction. In 1982 McGrath and Kravitz concluded that the area of team performance was dominated by "atheoretical" (even antitheoretical) viewpoints, and things have not improved since then. A related fourth problem is that much of the professional research on team training was designed to show that a particular type of training is effective, but not why, when, and for whom it is so: that is, the variables mediating the effectiveness of team training programs have been relatively ignored. Fifth, the nature and purpose of the team training

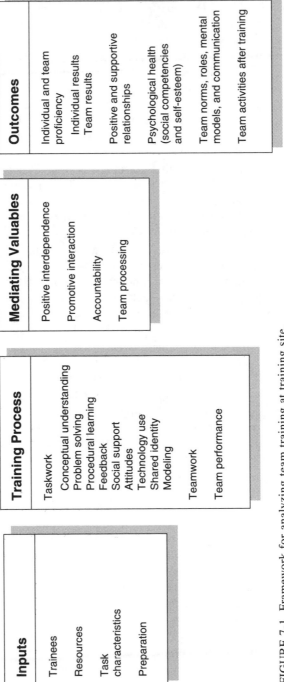

FIGURE 7-1 Framework for analyzing team training at training site.

being studied is rarely completely described. Researchers have tended to consider all training the same, without regard to the purpose of the training or the type of learning involved. To compare the results of different studies, reviewers need clear descriptions of the training methods used and the nature and purpose of the training. Finally, many of the studies lack methodological rigor, focusing far more on external validity (such as being conducted in a real-world setting) rather than internal validity (such as experimental control).

This chapter emphasizes the scientific literature. Some of the professional literature is cited to illustrate points, but the review covers primarily the knowledge generated in social and organizational psychology about some consequences of training individuals in teams and the effects of team structures on performance. The review of evidence in this chapter does not lead to firm conclusions. Rather, we draw from the literature general guidelines that support team training and specific ideas that merit further investigation.

INPUTS

For team training at a site, the inputs include the trainees, the resources required to conduct the training, the characteristics of the task, and preparatory activities of the team.

Trainees

Trainees can come as intact, cohort teams from a work site, individuals from different work sites, or as individuals who wish to qualify for a certain job. There are advantages to training cohort teams rather than individuals. According to the evidence reviewed by Katz and Kahn (1978), a traditional error in training programs is to train individuals while ignoring the systemic properties of the organization in which they work. Taking members out of the organization, giving them special training, and then returning them to the organization is a poor strategy for changing their performance because it ignores the power of role expectations, organizational norms, and other organizational variables in determining organizational behavior. When isolated individuals are trained and then returned to the job setting, the organizational pressures on them tend to be towards going "back to practice as usual," which causes an abandonment and decay in what is learned (Katz and Kahn, 1978). Training intact teams seems to mitigate such pressures by providing a mutual redefinition of role responsibilities and job procedures and social support for implementing and maintaining the procedures learned in the training program.

Resources and Task Characteristics

The resources required to conduct training include personnel (instructors and support personnel), materials, and equipment. Besides classrooms, desks, overhead projectors, and so forth, equipment includes computers, electronic networking systems, and simulators. Although there has been research on the effectiveness of training for different types of tasks, perhaps the most important distinction is whether the task is simple or complex. Different types of training procedures are usually needed for simple and complex tasks.

Preparation

Prior to formal sessions, trainees can be prepared for a team training experience in a number of ways. First, trainees can be helped to set goals for what they will learn and how hard they will work during the training. Cohen (1990) found that trainees who set goals prior to training began with higher levels of motivation to learn. Second, an accountability system can be provided to motivate trainees to take the training seriously and to use what they learn on the job. Trainers can inform members that how hard they work and how much they learn during training will be directly assessed after the training is over. Baldwin and Magjurka (1991) found that trainees who entered training expecting some form of follow-up activity or assessment afterward reported stronger intentions to transfer what they learned to the job. The fact that an organization would require them to prepare a posttraining report or undergo an assessment meant that they were being held accountable for their learning and apparently conveyed the message that the training was important.

Third, trainers can lessen constraints to using what is learned on the job. Trainees can be assured that what they learn in training will be used on the job and shown how constraints for doing so will be reduced. Mathieu et al. (1990) found that trainees who reported many situational constraints in their jobs (e.g., lack of time, equipment, and resources) entered training with lower motivation to learn. The trainees had little incentive to learn new skills when they worked in an environment in which the skills could not be applied.

Fourth, trainers can create positive expectations toward the training. In a study of five companies, Cohen (1990) found that trainees with more supportive supervisors entered training with stronger beliefs that training would be useful. Supervisors can show their support for training by discussing it with an employee, establishing training goals, providing time to prepare, and generally encouraging the employee.

Fifth, the more members value the training, the more likely they are to volunteer to participate in it. Volunteering to participate in the training, compared with mandatory attendance, tends to be related to higher motivation to learn, greater learning, and more positive trainee reactions (Cohen, 1990; Hicks and Klimoski, 1987; Mathieu et al., 1990). An exception may be when the history of training has been very positive. Baldwin and Magjurka (1991) found that engineers who had several previous positive training experiences, and who perceived the training to be mandatory, reported greater intentions to apply what they learned back on the job than engineers who did not have positive experiences, and who viewed their attendance as voluntary. Mandatory attendance may, however, be demoralizing when training is not valued.[1]

TRAINING PROCESSES

Training programs try to ensure that trainees gain proficiency in both taskwork procedures and teamwork procedures and that the performance of the team as a whole is enhanced. In most work situations, taskwork and teamwork are so interrelated that it is difficult to separate them. No matter how great individual taskwork skills may be, they will be ineffective if they are not coordinated with the supporting efforts of teammates. In work (performance) situations, both individual technical skills and skills in interacting and coordinating efforts with other team members are needed to succeed and, therefore, both have to be learned and practiced. In reviewing the research, however, we consider separately each of the parts of the training process.

Taskwork

This section considers in detail nine components of taskwork that are relevant to the likelihood of successful training, transfer, and maintenance in team training:

1. conceptual understanding;
2. applying conceptual understanding;
3. procedural learning;
4. feedback;
5. social support;
6. relevant attitudes;
7. use of technology;
8. positive professional identity among team members; and
9. behavioral models.

Conceptual Understanding

Transfer to the actual job situation and long-term maintenance of the learned procedures and skills depend on trainees' conceptually understanding what they are learning for several reasons. First, jobs are becoming more complex, and work requirements at all levels are becoming cognitively more demanding. Second, learning of a complex task can be facilitated by helping a learner develop an accurate and efficient mental conceptualization or mental model of the material that must be understood before the task is undertaken. Conceptual models are useful when they allow a trainee to infer the exact procedures for operating a device or completing a procedure or when the model is necessary to generalize the procedures to situations that were not trained explicitly (see Chapter 3; also see Gentner and Gentner, 1983; Kieras, 1988; Kieras and Bovair, 1984). Conceptual models are most helpful for dealing with complex problems when they organize material hierarchically rather than linearly (Eylon and Reif, 1984). Learning a conceptual model may not be useful when procedures are easily learned by rote mastery, when a particular device is so simple that the trainee does not need to make inferences about how the device works, when the conceptual model is too difficult or complicated for a trainee to acquire, or when the model does not support inferences that the trainee needs to make (Gentner and Gentner, 1983; Kieras, 1988; Kieras and Bovair, 1984).

Third, in job settings, complex work is done primarily by teams. In order for team members to work together effectively, trainees must develop conceptual understandings that are shared by all team members. Cannon-Bowers et al. (1990) and Orasanu and Salas (1993) suggest that shared or overlapping mental models among team members (created by such practices as cross-training) should enhance the use of implicit coordination strategies by enabling team members to anticipate behavior and information needs more accurately. Fourth, when trainees are provided with general principles governing successful or competent performance in both the training and real-world settings, transfer of training is generally facilitated (see Chapter 3).

In order to maximize cognitive understanding, training programs may emphasize competition among trainees, individualistic work by trainees, or cooperative efforts by learning teams. Miller and Hamblin (1963) concluded from a review of research that the superiority of cooperative teams over competitive and individualistic learning increases as the learning task becomes more conceptual and difficult. This conclusion was also supported by more comprehensive reviews (D.W. Johnson and R.T. Johnson, 1974, 1989; D.W. Johnson et al., 1981). In addition, in their meta-analysis, Johnson and Johnson (1989) found that both quality of individual reasoning strategies and level of individual cognitive processes were higher when persons learned in cooperative teams rather than competitively or individually (effect sizes of 0.79 and 0.97, respectively).[2] Taken together, the evidence indicates that when complex conceptual learning is required, individual performance is enhanced more by learning in teams than by learning individually (competitively or individually).

Applying Conceptual Understanding

Besides engaging in abstract, conceptual thinking about what is being learned, trainees need to develop the ability to apply that capacity for abstract thought to complex real-world job problems that involve the use of scientific and technical knowledge, are nonstandard and full of ambiguities, and have more than one right answer. In a recent meta-analysis, Qin (1992) identified 63 studies, conducted between 1929 and 1989, that examined the relative success of cooperative and competitive efforts on individual problem solving. She classified the studies into several kinds of problem solving: linguistic, solved through written and oral language; nonlinguistic, solved through symbols, math, motor activities, actions; well defined, clearly defined with well-defined operations and solutions; and ill defined, lacking clear definitions, operations, solutions. She found that members of cooperative teams outperformed individuals who worked competitively on all four types of problem solving (effect sizes of 0.37, 0.72, 0.52, and 0.60, respectively). Adults and secondary students working cooperatively performed better on linguistic, nonlinguistic, and well-defined problem solving than did children.

Procedural Learning

The ultimate aim of training is procedural learning, that is, for trainees to be competent in performing a job. Only a few studies have compared team training with individual instruction on tasks that appear to predominantly rely on procedural learning. Two studies conducted in a naval job training program have found that, compared with traditional naval training involving competitive and individual activities, training in teams resulted in greater conceptual mastery of the procedures taught, greater independent functional ability to perform job functions, a zero failure rate, and lower attrition from the program (Holubec et al., in press; Vasquez et al., 1993). Performance on a computer-assisted problem-solving task involving map reading and navigational skills was found to be higher in cooperative than in competitive or individual instruction (R.T. Johnson et al., 1985, 1986). A related study found similar results for the learning of map reading skills (Yager et al., 1985). Martino and Johnson (1979) compared cooperative and individual instruction on learning how to swim; students taught in cooperative pairs learned how to perform more swimming skills than did students taught individually. Similarly, subjects taught the golf skill of putting performed better when they were taught cooperatively than when they were taught competitively or individually (R.T. Johnson et al., 1983).

A basic principle of training design is that, whatever is being taught, trainees must actively "produce" that during training. Production facilitates both learning and retention (Perry and Downs, 1985). Performing the actual procedures and skills being taught during training complements the learning of more general concepts to improve posttraining performance (see Chapter 3).

Feedback

Feedback can come from many sources, including oneself, technological devices, and other people. Interpersonal feedback from teammates may have a number of benefits. First, it personalizes the learning situation. Personal feedback has been found to increase performance to a greater extent than impersonal feedback (Acheson, 1964; Fuller et al., 1969; Morse et al., 1970; Steiner, 1967; Tuckman et al., 1969). Second, to the extent that interpersonal feedback tends to be subjectively vivid, the information provided may be attended to more highly (Borgida and Nisbett, 1977; Hamill et al., 1980; Nisbett et al., 1976; Taylor and Thompson, 1982). Statistical data summaries and impersonal information sources are less vivid than face-to-face interactions. Third, peers can provide immediate and sustained remediation after a trainee gives an incorrect answer, supportively probing, providing cues, repeating the question, rephrasing the question, or allowing more time for the trainee to answer, all of which is important for achievement (Rowe, 1974; Webb, 1982). Fourth, teams provide a cooperative context for feedback. Trainees process the feedback they receive from collaborators differently than the feedback they receive from competitors (or trainers). Teams are especially helpful in continually monitoring members' learning and providing immediate interpersonal feedback and remedial help and assistance.

Social Support

Social support is the exchange of resources intended to enhance mutual well-being and the existence and availability of people on whom one can rely for assistance, encouragement, acceptance, and caring (D.W. Johnson and R.T. Johnson, 1989). A social support system consists of others who collaboratively share trainees' tasks and goals, who provide trainees with emotional concern (such as caring, reassurance, trust), instrumental aid (such as materials, tools, skills), information and advice, and feedback about the degree to which certain behavioral standards are met, all of which help trainees mobilize their psychological resources in order to complete the training program successfully. Social support directly and indirectly promotes achievement and productivity, psychological well-being, physical health and management of stress.

Social support is related to achievement, successful problem solving, persistence on challenging tasks under frustrating conditions, lack of cognitive interference during problem solving, satisfaction, high morale, attendance or lack of absenteeism, retention, academic and career aspirations, more appropriate seeking of assistance, and greater compliance with regimens and behavioral patterns that increase health and productivity (Bowlby, 1969, 1973, 1980; Cohen and Willis, 1985; Sarason et al., 1983). And social support directly reduces stress by providing the caring, information, resources, and feedback individuals need to cope with the stress inherent in participating in challenging training (see LaRocco et al., 1980; Seers et al., 1983). Indirect reduction of stress occurs when social support decreases the number or severity of stressful events during training (see, e.g., Kessler et al., 1985).

A predictable human tendency is to seek social support in times of stress, fear, sorrow, or high excitement. One of the earliest researchers to examine this tendency experimentally was Schachter (1959). He frightened subjects with the threat of shock, then examined the extent to which they chose to be with others. He argued that fear promoted affiliation for two reasons—to gain information about the stressful situation and to directly reduce the fear. In difficult training programs, therefore, where trainees experience considerable anxiety and pressure to achieve, teams may be effective by providing members with support that reduces anxiety (Schachter, 1959) and increases feelings of self-control and self-esteem (Cutrona and Troutman, 1986). A meta-analysis of over 106 experimental studies comparing the relative effects of teams versus individual efforts on social support provides evidence that team experiences promoted greater social support than did competitive or individual experiences (D.W. Johnson and R.T. Johnson, 1989). Teams can provide a social support system for their members as they work together to maximize their own and each other's productivity.

Positive Attitudes

Such attitudes as commitment to quality work, commitment to continuous improvement, and self-efficacy can be inculcated or strengthened during a training program. It is through interpersonal influences that attitudes are typically acquired and behavioral patterns are changed. Teams thus have several advantages over working alone when a training program is designed to inculcate attitudes that may promote the acquisition of training.

The more a team becomes a reference group for members, the more it will influence members' attitudes and values (D.W. Johnson and F. Johnson, 1994; Watson and Johnson, 1972). Attitudes and commitments to engage in specified behavior patterns that are made public and discussed in small groups are more likely to be adopted than are those that are private, especially when peers hold one accountable to fulfill one's commitments (D.W. Johnson, 1981; Lewin, 1943; Radke and Caso, 1948; Radke and Klisurich, 1947). During discussion, a norm of commitment seems to be created. This norm prescribes that individuals carry out those actions that they have promised or committed themselves to perform. It is strengthened when group members are unanimously committed to the course of action. Orbell et al. (1988), for example, observed that high rates of promising to cooperate during group discussion are followed by high rates of actual cooperation, when *all* members agreed to follow through on the action. When as few as one member disagreed, the correlation between promises and actions was negligible.

People are most likely to accept new attitudes and behaviors when they come into contact with visible and credible models who demonstrate the recommended attitudes and behavior patterns and directly discuss their importance (Aronson and O'Leary, 1982-1983; Goldman, 1940; Nisbett et al., 1976; Rogers and Shoemaker, 1977). Discussing information with peers in ways that promote active cognitive processing often produces attitude change and induces commitment to behave in prescribed ways. Active cognitive involvement in the persuasion situation is crucial for attitude change (Cook and Frey, 1978; Petty, 1977). In addition, people are particularly prone to increase their own commitment to a cause that they have attempted to persuade others to adopt (Nel et al., 1969).

In addition to the general attitude effects, learning as part of a team tends to promote more positive attitudes toward the task being worked on and the experience of doing so than does learning by oneself competitively or individually (D.W. Johnson and R.T. Johnson, 1989). Most individuals, furthermore, prefer cooperative over competitive and individual training experiences (DeVries and Edwards, 1973; D.W. Johnson and R.T. Johnson, 1976; D.W. Johnson et al., 1976; R.T. Johnson, 1976; R.T. Johnson et al., 1973, 1974; Wheeler and Ryan, 1973).

Use of Computers

The use of computers in training requires trainees concurrently to learn how to use the technology and to master the information, skills, procedures, and processes being presented within the technology. There is reason to believe that teams better manage the dual demands of the learning situation and make better use of computers than do individuals. Computer-assisted team learning, compared with individual efforts at the computer, promoted higher quantity and quality of daily achievement, greater mastery of factual information, greater ability to apply a learner's factual knowledge in test questions requiring application of facts, greater ability to use factual information to answer problem-solving questions, and greater success in problem solving (D.W. Johnson et al., 1986a, 1989, 1990; R.T. Johnson et al., 1985, 1986). In addition, working as part of a team at the computer promoted greater motivation to persist on problem-solving tasks and greater success in operating the computer program.

Technology such as electronic mail, bulletin boards, and conferences can be used to create teams made up of individuals who are widely separated geographically. In an electronically networked team, interaction no longer is face to face, and trainees may depend on one another differently than they do in face-to-face teams. "Meetings" only require that team members be at their terminals, and communication between meetings can be asynchronous and extremely fast in comparison with telephone conversations and interoffice mail. Participation may be more equalized and less affected by prestige and status (McGuire et al., 1987; Siegel et al., 1986). Electronic communication, however, relies almost entirely on plain text for conveying messages, text that is often ephemeral, appearing on and disappearing from a screen without any necessary tangible artifacts. It becomes easy for a sender to be out of touch with his or her audience. And it is easy for the sender to be less constrained by conventional norms and rules for behavior in composing messages. Communicators can feel a greater sense of anonymity, detect less individuality in others, feel less empathy, feel less guilt, be less concerned over how they compare with others, and be less influenced by social conventions (Short et al., 1976; Kiesler et al., 1984). Such influences can lead both to more honesty and more "flaming" (name calling and epithets).

While electronic communication has many positive features, face-to-face communication has a richness that electronic communication may never match. There is evidence that up to 93 percent of people's intent is conveyed by facial expression and tone of voice, with the most important channel being facial expression (Druckman et al., 1982; Meherabian, 1971). Harold Geneen, the former head of ITT, believed that his response to requests was different face to face than through teletype. "In New York, I might read a request and say no. But in Europe, I could see that an answer to the same question might be yes . . . it became our policy to deal with problems on the spot, face to face" (cited in Trevino et al., 1987). For this and other reasons (such as lack of effective groupware), training programs may be most effective when they use face-to-face rather than electronic teams. Team members may also benefit more from the social support function and vividness of feedback provided directly by other members.

Positive Professional Identity

An important aspect of training programs is to create, modify, and extend a trainee's professional identity and esteem. Attending Marine bootcamp, for example, is supposed to result in a trainee's adopting a new identity as a "Marine." Being trained to be an air-traffic controller is supposed to result in a trainee adopting a new identity as an "air-traffic-controller." Most training programs are aimed at inculcating an identification with the job the person is being trained to do. Identity has at least four properties (Miller and Harrington, 1990): relational, who one is in relation to others; situational; interactive, in interaction with other people; and affective. A person's social identity is substantially determined by the groups to which he or she belongs (Miller and Harrington, 1990). The more positive a person perceives the group to be, the more positive the implications of membership in that group for the person's self-identity. Team training typically builds a stronger, healthier, and more positive professional identity than does individual training (D.W. Johnson and R.T. Johnson, 1989). The new identity resulting from the training program helps trainees establish their membership in subsequent work teams.

Behavioral Modeling

Within learning teams there are visible and credible models who demonstrate the procedures being learned. Although the research on behavioral modeling is not consistent (Druckman and Bjork, 1991), observing skilled team members engage in a procedure or skill can facilitate learning.

Teamwork

In many work situations, problems and even the work is so complex that multiple experts and multiple sources of information are needed. To deal with that complexity, people doing many jobs have to work in teams. Teamwork competencies thus become essential aspects of those jobs. The taskwork cannot be done unless the individuals function as team members. This function can be aided by the development of teamwork skills.

Like all skills, teamwork skills need to be learned to an automatic level. If teamwork skills are not emphasized during training and if individuals do not learn the interpersonal and small group skills they need to function as team members, the taskwork will suffer.

There are several explanations for potential interference between taskwork and teamwork. Our proposal is that, if teamwork skills are not well learned, team members have an internal conflict between attending to the task and learning how to coordinate efforts with others (Baron et al., 1978). If a team member tries to attend to more than he or she can manage, the resulting conflict leads to drive (arousal) and stress, which in turn produces social impairment on difficult tasks.

Second, trying to learn teamwork skills while doing taskwork may cause attention overload. Attention overload occurs when a team member tries to attend to more things (such as taskwork and teamwork both) than he or she has the capacity to process. When people are bombarded with attentional demands, their focus of attention actually shrinks (see, e.g., Geen, 1976, 1980), causing deterioration of taskwork efforts.

Third, when one or more team members are not socially skilled and do not participate effectively in the team, they may distract the other team members from effective taskwork.

Fourth, trying to learn teamwork skills while doing taskwork may make team members self-conscious and self-aware. Self-awareness generally results in team members' "trying harder" to perform well (Duval and Wicklund, 1972; Carver and Scheier, 1981). One possible result of self-awareness is withdrawal from the task. By paying close attention to how well they are performing, self-conscious team members may experience a decrease in their desire to excel, as in the frequently observed phenomenon of stage fright.

Fifth, trying to learn teamwork skills while doing taskwork may interfere with team members' presenting a positive image of themselves. Self-presentation involves projecting a positive self-image ("looking good") to onlookers (e.g., Bond, 1982). Social impairment sometimes occurs on difficult tasks because initial failures produce embarrassment, which then disrupts performance.

Since both taskwork and teamwork proficiencies are required in many job situations, it is important that training programs emphasize both. The failure to teach teamwork skills in these situations can result in subsequent interference between taskwork and teamwork job demands.

MEDIATING VARIABLES

Because training in teams has been found to be have certain advantages, compared with individual training, does not mean that it will be more effective under all conditions. There are a number of variables that tend to mediate the effectiveness of team training. They include the degree of positive interdependence, face-to-face promotive interaction, individual accountability, and team processing.

Positive Interdependence

One apparent constraint on the observation of higher achievement for team training than individual training is that the team should have high positive interdependence. Positive interdependence is defined to exist when team members perceive that they are linked with teammates so that they cannot succeed unless their teammates do (and vice versa) or that they must coordinate their efforts with the efforts of their groupmates to complete a task (Deutsch, 1962; D.W. Johnson and R.T. Johnson, 1989). When positive interdependence is clearly understood, it highlights that each member's efforts is required and indispensable for group success (i.e., there can be no "free riders") and each member has a unique contribution to make to the joint effort because of his or her resources, or role, and task responsibilities.

There are a number of ways that positive interdependence can be structured within a team. One view is that a team needs to have positive goal interdependence: team members should realize that they have a mutual set of goals that all are striving to accomplish and that success depends on all members reaching the goal; otherwise, it is not a team (D.W. Johnson and R.T. Johnson, 1989).[3]   Other methods of structuring positive interdependence that supplement and support the positive goal interdependence include: positive reward interdependence, when each team member group is given the same reward for successfully attaining the team's goals; positive role interdependence, when team members are assigned complementary and interconnected roles; positive task interdependence, when a division of labor is created so that the actions of one team member have to be completed if another team member is to complete the next actions; positive resource interdependence, when each member has only a portion of the information, resources, or materials necessary for the task to be completed; and identity interdependence, which exists when a team establishes a mutual identity through a name, flag, motto, or song (D.W. Johnson et al., 1991).

In a series of studies to determine the relative effects of the types of interdependence on performance after a group has studied as a team, it was found that team membership is not enough to promote higher individual achievement; it also took positive goal interdependence (Hwong et al., in press). Knowing that one's performance affects the success of teammates seems to create "responsibility forces" that increase one's efforts to achieve. Interaction among individuals is not enough either. In a series of studies that investigated whether the relationship between teamwork and individual achievement was due to the opportunity to interact with peers or to positive goal interdependence, researchers consistently found that individuals achieved more under positive goal interdependence than when they worked individually but had the opportunity to interact with others (Lew et al., 1986a, 1986b; Mesch et al., 1986, 1988). Hagman and Hayes (1986) found that teams of two, three, and four members working together within an individual structure achieved at a lower level than did individuals who studied as cooperative teams. They concluded that without positive interdependence, there was no advantage to having individuals interact with one another while they work.

The results of the Mesch and Lew studies also indicate that, while positive goal interdependence is sufficient to produce higher individual achievement after studying as a team rather than individually, the combination of goal and reward interdependence is even more effective. The impact of the two types of outcome interdependence seems to be additive. Frank (1984) demonstrated that working both to achieve a reward and to avoid the loss of a reward produced higher individual achievement after studying as a team than after studying individually. D. W. Johnson and R. T. Johnson (1994) found goal interdependence promoted higher achievement than did resource interdependence. A study by D.W. Johnson et al. (1990) demonstrated that goal interdependence alone increased achievement, and the combination of goal and resource interdependence increased achievement even more. The use of resource interdependence alone seemed to decrease individual achievement and lower productivity after studying as a team rather than studying individually.

Finally, there is evidence that positive interdependence does more than motivate individuals to try harder. Positive interdependence seems to facilitate the development of new insights and discoveries through promotive interaction (Gabbert et al., 1986; D.W. Johnson and R.T. Johnson, 1981; D.W. Johnson et al., 1980; Skon et al., 1981).

Face-to-Face Promotive Interaction

In order for team training to promote higher achievement than individual training, team members must promote each other's success. Promotive interaction can be defined as individuals encouraging and facilitating each other's efforts to achieve, complete tasks, and produce in order to reach the team's goals (D.W. Johnson and R.T. Johnson, 1989). Positive interdependence can result in promotive interaction. Although positive interdependence in and of itself may have some effect on outcomes, the face-to-face promotive interaction among individuals fostered by positive interdependence appears to be the most powerful influence on efforts to achieve, caring and committed work relationships, and psychological adjustment and social competence.

Promotive interaction is characterized by team members' behavior in at least eight ways: (1) providing each other with efficient and effective help and assistance; (2) exchanging needed resources, such as information and materials, so that information can be processed efficiently and effectively; (3) providing each other with feedback in order to improve their subsequent performance on assigned tasks and responsibilities; (4) challenging each other's conclusions and reasoning, which promotes higher quality decision making and greater insight into the problems being considered; (5) advocating the exertion of effort to achieve mutual goals; (6) influencing each other's efforts to achieve the team's goals; (7) acting in trusting and trustworthy ways; and (8) being motivated to strive for mutual benefit.

For promotive interaction to occur, however, the development of appropriate social skills is required. A team's function is impaired if members do not have and use the interpersonal and small group skills needed to coordinate their efforts, namely, communication, leadership, decision-making, and conflict-management skills (Cartwright and Zander, 1968). A number of studies have demonstrated that the more these skills are used, the more productive a team is (Lew et al., 1986a, 1986b; Mesch et al., 1986, 1988) and the more positive the relationships among group members (Putnam et al., 1989). Cooperation, furthermore, promotes more frequent, effective, and accurate communication than either competitive or individual situations (D.W. Johnson, 1974). In cooperative situations, communication is relatively open, effective, and accurate; in competitive situations, communication tends to be closed, ineffective, and inaccurate (Bonoma et al., 1974; Crombag, 1966; Deutsch, 1962; French, 1951; Grossack, 1953; Krauss and Deutsch, 1966).

Promotive interaction may have a number of effects. First, there are cognitive insights and understandings that can come from explaining one's conclusions and views to others (e.g., Spurlin et al., 1984; Murray, 1983; Yager et al., 1985). Second, it is within face-to-face interaction that the opportunity for a wide variety of social influences and patterns emerge (see, e.g., Coleman, 1961; Hulten and DeVries, 1976). Third, the verbal and nonverbal responses of group members can provide important feedback concerning each other's performance (e.g., Lockhead, 1983). Fourth, it can provide an opportunity for peers to pressure unmotivated team members to do their share of the work (e.g., Deutsch, 1949; Crombag, 1966). Finally, the interaction involved in completing the work allows team members to get to know each other as persons, which in turn forms the basis for caring and committed work relationships.

Accountability

Individual accountability exists when the contributions that each team member makes to the team effort are assessed and the results are given back to the team and the individual. It minimizes the likelihood of social loafing, which is one of the major obstacles to group effectiveness. When groups work on tasks for which it is difficult to identify members' contributions, when there is an increased likelihood of redundant efforts, when there is a lack of group cohesiveness, and when there is lessened responsibility for the final outcome, some members will contribute less than otherwise to goal achievement (Harkins and Petty, 1982; Ingham et al., 1974; Kerr and Bruun, 1981; Latane et al., 1979; Moede, 1927; Petty et al., 1977; Sanna, 1992; Williams, 1981; Williams et al., 1981). Social loafing can be avoided by making each team member individually accountable for doing his own share of the work.

Individual accountability can be enhanced in several ways. First, social loafing can be avoided by clearly structuring positive interdependence so feelings of personal responsibility for the group's final outcome are high. Personal responsibility adds the concept of "ought" to members' motivation—one ought to do one's part, pull one's weight, contribute, and satisfy peer norms. Second, since individual accountability increases as the size of the team decreases (Messick and Brewer, 1983), teams can be kept small. Third, when it is made clear how much effort each member is contributing (i.e., there is individual assessment of each member's contributions), individual accountability is high. The more that group members are provided with information about the level of productivity and helpfulness of each member, the more individually accountable each member will be and the better members will be able to support and assist each other. Finally, when team members are assigned roles to ensure a lack of redundancy, individual accountability is high—a member cannot depend on another member to accomplish his or her assignment. However, this advantage is offset by the safety implications of a lack of redundancy. The challenge is to balance the motivating effects of lack of redundancy with the obvious protection that redundancy provides against individual error or unexpected occurrences.

Team Processing

As defined here, process is an identifiable sequence of events taking place over time. Team processing occurs when members discuss the sequence of events instrumental in achieving their goals and maintaining effective working relationships among members (D.W. Johnson and F. Johnson, 1994). Effective teamwork is influenced by whether or not teams reflect on and discuss how well they are functioning. Team members process when they describe what member actions were helpful and unhelpful and make decisions about what member actions to continue or change. Such processing enables teams to focus on group maintenance, facilitates the learning of social skills, ensures that members receive feedback on their participation, and reminds members to practice social skills consistently.

Although it is well accepted in the group dynamics literature that to be productive, teams have to "process" how well they are working and take action to resolve any difficulties members have in collaborating productively, there is actually very little evidence on the relationship between team processing and team productivity. Most of the research examines effects on individual outcomes. Yager et al. (1985) found that team members scored higher on individual measures of learning and retention when team processing occurred than did individuals in teams that did not process or individuals who studied alone. The combination of team processing and feedback from a supervisor produced greater individual and group problem-solving success than did supervisor feedback alone or neither (D.W. Johnson et al., 1990). Feedback to individual team members about their performance is more effective than overall team feedback in increasing productivity (Archer-Kath et al., in press).

Team processing may promote individual self-monitoring, which can promote a sense of self-efficacy (i.e., the expectation of successfully obtaining valued outcomes through personal effort) rather than helplessness. Sarason and Potter (1983) examined the impact of individual self-monitoring of thoughts on self-efficacy and successful performance and found that having individuals focus their attention on self-efficacious thoughts is related to greater task persistence and less cognitive interference. They concluded that the more that people are aware of what they are experiencing, the more aware they will be of their own role in determining their success. The greater the sense of self-efficacy and joint-efficacy promoted by group processing, the more productive and effective group members and the group as a whole become.

Monitoring one's own and one's collaborators' actions begins with deciding on which behaviors to focus one's attention. Individuals can focus either on positive and effective behaviors or negative and ineffective behaviors. Effective processing focuses primarily on positive rather than negative behaviors.[4] Sarason and Potter (1983) found that when individuals monitored their stressful experiences they were more likely to perceive a program as having been more stressful than did those who did not; but when individuals monitored their positive experiences, they were more likely to perceive the group experience as involving less psychological demands, were more attracted to the group and had greater motivation to remain members, and felt less strained during the experience and more prepared for future group experiences. When individuals are anxious about being successful and are then told they have failed, their performance tends to decrease significantly, but when individuals anxious about being successful are told they have succeeded, their performance tends to increase significantly (Turk and Sarason, 1983).

OUTCOMES

Although team training is used extensively, there is little direct evaluation of its effectiveness on team outcomes. Lassiter et al. (1990) found that teams in a skill-oriented training program demonstrated better communication skills than those in a lecture-based training program or a no-training control group. Several commercial airlines have established team training programs for air crews, but the results on training effectiveness have been mixed (Cannon-Bowers et al., 1991; Helmreich and Wilhelm, 1989; Helmreich et al., 1990). One reason that more research has not been conducted is the lack of methods for analyzing team tasks, behaviors, and skills (Modrick, 1986; Morgan and Salas, 1988; O'Neil et al., 1992). Without valid and reliable dependent (outcome) measures, programmatic research on team training is difficult. Team training, furthermore, has tended to ignore the development of teamwork skills and behaviors that are demanded by the interaction requirements of the team task. What is indicative of the effectiveness of team training is the research comparing the relative effects of team and individual training on subsequent knowledge and proficiency. This section first considers that work and then reviews other areas of research that have compared outcomes for individuals in individual, competitive, and team or group training.

Individual Proficiency and Team Productivity

A recent meta-analysis has been conducted on the effectiveness of team versus individual training for adults (18 years and older) (D.W. Johnson and R.T. Johnson, 1994). The studies included were divided into those using individual achievement and proficiency as the dependent (outcome) measure and those using team productivity as the dependent measure. Although a variety of training tasks were used, all studies separated the training session from the evaluation of proficiency or productivity.[5] The individual training programs were classified as either structuring interpersonal competition among trainees or having trainees work on their own. The results are reported as effects obtained on outcomes across many studies. High effect sizes indicate strong relationships between type of training programs and proficiency: for example, subjects trained in teams out-performed those trained individually in most or many, but not necessarily all, studies.

Individual Results

More than 120 studies have compared the relative efficacy of team and individual training on individual knowledge and proficiency (D.W. Johnson and R.T. Johnson, 1994). Although the first study was conducted in 1924, 70 percent of the studies have been conducted since 1970. A meta-analysis of these studies suggests that overall, team learning promoted higher individual knowledge and proficiency than did individual learning structured competitively or individually (effect sizes of 0.54 and 0.51, respectively). When only the methodologically high quality studies were included, team learning still promoted greater individual achievement than did competitive or individual efforts (effect sizes of 0.61 and 0.35, respectively). These results indicate that there is greater team-to-individual transfer than individual-to-individual transfer. The meta-analysis results, however, do not define the conditions under which team-to-individual transfer will be greatest.

Hagman and Hayes (1986) conducted two studies in which they demonstrated that the superiority of team-to-individual transfer over individual-to-individual transfer increased as subjects worked toward a team (rather than an individual) goal and as the size of the team was reduced. Teams in which members interacted with each other and discussed the material being learned and received a team reward had the greatest amount of team-to-individual transfer. In a study involving children as subjects, learning in a team resulted in greater individual transfer than did learning as an individual for complex higher-level tasks, but not for simple lower-level tasks (Gabbert et al., 1986). The studies comparing team and individual training used a wide variety of tasks. The tasks were classified into those that required verbal skills to complete (such as reading, writing, and oral presentation), mathematical skills to complete, or procedural skills to present (such as sports like swimming, golf, and tennis). When the results were analyzed for type of task, team training showed better transfer than individual training, structured either competitively or individually, on verbal tasks (effect sizes of 0.36 and 0.66, respectively), on mathematical tasks (effect sizes of 0.45 and 1.32, respectively), and on procedural tasks (effect sizes of 0.95 and 1.06, respectively). These results may be taken to indicate that training in teams promotes higher individual proficiency and knowledge than does individual training on all three types of tasks. The adult studies did not include simple rote or decoding tasks, but the research on children and adolescents indicates that individual training (structured competitively) may be just as effective as team training when very simple tasks are used (D.W. Johnson and R.T. Johnson, 1989).

Team Results

Since 1928, more than 57 studies have been conducted on the relative effectiveness of team and individual training on team productivity (D.W. Johnson and R.T. Johnson, 1994). Twelve percent of the studies were conducted before 1930, 15 percent from 1930-1960, 43 percent in the 1960s, and 30 percent in the 1970s. A meta-analysis of the results indicated that team training led to higher productivity than did individual training, structured either competitively or individually (effect sizes of 0.63 and 0.94, respectively). When only the methodologically high quality studies were included in the analysis, team learning was still more effective than competitive or individual efforts (effect sizes of 0.96 and 0.66, respectively). Teams tend to make better decisions and solve problems better than do individuals. When the results were analyzed for type of task, team training resulted in better performance than individual training, structured competitively and individually on verbal tasks (effect sizes of 0.73 and 1.47, respectively), on mathematical tasks (effect sizes of 0.26 and 0.86, respectively), and on procedural tasks (effect sizes of 1.37 and 0.95, respectively). These results indicate that team training promotes higher team performance than does individual training on all three types of tasks.[6] Other evidence suggests, however, that on brainstorming tasks individuals may do just as well as teams (see Dunnette et al., 1963).

Positive Relationships and Social Support

Training is often aimed at affecting relationships among trainees, as well as learning. Both long-term networking of trainees and increasing the positiveness of relationships among diverse trainees may be important goals of training programs. Since the 1940s research conducted on individual proficiency has also examined the quality of relationships among trainees (D.W. Johnson and R.T. Johnson, 1994). A meta-analysis of this research indicated that team training tended to promote greater interpersonal attraction among trainees than did individual efforts structured competitively (effect size, 0.68) or individualist (effect size, 0.55). Similar results were found in studies focusing on group productivity (effect sizes, 0.64 and 0.39, respectively).

Building positive relationships among trainees may be especially important when the trainees are heterogeneous in terms of ethnicity, handicapping conditions, and gender. More than 61 studies have been conducted comparing the relative effects of team and individual training (structured either competitively or individually) on interpersonal attraction between majority and minority individuals (D.W. Johnson and R.T. Johnson, 1989). Team training promoted significantly better relationships between white and minority individuals than did competition (effect size, 0.52) or individual efforts (effect size, 0.44). Individual efforts promoted more positive cross-ethnic relationships than did competition (effect size, 0.65), but since only three studies have been conducted, this finding is only suggestive. When only the high-quality studies were included in the analysis, the advantage of team over competitive and individual efforts was even more apparent (effect sizes of 0.68 and 0.53, respectively). In 41 studies comparing the relative effects of team and individual training on interpersonal attraction between handicapped and nonhandicapped individuals (D.W. Johnson and R.T. Johnson, 1989), team training resulted in greater interpersonal attraction between handicapped and nonhandicapped individuals than did competitive training (effect size, 0.70) or individual training (effect size, 0.64). Individual experiences tended to promote somewhat more positive cross-handicapped relationships than did competitive training (effect size, 0.16) in the five studies conducted. Only a few studies have compared the relative effects of team and individual training on interpersonal attraction between males and females. The results indicated that team training promoted more positive cross-gender relationships than did individual training (Warring et al., 1985), and cross-gender friendships may be more difficult to promote than cross-ethnic friendships between trainees of the same sex (Cooper et al., 1980).

In addition to interpersonal attraction or liking, relationships among trainees may be characterized by social support. Social support involves the exchange of resources intended to enhance mutual well-being and the existence and availability of people on whom one can rely for emotional, instrumental, informational, and appraisal aid. In a meta-analysis of studies focusing on individual performance, team training promoted greater social support than did individual efforts structured competitively (effect size, 0.60) or individually (effect sizes, 0.61 and 0.51, respectively) (D.W. Johnson and R.T. Johnson, 1994). Studies focusing on team performance found that cooperation promoted greater social support than did competitive efforts (effect size, 0.13) or individual efforts (effect size, 0.38).

Social support is not a trivial factor. It is associated with several positive outcomes: achievement and productivity; physical health—individuals involved in close relationships live longer, get sick less often, and recover from illness faster than do isolated individuals; psychological health—by preventing neuroticism and psychopathology, reducing distress, and providing resources such as confidants; and constructive management of stress—by providing the caring, resources, information, and feedback needed to cope with stress and by buffering the impact of stress on the individual. These relationships are bidirectional, with support and health influencing each other in a recursive fashion. Social support and stress are related in that the more social support individuals have, the less the stress they experience, and the better able they are to manage the stresses they do have (Cohen and Willis, 1985; Kessler and McLeod, 1985).

In research on team training, two types of social support have been examined. Social support can be aimed at promoting a person's task success or it can be aimed at the trainee as a person. Caring about how much a person achieves and wanting to be a person's friend were perceived to go hand in hand; there was little difference between the levels of task and personal support perceived from peers and superiors (D.W. Johnson and R.T. Johnson, 1989). There seems to be a "halo effect" in team situations— superiors as well as peers are perceived to be more supportive of the trainee as a person as well as of the trainee's task success.

Psychological Health, Social Competence, and Self-Esteem

Training programs are often aimed at inculcating a professional identity, self-esteem, and the ability to cope with adversity under highly stressful conditions. Training for managing emergencies within nuclear power plants or pilot training for commercial airlines, for example, are aimed at making sure the learned procedures will be correctly used when one's own life and the lives of others are at stake. Thus, training is aimed at promoting trainees' psychological health and ability to adjust psychologically to changing conditions and situations. And since training programs often assume that the knowledge and procedures learned will be used in teams in work situations, trainees are expected to pick up the social competencies needed to coordinate and integrate their efforts with those of others.

Several studies have directly measured the relationship between social interdependence and psychological health (Crandall, 1982; Haynes, 1986; N. James and Johnson, 1983; S. James and Johnson, 1988; D.W. Johnson et al., 1984, 1986b; D.W. Johnson and Norem-Heibeisen, 1977). The samples studied included university students, older adults, suburban high school seniors, juvenile and adult prisoners, step-couples, and Olympic hockey players. The results indicated that cooperative attitudes are highly correlated with a wide variety of indices of psychological health, competitiveness was in some cases positively and in some cases negatively related to psychological health, and individual attitudes were negatively related to a wide variety of indices of psychological health.

Studies focusing on individual proficiency that compared teams and individual efforts on self-esteem found that team training promoted higher self-esteem than did individual training structured competitively or individually (effect sizes, 0.47 and 0.29, respectively). Studies focusing on group productivity found that team training promoted higher self-esteem than did competitive efforts (effect size, 0.86) or individual effort (effect size, 0.68). The level of self-esteem is affected not only by being part of a team effort, but also by the process by which individuals make judgments about their self-worth. In four studies of 821 white, middle-class, high school seniors in a midwestern suburban community, Norem-Hebeisen and Johnson (1981) found that cooperative experiences promoted basic self-acceptance, freedom from conditional acceptance, and seeing oneself positively compared to peers. Competitive experiences were related to conditional self-acceptance, and individual attitudes were related to basic self-rejection, including anxiety about relating to other people. Cooperative, team-based experiences seem to result in internalizing perceptions that one is known, accepted, and liked as one is; internalizing mutual success; and developing multidimensional views of oneself and others that allow for positive self-perceptions (D.W. Johnson and R.T. Johnson, 1989).

Changes in Team Structure and Procedures

When intact teams are taken from a job situation, given training as a team, and then returned to the work setting, the training often focuses on changing the way the team functions and operates, as well as increasing the proficiency of its individual members. On the basis of the broad literature on group dynamics, it is assumed that such team training will be more effective in changing a team's norms, roles, communication patterns, shared mental models, and team processing procedures than will individual training (Baron et al., 1992; Cartwright and Zander, 1968).

One of the most important procedures for teams to learn is how to make effective decisions. Decision making typically involves considering possible alternatives and choosing one (D.W. Johnson and F. Johnson, 1994). Doing so often requires that team members be advocates for points of view and information that the team is not considering. Airplane cockpit crews are a good example. A factor in more than two-thirds of air accidents is a failure of crew members to use their information expeditiously to cope with safety hazards (Cooper et al, 1979). Among the factors involved in crashes are the reluctance of first officers to disagree with pilots and the focus of crew members on a minor problem so that they forget to pilot the plane (Blake et al., 1989; Foushee, 1984). Crews that communicated extensively, acknowledged each other's communication attempts, made commands, disagreed, and felt less angry and embarrassed have been found to make fewer errors and crashes in simulated flights (Cooper et al., 1979; Foushee et al., 1986; Foushee and Manos, 1981; Ruffell-Smith, 1979; Tjosvold, 1990c).

By definition, all decision-making situations involve some conflict as to which of several alternatives should be chosen (D.W. Johnson and F. Johnson, 1994; Tjosvold, 1991). During training, trainees need to be taught the procedures and skills required to advocate their points of view when decisions have to be made. The procedure for doing so is controversy. Controversy exists when one person's ideas, information, conclusions, theories, and opinions are incompatible with those of another, and the two seek to reach an agreement (D.W. Johnson and R.T. Johnson, 1979, 1989). Controversy can be a powerful decision-making tool. The alternative solutions to the problem being faced can be identified, with each major alternative assigned to an advocacy group of team members who have the responsibility of preparing, presenting, and advocating the "best case" for each of the alternatives. The team then synthesizes the best reasoning from all perspectives into the group's decision. Research indicates that controversy tends to increase quality of decision making and problem solving, creativity of problem solving, more efficient exchange of expertise, more involvement in the task, greater interpersonal attraction among participants, and higher self-esteem (D.W. Johnson and R.T. Johnson, 1989). For example, electronic discussion groups with a planted group member who criticized others produced more new ideas and achieved more than did groups whose planted member was highly supportive (Connolly et al., 1990).[7]

Team Activities After Training

Teams can influence the transfer and maintenance of what is taught in a training program by highlighting implementation goals, encouraging immediate use, holding trainees accountable for using what they have learned, providing social support for using what was learned, providing a climate for transfer, and giving feedback and social rewards for transfer. In a series of studies, Tjosvold (1990a) and Tjosvold and McNeely (1988) found that the more a team is focused on cooperative goals of implementing new practices, the greater the innovation and restructuring of work that takes place, even when team members have quite diverse perspectives.

Teams can ensure that opportunities to use what is learned are available and the new procedures and skills are immediately practiced. In a study of managers at the Internal Revenue Service, Pentland (1989) found that attempts to practice trained computer skills immediately on returning to the job had a major impact on long-term retention of the skills. In a study of Air Force technical trainees, Ford et al. (1991) noted that there were significant differences in opportunity to apply the training and wide variations in the length of time before trainees first performed the tasks for which they had been trained. Supervisor and peer support were found to be related to the extent to which airmen had opportunities to perform the trained tasks.

Teams create an expectation that each trainee will be held accountable for using the training. Baldwin and Magjurka (1991) found that trainees who expected to be held accountable for what they learned left training with stronger intentions to transfer. Marx and Karren (1990) found that trainees were more likely to apply time management skills when follow-up occurred 3 weeks after a time management course. Teams can provide social support for using what trainees have learned by meeting regularly to ensure that members are implementing what was learned regularly, appropriately, and with fidelity, and receiving the help they need to solve implementation problems (Baldwin and Ford, 1988).

Teams can provide a positive transfer climate for trainees. Transfer climate can be defined as reminding trainees to use their training through goal cues, social cues, and task and structural cues. Rouillier and Goldstein (1991) conducted a study of assistant managers who completed a week-long training program and were then randomly assigned to 1 of 102 organization units. In units with a more positive transfer climate, trainees demonstrated significantly more trained behaviors, even when the outcomes were controlled for learning and for unit performance. Teams are ideal for providing trainees with the goal, social, and task cues conducive to transfer and maintenance.

Teams can provide feedback about and reinforcement for transfer of what was learned from the training to the job situation. After training, paraprofessionals at a facility for the handicapped were assigned to pairs and instructed to provide their partners with feedback and reinforcement (Fleming and Sulzer-Azaroff, 1990). The researchers concluded that the peer support increased the maintenance of the procedures and skills learned during training. Stable and enduring performance of newly learned skills in application settings, furthermore, is very much dependent on real-life reinforcement contingencies. Supplemental programs, such as follow-up teams, can provide the rewards trainees need to maintain their new behaviors.

Transfer of what is learned during training to the job is affected by how the work organization structures the posttraining situation. If, for example, the organization has clear goals, pay incentives, and job aids for using what was learned, transfer is encouraged (Tjosvold, 1990a, 1990b, 1990d; Tjosvold and McNeely, 1988). But if using the new skills is ridiculed by peers who did not take the training and if job responsibilities have not been modified to require the use of the new competencies, then transfer is discouraged. And if necessary equipment is lacking, the use of the new competencies on the job may be actually prohibited. Although it seems logical that such posttraining influences affect transfer, there is very little empirical evidence on the issue. Baldwin and Ford (1988) found only seven studies that examined the influence of the work environment on the transfer of training. In these seven studies, social support seemed to be the most important influence on transfer.

CONCLUSIONS

As noted at the beginning of this chapter, training is instruction aimed at procedural knowledge and proficiency. Teams are used in training programs to increase members' procedural knowledge and proficiency of taskwork, members' procedural knowledge and proficiency of teamwork, and team productivity. These training goals can be achieved through a process construed in terms of the framework developed in this chapter (see Figure 7-1). Team training programs can take place at a training site or a job site. The training process is a combination of inputs, training processes, mediating variables, and outcomes. The inputs include trainees, resources, task characteristics, and pretraining activities of teams. The training processes are the procedures used to teach both taskwork and teamwork and to increase team performance. The mediating variables are positive interdependence, face-to-face promotive interaction, individual accountability, and team processing. The outcomes are individual proficiency and team productivity, positive relationships and social support, psychological health and self-esteem as well as social competencies, team changes, and posttraining team activities.

Guidelines for Research and Practice

On the basis of the research reviewed in this chapter, a number of suggestions can be made about using teams in training. The suggestions are also guidelines for trainers on how best to structure training in teams. And they can be regarded as hypotheses to be explored in further research.

Team training may work better if attention is paid to how the inputs to training are assembled. Sending cohort, intact teams to be trained who will work together subsequent to the training will tend to increase the positive effects of the training. Team training will be more successful if pretraining teams are organized and focused on helping trainees set goals for what they will learn, alerting members that what they learn will later be assessed on the job, reducing the constraints for using the procedures and knowledge learned, creating positive expectations toward the training, and ensuring that supervisors support the training.

Team training can promote the simultaneous learning of both taskwork and teamwork skills: every session on taskwork becomes also a session on teamwork. In order to complete the tasks designed to teach participants taskwork procedures and proficiencies, trainees must clarify and implement the assignments (develop clear team goals), ensure that there is clear two-way communication among all team members, hold all members accountable for participating and providing their skills, and matching the decision-making procedures to the needs of the situation (including constructive conflict among group members). Trainees in individual training settings do not provide opportunities to develop these skills.

Team training also provides opportunities to better master the taskwork procedures being taught and to increase the likelihood of transferring the procedures to the job situation and maintaining their use. Team training provides a setting in which trainees can practice and master many aspects of taskwork: construct and extend conceptual understanding of what is being learned through explanations and discussion; use the shared conceptual models learned in flexible ways to solve problems jointly; jointly perform the procedures learned; receive other team members' feedback as to how well the procedures are performed; receive social support and encouragement to extend one's competencies; be held accountable by peers to practice until the procedures and skills are well learned; acquire the attitudes (such as continuous improvement) needed to refine the procedures learned; jointly master the use of the relevant technological devices; experience the stimulus variability inherent in working as part of a team; establish a positive and shared identity with other team members and with future colleagues, and observe the most outstanding team members as behavioral models to be emulated. These opportunities are not guaranteed, and they do not automatically occur in every team, but the likelihood of their occurrence exists when teams are used for training. The likelihood of their occurrence is very low when teams are not used.

Team training creates opportunities for a variety of positive outcomes. Individual proficiency tends to be increased, as well as productivity. As trainees work together to complete assignments, positive and supportive relationships tend to develop, even among trainees from different ethnic and gender groups. Working together and developing positive relationships also contributes to increased psychological health, self-esteem, and social competencies.

Completing a training program together can change a team's norms, roles, communication patterns, and decision-making procedures. Individual training programs do not have the potential for resulting in such multiple outcomes.

If teams are to be effectively used in training programs, the essential mediators should be structured in a disciplined and diligent way. Instructors must carefully structure positive interdependence to ensure that all trainees are committed to each other's success and each other as persons. Trainees must meet in teams and promote each other's learning face to face. Each trainee must be held accountable by his or her peers to maximize the effort to learn. In addition, each team must be held accountable for meeting the criteria set for successful performance. The teamwork skills required to coordinate efforts to complete joint assignments must be directly taught and learned. Finally, team members must gather data on their progress and plan how to improve the process they are using to learn. Without the disciplined application of these mediators of team effectiveness, the potential of training teams may not be realized.

Teams should be used in posttraining work situations to ensure that trainees engage in actions conducive to transfer and long-term maintenance of what was learned. Posttraining teams can be organized to ensure that trainees provide each other with opportunities for using what they learned, hold each other accountable for doing so, support each other's efforts to engage in a continuous improvement process to increase the quality of their application, and generally create a positive transfer climate.

Future research on the use of teams in training programs should be neither atheoretical nor nonpractical. Research is needed that directly tests the theoretical propositions about what makes team training programs effective. Validated theories can then be used to redesign training programs.

Obstacles to Team Training

The use of teams in training is not a panacea that solves all problems experienced by training programs. There are many ways that the use of teams in training programs can go wrong. There are tasks, for example, on which individuals may outperform a group (such as driving a car).

There are conditions under which the use of teams in training programs may be counterproductive. The most obvious is the use of poorly structured teams. Placing several trainees in the same room and calling them a team does not make them one. There is no advantage to telling trainees to work together if there is no positive interdependence, promotive interaction, individual and team accountability, use of social skills, and group processing. If teams are going to be used effectively in training programs, the mediating variables must be structured in a disciplined way. A second obstacle is lack of instructor training. Using teams effectively is a complex process that requires a clear understanding of the basic mediating variables and their application for a specific training purpose. Instructors who have spent years training individuals cannot be expected to be automatically knowledgeable and skilled in using teams for training purposes.

If training promotes a very strong team identity, several unfortunate outcomes can result. Members can overestimate the value of their group and its position and underestimate the value of other teams and their positions. For example, Blake and Mouton (1962), demonstrated that team members knew and understood their own position in negotiations far better than they knew and understood the opposing position, even after studying both for some time. When the ingroup-outgroup bias is extreme, teams can become closed brotherhoods or microsocieties that lose touch with external realities and the organization's goals (see Chapter 6). A fourth obstacle to effective team training is the possibility that team goals may be valued more than an organization's overall goals. If team goals are isolated from and not made interdependent with the goals of the rest of the organization, team members may be more committed to the short-term objectives of the team than to the organization's goals. Fifth, when training becomes a discrete event separated from the ongoing work situation and organizational life, the training can become irrelevant or even counterproductive. Of course, this phenomenon is not unique to team training.

Finally, as noted above, a major obstacle to team training can be the lack of trainees' teamwork skills. The inability of trainees to work as part of a team can interfere with their taskwork, through such mechanisms as attention overload, distraction, self-consciousness, and embarrassment.

There is a face validity to the use of teams in training that may be deceptive. Since most tasks impose greater mental and physical demands than one individual can perform in isolation, work teams may become the rule, not the exception. When work teams are used, complex mixtures of taskwork and teamwork are usually required. This does not mean, however, that teams should be used for every assignment in training programs. To practitioners, this cautionary note may seem strange, as the majority of training is currently structured so that trainees work alone, either independent from or in competition with their peers. Although the use of teams in training programs should be increased dramatically, this does not mean that individual work should be stopped or that all training activities should take place in teams. Individual practice, for example, is usually necessary. Instructors need to be trained to integrate their use of team and individual procedures. Since poorly structured teams may be counter-productive, furthermore, instructors have to know how to be judicious consumers who can tell the difference between teams in which the mediating processes have been carefully structured and groups in which they have not. Thus, training program staff have the difficult responsibility of increasing the use of well-structured teams while stopping the use of poorly structured ones.

NOTES

[1]It should be noted that these facilitatory practices during the preparatory period need not be limited to training in teams. Trainers of individuals could also profit from goal setting, and trainees can benefit from reduced constraints or application, positive expectation, and motivation.

[2]Unlike the effect sizes reported in Chapter 6, those reported here are not correlation coefficients. Each is calculated as the difference between the experimental and control group averages divided by the pooled sample standard deviation. This ratio can be greater than 1.00 (see Hedges and Olkin, 1985).

[3]Most of the contemporaneous research on positive interdependence has been done by D.W. Johnson and his colleagues at Minnesota. The research has extended the original work on this topic by Deutsch (1949). Another view on the role of interdependence in training, referred to as process interdependence, is discussed in Chapter 5.

[4]We note, however, that making and correcting errors during training has been shown to have positive effects on long-term performance (Druckman and Bjork, 1991:Chapter 3).

[5]Typically, however, these studies do not bring subjects to a criterion of performance before the training is completed.

[6]The teams in these studies were organized and trained to the task. The advantage for teams may largely dissipate for ad hoc freely interacting teams. Indeed, early research by Taylor (1954), Marquart (1955), and Lorge and Solomon (1955) showed that group problem-solving efforts were not routinely superior to individual efforts when an appropriate baseline for comparison was used. (This issue is discussed in Druckman and Bjork, 1991:Ch.12).

[7]Another way to analyze team decision making is to examine rules, either implicit or explicit, by which individual judgments are combined to yield a team decision (e.g., Smoke and Zajonc, 1962).

PART IV

Mental and Emotional States

In this part we discuss the implications of a person's emotional state for performance. The chapters provide a sampling of ways to alter states in order to influence performance.

Concentrating on perceptions of self-confidence, in Chapter 8 we review studies on achievement motivation, career development, health and exercise behavior, anxiety disorders, and sport and motor performance.

In Chapter 9, we focus primarily on hypnosis, but we also discuss restricted environmental stimulation (REST) and revisit issues concerned with meditation and sleep learning. For hypnosis, the chapter evaluates claims made about its effectiveness in such areas as pain control, strength, learning, sensory acuity, time perception, and memory. For REST, we evaluate the implications of a number of experiments that explore its effects on relaxation, learning, endurance, and so on. For this second look by the committee at the meditation literature, we focus particularly on Transcendental Meditation, evaluating the results obtained from meta-analyses performed on numerous experiments. Finally, for sleep learning, we consider recent work, which was stimulated by the committee's first report.

8

Self-Confidence and Performance

Self-confidence is considered one of the most influential motivators and regulators of behavior in people's everyday lives (Bandura, 1986). A growing body of evidence suggests that one's perception of ability or self-confidence is the central mediating construct of achievement strivings (e.g., Bandura, 1977; Ericsson et al., 1993; Harter, 1978; Kuhl, 1992; Nicholls, 1984). Ericsson and his colleagues have taken the position that the major influence in the acquisition of expert performance is the confidence and motivation to persist in deliberate practice for a minimum of 10 years.

Self-confidence is not a motivational perspective by itself. It is a judgment about capabilities for accomplishment of some goal, and, therefore, must be considered within a broader conceptualization of motivation that provides the goal context. Kanfer (1990a) provides an example of one cognitively based framework of motivation for such a discussion. She suggests that motivation is composed of two components: goal choice and self-regulation. Self-regulation, in turn, consists of three related sets of activities: self-monitoring, self-evaluation, and self-reactions. Self-monitoring provides information about current performance, which is then evaluated by comparing that performance with one's goal. The comparison between performance and goal results in two distinct types of self-reactions: self-satisfaction or -dissatisfaction and self-confidence expectations. Satisfaction or dissatisfaction is an affective response to past actions; self-confidence expectations are judgments about one's future capabilities to attain one's goal. This framework allows a discussion of self-confidence as it relates to a number of motivational processes, including setting goals and causal attributions.

One theoretical perspective of self-confidence that fits well in Kanfer's (1990b) framework of motivation and has particular relevance to enhancing self-confidence in a variety of domains of psychosocial functioning is self-efficacy theory (Bandura, 1977, 1986). Self-efficacy theory is also useful in guiding the development of motivational programs because self-beliefs of confidence operate in most of the approaches to cognitive theories of motivation, particularly goal-setting theory and attribution theory (Bandura, 1990).

This chapter provides an overview of the self-efficacy concept of self-confidence and its relationship to other cognitively based motivational processes that influence learning and performance; it does not attempt to integrate the different theories of motivation that incorporate self-confidence constructs. (For summaries and comparisons of cognitive theories of motivation, see Frese and Sabini, 1985; Halisch and Kuhl, 1987; Kanfer, 1990b; Pervin, 1989.) We first define self-confidence and related concepts. Next, an overview of self-efficacy theory is given, along with a review of the relevant research. The third section covers applications of techniques for enhancing self-confidence. Lastly, we note the research questions that follow from what is currently known.

"SELF-CONFIDENCE" AND RELATED CONCEPTS

Terms such as "self-confidence," "self-efficacy," "perceived ability," and "perceived competence" have been used to describe a person's perceived capability to accomplish a certain level of performance. Bandura (1977) uses the term "self-efficacy" to describe the belief one has in being able to execute a specific task successfully (e.g., solving a math problem) in order to obtain a certain outcome (e.g., self-satisfaction or teacher recognition) and, thus, can be considered as situationally specific self-confidence.[1] Self-efficacy is not concerned with an individual's skills, but, rather, with the judgments of what an individual can accomplish with those skills (Bandura, 1986). Bandura (1986, 1990) distinguishes between "self-efficacy" and "self-confidence": self-confidence refers to firmness or strength of belief but does not specify its direction; self-efficacy implies that a goal has been set. We do not adopt Bandura's distinction, but use the term "self-confidence" because it is more familiar to most individuals. "Self-confidence," as the term is used here, is the belief that one can successfully execute a specific activity, rather than a global trait that accounts for overall performance optimism. For example, one may have a lot of self-confidence in one's ability at golf but very little self-confidence in one's tennis skills.

"Perceived competence" and "perceived ability" are terms that have been used in the research literature on achievement and mastery motivation. They indicate the perception that one has the ability to master a task resulting from cumulative interactions with the environment (Harter, 1981; Nicholls,

1984). In sports and physical movement, Griffin and Keogh (1982) developed the concept of "movement confidence" to describe a person's feeling of adequacy in a movement situation; Vealey (1986) used the term "sport confidence" to define the belief or degree of certainty individuals possess about their ability to be successful in sport. Some organizational psychologists use the term "state expectancy" in essentially the same manner as Bandura's (1977) concept of self-efficacy (Eden, 1990).

Some terms related to self-confidence are occasionally confused with the construct. Some authors (e.g., Kirsch, 1985) have tried to implement Bandura's (1977) concept of self-confidence (self-efficacy) as an expectancy construct. Bandura distinguishes judgments of personal efficacy from the expectancy construct in expectancy-by-value theories (e.g., Fishbein and Ajzen, 1975; Triandis, 1977): self-confidence is a judgment of one's ability to perform at a certain level; expectancies pertain to the outcomes one expects from a given level of effort. In essence, confidence expectations are concerned with beliefs about one's competence and outcome expectations are concerned with beliefs about one's environment. For example, a person may believe that running a marathon in less than 2 hours will lead to social recognition, money, and self-satisfaction (outcome belief), but may question whether she can actually run that fast (confidence belief). Similarly, a woman may believe that Karate self-defense techniques will deter assault (outcome belief), but may doubt her capability to be effectively aggressive against a powerful assailant (confidence belief).

Bandura (1986) asserts that, in a responsive environment that rewards performance achievements, the outcomes people expect depend heavily on their self-confidence that they can perform the skill. However, in an environment in which outcomes are fixed at a minimum level of performance or in which a social condition restricts people's ability to perform successfully or control their circumstances, outcome and confidence expectations would not be causally linked. For example, a concentration camp inmate could have confidence that he or she is efficacious enough to maximize his or her survival probability without violating personal ethics while simultaneously believing that this survival probability is not very high at all. Such individuals may give up trying, not because they doubt their own capabilities, but because they expect their efforts to be futile. This type of outcome-based futility is hypothesized to lead to pessimism or learned helplessness (Bandura, 1986).

"Self-concept" represents a composite view of oneself that is developed through evaluative experiences and social interactions. As Bandura (1986) has noted, however, a person's self-conceptions become more varied across activities with increasing experience. Thus, global measures of self-concept will not predict the intra-individual variability in a performance situation as well as self-confidence perceptions that vary across activities and circumstances. Rather, global measures of self-concept are helpful to understanding one's total outlook toward life. However, it should be noted that people's self-concepts have also been shown to be malleable in certain situations (Markus and Kunda, 1986). (For a thorough discussion of self-concept, see Hattie, 1992.)

"Self-esteem" is another global construct related to self-confidence and self-concept and pertains to one's personal perception of worthiness. Although self-confidence and self-esteem may be related, individuals can have one without necessarily having the other. Certain individuals may not have high self-confidence for a given activity, but still "like themselves"; by contrast, there are others who may regard themselves as highly competent at a given activity but do not have corresponding feelings of self-esteem. (For a thorough discussion of the concept of self-esteem with respect to work behavior, see Brockner, 1988.)

Other related concepts include locus of control, optimism or pessimism (learned helplessness), healthy illusions, and level of aspiration. Rotter's (1966) notion of locus of control is concerned with a person's generalized expectancies about his or her ability to control reinforcements in life: individuals who tend to perceive events as internally controlled behave more self-determinedly; those who tend to perceive events as beyond their control behave more fatalistically. Although an internal locus of control orientation may create a high sense of confidence, the two constructs must be distinguished. Bandura (1986) points out that locus of control is based on outcome expectancies rather than confidence expectancies. For instance, people who believe that their physical health is personally determined but find it is failing despite their efforts to improve it would experience low self-confidence. Studies have shown that task-specific self-confidence expectancies are better predictors of successful behavior in specific situations than are general measures of perceived control (Kaplan et al., 1984; Manning and Wright, 1983).

Optimism and pessimism have been defined by some authors in terms of generalized expectancies for internal or external locus of control (Scheier and Carver, 1992). Scheier and Carver (1992:203) define "dispositional optimism" as the "tendency to believe that one will generally experience good vs. bad outcomes in life." Optimism and pessimism have also been conceptualized within an attributional or explanatory style framework (Abramson et al., 1978; Peterson and Bossio, 1991). In an attributional view, individuals base their expectations for controlling future events on their causal explanations for past events. Optimism is the tendency to attribute negative events to causes that are unstable, specific, and external; pessimism or learned helplessness is the tendency to attribute negative events to causes that are stable, global, and internal. Optimism and pessimism or learned helplessness are considered to be much more global concepts than task-specific self-confidence and, thus, are more resistant to short-term interventions to change them. In addition, optimism and pessimism emphasize perceptions of controllability of the environment rather than the sense of personal agency to control the environment.

A concept similar to optimism has been described as healthy illusions (Taylor and Brown, 1988) or positive denial (Lazarus, 1979), which involves a slight distortion of reality in the positive direction. Such illusions can help sustain one's hopes of success, keep morale high, and lower anxiety (Hackett and Cassem, 1974). As Peterson and Bossio (1991) explain in relation to severe illnesses, the immediate denial of the severity of an illness allows individuals to face crises slowly, which helps their motivation to recover. However, if denial or illusion is too far removed from reality, it can get in the way of recovery and taking action to improve one's situation or performance.

Level of aspiration, first conceptualized in the 1930s within the scientific analysis of goal-striving behavior, is concerned with people's estimation of their subsequent performance prior to trying a task. An early investigator (Frank, 1935:119) defined it specifically as "the level of future performance in a familiar task which an individual, knowing his level of past performance in that task, explicitly undertakes to reach." Once a level of aspiration has been set, the individual performs, examines the discrepancy between the level of aspiration and the performance, and reacts with feelings of success or failure (depending on discrepancy). These reactions could lead to trying harder, leaving the activity altogether, or continuing with a readjusted level of aspiration (Lewin et al., 1944). Early investigations on levels of aspiration were the precursors to modern research on various cognitive aspects of goal-setting, self-appraisal, and feeling of satisfaction regarding relative success and failure. Much of the basis for current views on self-regulation in terms of self-monitoring, self-evaluation, and self-reaction can be found within the level-of-aspiration paradigm (see Bandura, 1982; Carver and Scheier, 1990).

The earlier research, most of which occurred in the 1930s and 1940s (see, e.g., Festinger, 1942; Frank, 1935, 1941; Lewin et al., 1944), tried to determine the factors that influence the fluctuations in a person's level of aspiration (e.g., success and failure of comparison groups) or studied how well personality traits correlated with the phenomenon. One general finding in relation to success and failure was that subjects raised their level of aspiration after success and lowered it after failure. However, Bandura has shown that this finding does not automatically occur in real-life tasks: "Having surpassed a demanding standard through laborious effort does not automatically lead people to raise their aspiration" (Bandura, 1986:348). Whether one raises one's level of aspiration or not depends more on one's level of task-specific self-confidence. This is the additional self-evaluation mechanism that Bandura (1977) has added to the old paradigm and the self-regulation model. In contrast, Carver and Scheier (1990) emphasize the rate of discrepancy reduction or rate of progress made toward a goal over time in determining one's level of aspiration.

Although many of the concepts related to self-confidence are investigated from different perspectives, the phenomenon of interest for most of them is the cognitive process by which a person regulates thoughts and action to attain desired outcomes or to control events in his or her life.

THEORETICAL PERSPECTIVES

Self-efficacy theory was developed within the framework of a social cognitive theory (Bandura, 1986). Bandura poses self-confidence as a common cognitive mechanism for mediating people's motivation, thought patterns, emotional reactions, and behavior. The theory was originally proposed to account for the different results achieved by the diverse methods used in clinical psychology for treating anxiety. It has since been expanded and applied to other domains of psychosocial functioning, including motivation, cognitive skill acquisition, career choice and development, health and exercise behavior, and motor performance. (For reviews on specific domains, see Feltz, 1988b; Lent and Hackett, 1987; McAuley, 1992; O'Leary, 1985; Schunk, 1984a). The theory has also been found to be equally predictive cross-culturally (Earley, 1993; Matsui, 1987; Matsui and Onglatco, 1991).

Self-Confidence Information

Self-confidence beliefs, defined as people's judgments of their capability to perform specific tasks, are a product of a complex process of self-persuasion that relies on cognitive processing of diverse sources of confidence information (Bandura, 1990). These sources of information include performance accomplishments, vicarious experiences, verbal persuasion, and physiological states.

Performance accomplishments are supposed to provide the most dependable confidence information because they are based on one's own mastery experiences. One's mastery experiences affect self-confidence beliefs through cognitive processing of such information. If one has repeatedly viewed these experiences as successes, self-confidence will increase; if these experiences were viewed as failures, self-confidence will decrease. Furthermore, the self-monitoring or focus on successes or failures should have differential effects on behavior and self-confidence, depending on which is monitored (Bandura, 1986): focusing on one's successes should provide more encouragement and greater confidence than focusing on one's failures.

The influence that performance experiences have on perceived self-confidence also depends on the perceived difficulty of the task, the effort expended, the amount of guidance received, the temporal patterns of success and failure, and one's conception of a particular "ability" as a skill that can be acquired versus an inherent aptitude (Bandura, 1986). Bandura has argued that performance accomplishments on difficult tasks, tasks attempted independently, and tasks accomplished early in learning with only occasional failures carry greater confidence value than easy tasks, tasks accomplished with external aids, or tasks in which repeated failures are experienced early in the learning process without any sign of progress.

Confidence information can also be derived through a social comparison process with others (Festinger, 1954). Vicarious sources of confidence information are thought to be generally weaker than performance accomplishments; however, their influence on self-confidence can be enhanced by a number of factors. For instance, the less experience people have had with performance situations, the more they will rely on others in judging their own capabilities. The effectiveness of modeling procedures on one's self-confidence has also been shown to be enhanced by perceived similarities to a model in terms of performance or personal characteristics (George et al., 1992; Gould and Weiss, 1981).

Persuasive techniques are widely used by instructors, managers, coaches, parents, and peers in attempting to influence a learner's confidence, motivation, and behavior. In acquiring expert performance, Ericsson and his colleagues put a great deal of emphasis on parents' and teachers' expectations and verbal persuasions that a child is "talented" as a major influence on the child's self-confidence, motivation, and perceived protection "against doubts about eventual success during the ups and downs of extended preparation" (Ericsson et al., 1993:399). Persuasive information includes verbal persuasion, evaluative feedback, expectations by others, self-talk, imagery, and other cognitive strategies. Self-confidence beliefs based on this type of information, however, are likely to be weaker than those based on one's accomplishments, according to the theory. In addition, persuasive techniques are thought to be most effective when the heightened appraisal is slightly beyond what the person can presently do but still within realistic bounds because people are generally aware that better performances are achievable through extra effort (Bandura, 1986). The extent of persuasive influence on self-confidence has also been hypothesized to depend on the prestige, credibility, expertise, and trustworthiness of the persuader.

The causal attributions that one makes regarding previous achievement behavior also can be thought of as a source of self-persuasive information in formulating future confidence expectations. Causal attributions for previous behavior have been shown to predict confidence expectations (McAuley, 1990; Schunk and Cox, 1986). (This relationship is discussed in more detail below.)

Confidence information can also be obtained from a person's physiological state or condition. Such information is provided through cognitive appraisal (Bandura, 1986), such as associating physiological arousal with fear and self-doubt or with being psyched up and ready for performance. Eden (1990) also suggests that the stress one experiences in work can influence confidence judgments about one's coping capacity for the job. Bandura (1986) also notes that physiological sources of self-confidence judgment are not limited to autonomic arousal.[2] People use their levels of fitness, fatigue, and pain in strength and endurance activities as indicators of their physical inefficacy (Feltz and Riessinger, 1990; Taylor et al., 1985).

These four categories of confidence information—performance accomplishments, vicarious experience, persuasion, and physiological states—are probably not mutually exclusive in terms of the information they provide, though some are more influential than others. How various sources of information are weighted and processed to make judgments given different tasks, situations, and individual skills is as yet unknown. The consequences of these judgments, however, are hypothesized to determine people's levels of motivation, as reflected in the challenges they undertake, the effort they expend in the activity, and their perseverance in the face of difficulties. People's self-confidence judgments can also influence certain thought patterns and emotional reactions (e.g., pride, shame, happiness, sadness) that also influence motivation (Bandura, 1986). For instance, self-confidence beliefs may influence people's success or failure images, worries, goal intentions, and causal attributions.

Self-Confidence, Behavior and Thought Patterns, and Motivation

Bandura (1977) states that self-efficacy (self-confidence) is a major determinant of behavior only when people have sufficient incentives to act on their self-perception of confidence and when they possess the requisite skills. He predicts that self-confidence beliefs will exceed actual performance when there is little incentive to perform the activity or when physical or social constraints are imposed on performance. An individual may have the necessary skill and high self-confidence beliefs, but no incentive to perform. Discrepancies will also occur, according to Bandura, when tasks or circumstances are ambiguous or when one has little information on which to base confidence judgments.

How individuals cognitively process confidence information also influences the relationship between self-confidence and behavior (Bandura, 1977). For example, successes and failures may be distorted in importance. People who overweigh their failures are believed to have lower expectations than those with the same performance levels who do not overweigh their failures.

The relationship between self-confidence expectations and performance accomplishments is also believed to be temporally recursive (Bandura, 1977:194): "Mastery expectations influence performance and are, in turn, altered by the cumulative effect of one's efforts." Bandura (1990) has emphasized the recursive nature of the relationship between self-confidence and thought patterns as well. The relationship between the major sources of confidence information, confidence expectations, and behavior and thought patterns, as predicted by Bandura's theory, is presented in Figure 8-1.

As just discussed, people's self-confidence beliefs are hypothesized to influence certain thought patterns and emotional reactions as well as behavior. Two thought patterns of particular interest to the study of performance motivation are goal intentions and causal attributions; a third thought pattern that can influence self-confidence beliefs is how one thinks about ability.

Self-confidence beliefs have been shown to influence future personal goal-setting and to mediate the relationship between goal intentions and motivation (Earley and Lituchy, 1991). Research has also shown that the stronger people's self-confidence beliefs (assessed independently from their goals), the higher the goals they set for themselves and the firmer their commitments are to them (Locke et al., 1984). In addition, as noted above (Kanfer, 1990a), motivation based on goal intentions is mediated by self-regulatory influences that include two types of self-reactive influences: affective self-evaluation (satisfaction/dissatisfaction), and perceived self-efficacy for goal attainment. Bandura (1990) includes a third type of self-reactive influence: adjustment of personal standards. Figure 8-2 summarizes, schematically, Kanfer's and Bandura's ideas of motivation that are based on goal intentions.

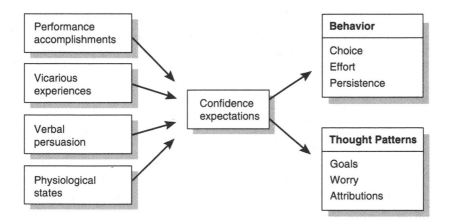

FIGURE 8-1 Relationship between sources of confidence information, confidence expectations, and behavior/thought patterns.

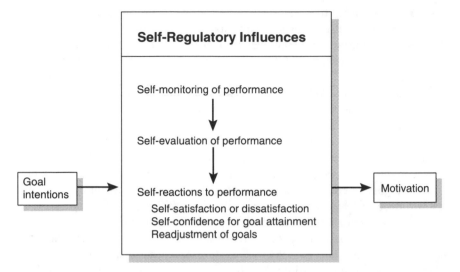

FIGURE 8-2 Conceptions of motivation based on goal intentions.

When performances fall short of people's personal goals (or level of aspiration), they become dissatisfied. Whether this dissatisfaction serves as an incentive or disincentive for enhanced effort is partly influenced by a person's self-confidence for goal attainment and the degree of the discrepancy (Bandura, 1986; Carver and Scheier, 1990). Bandura (1986) predicts that, in general, in the face of negative discrepancies between personal goals and attainments, those who have high self-confidence beliefs will heighten their level of effort and persistence and those who have self-doubts will quickly give up. However, if the degree of the negative discrepancy is perceived as quite large, people's self-confidence for goal attainment will be undermined. In this situation, research has shown that highly self-confident individuals will readjust their goals so as not to further undermine their self-confidence; those with little sense of self-confidence to begin with will become discouraged and abandon their goal altogether (Bandura and Cervone, 1983).

Bandura (1986, 1990) also suggests that confidence beliefs and causal attributions are reciprocal determinants of each other. According to Bandura, self-confidence beliefs help shape causal ascriptions for future behavior. People with self-beliefs of confidence have been shown to attribute failure to lack of effort; people with low self-beliefs of confidence ascribe their failures to lack of ability (Collins, 1982). Causal attributions also play a role in the formation of future confidence expectations (McAuley, 1990; Schunk and Cox, 1986). Successes are more likely to enhance self-confidence if performances are perceived as resulting from ability rather than from luck. Conversely, individuals can talk themselves out of succeeding by attributing prior failure to inherent ability rather than to bad luck or reduced effort. Studies using causal analyses also indicate that the effects of causal attributions on performance are mediated through self-confidence beliefs (Schunk and Gunn, 1986; Schunk and Rice, 1986).

As noted above, the way that people construe ability may also influence self-confidence beliefs and other self-regulatory factors. Two conceptions of ability have been identified that lead to the development of two goal orientations (Dweck and Leggett, 1988; Elliott and Dweck, 1988; Nicholls, 1984). The first is the conception of ability as an acquirable skill: people who conceive of ability in this way adopt a learning or mastery goal (Ames, 1984; Dweck and Leggett, 1988; Nicholls, 1984). This type of goal-orientation is well suited for skill development because people seek to improve their competence, judge their capabilities in terms of personal improvement, and regard errors as a natural part of the skill-acquisition process. Furthermore, when performance falls short of their goals, they attribute the discrepancy to inadequate effort, and their self-confidence beliefs remain minimally affected.

The second conception of ability is as a more or less inherent aptitude or entity conception: people who have an entity conception of ability adapt a performance or ability-focused goal (Ames, 1984; Dweck, 1986; Nicholls, 1984). People with this conception of ability seek to prove their competence or demonstrate their ability; they avoid demonstrating low ability and use social comparison processes to judge their ability relative to others. This type of goal-orientation is not well suited for skill development because people view errors as a threat to being able to demonstrate their ability and, thus, they avoid adopting challenging goals. When a negative discrepancy occurs between their goals and current performances, they attribute it to low ability. Research has shown that this type of ability conception increases a person's vulnerability to the adverse effects of failure (Elliott and Dweck, 1988; Jourden et al., 1991; Wood and Bandura, 1989). The feeling of failure and the attribution to low ability may also lead to dissatisfaction and a decrease in confidence beliefs and subsequently to goal abandonment. It also diverts attention away from the task and to worry (Kanfer, 1990a). The negative effects of an inherent aptitude conception are most distinct among people with low self-confidence in their ability (Kanfer, 1990a).

The structure and demands of a learning environment establish a motivational climate that can evoke different goal orientations (see Ames, 1992). For instance, schools often establish learning environments that include evaluating student achievement on the basis of normative standards and with extrinsic rewards. This structure encourages learners to use social comparison processes to judge their ability and adopt a performance-goal orientation instead of a mastery-goal orientation. Students, especially those who lack skills and self-confidence, do far better in school settings that foster a mastery orientation by designing activities for individual challenge, using flexible and heterogeneous grouping arrangements, helping students develop self-management and self-monitoring skills, recognizing individual progress, and involving them in self-evaluation (Ames, 1992).

Team Confidence

Much of the research on self-efficacy (self-confidence) beliefs has focused on the individual level of behavior. However, in many organizational settings, such as business, military, or sport, individuals perform as members of teams rather than just as individuals. Thus, many of the challenges and difficulties people face in organizations reflect team problems requiring team efforts to produce successful performance.

Bandura (1977, 1986) distinguishes between self-efficacy (self-confidence) and perceived collective efficacy (team confidence) in his theory of self-efficacy. Self-efficacy refers to people's judgments of individual capabilities and effort; collective efficacy or team confidence refers to people's judgments of group capabilities and influences "what people choose to do as a group, how much effort they put into it, and their staying power when group efforts fail to produce results" (Bandura, 1986:449). In this view, teams with high collective confidence beliefs should outperform and should persist longer than teams with low perceived collective confidence. Prior to the development of Bandura's theory, Bird and Brame (1978) found team confidence to be the most powerful discriminator of winning and losing teams.

Similarly to self-confidence, the confidence of a team or organization is most likely influenced by diverse sources of confidence information. As with self-confidence beliefs, performance accomplishments of the team are predicted to be the most powerful source of information for team confidence beliefs. Organizations that have an outstanding record of performance undoubtedly cultivate a strong sense of confidence among their members. Likewise, as Eden (1990) noted in his description of organizationwide self-fulfilling prophecies, a serious performance failure—such as the Challenger space shuttle disaster of the National Aeronautics and Space Administration—can decrease the collective confidence of the organization's members, which, in turn, can influence subsequent failures. The perceived collective confidence of a team or group might also be influenced through a collective social comparison process with other teams. It is also possible that reciprocal social influences within a team can raise or lower collective confidence for team performance. For example, the modeling of confidence or ineffectiveness by one member of the group may influence the rest of the group's sense of confidence (Bandura, 1990). In addition, just as persuasive information can influence an individual's sense of self-confidence, collective efficacy theory suggests that it could also influence an entire group. Charismatic leaders seem to have such persuasive influence on their organization's members (Eden, 1990).

Bandura (1986) further suggests that team confidence is rooted in self-confidence. According to Bandura, a team that has a strong sense of collective confidence can enhance the perceived task-specific confidence of its members, although a team with a weak sense of collective confidence may not totally undermine the perceived self-confidence of its more resilient members (also see Parker, 1992). Members of a team who have weak beliefs in their own individual capabilities are unlikely to be easily transformed into a strong collective force.

In terms of the assessment of perceived team confidence, Bandura (1986) suggests that team confidence may be insufficiently represented as a predictor of team performance through just the sum of the perceived personal confidences of its members, especially on highly interactive tasks or in situations in which members must work together to achieve success. A study of predicting team performance on the basis of individual performances provides some evidence for the possible moderating influence of task type on the confidence-performance relationship in teams (Jones, 1974). Using baseball (which does not require a lot of interaction among team members for team outcome), Jones (1974) predicted team outcome 90 percent of the time. However, for basketball (which does require a lot of interaction), he predicted team outcome only 35 percent of the time. This outcome suggests that the average of team members' perceptions of their team's performance capability should be added to their personal confidence to execute their individual functions in a collective task to measure team confidence.

This construct of team confidence may be related to other constructs of group motivation. For example, a team's collective confidence beliefs may also be influenced by the nature of its collective goals. As interpreted from Bandura (1986), effective team performance would require the merging of diverse individual goals in support of common group goals. If a team consists of a group of members who are all pursuing their own individual goals, they are not as apt to work together to achieve the necessary team goals to be successful, especially on highly interactive tasks. In addition, when the overall success of a team calls for sustained efforts over a long time, short-term intermediate goals may be needed to provide incentives, provide evidence of progress along the way, and sustain team confidence beliefs.

The attributions a team ascribes for its successes and failures may also influence team confidence. For example, an athletic team that defeats a difficult opponent with minimal effort may perceive itself to be highly confident. Conversely, if that same team worked very hard but lost to an easier opponent, perceived team confidence may weaken. Perceived team confidence may, in turn, influence the types of causal attributions that teams make about their performance (Bandura, 1986, 1990). Teams with little confidence may infer that poor performance was due to a lack of ability; highly confident teams may ascribe poor performance to a lack of effort.

Team confidence and cohesion may also be related. Both constructs have been shown to be positively associated with successful performance and persistence in the face of adversity (Spink, 1990). Thus, team confidence and team cohesion appear to share some common elements.

A team's collective confidence beliefs may similarly be related to a team's desire for success. For example, Zander (1971) found that groups with a strong desire for success outperformed groups with a weaker desire for success. Over time, when a group succeeded more often than it failed, members of that group were more interested in the activity and had a stronger desire for their group to perform well (Zander, 1971). Thus, successful outcome had a cyclical relationship with desire for success. Team confidence could also be part of this relationship. Successful performance can be expected to positively influence team confidence, which in turn should lead to behaviors and actions (e.g., setting higher goals, working harder) that enhance the ability of the group to succeed in the future, resulting in an even stronger desire for group success. This relationship may not hold for tasks that are not intrinsically motivating.

Social loafing may also be conceptualized in terms of team confidence. However, social loafing (conceptualized as the motivational losses in group performance) may represent the dark side of team confidence. In typical team performance situations, the evaluation potential for any one individual is not as strong as it would be for an individual performance, and this situation can give rise to social loafing. If individual team members believe that their team is highly capable of performing a task, they may loaf. Thus, high team confidence may actually undermine contributions to team performance unless there is individual identifiability. There has not yet been research to test this "undermining" assumption, but a considerable body of research has shown that increasing the identifiability and recognition of individual performances in groups reduces social loafing (e.g., Latané et al., 1979).

Some work suggests that self-confidence mediates the relationship between identifiability of performance and loafing (Sanna, 1992). Highly confident individuals whose performances were identifiable as part of a group's performance were less likely to loaf than were individuals with little confidence in the same situation. The results of this study suggest that when individual contributions toward team performance are identifiable, highly confident members may exert more effort toward performance than members whose confidence is not high. Increased individual effort towards performance usually facilitates successful team performance, which in turn may enhance perceived team confidence.

RESEARCH ON SELF-CONFIDENCE

Evidence for the effectiveness of self-confidence as an influential mechanism in human agency comes from a number of diverse lines of research in various domains of psychosocial functioning, including achievement motivation (Bandura and Cervone, 1983; Schunk, 1984a), career choice and development (Betz and Hackett, 1981), health and exercise behavior (DiClemente, 1981; McAuley and Jacobson, 1991), anxiety disorders (Bandura et al., 1982) and sport and motor performance (Feltz, 1982). Results of these diverse lines of research provide converging evidence that people's perceptions of their performance capability significantly affect their motivational behavior (Bandura, 1986).

This section is not an exhaustive review of all the research on self-confidence and psychosocial functioning; rather, we focus on work that is relevant to enhancing perceived self-confidence and the effects of self-confidence beliefs on performance. The first part of this section looks at research on the effect of various techniques for enhancing self-confidence beliefs; the second part considers the effects of self-confidence on performance; the third part looks at research on team confidence; and the fourth part considers how to apply those research findings.

Enhancing Self-Confidence

Performance-Based Confidence Information

As noted above, Bandura (1977) proposed that performance accomplishments provide the most dependable source of information on which to base self-confidence judgments because they are based on one's mastery experiences. Techniques based on such performance accomplishments as participant modeling, guided exposure, physical guidance, external aids, and task modification have been effective in enhancing both self-confidence beliefs and performance in a wide variety of areas, including: reducing phobic dysfunction (Bandura et al., 1982; Biram and Wilson, 1981); mastering high-risk skills (Brody et al., 1988; Feltz et al., 1979; Weinberg et al., 1982); enhancing personal empowerment over physical threats (Ozer and Bandura, 1990); and increasing interest in mathematical tasks (Campbell and Hackett, 1986). Research has also supported the superiority of performance-based information over other sources of confidence information (e.g., Bandura and Adams, 1977; Bandura et al., 1977; Feltz et al., 1979; Lewis, 1974; McAuley, 1985).

For example, Feltz et al. (1979) investigated the effectiveness of participant, live, and videotaped modeling on learning the back dive, a high-avoidance task. Participant modeling involved an expert's demonstration plus guided participation with the learner. On the first four performance trials (training period), the participant-modeling subjects were guided through the dives to ensure successful performance. On the second four trials (test period), the physical guidance was removed. As predicted, the participant-modeling treatment produced more successful dives and stronger confidence beliefs than either the live modeling or videotaped modeling treatments.

According to Bandura (1986), information acquired from mastery experiences does not influence self-confidence directly; rather, it depends on how the information is cognitively appraised, such as how difficult the task is perceived to be in comparison to the effort expended, how much external aid is received, the temporal pattern of one's successes and failures, and one's conception of ability. For instance, research in motor learning has shown that in initial learning the experience of a temporal pattern of early success followed by a series of failures resulted in less persistence at the task in the face of subsequent failure than the experience of early failure followed by a series of successes (Feltz et al., 1992). The early failure and subsequent success pattern was more representative of the typical learning pattern of a motor skill and, therefore, probably influenced perceptions of the skill as an acquirable one.

In another study researchers first induced different conceptions of ability—inherent aptitude or acquirable skill—for performance on a rotary pursuit task (a spinning disc with a quarter-sized target that a person tries to track and that records time on target) (Jourden et al., 1991).[3] Subjects who performed the task under the conception of ability as an acquirable skill showed increases in self-confidence, showed positive self-reactions to their performance, displayed widespread interest in the activity, and showed greater improvements in performance in comparison with those who performed the task under the inherent-aptitude conception of ability. These results suggest that instructors should use a positive approach, which emphasizes the learnability of the skill to be taught, to improve the speed and quality of skill acquisition, especially in the early phases.

Vicarious Confidence Information   Information gained through vicarious experiences has been shown to influence perceived confidence in such areas as muscular endurance performance (Feltz and Riessinger, 1990; George et al., 1992; Weinberg et al., 1979); physical activity (Corbin et al., 1984); competitive persistence (Brown and Inouye, 1978); problem-solving (Schunk, 1981; Zimmerman and Ringle, 1981); phobic behavior (Bandura et al., 1977); and management training (Gist, 1989a, 1989b; Gist et al., 1989). These techniques have included modeling and social comparison. Weinberg et al. (1979) manipulated subjects' confidence beliefs about competing on a muscular endurance task by having them observe their competitor (a confederate) on a related task. The confederate either performed poorly and was said to have a knee injury (belief of high self-confidence) or performed well and was said to be a varsity track athlete (belief of low self-confidence). Results indicated that the higher the induced self-confidence, the greater the muscular endurance. Subjects who competed against an "injured" (perceived as relatively weaker) competitor endured longer and had higher confidence expectations about winning against their opponent than those who thought they were competing against a varsity athlete—even though the subjects lost in both trials.

Modeling provides confidence information, according to Bandura (1986), through a comparative process between the model and the observer. George et al. (1992) demonstrated that a model who was similar to nonathletic observers in ability enhanced observers' confidence beliefs and endurance performance over a dissimilar model. In essence, the similar model seems to instill the attitude of "If he/she can do it, so can I." Also, the use of multiple models has been shown to enhance the modeling effect (Lewis, 1974). Bandura (1977) reasoned that observers would have a stronger basis on which to increase their own self-confidence if they could see a number of people of widely differing characteristics succeeding at a task.

Persuasory Confidence Information   For many kinds of performance, people are influenced by the opinions of others—teachers, coaches, peers, and managers—in judging their ability to perform a task. People may also try to persuade themselves that they have the ability to perform a given task through imagery and causal attributions for previous performances. Verbal persuasion by itself is of limited influence, and for treating phobias in clinical psychology it is often used in combination with other techniques, such as hypnosis, relaxation, or performance deception. However, in athletic, educational, and work situations, for which the fear component is unlikely to be as paralyzing as in chronic phobias, persuasive techniques by themselves may improve performance more successfully than in phobic behavior; but there has been little research on this possibility.

The few studies that have been conducted in motor performance report mixed results (Feltz and Riessinger, 1990; Fitzsimmons et al., 1991; Weinberg, 1985; Wilkes and Summers, 1984; Yan Lan and Gill, 1984). Weinberg (1985) found no effects on endurance performance with the use of dissociation and positive self-talk strategies, and Yan Lan and Gill (1984) found that providing subjects with bogus feedback and the suggestion that elevated arousal levels were indicative of good performance did not induce higher self-confidence. In contrast, Wilkes and Summers (1984) found persuasive techniques that tried to enhance confidence and emotional arousal influenced strength performance, but confidence-related cognitions did not seem to mediate the effect. Fitzsimmons et al. (1991) found that false positive feedback increased self-confidence judgments and future weightlifting performance. In addition, Feltz and Riessinger (1990) found significant effects on endurance performance using mastery imagery, with corresponding effects on self-confidence.

One explanation for the equivocal findings in these studies may be the differences in the degree of persuasive influence of their techniques and the extent of their subjects' personal experience on the task. In the Weinberg (1985) study, subjects were not told that the cognitive strategy they were to use would enhance their performance. There was no attempt at persuasion. In comparison, Wilkes and Summers (1984) instructed their subjects to persuade themselves that they were confident or to persuade themselves that they were "charged up."

The degree of persuasive influence also depends on the believability of the persuasive information. Yan Lan and Gill (1984) tried to lead subjects to believe that they had the same heightened pattern of physiological arousal as good competitors. However, there was no manipulation check that the subjects believed the persuasion. Fitzsimmons et al. (1991), in contrast, used pilot data to ensure that the deceptive feedback provided was believable.

The lack of persuasive effects in some of the research may also have been due to confounding with actual performance. All of the studies used multiple performance trials; thus, subjects may have formed perceptions on the basis of their performance experience that overshadowed much of the influence that the treatment variable had on self-confidence. This explanation is supported by research showing that the significant effects for endurance performance and self-confidence were short-lived after subjects experienced performance failure (Feltz and Riessinger, 1990).

A slightly different line of research in organizational behavior has shown consistent effects for instructors' expectancies on trainees' self-confidence and performance (Eden, 1990; Eden and Ravid, 1982; Eden and Shani, 1982). These studies induced military instructors to expect higher performance from some trainees than others. Not all of these studies measured self-confidence (or self-expectancy, as used in the studies), but those that did showed that high expectancy trainees had higher levels of self-confidence and performance than low expectancy trainees.

Performance Feedback Evaluation feedback about ongoing performances has also been used as a persuasive technique (Bandura, 1986). Instructors, managers, and coaches often try to boost perceived trainees' self-confidence by providing encouraging feedback. Positive feedback about ongoing performance has been shown to instill higher perceptions of confidence than no feedback at all (Vallerand, 1983). Also, feedback on causal attribution that credits progress to underlying ability or effort has been shown to raise perceived confidence more than no feedback or feedback that implies lesser ability (Schunk, 1983a). However, inappropriately high amounts of positive feedback can be detrimental to self-perceptions and motivation when used on individuals differentially because it implies low ability (Horn, 1985; Meyer, 1982). For instance, Horn (1985) found that the frequent use of positive reinforcement by coaches for less-skilled players resulted in lower perceived competence in those athletes, while the use of higher amounts of mistake-contingent criticism for highly-skilled players led to higher levels of perceived competence. Horn reasoned that the liberal use of praise given to low-skilled players was not performance-contingent and thus communicated to them that their coach held lower expectations for them.

In addition to its use as a persuasive technique, evaluative feedback can also add to enactive confidence information regarding ongoing performance as it conveys signs of progress. In order to be informative and motivative, feedback must be provided in reaction to defined performance standards or goals (Bandura, 1986). Otherwise, there is no basis on which to form internal comparisons to be able to evaluate ongoing performance. A wealth of research has shown that both feedback and goal setting are needed to enhance performance (Bandura and Cervone, 1983; Erez, 1977; Feltz and Riessinger, 1990; Locke and Latham, 1990; Strang et al., 1978). Even in the face of substandard performance, Bandura (1986) suggests that subjects' motivation and self-confidence may not be undermined if the discrepancy is only moderate and they are given knowledge of that discrepancy.

Causal Attributions   Studies that have examined the influence of causal attributions on self-confidence beliefs have either assessed the attributions that individuals have made for previous performances in relation to the confidence expectations for future performances (McAuley, 1990, 1991) or have manipulated attributional feedback concerning previous performance to examine the effect on subsequent confidence expectations (Schunk, 1983a, 1984a; Schunk and Cox, 1986; Schunk and Gunn, 1986). Much of this research, conducted on educational learning has generally shown that attributions made or induced for previous performance that are internal and subject to personal control (e.g., effort and ability) will raise self-confidence beliefs for subsequent performance. Therefore, helping individuals attribute good performance to ability, skill improvement, or hard work and their bad performances to lack of effort, lack of sufficient practice time, or use of an inappropriate strategy can be expected to improve their self-confidence beliefs and motivation for continued performance.

Physiological Confidence Information   The few studies that have investigated the influence of physiological or emotional states on self-confidence are equivocal (Feltz, 1982, 1988a; Feltz and Mugno, 1983; Juneau et al., 1986; Kavanagh and Hausfeld, 1986). For diving tasks, Feltz (1988a) found that perceived autonomic arousal, rather than actual physiological arousal, significantly predicted confidence judgments. Juneau et al. (1986) found that individuals who focused on their physical stamina as they mastered increasing workloads on a treadmill judged their cardiac confidence as more robust than those who focused on the negative signs. For strength tasks, however, Kavanagh and Hausfeld (1986) found that induced moods (happiness or sadness), as measured by self-reports, did not alter confidence expectations in any consistent manner. Bandura (1988) has argued that it is people's perceived coping confidence that is more indicative of capability than their perception of their physiological arousal condition. If people believe that they cannot cope with a potential threat, they experience disruptive arousal, which may further lower their confidence judgments that they can perform successfully. Evidence for this argument comes from research that has shown that it is not the frightful cognitions themselves that account for anxiety symptoms, but the perceived self-confidence to control them (Kent, 1987; Kent and Gibbons, 1987).

Contextual Influences

A number of instructional practices are important contextual influences on self-confidence that do not necessarily fit into any of the four principal sources of confidence information (Schunk, 1984b). In addition to evaluative and attributional feedback, these practices include goal setting and reward contingencies. Schunk (1985) has suggested that these contextual influences convey confidence information to learners by making salient certain cues that learners use to appraise their self-confidence.

The research on goal setting and self-confidence has generally shown that setting goals for oneself and attaining them, especially specific, difficult, and proximal goals, enhance perceptions of self-confidence (Bandura and Schunk, 1981; Locke et al., 1984; Manderlink and Harackiewicz, 1984; Schunk, 1983b; Stock and Cervone, 1990). Specific goals raise confidence expectations to a greater extent than more abstract goals because they provide more explicit information with which to gauge one's progress. Difficult goals raise confidence expectations more than do easy goals because they, too, offer more information about one's capability to achieve.

Although the research supports the setting of difficult goals, experts recommend that they be realistic (Locke and Latham, 1990). Garland (1983), however, has questioned the basis of the goal attainability assumption in setting difficult goals. Laboratory experiments on goal-setting have found positive relationships between goal difficulty and performance even when the goals assigned to individuals were difficult and beyond their reach (Weinberg, 1992). One factor that may resolve the differences between experts' recommendations and laboratory evidence is task type. The type of task used in goal-setting studies has been observed to mediate this positive relationship between goal difficulty and performance (Tubbs, 1986; Wood et al., 1987). Kanfer and Ackerman (1989) have provided a theoretical explanation for this mediating effect in terms of resource capacity and attentional demands of the task: that is, setting and striving for goals impose additional attentional demands on the individual. In learning complex tasks, such as air-traffic control operations, the benefits of goal-setting are difficult to realize because of the already high attentional demands of the task (Kanfer and Ackerman, 1989). In simple tasks, such as performing sit-ups, attentional demands are minimal, which leaves plenty of room available for engaging in the self-regulatory activity of goal-setting.

One problem in being assigned specific and difficult goals (versus selecting one's own goals) is that it may create a performance goal orientation that focuses one's attention on proving one's ability (Kanfer, 1990a:229): "The assigned performance goal sets the objective standard for proving one's ability." In a learning situation, the adoption of a difficult goal when trying to prove one's ability emphasizes the negative discrepancy and, thus, the feeling of failure, attribution to low ability, and a decrease in self-confidence about the task. Research is needed to determine whether assigning specific and difficult goals creates a performance goal orientation and whether assigning less specific goals might offset some of the negative motivational effects of assigning difficult goals, including a decreased sense of self-confidence.

In addition to specific and difficult goals, immediate goals are also easier to gauge in terms of progress than are distant goals. They make a task appear more manageable, provide an indication of progress, and affect self-evaluative reactions to performance (Stock and Cervone, 1990). A few studies have found no difference between immediate and distant goals (e.g., Bandura and Simon, 1977; Dubbert and Wilson, 1984), but many of the subjects assigned long-term goals in these studies were found to have spontaneously set short-term subgoals for themselves, which contaminated the findings. However, research on long-term goal-setting programs to improve the study skills and grades of college students suggests that relatively long-term plans and goals are most beneficial because they allow flexible choice among daily activities (Kirschenbaum, 1985; Kirschenbaum et al., 1981, 1982). One way to reconcile these divergent findings is to view them in terms of stages of skill acquisition. For instance, it may be argued that short-term goals facilitate performance and perceived competence in the early stages of skill acquisition, but as competence develops over time, moderately long-term goals allow greater flexibility and choice and may be viewed as less controlling than short-term goals (Manderlink and Harackiewicz, 1984).

In addition to examining goal-setting influences on self-confidence and performance in relation to stages of skill acquisition, examining them in relation to one's rate of progress may also explain divergent findings. Carver and Scheier (1981) propose that when one encounters difficulty in executing a higher order (more distant) goal, attention is shifted back to a lower order (more immediate) subgoal. As discrepancy toward the subgoal is reduced, attention shifts back to the higher order goal. As long as one is making good progress toward a long-term goal, one's attention does not need to shift to subgoals to feel confident and be successful. Future research is needed to determine under what conditions and with what tasks different goal-setting techniques enhance self-confidence and performance.

Another common instructional practice to enhance motivation is the use of rewards. Providing rewards (incentives) for desirable outcomes imparts information as well as motivation (Bandura, 1986). Informing learners that they can earn rewards on the basis of what they accomplish is hypothesized to influence their self-confidence for learning. As individuals work toward a task and note their progress, their sense of confidence can be validated through rewards. Rewards have been shown to heighten self-confidence beliefs more when they are contingent on performance than when offered simply for participation (Schunk, 1983c). As with feedback, rewards may actually reduce self-confidence beliefs if they are given in a noncontingent manner for some learners and not others or if they are distributed within a competitive reward structure (Ames, 1981); competitive reward structures emphasize social comparisons that can result in differential ability attributions (Schunk, 1985).

Effects of Self-Confidence on Performance

Numerous studies have examined the relationship between self-confidence and motivated behavior or performance across a number of tasks and situations (Bandura, 1986). Although these correlational results do not necessarily demonstrate a causal relationship between self-confidence and performance, they do provide convergent evidence of a consistent association between self-confidence and performance of at least a moderate magnitude. For instance, in sport and exercise, Feltz (1988b) found that the correlations between self-confidence and subsequent performance in 28 studies ranged from .19 to .73, with a median of .54. Other studies have experimentally manipulated perceived self-confidence levels and then measured subjects' motivation in coping behavior (Bandura et al., 1982), endurance performance (Feltz and Riessinger, 1990; Weinberg et al., 1979); problem solving (Cervone and Peake, 1986), and pain tolerance (Litt, 1988). In general, these diverse causal tests provide corroborating evidence that perceived self-confidence contributes significantly to motivated behavior and performance.

Attempting to demonstrate the causal influence of self-confidence on behavior and performance through experimental manipulation of self-confidence, however, has been criticized as leading to an arbitrary interpretation of the relationship of self-confidence to performance (Biglan, 1987). Biglan points out that when environmental variables are manipulated in order to manipulate self-confidence ratings, performance behavior or other factors are also affected. Environmental manipulations may influence some other variable (e.g., anxiety) that influences self-confidence and performance without any causal role for self-confidence. "Third variable" causes must be considered, but this is difficult to do in traditional experimental studies, especially when considering a network of causal relationships. In such situations, path analysis or structural-equation modeling is an appropriate method to investigate a network of causal relationships (Anderson and Evans, 1974; Cook and Campbell, 1979; Duncan, 1975). Path analysis and structural-equation modeling allow one to test whether the model presented fits a set of data adequately by comparing the observed relationships among the variables with the predicted relationships. These methods also permit an estimation of the relative indirect and direct contributions of effects. Causal modeling methods are not techniques for discovering causal directions, but, rather, for testing directions of causation that have already been specified by a model.

Causal modeling techniques have been used in a number of self-confidence studies to control for the contribution of other possible factors and to test the network of causal relationships posed by a theory (Dzewaltowski, 1989; Dzewaltowski et al., 1990; Earley and Lituchy, 1991; Feltz, 1982, 1988a; Feltz and Mugno, 1983; Garland et al., 1988; Hackett, 1985; Locke et al., 1984; McAuley, 1985, 1990; Ozer and Bandura, 1990; Schunk, 1981; Wood and Bandura, 1989; Zimmerman et al., 1992). In general, these studies have found self-confidence to be a major determinant of motivated behavior or performance and to be influenced by performance in a recursive fashion. For motor behavior and performance, existing self-confidence has been shown to predict initial performance, but as one gains experience on the task, performance also becomes a strong predictor of both future performance and self-confidence (Feltz, 1982, 1988a; Feltz and Mugno, 1983; McAuley, 1985). These results indicate that performance-based treatments may be affecting behavior through other mechanisms, as well as perceived self-confidence. One of the mechanisms not investigated in these studies on motor performance is goal effects. Path-analytic studies that have included goal effects have generally found that assigned goals influence both self-confidence and personal goals and that both variables, in turn, have direct effects on performance (Earley and Lituchy, 1991; Locke et al., 1984; Wood and Bandura, 1989; Zimmerman et al., 1992).

Team Confidence

Although team confidence is recognized as being important to group or team functioning, there has been little research on it (Bandura, 1986). Studies have examined group confidence in social dilemmas (Kerr, 1989), school systems (Parker, 1992), and sports (Feltz et al., 1989; Spink, 1990). Two of these studies (Feltz et al., 1989; Parker, 1992) found some support for

Bandura's (1986) proposition that an aggregate of group members' perceived confidence of the group as a whole would be more predictive of the group's performance than an aggregate of the members' judgments of their own confidence when there is at least a moderate level of interdependent effort required of the group.

Because school systems require at least a moderate level of interdependence among their teachers, Parker (1992) examined teachers' beliefs in their own instructional self-confidence and their beliefs about their schools' collective capability to predict schools' levels of academic achievements. Teachers were asked to rate their self-confidence in three teaching domains (reading, mathematics, and language), as well as their beliefs in the collective confidence of the school as a whole in the same three areas. Each teacher's self-confidence and school confidence ratings were then compared with the performances of the students in each teacher's school on a standardized test of reading, mathematics, and language proficiencies. The teachers' perceived confidence in their school's capability (perceived school confidence) predicted the academic achievements of the students in their school and that these collective confidence beliefs of the school were more predictive of the academic achievement of the students than were the teachers' beliefs of their own instructional self-confidence, thus, supporting Bandura's (1986) hypothesis.

Feltz et al. (1989) compared self-confidence and team confidence in the prediction of team performance of seven collegiate hockey teams across a 32-game season. A team confidence measure was constructed after conducting a conceptual analysis of the competence areas required in hockey (with the consultation of two collegiate hockey coaches). The resulting measure of team confidence had seven dimensions: (1) winning against opponents, (2) outskating opponents, (3) outchecking opponents, (4) forcing more turnovers than opponents, (5) bouncing back from poor performances more than opponents, (6) performing better in power play situations than opponents, and (7) performing better in short-handed situations than opponents. Initial analyses have indicated that team confidence was only slightly more predictive of team performance than was individual confidence. However, when wins and losses were analyzed by game, team confidence was more affected by losses than was individual confidence.

The construct of team or collective confidence is still in a rudimentary stage in terms of understanding and explaining motivation. Clearly, a greater understanding of its utility will come from rigorous and systematic research. Toward this end, Bandura (1990) suggests that advances in research on team confidence will be greatly influenced by the development of appropriate measures; specifically, measures of perceived team confidence need to be tied closely to explicit indices of group performance. This may be best accomplished by conducting conceptual analyses of the competence areas within a group's performance.

Although Bandura's theory of self-efficacy as a self-confidence concept is not without its criticisms (see Biglan, 1987; Eastman and Marzillier, 1984; Feltz, 1988b; Lee, 1989), research on self-confidence from divergent psychosocial domains of functioning and from different cultural environments (Earley, 1993; Matsui, 1987; Matsui and Onglatco, 1991) has consistently shown self-perceptions of ability to be an important and necessary cognitive mechanism in explaining motivated behavior and performance. However, self-confidence, as a common mechanism that mediates behavior, cannot be expected to account for all behavior change in human performance (Bandura, 1984). Even so, given the demonstrated importance of self-confidence in enhancing performance, numerous inferences can be drawn to help individuals develop and maintain self-confidence to improve motivation for performance.

Techniques for Enhancing Self-Confidence

In this section research and theory from self-efficacy, goal-setting, and attributions are used to speculate on practical ways to enhance self-confidence for motivation and performance. Applications for enhancing self-confidence are organized around techniques that are based on the four sources of confidence information within Bandura's theory of self-efficacy (Bandura, 1977): performance-based strategies, modeling, persuasion and communication, and anxiety-reduction strategies.

Performance-Based Approaches

Given that the relationship between self-confidence and motivated behavior or performance has been well documented, the important goal is to find ways to enhance self-confidence beliefs. Research has supported that the strongest and most durable determinant of self-confidence is the experience of mastery or performance accomplishments.

One way of facilitating performance mastery is through instructional strategies[4] (Schunk, 1985). The instructor can provide for maximum skill development through an instructional sequence of developmental or modified activities, breaking the skill into parts, providing performance aids, physical guidance, or a combination of these methods. For example, the instructor can physically guide learners through the movements, have them practice on a simulation training device, or design a series of progressive activities to challenge their improving skills. These successes should be based on relevant and realistic progressions: progress must be in small enough increments to ensure intermediary successes, which can lead to mastery of the final goal. Performance aids and physical guidance should be gradually removed as soon as possible, however, so that learners can engage in self-directed mastery experiences. As noted, self-directed experiences indicate higher levels of self-confidence to individuals than do externally guided experiences because the performance is attributed to a person's own effort and ability rather than external aids (Bandura, 1986).

A second effective means of ensuring performance accomplishments is through goal-setting—defining realistic performance standards toward which individuals strive. For complex tasks, the goals should be specific and challenging but attainable. For easy or routine tasks, the harder the goal, the better the performance. Assuming an individual has the requisite skills and commitments, working toward difficult goals can build a strong sense of confidence because the goals offer more information about the performer's capability to acquire knowledge and skills than do easier goals. Some individuals, however, may need some persuasive help to be convinced that the goals are not too difficult (Schunk, 1983b). In addition, for complex and difficult tasks, short-term goals should be used along with long-term goals. Similarly, when using short-term goals, the performer's perceptions of self-confidence for attainment of future goals should be monitored, as well as perceptions of self-confidence that result from goal attainment. As Stock and Cervone (1990) point out, goal-setting strategies will not help individuals who lack a sense of efficacy for attaining the subgoals or those who do not experience enhanced feelings of confidence when they attain the subgoals.

Feedback also appears necessary for goals to have maximum effectiveness in enhancing self-confidence and improving performance. Furthermore, when one is first learning complex tasks, self-confidence beliefs and success can be enhanced by emphasizing process-related (or learning) goals over outcome-related (or performance) goals. Rather than defining success through outcome measures, such as winning and losing or number of tasks completed, success should be redefined to include process variables, such as effort, form, and strategy. These process-related goals are important because they help individuals focus on the learnability of a skill rather than viewing the skill as requiring inherent aptitude (Jourden et al., 1991).

Modeling Others

When individuals have had no prior experience with a task, observing others (modeling) is one means of providing information by which to judge one's own capabilities. For instance, observing others engaging in threatening activities without adverse consequences can reduce inhibitions in observers (Lewis, 1974). The models can be similar in terms of personal characteristics (e.g., age, sex, race) and skill levels, but similarity in skills appears to be more salient to observers than personal characteristics (George et al., 1992). The content of the model's statements is also an influential factor in raising perceptions of efficacy (Gould and Weiss, 1981; Schunk,

1981). Models can provide information and strategies about how to perform the task as well as confidence statements.

The use of multiple demonstrators and coping models has also been shown to influence the effectiveness of demonstrations (Bandura et al., 1982; Lewis, 1974). Bandura (1986) has reasoned that the more different types of people observers see succeeding at a skill, the stronger the convictions will be that they, too, can succeed. Coping models, who initially exhibit difficulty on the task in the same way as learners do but gradually overcome those difficulties, provide the learners with information that this task can be accomplished through perseverance.

The U.S. Olympic Training Center has used observational techniques in a slightly different manner in an attempt to increase an athlete's confidence expectations and performance. In this self-modeling technique, videotapes of an athlete's performance is altered to eliminate the mistakes and then replayed a number of times for the athlete in hopes of altering the athlete's performance beliefs. Research has not yet been provided to determine the effectiveness of this technique with athletes; however, it has been shown to be effective with persons exhibiting deficient speaking skills by editing out the mistakes, hesitancies, and external aids from the videotapes and playing them back to the speakers (Dowrick, 1983).

Persuasion and Positive Communication

Although persuasion and communication techniques alone may be of limited value in enhancing self-confidence beliefs, they may be effective when used in conjunction with performance-based techniques and are provided in a manner contingent to performance. Because it is difficult to evaluate one's own progress in many activities, credible and expert observers can help stretch one's confidence beliefs through effective persuasion techniques. Persuasive information is probably most important during early stages of skill acquisition, when learners lack task experience and knowledge of their capabilities.

As discussed above, to be effective the persuasive information must be believable and, therefore, should be only slightly beyond what the learners can do at that time. For instance, if one is using imagery to try to help convince individuals that they can endure more muscular fatigue, manage potential threats safely, achieve greater athletic feats, or return to performance from injury, the imagery should be structured so that the individuals imagine themselves performing just slightly better than what they think they can do. As with setting goals, the imagery should be challenging but attainable. Mastery experiences should then be arranged to facilitate effective performance.

For individuals who are experienced at a task but are in a performance slump or plateau, false performance feedback (performance deception) has been used successfully to improve performance (Fitzsimmons et al., 1991). As with the other persuasion techniques, it is important that the deception is believable. For instance, if a coach is trying to improve an athlete's maximum press in weight lifting by persuading him to think he is lifting less weight than he is actually pressing, the difference between the two should be small. Instructors should also be aware that continually deceiving one's students may undermine the trust they need to have in order to attempt new skills.

A second category of persuasion techniques involves effective communication from instructor to learner. These strategies include performance feedback, rewards, causal attribution feedback, and positive communication. Performance feedback can provide clear information that learners are making progress toward their goals. As noted above, however, feedback must be given contingently in relation to defined performance standards or goals, and it must be given consistently to all learners so as not to create expectancy effects. If a wide discrepancy continues between performance and goals, short-term subgoals should be constructed to reduce the discrepancy.

Different types of performance feedback should be used, depending on a learner's phase of skill acquisition: progress feedback provides information on an individual's progress without regard to others; normative feedback compares an individual's progress in relation to others. Progress feedback should be used during the early phase of skill acquisition or with persons who are likely to perform more poorly in comparison with others because normative feedback can debilitate learning if used before an individual has developed a resilient sense of self-confidence for the task (Kanfer, 1990b). Normative feedback can be used during later phases of skill acquisition.

As with performance feedback, if rewards are used they must be clearly tied to performance progress in order to influence self-confidence (Schunk, 1983c, 1984a). The combination of performance-contingent rewards with short-term goals appears to enhance self-confidence beliefs better than either technique alone (Schunk, 1984a).

Attributional feedback and positive communication are especially important techniques when mistakes and setbacks occur. Because mistakes and failures are inevitable, the way in which an instructor communicates and interacts with a learner will have an important influence on the learner's self-confidence. Telling learners that their past failures were due to insufficient effort, rather than lack of ability, can help them meet their setbacks with renewed vigor and persistence because lack of effort can be rectified. But encouraging learners to emphasize external factors (e.g., bad luck or task difficulty) as the reason for a setback (as some athletic coaches do) could be a serious mistake if the mistake and attribution occur repeatedly, because the learners may start to perceive that the outcome is out of their control and not take responsibility for their performance.

Another caution in providing attributional feedback is that the difficulty of the task and a learner's actual efforts have to be taken into account. If an instructor tells a learner that her failure on a difficult task, for which she expended a lot of effort, was due to lack of effort, she is apt to interpret the feedback as lack of ability or start to distrust the instructor's feedback. In situations in which learners are expending great effort at difficult tasks and still not succeeding, the instructor needs to help them acknowledge the difficulty of the task and set up modified challenges that can be accomplished.

Positive communication by an instructor has been shown to be very helpful in reducing the negative affect that occurs in failure situations (Smith et al., 1979). Positive communication is performance contingent, but it focuses on positive aspects of performance while acknowledging mistakes, provides instructional feedback, and emphasizes the learning nature of task acquisition (Eden, 1990; Jourden et al., 1991). Most individuals feel discouraged and ashamed when they do not perform well and need the assurance and encouragement of the instructor in regard to their abilities. In response to a learner's mistakes, the instructor should not focus on the error itself, but instead find something positive and constructive to say about improving the performance. Four steps characterize this positive approach to mistakes. First, the learner's distress about the mistake is acknowledged. Second, the learner is complimented by the instructor's finding something about the performance that was correct. The compliment must be about an important and relevant aspect of the task; otherwise, it is likely to be discounted by the learners. Third, the instructor provides instructions on how the learner can improve the mistake. Fourth, the instructor ends with a positive note by encouraging the learner to keep trying. These four steps "sandwich" skill instructions between words of encouragement and praise. A positive communication style allays feelings of embarrassment and promotes a sense of self-confidence.

Anxiety Reduction

Some individuals may interpret increases in their physiological arousal as a fear that they cannot perform a skill successfully. Thus, it is believed that if the arousal of these individuals can be reduced through such techniques as relaxation and biofeedback, fears will decrease and self-confidence will increase. However, as Bandura (1988) argued, it is one's perceived coping confidence that plays a central role in controlling fear arousal: people with low perceived coping confidence tend to focus on the danger and fear cues; those with high levels of coping confidence concentrate on the task at hand (Keinan, 1988).

Helping individuals believe that they can exercise control over potential threats and frightful cognitions is the way to decrease fears and increase self-confidence. One way to help improve coping confidence is to teach individuals coping strategies to use to manage threatening situations, such as positive self-talk. Research has shown that positive self-talk can help individuals manage stressful situations if they believe that the technique will help them cope (Girodo and Wood, 1979). According to Bandura (1986), the persuasion that the technique will help the individual cope more effectively is what instills a sense of personal control, which enhances coping confidence.

Another technique that instructors can use to help improve coping confidence is to try to manipulate the environment to reduce the uncertainties of the situation. For example, sources of uncertainty might include how dangerous the situation is, how well one expects to perform, whether one will be asked to perform, or what one's coworkers, colleagues, or teammates will think. Uncertainty can be reduced by providing information of task requirements, providing assurance to the learner (or performer), and emphasizing realistic, short-term goals that take the attention away from long-range outcomes. Simulation training can also help to reduce uncertainties about stressors. However, simulation training that involves exposure to serious physical threats reduces anxiety only when it is perceived as successful (Keinan, 1988). Individuals who have low coping self-confidence might require some preparatory coping interventions before they are exposed to simulation training that is physically dangerous or threatening.

Self-confidence is a potent predictor of an individual's performance, given the appropriate skills and adequate incentives. The role of an instructor, manager, or coach, therefore, is to develop and sustain a learner's high level of self-confidence by ensuring performance success, using modeling and persuasion techniques, communicating effectively, and reducing anxiety-producing factors. These techniques can be used in combination with each other in various ways, depending on the task and the learner, to enhance self-confidence.

Many of these techniques can also be applied to enhance team confidence. For instance, if a team is having some difficulty achieving a task or solving a problem, the instructor or leader can design a series of progressive activities for the team and help them set short-term team goals that emphasize process variables (e.g., strategy) rather than outcome variables. Teams can also observe other, similar teams that persevere in the face of adversity or that demonstrate successful strategies about how to perform the group task. Self-modeling techniques, in which mistakes are edited out of a performance, can also be used to enhance confidence, although no research to date has explored the effectiveness of this technique with teams.

The communication techniques described can be used with teams as well as individuals. Team confidence can be expected to be enhanced when contingent performance feedback and rewards are provided to the team and when the feedback is positively focused and the causal attribution is appropriate to the difficulty of the task and the team's effort expenditure.

Lastly, as with individual coping confidence in threatening situations, team coping confidence can be enhanced and anxiety reduced by reducing the uncertainties that a team faces. Techniques for reducing uncertainties for teams also include simulation training, observing other teams performing the task, and providing as much information regarding the task as possible.

Four major categories of techniques have been described to enhance self- and team confidence. Evidence for the use of these techniques has come from an extensive and diverse research literature, but there are still a number of areas of research that are needed to better understand self-confidence and to enhance performance.

FUTURE RESEARCH DIRECTIONS

Most of the research and applications on self-confidence have been concerned with the influence of unidimensional confidence information on individual performance. Other areas that deserve attention are how people process multidimensional confidence information; the study of self-confidence over time and in different situations; the relationships among self-confidence, goals and goal orientations; individual differences in self-confidence; and team confidence.

Scant research has been conducted on how people process multidimensional confidence information and the heuristics they use in weighting and integrating these sources of information in forming their confidence judgments (Bandura, 1986). The importance of different types of information may vary across different types of activities and situations. For instance, in some sport and exercise situations, physiological information may be a more pertinent source of confidence information than previous performance. In addition, people may weight sources of information differently in different phases of skill acquisition. In processing multidimensional information, people may also misjudge or ignore relevant information in trying to integrate different information (Bandura, 1986). Results from research on these questions will help to understand how self-confidence expectations gain their predictive power; it will also have implications for the type and amount of confidence information provided to individuals for particular types of activities and situations.

Other motivational variables, such as goal orientations and conceptions of ability as they relate to goal setting and self-confidence, have received little attention in research except for Kanfer (1990a), who has noted that different goal orientations may be called for at different phases of skill acquisition. Research is needed to examine induced differential goal orientations in relation to goal-setting and self-confidence at different phases of skill acquisition and for different kinds of tasks (e.g., complex, physically threatening, mundane). Studying confidence judgments across extended periods of performance and across situations or tasks may be the most informative paradigm for testing the relative contribution of self- or team confidence and other cognitions to performance over time, as well as for testing changes in sources of confidence information.

Besides goal orientation and conceptions of ability, other individual difference variables—such as gender, gender role orientations, and self-focus (see Carver and Scheier, 1981) or action control (Kuhl, 1984)—may play a role in determining self-confidence. For instance, research has generally shown that males view themselves as more confident than females in achievement activities that have been stereotypically linked with males (Campbell and Hackett, 1986; Fennema and Sherman, 1978; Lirgg, 1991). Further research is needed to explore the extent to which individual differences mediate the relationship between confidence judgments and performance.

The resiliency of confidence beliefs may also be an important factor in the relationships between self- or team confidence and performance. Bandura (1986, 1990) has suggested that self-confidence must be resilient in order for one to persist and sustain effort in the face of failure. Ericsson et al. (1993) also allude to this in their discussion of the role of deliberate practice in the acquisition of expert performance. According to Bandura, experience with failures and setbacks is needed to develop this robust sense of self-confidence. Future research might examine how different patterns of success and failure influence the development of a robust sense of confidence. In addition, Bandura (1990) notes that when self-doubt sets in after failure, some individuals recover from their perceived low confidence more quickly than others. Similarly, some teams may be able to regain their sense of confidence after a setback more quickly than other teams. Knowing how and why some individuals and teams are able to regain their sense of confidence more quickly than others would be a valuable source of information for designing interventions that would help confidence recovery. Furthermore, although according to Bandura (1986, 1989), an optimistic sense of self-confidence is advantageous to continued effort and persistence, substantial overestimates of one's competence provide a dangerous basis for action (Baumeister, 1989). Research is needed to determine the optimal distortion necessary to foster the persistence needed for mastering various tasks.

In the area of team confidence, a number of other issues are in need of further investigation, such as sources of team confidence information, the relationship of team confidence to group attributions and other group motivation concepts, and the influence of team leaders on team confidence. Although Bandura (1986) postulated that teams are influenced by the same sources of confidence information as individuals, there may be other sources that are unique to a team. Perhaps social, community, or political support provides important team confidence information. For sports teams, the media may provide a source of team confidence information (although this may also be the case for individual athletes).

Research has also yet to examine the relationship between team confidence and other conceptual and theoretical perspectives of group motivation. For example, relationships between team confidence and team attributions, desire for team success, and social loafing have yet to be studied. Only one study has examined team confidence and team cohesion (Spink, 1990).

Lastly, the influence of team leaders may also provide some insight on team confidence and performance. Bandura (1990) has suggested that a performance slump, especially by a key member of the team or the team leader, could influence the confidence that other members have in the team's ability to be successful.

Similarly, managers' and team leaders' leadership confidence may affect team confidence and performance. Wood and Bandura (1989) found evidence that perceived managerial self-confidence both directly and indirectly influenced organizational performance by the effect it had on people's goal setting and use of analytic strategies. Other research has shown that a high sense of personal confidence enhances strategic thinking and facilitates organizational performance under varying levels of organizational complexity and goal assignments (Wood et al., 1990). It could be argued, therefore, that the confidence a team has in a key member or in its leader may also have an important effect on team effectiveness. In addition to the confidence a team has in its leader, the confidence that a leader has in his or her team may also affect team performance. Some support has been found for this argument (Chase et al., 1993), but further research is required to link antecedents and consequences of such confidence beliefs.

In addition to leadership confidence, different kinds of leaders' behaviors may also influence individual and team confidence for certain tasks and certain team members. Research on leadership behavior has suggested a path-goal theory of leadership: this theory argues that the central function of a leader is to create positive performance expectancies (or self-confidence beliefs) among team members (subordinates) (Evans, 1974; Fulk and Wendler, 1982; House and Mitchell, 1974). Certain leader behaviors (supportive, directive, participative, and achievement oriented) are hypothesized to differentially influence the self-confidence and effort-performance expectancies among team members, depending on the task and its characteristics. For instance, supportive leadership behavior (e.g., concern for welfare of team members) should lead to increased self-confidence among team members for tasks that are stressful, boring, tedious, or dangerous, but not for tasks that are interesting and enjoyable and for which team members are confident in their ability to complete the task. Leadership behaviors that are directive (e.g., giving specific guidance, close supervision), participative (e.g., consulting with team members), and achievement oriented (e.g., setting challenging goals) should increase self-confidence when the task is unstructured and complex, but not when the task is simple, repetitive, or highly structured. Although Yukl (1989) suggests that the theory has yet to be adequately tested, it can provide a framework in which to investigate possible moderating variables of leadership influences on both self-confidence and team confidence.

NOTES

[1]The large number of citations in this chapter to Bandura's work reflects the fact that most of the research on self-efficacy has been done in his laboratory. One advantage of relying on the research of one team of investigators is that the work displays an analytical progression as later studies build on the results obtained from earlier work. Another advantage of Bandura's work is that the approach identifies sources of confidence information that provide a basis for practical ways of enhancing performance, as discussed below. A disadvantage is that this work is based largely on a particular theoretical perspective, which may not be the only framework for studying the relationship between self-confidence and performance.

[2]Autonomic arousal is the physiological arousal that is under the control of the autonomic nervous system (e.g., changes in heart rate, respiration rate, adrenaline in the blood).

[3]Although the subjects in the "inherent aptitude" condition were deceived, they were fully debriefed, told of the difficult nature of the task and assured that it did not indicate "aptitudes."

[4]In clinical psychology, these strategies are referred to as participant modeling or performance desensitization.

9

Altering States of Consciousness

Consciousness can be characterized as a state of mental alertness and awareness. Conscious people experience concurrent, retrospective, or prospective awareness of events in their environment—an awareness that exists even in the absence of their ability to report it to others. Consciousness can also be characterized as the experience of voluntariness. People experience themselves as deliberately focusing attention on one object or idea rather than another and choosing among them to respond to environmental demands or to achieve personal goals—goals of which they are aware.

A person is in an altered state of consciousness to the extent that these monitoring and controlling functions have been modified or distorted (Farthing, 1992; Kihlstrom, 1984). For example, a person may be unaware of current or past events that nonetheless are affecting his or her experience, thought, and action; or a person may represent objects and events in a manner that is radically discordant with objective reality; or a person may be unable to exert ordinary levels of voluntary control over attention and behavior. Yet, in contrast, an individual in an altered state of consciousness may be *more* aware of events than usual or otherwise able to transcend the limits of normal voluntary control. In this respect, altered states of consciousness are relevant to enhancing human performance.

An altered state of consciousness can be defined by four features (Kihlstrom, 1984): (1) operationally, as the product of a particular induction technique; (2) phenomenologically, as an individual's subjective report of altered awareness or voluntary control; (3) observationally, as changes in overt behavior corresponding to a person's self-report; and (4) physiologically, as a particular pattern of changes in somatic functioning. In principle, every altered state of consciousness would be associated with a unique combination of these four attributes. For example, dreaming sleep is induced by going to bed, closing one's eyes, and counting sheep; by subjective reports of a lapse in consciousness or dreaming; by observable behaviors such as closed eyes, prone position, and slow breathing; and by high-frequency, low-amplitude, desynchronized brain waves accompanied by rapid, synchronous eye movements. However, such clear specification of the four features does not characterize most altered states of consciousness.

In some instances, this lack of clear specification reflects the state of current technology and incomplete knowledge from available experimental work. But it is also not clear that the relationship between mind and brain is such that it will ever be possible to specify unique psychophysiological correlates of different states of consciousness. Accordingly, in this chapter, we consider the effects on human performance of a number of conditions that are conventionally defined as altered states of consciousness. Chief among these is hypnosis, a technique that has been widely used in attempts to enhance human performance. We also discuss restricted environmental stimulation and update the committee's previous reviews of sleep learning and meditation (see Druckman and Swets, 1988:Ch.4; Druckman and Bjork, 1991:Ch.7).

HYPNOSIS

Hypnosis is a social interaction in which one person, a hypnotist, offers suggestions to another person, a subject, for experiences involving alterations in perception, memory, and the voluntary control of action. Hypnosis is typically induced by suggestions for relaxation, focused attention, and closing one's eyes. After a subject's eyes have closed, the procedure continues with suggestions for various sorts of imaginative experiences. The range of such experiences is very broad: a hypnotist may ask a subject to extend his arm and suggest that he is holding a very heavy object, whose weight is pressing the hand and arm down; a hypnotist may ask a subject to interlock her fingers and suggest that her hands are glued together so that they cannot be pulled apart; a hypnotist may suggest that there is a voice asking questions over a loudspeaker, to which the subject should reply; a hypnotist may suggest that a subject cannot smell an odorous substance held near his nose; or a hypnotist may suggest that a subject is growing younger and reliving an experience from early childhood. A subject may also be given a posthypnotic suggestion: for example, that after hypnosis, when the hypnotist picks up a pencil, the subject will stand up, stretch, and change chairs—but forget that he had been told to do so. A subject may also receive a suggestion that upon awakening she will be unable to remember the events and experiences that transpired during the hypnotic session;

after the session, she may indeed display a posthypnotic amnesia, but when the hypnotist gives the prearranged cue, she may well execute the suggested behavior. Typically in these situations, the subjects are unaware that they are carrying out a posthypnotic suggestion until the suggestion for amnesia has been canceled by a prearranged cue. These experiences and their accompanying behaviors are often associated with a degree of subjective conviction bordering on delusion and an experience of involuntariness bordering on compulsion.

Hypnosis has a long history, by some accounts extending back to a version of suggestive therapeutics practiced by the ancient Greeks and Romans in the temples of Aesculapius, and the technique of "animal magnetism" promoted by Franz Anton Mesmer in eighteenth-century Vienna and Paris. The term "hypnosis" itself was coined by Braid in 1842-1843; interest in the technique was revived by French neuropsychiatrists, particularly Hippolyte Bernheim, Jean Baptiste Charcot, Pierre Janet, and A. A. Liebeault in the late nineteenth century and brought into academic psychology in the early twentieth century by William James, Morton Prince, and Boris Sidis. Hypnosis then became a salient topic for psychological research, with pioneering programmatic investigations by P. C. Young, Clark L. Hull, and Milton H. Erickson, among others. The modern era of hypnosis research was inaugurated in the 1950s by the systematic work of Martin T. Orne, Ernest R. Hilgard, and Theodore X. Barber.

The most important finding from 100 years of formal research is that there are wide individual differences in response to hypnotic suggestions (Hilgard, 1965). These differences are measured by standardized scales of hypnotizability such as the Stanford Hypnotic Susceptibility Scale, which are constructed as work-samples of hypnotic performance. The distribution of scores on such scales is quasinormal: relatively few subjects score at the very highest levels of the scale, relatively few are entirely refractory to hypnosis and respond to hypnotic suggestions to at least some degree. The available evidence indicates that hypnotizability is a cognitive skill that reaches a peak in the years immediately before adolescence, remains highly stable during most of adulthood, and may decline during middle and old age. There is some controversy over whether hypnotizability can be modified by cognitive-behavioral interventions.

A great deal of research has attempted to isolate correlates of hypnotizability within the larger domain of personality and cognitive assessment, which would permit the confident prediction of hypnotic responsiveness. While hypnotizability is essentially unrelated to conventional personality characteristics, as measured by such well-known instruments as the Minnesota Multiphasic Personality Inventory and the California Psychological Inventory, hypnotizability has been found to be related to individual differences in "hypnosis-like" experiences in the ordinary course of everyday living, in which attention is tightly focused, imagined events become real, or a person loses touch with objective reality. For example, a classic paper by Tellegen and Atkinson (1974) showed that hypnotizability was modestly but significantly related to "absorption," defined as a person's tendency to completely commit his or her cognitive resources to a "unified representation" of attentional objects; or, alternatively, as a person's disposition to enter stages of cognitive restructuring marked by narrowed or expanded attention (for a review, see Roche and McConkey, 1990). Interestingly, scores on Tellegen's absorption scale do not correlate with scores on extraversion or neuroticism, the two major dimensions represented in the usual personality inventories. Thus, it is not surprising that those instruments have not proved useful to measure hypnotizability. But absorption is related to a broader construct of openness to experience, which has been promoted by McCrae and Costa (1985) as one of the five major dimensions of personality—but a dimension that had been largely ignored in earlier psychometric work on individual differences (for a review, see Glisky et al., 1991).

Although we have characterized hypnosis as a social interaction, involving a hypnotist and a subject, it should be understood that in a very real sense all hypnosis is self-hypnosis (L. S. Johnson, 1981; Orne and McConkey, 1981). A hypnotist does not hypnotize a subject: rather, a hypnotist functions somewhat like a coach or tutor, who helps a subject hypnotize him- or herself. A number of investigations have shown that, with only minimal instructions and practice, subjects can successfully learn to induce hypnosis in themselves (Fromm et al., 1981; L. S. Johnson, 1979; L. S. Johnson et al., 1983; L. S. Johnson and Weight, 1976; Ruch, 1975; Shor and Easton, 1973). However, we note that much of what is described as "self-hypnosis" in the clinical and self-help literature is really only suggestions for relaxation, imagery, and reverie. Yet, hypnosis need not involve relaxation— subjects have been successfully hypnotized while engaged in vigorous exercise (Banyai and Hilgard, 1976)—and it goes beyond imagery and reverie to produce subjectively compelling alterations in conscious awareness and control. The rest of this section reviews the use of hypnosis for a wide variety of purposes, including enhancing performance.

Analgesia and Pain Control

To begin, many limitations on performance are caused by physical pain and hypnosis has long been acknowledged as an effective technique for pain control. Hypnosis, in its earlier form of animal magnetism, was used in major surgery as early as 1821; in fact, the reports by Elliotson (1843) and Esdaile (1850, written in 1846) were substantially responsible for the revival, at midcentury, of medical and scientific interest in the phenomenon. The introduction in the late 1840s of chemical anesthetics such as ether and chloroform supplanted these psychological techniques, but they were re-vived in the twentieth century along with general scientific interest in hyp-nosis. The voluminous clinical and experimental literature on hypnosis for pain relief has been summarized by Hilgard and Hilgard (1975, 1983) and others (Chaves, 1989; D'Eon, 1989; Turner and Chapman, 1982; Wadden and Anderton, 1982).

A large number of clinical studies indicate that hypnosis can effectively relieve pain in a substantial proportion of patients that are suffering pain from a wide variety of causes, including burns, cancer, child birth, and dental work. Hypnosis has also been used as the sole analgesic agent in a number of major surgeries, including those for abdominal, breast, cardiac and genitourinary reasons, and for the repair of fractures and dislocations. Although it is likely that fewer than 10 percent of ordinary patients can tolerate major surgery under hypnosis alone, it appears that approximately 50 percent of patients can gain significant pain relief in other procedures and the likelihood of effective analgesia increases in patients who are hyp-notizable. This conclusion is underscored by recent clinical studies of pain secondary to the treatment of cancer. For example, Reeves et al. (1983) obtained significant reduction in pain among hypnotizable, but not insus-ceptible, patients undergoing tumor destruction by hyperthermia (this pain is not usually affected by chemical analgesics). Similarly, Hilgard and LeBaron (1984) found that more than half of a group of hypnotizable chil-dren experienced palpable relief of pain during bone-marrow aspirations for treatment of leukemia; none of the insusceptible children did so.[1]

The comparative effectiveness of hypnotic analgesia was evaluated in a provocative study conducted by Stern and his associates (Stern et al., 1977), who exposed volunteer subjects to both the ischemic pain induced when blood-flow to the forearm is cut off by a tourniquet and the cold-pressor pain induced by immersion of the forearm in cold water (both are excellent laboratory analogues of clinical pain). Pain was treated by a number of agents, including hypnosis, morphine, diazepam, aspirin, and acupuncture, as well as placebos for acupuncture and each of the chemical agents. Hyp-nosis proved to be more effective with both types of pain than any other technique; morphine was the next most effective treatment; acupuncture was the third; valium and aspirin were not more effective than placebos. Hypnotizability was related to the effectiveness of hypnosis, but not that of any of the other treatments.[2] Other studies also indicate that hypnosis is superior to acupuncture (Knox and Shum, 1977; Knox et al., 1978, 1979, 1981). Hypnosis is at least as effective as biofeedback in the treatment of chronic pain, and it requires less equipment (Elton et al., 1980).

Although research clearly documents the effectiveness of hypnotic anal-gesia, its mechanisms are still subject to debate. Pain is often analyzed in two components: sensory pain, which informs a person of the location and extent of insult, injury, or disease; and suffering, which has to do with the meaning of pain to the person experiencing it. In hypnotizable subjects, at least, hypnosis has equivalent effects on both sensory pain and suffering (Knox et al., 1974); and the analgesic effects of pain as not mediated by the sedative effects of hypnosis-induced relaxation (Greene and Reyher, 1972; Hilgard et al., 1974). Moreover, a clever study showed that hypnotic analgesia is not merely a placebo effect (McGlashan et al., 1969). In this study, insusceptible subjects were convinced through a surreptitious manipulation during a pretest involving painful electric shock that they could respond positively to suggestions for hypnotic analgesia. These subjects did show some reduction in ischemic pain when given hypnotic suggestions for analgesia but the extent of the reduction was no greater than achieved by a placebo for people who thought they were getting Darvon (a chemical painkiller). The hypnotizable subjects showed much greater reductions in pain, both compared with the insusceptible subjects and with their own performance with a placebo. All active agents have a placebo component, and hypnosis is no exception: apparently, insusceptible subjects can derive some measure of pain relief from the placebo component in hypnotic analgesia; but for hypnotizable subjects, the benefits of hypnosis far outweigh those of placebo.

Although it has been speculated that endogenous opiates (endorphins) play a role in hypnotic analgesia, research does not support this view. For example, narcotic antagonists such as naloxone do not block hypnotic analgesia (J. Barber and Mayer, 1977; Goldstein and Hilgard, 1975; Spiegel and Albert, 1983). Nor are there any changes in blood concentrations of endorphins during hypnotic analgesia (De Benedittis et al., 1989; Domangue et al., 1985; Guerra et al., 1985; Olness et al., 1980).[3]

The endorphin results suggest that the most appropriate explanation for hypnotic analgesia is to be found at the psychological, rather than the biological, level of analysis. There are two competing explanations for a psychological effect. According to Hilgard (1977, 1986), highly hypnotizable subjects reduce their awareness of pain through dissociation—by erecting an amnesia-like barrier that diminishes their awareness of the pain. The pain is still registered, as indicated by physiological responses to the stimulus, but the pain is not consciously felt or is, at least, substantially reduced. In contrast, Spanos (1989) and Chaves (1989) argue that hypnotic analgesia is mediated by self-distraction, stress-inoculation, reinterpretation, and other tension-management techniques. Their research indicates that successful response to hypnotic suggestions is often accompanied by the deliberate use of cognitive strategies, such as distraction or pleasant imagery. One dimension of coping appears to be related to individual differences in pain perception in both hypnosis and the normal waking state.

There is little doubt that cognitive strategies can reduce pain (Turk et al., 1983), and they may be of considerable value for subjects who are insusceptible to hypnosis. But recent research support the view that analgesia in highly hypnotizable individuals may be achieved by means of a dissociative mechanism. In an important study by Miller and Bowers (1986), individuals classified as low or high in hypnotizability were subjected to cold-pressor pain under one of three conditions: stress inoculation, in which subjects were instructed to use certain cognitive strategies to cope with pain (self-distraction, imaginative transformation of the stimulus, fantasies incongruent with the pain experience, avoidance of "catastrophizing"); hypnotic suggestions for analgesia; and stress-inoculation instructions masquerading as hypnotic suggestions. The results, based on reports of both pain intensity and subjective distress, were clear: all three conditions produced significant amounts of pain relief in comparison with no-treatment baselines. However, the success of stress inoculation, regardless of whether it was defined as hypnosis, was not correlated with hypnotizability, while the success of hypnotic analgesia was strongly associated with hypnotizability. Moreover, while 92 percent of the subjects in the stress inoculation conditions reported using cognitive strategies to control pain (as they were instructed), such reports were made by only 17 percent of subjects in the hypnotic analgesia condition. The fact that coping can be taught leaves open the possibility for successful cognitive control of pain even in subjects who are insusceptible to hypnosis.

The more important finding is that hypnotic analgesia is mediated by processes other than the usual cognitive control strategies and seem to involve some dissociation of the experience of pain from conscious awareness. Hypnotic analgesia was superior to stress inoculation for hypnotizable subjects, but not for their insusceptible counterparts. A later study by these same investigators (Miller and Bowers, 1993; see also Bowers and Davidson, 1992; Spanos and Katsanis, 1989) found that stress inoculation techniques, as practiced by both hypnotizable and insusceptible subjects, distracted subjects from performance on a simultaneous cognitive task; however, such interference did not occur in the hypnosis condition, especially among the high hypnotizables. Thus, while stress inoculation does appear to be effective in reducing pain, it does not seem to be involved in the hypnotic analgesia experienced by hypnotizable subjects.

In order to reduce the debilitating effects of pain and fatigue on performance, it seems reasonable to teach cognitive strategies such as self-distraction and stress inoculation, which can effectively reduce pain in a wide segment of the population. However, these strategies can also have detrimental effects on ongoing task performance by using cognitive resources. Hypnotic analgesia might be more effective than stress inoculation, but even if it is not, it appears to produce its effects in a manner that does not interfere with other ongoing tasks. Accordingly, individuals who have at least a moderate capacity for hypnosis (and especially those who are highly hypnotizable) might also be taught to reduce pain through self-hypnosis. Even if hypnotic suggestion does not enhance human performance per se, hypnotic analgesia appears to offer some promise for regulating pain and, thus, indirectly enhancing performance in those individuals who have a capacity for hypnosis.

Strength and Endurance

Almost from the beginning of the modern period of research, there have been claims that hypnotized individuals are able to transcend their normal nonhypnotized capacities, showing dramatic improvements in muscle strength, sensory acuity, intelligence, and even clairvoyance. Hypnosis is also frequently used by professional and amateur athletes in both team and individual sports (for reviews, see W. R. Johnson, 1961; Morgan, 1980). However, these claims for hypnotic enhancement of human performance have rarely been subjected to empirical verification.

The history of empirical studies goes back to the nineteenth century revival of hypnosis in France. Rieger (1884) reported an "immensely increased capacity to resist gravity and fatigue" in an experiment in which the task was to hold one's arm in a horizontal position for an indefinite period of time. Similarly, Charcot (1889) reported that a hypnotized subject placed in such a position showed "excellent performance," with no tremor and normal rates of respiration. This was consistent with Charcot's contention that catalepsy was, along with lethargy and somnambulism, one of three stages of hypnotic depth. But Hull (1932:229) remarked that "it would be difficult to imagine a more thoroughly bad experiment" than Charcot's. In a careful experiment performed in Hull's own laboratory, Williams (1930) asked seated subjects to hold their arms in a horizontal position and measured both deviations from horizontal and amount of tremor with a recording device attached to the wrist by a thread. He found no significant differences between hypnosis and a control condition. With respect to resistance to fatigue, Nicholson (1920) carried out an experiment using a Mosso ergograph, in which subjects were required to flex their index fingers in order to pull a three-kilogram weight. Measuring the amount of work performed over a 10-minute period, he obtained a large difference between hypnosis and control conditions and concluded that in hypnosis "the capacity for work seemed endless." However, a careful repetition of the experiment by Williams (1929), in which hypnotized subjects received suggestions both for resistance to fatigue and anesthesia to pain, showed only a very small difference between the hypnosis and control conditions.

Concerning grip strength, Hadfield (1924) reported dramatic improvements in performance with a hand dynamometer, but Young (1925, 1926) reported no differences between conditions at any level of hypnotizability.

Over subsequent decades, continuing research on strength and endurance produced a similar mix of positive (Manzer, 1934; Wells, 1947) and negative (e.g., Eysenck, 1941; W. R. Johnson and Kramer, 1960, 1961; W. R. Johnson et al., 1960) results; to further complicate the picture, some investigators, such as Roush, reported positive results with some tests and negative results with others (Mead and Roush, 1949; Roush, 1951).

These earliest studies of the hypnotic enhancement of muscular performance present a number of difficult conceptual and methodological problems. For example, hypnosis, as defined at the outset, is an essentially subjective experience: a subject experiences the world as different from what it is objectively. Put another way, an important aspect of hypnosis is the fact that the imagined state of affairs is not the same as the objective state of affairs. Thus, it is not at all clear that subjects who have received suggestions that they are stronger (for example), should actually grow stronger—any more than that subjects who receive suggestions for age regression should grow smaller in the chair. Yet there is enough research on the "self-fulfilling prophecy" to lend credence to the idea that a person's belief that he or she is stronger might actually lead to enhanced performance on tasks of strength and endurance—although there is no basis for believing (nor any research) that any observed increase will reach superhuman levels.

Modern consideration of this early literature and modern research have suggested some standards for acceptable research. From a psychometric point of view, for example, any specific effect of hypnosis should be correlated with hypnotizability. If ostensibly hypnotic effects are independent of hypnotizability, they may reflect nothing more than expectancies associated with the hypnotic setting or procedures or the efforts of highly motivated individuals to try harder under hypnotic conditions. Expectational and motivational effects are not uninteresting, but the general view is that hypnosis adds something special to them: this extra factor should be correlated with hypnotizability. However, expectations and motivations concerning hypnosis might well be higher in hypnotizable subjects than in those who are insusceptible to hypnosis.

Consider, for example, a study by Orne (1959), in which subjects were asked to hold a 1-kilogram weight at arm's length for as long as possible. The subjects were tested first in hypnosis and then in the normal waking state. Before the nonhypnotic test, however, they were informed (incorrectly) that other subjects had been able to perform even better than they and were paid a bonus for achieving that level. All of the subjects were able to surpass their hypnotic performance when appropriately motivated in the normal waking state. Orne (1965, 1966) concluded that, at least in the context of performance enhancement, hypnosis was only "one of many motivational techniques which will induce an individual to exert himself more than usual" (1965:291-292).

This possibility has led to the development of a number of experimental designs for studying the effects of hypnosis on performance while taking account of the effects of positive expectations and motivations. In the 1960s, for example, T. X. Barber (1969) introduced the task-motivation design, in which hypnotized subjects are compared to controls who have been exhorted to give maximal performance in the normal waking state. The "task-motivation" instructions employed by T. X. Barber (1969:46) were phrased as follows:

> You did not do as well as you really could. Some people think it is difficult to do this task, and therefore do not really try hard. However, everyone is able to do this if they really try. I myself can do it quite easily, and all the previous subjects that participated in this experiment were able to do it when they realized it was an easy thing to do. I want you to score as high as you can because we're trying to measure the maximum ability of people. If you don't try to the best of your ability, this experiment will be worthless and I'll tend to feel silly. On the other hand, if you try to imagine to the best of your ability, you can easily imagine and do all the interesting things I tell you and you will be helping the experiment and not wasting any time.

The general finding of Barber's research was that the performance of task-motivated subjects equalled that of hypnotic subjects. For example, T. X. Barber and Calverley (1964b) took baseline measures of grip strength and weight-holding endurance in a group of subjects and then repeated the tests in hypnotic and task-motivation conditions. There were no effects of either hypnosis or task-motivation on strength of grip. Hypnosis increased endurance, but only when accompanied by task motivation instructions and nonhypnotic task motivation produced even greater increases. Similarly, Levitt and Brady (1964), in a study of highly hypnotizable subjects, found no difference between hypnosis and task motivation. Barber's research has often been criticized for failing to take account of individual differences in hypnotizability, leaving open the possibility that his design obscured performance improvements that occurred among especially hypnotizable subjects. That is, genuine performance enhancements observed in the relatively small number of highly hypnotizable subjects may have been swamped by the lack of enhancement observed in the relatively large number of subjects of low and moderate hypnotizability. Nevertheless, the very fact that unselected task-motivated subjects showed levels of performance better than those of unselected hypnotic subjects underscores the problem of controlling for motivation, in comparison with hypnosis per se.

In his analysis of the performance effects of hypnosis, Orne has underscored the "demand characteristics" inherent in most hypnosis research, by which an experimenter communicates an expectation that performance will be improved in hypnosis, leading to apparent gains that in fact are artifactual (Orne, 1959, 1962). For example, when the same subjects are tested in both hypnotic and nonhypnotic conditions, it may be clear to them that hypnosis is of interest, leading them to hold back on their nonhypnotic performance (Evans and Orne, 1965). Counterbalancing the order of testing, which controls for the effects of fatigue, does not eliminate this possibility. The only solution is to get a baseline that is truly independent of hypnosis, a feature that is rare in this body of research.

In another approach, Slotnick and London (1965) attempted to cope with the problem that the mythology of hypnosis leads most people to expect that hypnosis will improve their performance—even more so to the extent that they are hypnotizable (see also London and Fuhrer, 1961). That is, differences in responses to hypnotic suggestions may be an artifact of differences in expectations related to self-perceptions of hypnotizability. They invented a way of convincing insusceptible subjects that they were, in fact, hypnotizable (Slotnick and London, 1965:40).

> Most people wonder just how well they have been responding to the suggestions that are given . . . . The fact is that your performance earlier indicated clearly, in some of its significant details, that you would be an excellent subject for the purposes of the experiment we are doing now. Because you *are* a good subject, we want you to participate in the hypnotic phase of this experiment.

Somewhat surprisingly, under these conditions insusceptible subjects showed greater improvements following hypnotic suggestion than hypnotizable subjects. London and Fuhrer (1961) found the highest scores for both dynamometer strength and weight endurance among insusceptible subjects given exhortations for enhanced performance, regardless of whether these exhortations were delivered in hypnosis. Other investigations confirmed the basic finding that hypnosis did not improve performance over appropriately motivated nonhypnotic conditions (Evans and Orne, 1965; Rosenhan and London, 1963; Slotnick and London, 1965), indicating that "hypnosis, as such, adds nothing magical to performance" (London and Fuhrer, 1961:332). Publication of these experiments essentially ended this line of research.

Nevertheless, a follow-up experiment by Slotnick et al., (1965), which has been largely ignored, offers some reasons for reopening this research. In this experiment, highly hypnotizable subjects were asked to lift a 2.5-kilogram weight and hold it at shoulder height. In one condition, the subjects were given exhortations for maximal performance, similar to those used by London and Fuhrer. In the other condition, they were given the same exhortation followed by "involving" instructions, in which the subjects were asked to imagine themselves becoming "stronger and more capable." Among these hypnotizable subjects, performance was significantly greater with the involving instructions than exhortation of the sort used by previous investigators.

Although the Slotnick et al. (1965) experiment needs to be repeated in a full version of the London-Fuhrer design, it suggests that significant improvements can be obtained by treatments that capitalize on the ability of hypnosis to alter perception, especially self-perception, in hypnotizable people. That is, the key to hypnotic enhancement of human performance may lie not in the ability of hypnotic suggestions to passively augment performance, but rather in the interaction of involving suggestions to interact with the capacity for absorption and imagining characteristics of hypnotizable individuals. In the absence of a definitive study, however, the conclusion about the hypnotic enhancement of muscular performance must be negative: hypnotized subjects, even those who are highly hypnotizable, do not appear to be capable of exceeding the performance of highly motivated unhypnotized subjects. And even if the Slotnick et al. findings were to be confirmed, the conclusion would be that hypnosis improves performance to the extent that it increases the subject's involvement in the task at hand.

Learning

A history similar to that for strength and endurance can be given for studies of the effects of hypnosis on learning capacity. This line of research received some impetus from the reports of many nineteenth-century authorities that mesmerized or hypnotized subjects gave evidence of transcending of normal capacity: changes ranging from increases in verbal fluency and physical strength to clairvoyance. Nevertheless, an early study by Gray (1934) answered the question only weakly in the affirmative: a small group of poor spellers improved their spelling ability somewhat when the learning occurred in hypnosis. Similarly, Sears (1955) reported that subjects who learned Morse code in hypnosis made fewer errors than those whose learning took place under nonhypnotic conditions.

More dramatic results were reported in a series of studies by Cooper and his associates, using hypnotic time distortion and hallucinated practice. Subjects were asked to hallucinate engaging in some activity, and at its conclusion were given suggestions that a long interval had passed (e.g., 30 minutes) when the actual elapsed time had been considerably shorter (e.g., 10 seconds). The idea was that this expansion of subjective time would effectively increase the amount of study, or practice, that could be performed per unit of objective time. Cooper and Erickson (1950, 1954) reported, for example, that hallucinated practice led to marked improvement in a subject's ability to play the violin. A more systematic study by Cooper and Rodgin (1952), concerned with the learning of nonsense syllables, also had positive results. Unfortunately, there were no statistical tests of the differences between treatment conditions. Even so, the effects of hypnotic time distortion and hallucinated practice were seen only on the immediate test: the superiority of hypnosis virtually disappeared at retest, 24 hours later. Another study, by Cooper and Tuthill (1952), found no objective improvements in handwriting with hallucinated practice in time distortion, even though the subjects generally perceived themselves as having improved. More recent experiments also yielded negative results (T. X. Barber and Calverley, 1964a; Edmonston and Erbeck, 1967).

In contrast, Krauss et al. (1974) reported positive findings in a study of verbal learning in which hypnotized subjects were allotted 3 minutes to study a list of words, but were told they had studied it for 10 minutes. Unfortunately, R. F. Q. Johnson (1976) and Wagstaff and Ovenden (1979) failed to replicate those results: in fact, their subjects did worse under time distortion than in control conditions. In the most comprehensive study to date, St. Jean (1980) repeated the essential features of the Krauss et al. design, paying careful attention to details of subject selection and the wording of the suggestion. Although highly hypnotizable subjects reported that they experienced distortions of the passage of time, as suggested, there were no effects on learning.

The combination of time distortion and hallucinated practice is ingenious, but of course it makes some assumptions that are not necessarily valid. First, can mental practice substitute for actual physical practice? There is in fact considerable evidence for this proposition (Feltz and Landers, 1983), and since hypnotic hallucinations are closely related to mental images, there is no reason to think that hallucinated practice might not also be effective. But time distortion is another matter: the assumption is that the hallucination of something is the same as the thing itself, and there is no reason or evidence for this assumption. In fact, such an assumption flies in the face of a wealth of research on hypnotic hallucinations, which shows that they are inadequate substitutes for the actual stimulus state of affairs (Sutcliffe, 1960, 1961; Kihlstrom and Hoyt, 1988). Thus, while hypnosis, and hypnotic suggestion, can produce distortions in time perception just as they can produce other distortions in subjective experience, these distortions do not necessarily have consequences for learning and memory (St. Jean, 1989).

A rather different approach to the question has been taken by investigators who have offered subjects direct suggestions for improved learning, without reference to time distortion or hallucinated practice (e.g., Fowler, 1961; Parker and Barber, 1964). Unfortunately, interpretation of such studies is difficult because of the same methodological problems encountered in the studies of muscular strength and endurance. For example, the induction of hypnosis might merely increase the motivation of subjects to engage in the experimental task, independent of any effects of hypnosis per se. Moreover, subjects may respond to the demand characteristics of such an experiment by holding back on their performance during baseline tests and other nonhypnotic conditions, which would result in an illusory improvement under hypnosis. As in the studies of strength and endurance, some of the problems have been addressed by studies using the paradigm invented by London and Fuhrer (1961), in which hypnotizable subjects are compared with objectively insusceptible subjects who have been persuaded that they are responsive to hypnosis.

As noted above, studies of muscular performance using the unadorned London-Fuhrer design have generally found that when subjects are given hypnotic exhortations for enhancement, hypnotizable subjects and insusceptible subjects who believe that they are hypnotizable perform the same. Measures of rote learning show similar results (Evans and Orne, 1965; London et al., 1966; Rosenhan and London, 1963; Schulman and London, 1963). Thus, the available evidence suggests that hypnotic suggestions do not enhance the learning process. However, most of these studies have used a hypnotic induction based on suggestions for relaxation and sleep, which might interfere with both motor performance and learning. Relaxation is not necessary for hypnosis, however (Banyai and Hilgard, 1976), and it remains possible that different results would be obtained if the suggestions were for an active, alert form of hypnosis. Moreover, suggestions that capitalize on a hypnotized subject's capacity for imaginative involvement may prove to be better than mere exhortations (Slotnick et al., 1965). In sum, the question of the possibility of hypnotic enhancement of learning and performance is not closed.

Sensory Acuity and Perceptual Accuracy

Exactly the same considerations apply to studies of the effects of hypnosis on sensory-perceptual acuity (for example, word-recognition thresholds) that apply to learning. In response to suggestions, subjects may very well experience themselves as seeing and hearing objects more clearly and easily—in the absence of any objective change in sensory acuity. The question is whether these changes in subjective experience reflect actual changes in objective performance in tasks involving sensory detection and discrimination, that is, whether a true hyperesthesia can be induced by means of hypnosis. Early authorities, such as Braid (1843) and Bramwell (1903), concluded that this was possible: Bergson (1886) even reported that a hypnotized boy could read, out of the cornea of a man standing in front of him, the letters on a page that the man was holding behind the boy's head.

Beside such dramatic claims, the results of formal research have been much less positive. Again, the earliest investigator in this area was Young (1925), who investigated changes in tactile pressure sensitivity: despite suggestions for heightened sensitivity and the belief of the subjects that they were responding positively to the suggestions, tactile thresholds were actually higher in hypnosis. In a follow-up study, Young (1926) found no effect of hypnosis on the ability to detect subtle differences among postage stamps. Sterling and Miller (1940) likewise failed to find differences in figure-recognition and visual and auditory detection attributable to hypnosis.

Zamansky and his associates revived interest in the question and developed special procedures to evaluate order effects driven by expectancies generated by the comparison of hypnotic and nonhypnotic conditions. In their first study (Scharf and Zamansky, 1963), these investigators obtained a significant reduction in sensory thresholds for subjects who received hypnotic suggestions and a smaller reduction for subjects who received waking suggestions. Detailed analysis (and postexperimental interviews) led these investigators to speculate that the subjects, expecting to be hypnotized on subsequent trials, may have artificially elevated their thresholds on baseline tests. To test this possibility, they replicated tests but did not inform the subjects about the hypnotic test until after the baseline test had been completed. Under these circumstances, baseline thresholds were high in both hypnotic and control conditions: postexperimental interviews indicated that subjects expected to be hypnotized in both conditions (because they could not distinguish between hypnotic and control baselines) and elevated their pretest thresholds accordingly. A later study, with even more careful manipulation of subjects' expectations, showed that baseline thresholds were higher when subjects expected to be subsequently hypnotized (Zamansky et al., 1964).

The Zamansky-Scharf studies underscore the difficulty in performing valid comparisons between hypnotic and nonhypnotic conditions: subjects are capable of modulating their nonhypnotic performance in such a way as to leave considerable room for improvement in hypnosis. This possibility cannot be controlled by conventional counterbalancing; it can only be eliminated by the very difficult strategy of keeping subjects ignorant of the hypnotic tests until baseline testing has been completed. Obviously, holding back on nonhypnotic baselines is a possibility in the studies of strength, endurance, and learning reviewed above. The fact that the nonhypnotic tests may have been unrepresentative of subjects' true nonhypnotic capacity only accentuates the need for caution in interpreting the few positive results obtained in those studies.

This is an area that cries out for application of modern signal-detection theory (Green and Swets, 1966; Pastore and Scheirer, 1974) because of the distinction that approach makes between actual sensitivity and decision criterion. Studies using classical psychophysical techniques for threshold-determination are not able to discriminate between changes in sensitivity and changes in response criterion. Consider, for example, subjects in Young's (1925) study, who are asked to indicate whether they have been touched by one of two stimuli, strong or weak. Increased sensitivity is indicated by an increase in detection of the weak stimulus. But subjects who wished to appear highly sensitive could simply indicate that they felt the stimulus on each trial. Such subjects would show a high rate of "hits," appearing to detect the stimulus each time it was presented; however, they would also show a high rate of "false alarms," indicating that they felt the stimulus even on "catch trials" when it had not in fact been applied. Signal-detection theory takes account of both hits and false alarms and produces a estimate of a subject's sensitivity that is uninfluenced by the subject's response criterion.

In one portion of a larger experiment focusing on hypnotic deafness (which, as an ostensible impairment of human performance, is beyond the scope of this volume), Jones and Spanos (1982) gave subjects suggestions for increased auditory acuity. Hypnotizable subjects did show a slight, nonsignificant increase in sensitivity under these conditions, but they also showed significantly lower levels of sensitivity in a baseline condition— thus suggesting, as in the work of Zamansky and Scharf, that they were holding back in the control test. There was also a change in response bias, with hypnotizable (but not insusceptible) subjects showing an increased bias toward reporting that the signal was present, even when it was not. Although these results are not clear-cut—for example, response criterion did not show a comparable shift in the other direction when hypnotizable subjects were given suggestions for *decreased sensitivity*—they do underscore the problem of response bias in tests of the hypnotic enhancement of performance.

Although hypnosis does not appear to enhance the performance of people whose sensory and perceptual abilities are intact, it may have positive effects on those whose capacities are impaired. In a provocative paper, Graham and Liebowitz (1972) examined the effects of hypnotic suggestion on visual acuity in myopes—that is, people who suffer an impairment in distance vision. The task was to determine the orientation of the break in a series of 19 rows of "Landolt Cs": from the top row to the bottom, the size of the break in the letter "C" progressively diminished. After threshold determination, subjects were hypnotized and given suggestions to relax their eye muscles in order to permit clearer vision; they were also given the same suggestions posthypnotically. Over a period of 3 weeks, the subjects' visual acuity increased, both in and out of hypnosis, as confirmed by independent optometric examination; the extent of improvement was greater than that observed in nonhypnotized controls. A follow-up study showed that the improvements were only observed in highly hypnotizable subjects: measurements with a laser scintillation technique indicated that the improvements were not a function of accommodation or other structural changes in the eyes.

A conceptual replication of this experiment was reported by E.P. Sheehan et al. (1982), who improved on the methodology by carefully matching hypnosis and control subjects for hypnotizability and degree of myopia; they also supplemented the conventional threshold assessments with signal-detection procedures in which the subjects had to distinguish between open and closed lines, the gaps in which were equivalent to those of the "Landolt Cs" used by Graham and Liebowitz (1972). The hypnotic subjects showed a significant improvement on the signal-detection measure of accuracy, but no change in response bias, in comparison with the waking controls. However, there was no correlation between improvement and hypnotizability. Although Wagstaff (1983) questioned their statistical analysis, Smith et al. (1983) were able to defend their procedures. In addition, a secondary analysis by Tataryn (1992) showed that the improvement in acuity corresponded to a fairly substantial experimental effect.

Time Perception

A rather large research literature exists on hypnosis and the perception of time.[4] In the nineteenth century, many investigators claimed that hypnotized subjects were extraordinarily accurate in time perception. For example, Bramwell (1903) gave suggestions to a subject that she should perform some act after a specified interval (in one instance, 4,453 minutes—or 3 days, 2 hours, and 13 minutes) and found that she was accurate (within 5 minutes) on the vast majority of trials—a feat that Bramwell considered to be beyond the capacity of normal subjects. Unfortunately, Bramwell neglected to make the same request of unhypnotized controls, and it is not at all clear that individuals of normal intelligence are incapable of carrying out the elementary arithmetic operations involved. In any event, these early claims have not been upheld by more formal experiments.

Some experiments in this area involve intentional, prospective procedures in which subjects are instructed to perform some response after the passage of a specified interval of time. In one such experiment, Stalnaker and Richardson (1930) found no differences between hypnotic and control intervals in the estimation of intervals of one to three minutes. Sterling and Miller (1940) also found no effect, but Eysenck (1941) reported greater accuracy in hypnosis (for a review of the early literature, see Loomis, 1951). More recently, Tebecis and Provins (1974) found that the prospective estimations of hypnotizable subjects were no more accurate in hypnosis than in the normal waking state. Overall, the experimental literature, which is somewhat sparse, has yielded a mix of results that tend to support negative conclusions (for a recent review, see St. Jean, 1989)—although none of these modern investigations concerned extremely long time intervals of the sort studied by the early researchers.

Another procedure, more recently introduced, involves incidental, retrospective time estimation: without any warning, subjects are asked to estimate how much time has passed since an event specified by the experimenter. With this approach, Schwartz (1978, 1980) and Bowers (1979; Bowers and Brenneman, 1979) found a general tendency of subjects to retrospectively underestimate the length of time that they had been hypnotized, but this tendency was independent of hypnotizability. A series of studies by St. Jean (St. Jean and MacLeod, 1983; St. Jean and Robertson, 1986; St. Jean et al., 1982) confirmed this general finding, which appears to be unrelated to hypnosis per se, but rather to the fact that hypnotic subjects are engaged in demanding, interesting tasks.

Of course, time is not a sensory modality like vision or audition. Although the passage of time can be measured objectively, there is no proximal stimulus for time, and no receptor organs that can extract information about the duration of the interval between two events. Ultimately, time perception is a matter of judgment and inference, and its underlying mechanisms remain largely unknown (Doob, 1971; Fraisse, 1984; Gibbon and Allan, 1984; Ornstein, 1969).

Memory

In recent years there has emerged a considerable literature on the use of hypnosis to enhance memory for knowledge acquired outside hypnosis—what is known as hypnotic hypermnesia (vivid recall). The most prominent question investigated is whether hypnotic suggestion can enhance the memories of witnesses and victims of crime, but essentially the same question can be asked about the prospects for improving memory "bandwidth" in other applied situations. (For a complete review, see Kihlstrom and Barnhardt, 1993, on which this section is based.)

Laboratory studies of hypnotic hypermnesia have a history that extends back to the beginnings of the modern period of hypnosis research (for recent reviews, see Erdelyi, 1988; Kihlstrom and Barnhardt, 1993; Smith, 1983). For example, Young (1925, 1926) taught his subjects lists of nonsense syllables in the normal waking state and then tested recall in and out of hypnosis, each time motivating subjects for maximal recall. There was no advantage of hypnosis over the waking test. Later experiments with nonsense syllables also failed to find any effect of hypnosis, although studies that used meaningful linguistic or pictorial material have sometimes shown hypermnesia effects. For example, Stalnaker and Riddle (1932) tested college students on their recollections for prose passages and verse that had been committed to memory at least 1 year previously and found that hypnotic suggestions for hypermnesia produced a significant enhancement over waking recall. Although this kind of laboratory evidence suggests support for the use of hypnosis to enhance memory, the effects achieved in the laboratory (though sometimes statistically significant) are rarely dramatic. Moreover, it is fairly clear that any gains obtained during hypnosis are not attributable to hypnosis per se, but rather to hypermnesia effects of the sort that occur in the normal waking state. At least four investigations (Nogrady et al., 1985; Register and Kihlstrom, 1987, 1988; Whitehouse et al., 1991) found significant increments in memory for pictures or words in trials conducted during hypnosis but these increments were matched or exceeded by gains made by control subjects tested without hypnosis.

Most important, it seems clear that increases in valid memory (or "hit rate") may be accompanied by an equivalent or greater increase in confabulations and false recollections ("false alarms"). In an experiment by Stalnaker and Riddle (1932), for example, hypnosis produced a substantial increase in confabulation over the normal waking state, so that overall memory accuracy was very poor. The hypnotized subjects were apparently more willing to attempt recall and to accept their "memories"— however erroneous they proved to be. These conclusions are supported by more recent experiments by Dywan (1988; Dywan and Bowers, 1983) and Nogrady et al. (1985), who found that hypnotic suggestions for hypermnesia produced more false recollections by hypnotizable than insusceptible subjects. Whitehouse et al. (1991) found that hypnosis increased subjects' confidence of memory reports that had been characterized as mere guesses on a prehypnotic test. Dywan and Bowers (1983) have suggested that hypnosis impairs the process of reality monitoring, so that hypnotized subjects are more likely to confuse imagination with perception (M. K. Johnson and Raye, 1981).

Proponents of forensic hypnosis often discount these sorts of findings on the ground that they are obtained in sterile, laboratory investigations that bear little resemblance to the real-world circumstances in which hypnosis is actually used; but the evidence supporting this assertion is quite weak. Reiser (1976), a police department psychologist who has trained many investigators in hypnosis, claimed that the vast majority of investigators who tried hypnosis found it to be helpful, but such testimonials cannot substitute for actual evidence. In fact, a study by Timm (1981), in which police officers themselves were witnesses to a mock crime (after having been relieved of their firearms through a ruse!), found no advantage for hypnosis. A later study by Geiselman et al. (1985), using very lifelike police training films as stimuli and actual police officers as investigators, found that the benefits of hypnosis were matched by unhypnotized subjects led through a "cognitive interview" capitalizing on various cognitive strategies. In sum, the available evidence does not indicate that hypnosis has any privileged status as a technique for enhancing memory.

In evaluating the effects of hypnosis on the recovery of forgotten memories, it is important to remember that hypnosis entails enhanced responsiveness to suggestion. Therefore, if memory is tainted by leading questions and other suggestive influences, as Loftus's (1975) work suggests, these elements may be even more likely to be incorporated into memories that have been refreshed by hypnosis. Putnam (1979) exposed subjects to a variant of Loftus's paradigm, in which subjects viewed a videotape of a traffic accident followed by an interrogation that included leading questions. Those subjects who were interviewed while they were hypnotized were more likely to incorporate the misleading postevent information into their memory reports (see also Sanders and Simmons, 1983; Zelig and Beidelman, 1981). Register and Kihlstrom (1987), using a variant of Loftus's procedure introduced by Gudjonsson (1984), failed to find that hypnosis increased interrogative suggestibility, but did find that errors introduced during the hypnotic test did carry over to subsequent nonhypnotic tests. An extensive and complex series of studies by Sheehan and his colleagues (reviewed by P. W. Sheehan, 1988a, 1988b) found that subjects tested during hypnosis were more confident in their memory reports than were those tested in the normal waking state—regardless of the accuracy of the reports.

The situation is worsened when the suggestions are more explicit, as in the case of hypnotically suggested paramnesias—a confusion of fact and fantasy (for a recent review, see Kihlstrom and Hoyt, 1990). Laurence and Perry (1983) suggested to a group of hypnotized subjects that on a particular night they had awakened to a noise. After hypnosis, a majority of subjects remembered the suggested event as if it had actually occurred; almost half of the subjects maintained this belief even when told that the event had been suggested to them by the hypnotist. Similar results have been obtained by a number of investigators, although the precise conditions under which the pseudomemory effect can be obtained remain obscure. Equally important, it remains unclear whether the pseudomemories reflect actual changes in stored memory traces or biases in memory reporting—an issue that also has been raised in the postevent misinformation effect observed outside hypnosis (e.g., McCloskey and Zaragoza, 1985; Metcalfe, 1990; Loftus et al., 1985; Tversky and Tuchin, 1989).

Direct suggestions for hypermnesia are often accompanied by suggestions for age regression: that the subject reverts to an earlier period in his or her own life, relive an event, and act in a manner characteristic of that age (for recent reviews, see Kihlstrom and Barnhardt, 1993; Nash, 1987).[5] With respect to the reinstatement of childlike modes of mental functioning, As (1962) found a college student who had spoken a Finnish-Swedish dialect until age 8, but who no longer remembered the language; his knowledge of the language improved somewhat under hypnotic age regression. More dramatic findings were obtained by Fromm (1970) in a *nisei* student who denied any knowledge of Japanese; when age regressed, she broke into fluent, childish Japanese.

In contrast, experimental studies have found no convincing evidence favoring the reinstatement of childlike modes of mental functioning, whether these are defined in terms of physiological responses (e.g., the Babinski reflex, in which the toes fan upward in response to plantar stimulation), scores on achievement tests, reversion to preconceptual (Werner) or preformal (Piaget) modes of thought (e.g., failing to predict the order in which three spheres will emerge from a hollow tube after it has been rotated through half or whole turns; defining right or wrong in terms of what is rewarded or punished), or perceptual processes (e.g., changes in magnitude of the Ponzo and Poggendorf illusions; the return of eidetic imagery ostensibly prominent in children). Nash (1987) also found that age regression does not necessarily revive specific childhood memories. It may, however, reinstate childlike modes of emotional functioning.

A third component of age regression, revivification, is conceptually similar to the recovery of memory in hypermnesia. In fact, Young (1926) was able to elicit a substantial number of early recollections, whose accuracy was independently verified, in two hypnotizable subjects. And more recently, Hofling et al. (1971) compared subjects' recall of personal experiences to actual diary entries made at the time and found superior memory during hypnosis in comparison with a nonhypnotic session. Unfortunately, neither of these experiments examined false recollections that may have been produced by the subjects. The obvious difficulty in obtaining independent verification effectively prevents many more studies of this sort from being done in order to understand better the conditions under which these improvements in memory might be obtained.

In the absence of independent confirmation, it should be understood that the apparent enhancement of memory occurring as a result of hypnosis may be illusory. But even independent confirmation does not guarantee that hypnosis itself is responsible for the appearance of revivification: the enhancement of memory may come from general world knowledge or cues provided by the experimenter, rather than improved access to trace information. The salient cautionary tale is provided by True (1949), who reported that age-regressed subjects were able to identify at better than chance levels the day of the week on which their birthdays, and Christmas, fell in their 4th, 7th, and 10th years. But the experimenter in question knew the answers to the questions as they were asked: when the experimenter is kept blind to the correct answer, response levels fall to chance (O'Connell et al., 1970). In general, when the testing environment is controlled in such a manner as to eliminate potentially informative cues, there is no evidence that age regression can enhance memory for past experiences. There is often an experience of increased memory but like so much else about hypnosis, the experience is illusory.

Forensic Hypnosis

Despite the poverty of evidence supporting the idea that memory can be enhanced by hypnotic suggestions, hypnosis has come to be used by police officers, attorneys, and even judges in an effort to refresh or bolster the memories of witnesses, victims, and suspects in criminal investigations. Although hypnosis does appear to have been helpful in some cases, a number of instances have been recorded in which the memories produced by hypnotized witnesses and victims have proved highly implausible or even false (Orne, 1979). The inherent unreliability of hypnotically elicited memories—the difficulty of distinguishing between illusion and reality, the susceptibility of hypnotically refreshed memory to distortion by inadvertent suggestion, and the tendency of subjects to enhance the credibility of memories produced through hypnosis—creates problems in the courtroom or in any environment in which the factual accuracy of hypnotically refreshed memory is critical (Orne et al., 1984, 1988).[6]

For these reasons, and in response to a number of cases that were prosecuted on the basis of evidence that later proved to be incorrect, both the medical establishment (American Medical Association, 1985) and the courts have begun to establish guidelines for the introduction and evaluation of hypnotically elicited memories. In some sense, of course, these guidelines are superfluous: because there is no evidence that hypnosis enhances memory, there is no reason to use it at all for this purpose. In fact, the current dominant position in the state courts appears to be a per se exclusion of all hypnotically elicited evidence, and some courts have gone so far as to exclude from testimony even the prehypnotic memories of a witness who has been subsequently hypnotized, on the grounds that hypnosis may distort prehypnotic as well as hypnotic memories—for example, by inflating the subject's confidence in what he or she had already remembered (Scheflin and Shapiro, 1989).

However, it seems clear that investigators, persuaded by anecdotal evidence of the efficacy of hypnosis in individual cases, will continue to use hypnosis for this purpose, despite the scientific evidence. Accordingly, some guidelines for the use of hypnosis seem necessary at this time. Those who use hypnosis to enhance memory should be aware of the dangers posed by its use and should conform their procedures to the sorts of procedural safeguards, adopted in many legal jurisdictions, to minimize the possibility that the witness' independent memory will be contaminated by hypnosis, and to maximize the likelihood that such contamination will be detected if it has occurred.

One set of guidelines, based on those proposed by Orne (1979) and adopted in the United States by the Federal Bureau of Investigation (Ault, 1979), has been proposed by Kihlstrom and Barnhardt (1993:106-114):

(1) There should be a prima facie case that hypnosis is appropriate. Memories that have not been properly encoded are not likely to be retrieved, even by heroic means. Thus, hypnosis will be of no use in cases where the witness did not have a good view of the critical events, was intoxicated, or sustained head injury at the time of the crime.

(2) For the same reason, there should be an objective assessment of the subject's hypnotizability, using one or another of the standardized scales developed for this purpose. Hypnosis will be of no use with subjects who are not at least somewhat hypnotizable.

(3) The hypnotist should be an experienced professional, knowledgeable of basic principles of psychological functioning and scientific methods. Forensic hypnosis raises cognitive issues, such as the nature of memory, and clinical issues, such as the subject's emotional reactions to any new information yielded by the procedure, and the hypnotist must be capable of evaluating and dealing with the situation on both counts.

(4) The hypnotist should be a consultant acting independently of any investigative agency, either prosecution/plaintiff or defense/respondent, so as to emphasize the goal of the procedure: collecting information rather than supporting a particular viewpoint.

(5) The hypnotist should be informed of only the barest details of the case at hand in order to minimize the possibility that his or her preconceptions will influence the course of the hypnotic interview. A written record of all information transmitted to the hypnotist should be preserved.

(6) A thorough interview should be conducted by the hypnotist, in advance of the hypnotic session, in order to establish a baseline against which any subsequent changes in memory can be evaluated.

(7) Throughout the prehypnotic and hypnotic interview, the hypnotist and the subject should be isolated from other people, especially those who have independent knowledge of the facts of the case, suspects, etc., so as to preclude the possibility of inadvertent cuing and contamination of the subject's memory.

(8) A complete recording of all interactions between hypnotist and subject should be kept to permit evaluation of the degree to which any influence may have occurred.

Because these standards are difficult to meet, and because of the continuing legal controversy attached to forensic hypnosis, investigators are advised to confine their use of hypnosis to the gathering of investigative leads. Under these circumstances, hypnotically refreshed memories are not introduced into evidence, and cases are based solely on independently verifiable evidence.

Hypnosis has the potential to permanently distort a person's memory, and it can increase the likelihood of both unintended confabulations and the influence of leading questions and other misinformation. The confusion between illusion and reality that is part and parcel of the hypnotic experience may be fascinating in the laboratory and perhaps useful in the clinic, but it is problematic in the real world, outside the laboratory or doctor's office. The myths surrounding the wonders of hypnosis may lead consumers of hypnotically elicited memories to inappropriately inflate their confidence in what they remember or to inappropriately accept such memories as accurate.

TRANSCENDENTAL MEDITATION

Meditation can be defined as a broad class of ritual techniques designed to alter the deployment of attention, and thus consciousness itself, in the hope that the practitioner will achieve a higher level of personal and spiritual growth. In some practices, the alteration of attention is toward focused concentration on a single stimulus, image, or idea; in others, the alteration of attention is toward an expanded awareness encompassing everything that is available to consciousness. Meditation has a place in a wide variety of religious traditions, both East and West: many Hindus, Buddhists, Jews, Christians, and Muslims, among adherents of other religions, practice meditation as an important part of their devotional lives— for example, as a way of achieving union with God or transcending the boundaries of worldly, corporeal existence. In this century, moreover, a number of avowedly secular systems of meditation have been developed to enable individuals to reduce stress and increase feelings of well-being, independent of their religious beliefs and practices. In either form, it seems clear that the disciplined practice of meditation might have positive effects on human performance.

Accordingly, the committee's second report, *In the Mind's Eye* (Druckman and Bjork, 1991), included a broad overview of the relevant literature on the effects of meditation. In light of extraordinary claims for performance enhancement made by some enthusiasts, the committee's initial work focused on methodological problems in evaluating research on meditation. For example, much research on religious and mystical forms of meditation necessarily uses adherents of the particular religious tradition as subjects; as a consequence, it is difficult to separate the effects of meditation per se from those of religious belief or from changes in life-style that are conditioned on such belief. For example, it would be no surprise to find that meditators are less prone to coronary heart disease if the meditators are also vegetarians. In addition, in many studies that show differences between meditators and nonmeditators, a key question is whether individuals who choose a life-style of disciplined meditation may have possessed the characteristic in question even before they began meditating. Moreover, the confounding of practice with belief raises questions of generalizability: If the rationale for a particular meditative practice is to be found in a particular religious tradition, are the salutary effects of this practice available to individuals who do not share those beliefs or practice that life-style?

In addition, most meditative practices consist of several components, including seated or prone posture, relaxation, attention to one's breathing or to a word or phrase serving as a "mantra," and the development of a passive frame of mind. The heterogeneity within meditative practices makes it difficult to select appropriate control procedures. Many studies of the effects of meditation have no control group at all, and many of the remainder simply compare meditators to individuals who do not meditate. But it is clearly not sufficient to compare one group of people who meditate with another group of people who do nothing. Even if such a comparison showed differences that favor meditation, the specific factors that are responsible for the effect would still not be known. For example, the positive effects might be due solely to the subject's state of relaxation, and not to posture, breathing, the mantra, or mental passivity. A properly designed analysis of the effects of meditation would analyze its components and then systematically vary them: for example, there would be a group that sits prone and focuses on a mantra but does not relax and does not maintain a passive state of mind. As an extreme example, study of religious meditation would include a control group who practiced all of the components of the meditative discipline in question without adhering to the religious belief that ostensibly underlies that discipline.

In its previous report, the committee lamented that few if any studies met this standard, making it difficult to draw firm conclusions about the effects, or even the potential, of meditation. Many of the studies of meditation we reviewed lacked even elementary controls for relaxation. Even the results of the best controlled studies often showed that the effects of meditation are often duplicated in individuals who simply rest quietly in chairs for an equivalent amount of time or who engage in progressive muscle relaxation. It is not clear that the effects obtained from the controlled, peaceful confines of the meditation room or research laboratory would generalize to the real world—a battlefield, a corporation, or an assembly line. This methodological situation has not changed. At the same time, however, the committee is aware of the existence of a large body of literature pertaining to the effects of one particular meditative discipline: the transcendental meditation (TM) technique, and the TM-Sidhi program, introduced by the Maharishi Mahesh Yogi and based on the Vedic tradition of Hinduism. In light of the high degree of popular interest in this technique, the committee decided to review the research on TM as part of its continuing work. Even with this narrow focus, however, the task is daunting: one collection of papers pertaining to TM, entitled *Scientific Research on Maharishi's Transcendental Meditation and TM-Sidhi Program*, contains 430 articles in 5 volumes. Accordingly, this section focuses only on the studies summarized in three published meta-analyses of the effects of TM: on physiological arousal (Dillbeck and Orme-Johnson, 1987); on relaxation and anxiety (Eppley et al., 1989); and self-actualization and psychological health (Alexander et al., 1991).

Theory and Practice

In TM, practitioners begin by assuming a comfortable posture, relaxed but alert, in an environment free of interruptions. After a few minutes of quiet relaxation, they close their eyes and mentally repeat a Sanskrit sound, or mantra, which provides a focus of attention. After about 20 minutes, they stop attending to the mantra and open their eyes but remain comfortably relaxed for a few more minutes before beginning (or resuming) their ordinary business. This cycle is performed twice daily, typically in early morning and late afternoon. It may be practiced individually or in groups. The purpose of the regimen is to shift the person from an active mode of consciousness, oriented toward the external world, to a more passive state oriented toward one's internal, subjective experience. Disciplined practice of TM, which is taught according to a standardized syllabus for a fee by certified trainers, eventually results in a state characterized as "pure consciousness," or samadhi, in which thought ceases but awareness is maintained. The regular achievement of this state of contentless awareness, through TM, is held to have a wide variety of beneficial effects for the person.[7]

The practice of TM is based on a classification of consciousness into seven qualitatively distinct states, including the waking, sleeping, and dreaming familiar in ordinary life, but also extending to four other states that may be achieved as a result of the disciplined practice of meditation: transcendental consciousness reflects the temporary breakdown of the usual cognitive boundaries between the knower, the object of knowledge, and the process of knowing; cosmic consciousness is achieved when transcendental consciousness becomes a permanent feature of mental life, maintained not only in waking but also in sleeping and dreaming; refined cosmic consciousness entails the further breakdown of the distinction between self and object, although there is still some residual awareness of self; finally, unity consciousness involves the complete disintegration of the sense of self and of any boundary between the individual and the universe.

In developing TM as a "science of creative intelligence," Maharishi and his disciples have sought to connect the rather obscure (to a Westerner) concepts of Vedic psychology with the rather more familiar concepts of cognitive and personality psychology (for a summary, see Alexander et al., 1991).[8] Thus, the achievement of transcendental consciousness is likened to Maslow's concept of self-actualization, and its effects are likened to Maslow's peak experiences, involving "cognition of being," or B-cognition. Similarly, the distinction between transcendental and cosmic consciousness is analogous to Maslow's distinction between "peakers," who have frequent peak experiences, and "transcenders," for whom the peak experience is more stable. In another line of argument, the successive achievement of higher states of consciousness is sometimes attached to Piaget's stages of cognitive development (Alexander and Langer, 1990). Whereas Piaget emphasized the child's developing ability to form and manipulate mental representations of the external world, the implication of Vedic psychology is that there are "postrepresentational" stages in which the distinction between an object and its mental representation progressively disintegrates. Thus, just as a child who has learned formal operations has abilities that one in the sensorimotor stage does not, an adult who is capable of cosmic consciousness is held to be capable of feats that are simply beyond the reach of one whose consciousness is limited to waking, sleeping, and dreaming.

Physiological Effects

In a reply to Holmes's (1984) critical review of the effects of meditation on autonomic arousal, Dillbeck and Orme-Johnson (1987) briefly reviewed the results of 32 (not 31 as indicated in the paper) studies of the physiological effects of TM; 23 of these papers had appeared in refereed journals. All of the studies employed a pretest-posttest design, in which measures of physiological arousal were taken before and during a period of TM or eyes-closed rest. Some of the studies involved only TM; other studies compared both TM and rest in the same experiment. From each study, the investigators were able to extract information on the effects of TM or rest on one or more of five measures of physiological arousal. For three of these measures—basal galvanic skin response (GSR), respiration rate, and plasma lactate level—TM produced greater reductions from baseline than did eyes-closed rest. For the remaining two measures (spontaneous GSRs and heart rate), the differences were in the same direction, but not significant. For four of the variables (all but basal GSR), there were also significant baseline differences between meditators and nonmeditators, indicating that subjects who were experienced in meditation showed lower levels of arousal even when they were not meditating.

Unfortunately, this conclusion is somewhat weakened by a crucial design feature of the research: in most of the studies reviewed, there is a confounding of subjects and experimental conditions in that experienced meditators are placed in the meditation condition, while subjects in the rest condition have no experience with the technique. For example, in a study by Orme-Johnson (1973), meditators had lower baseline levels of spontaneous GSRs and showed greater decreases in spontaneous GSRs while meditating in comparison with control subjects. However, one group of subjects assigned to the meditation condition had practiced TM twice a day for an average of 15 months; another group had practiced TM for an average of 24 months. In contrast, none of the subjects assigned to the rest condition had any experience with TM (some were on a waiting list for TM instruction). Similarly, in a study by Jevning et al. (1978) plasma lactate levels declined during TM, but not during a control period of rest: but, again, the subjects in the TM group had been practicing TM twice a day for an average of a year, while those in the control group had not practiced TM. According to Jevning et al. (1992:416), "most recent investigations [of TM] have studied the long-term meditator," defined as an individual who has been regularly meditating for at least 5 years, usually has had additional meditation experience at special courses, and is often him- or herself an instructor of TM. Generally, subjects in control groups do not have any similar kind of experience.

The consequences of this confounding problem are twofold: it is possible that experienced meditators would show decreases in physiological arousal during an eyes-closed rest period, without meditating, that are similar to those shown when they are actually meditating; alternatively, it is possible that subjects who had practiced eyes-closed rest (i.e., without meditating) for 20 minutes a day, twice a day, for 15-24 months would show decreases in physiological arousal during an eyes-closed rest period that are comparable to those shown by the meditators during meditation. Comparisons of this sort may be impossible—experienced meditators may find it difficult to rest with their eyes closed without slipping into meditation, and individuals who routinely practice eyes-closed rest may be hard to find. But without such rigorous comparisons, it is not possible to draw definitive conclusions about the effects of TM on physiological arousal.

Relaxation, Anxiety, and Self-Actualization

Similar problems are encountered in the second review, concerning relaxation and anxiety (Eppley et al., 1989). In this case, comparisons were made between TM and other meditation techniques, progressive muscle relaxation (including Benson's "relaxation response," which is a secularized version of TM), and other relaxation techniques such as electromyographic biofeedback, in which subjects are taught techniques for reducing activity in the skeletal musculature. There were 105 separate studies, of which 47 appeared in peer-reviewed journals. Trait anxiety, as a characteristic of personality, was measured by the Spielberger State-Trait Anxiety Inventory or similar measure. The salient finding was that practitioners of TM showed substantially lower levels of trait anxiety than did those who practiced the other comparison techniques. Similarly, a meta-analysis of 34 articles (17+ by Alexander et al., 1991) found a greater effect of TM than comparison meditation or relaxation treatments on self-actualization, as measured by scores on the Personal Orientation Inventory or similar instruments.

The trait-anxiety meta-analysis was much more extensive than the one on somatic arousal, and so the investigators were able to develop statistical controls for a wide variety of potentially confounding variables. Again, however, a combination of subject-selection procedures and the special characteristics of TM undermine the strength of the positive conclusions about TM. Eppley et al. (1989) show that, across experiments, the subjects in the TM conditions practiced the technique for an average of 2.5 months, while the other techniques had been practiced for an average of 1.6 months. Similarly, TM practitioners had received an average of 5.5 hours of instruction in the first week, compared with 1.5 hours for the others. And TM participants had an average of 14 practice sessions per week following instruction, compared with 10.1 sessions for the other techniques. Thus, at the time the comparisons were made, TM practitioners had experienced an average of 140 sessions (2.5 months at 14 sessions per week), while the subjects in the other groups had an average of only 64.6 (1.6 months at 10.1 sessions per week). In an attempt to control for potentially confounding differences between the groups, Eppley et al. (1989) statistically adjusted for the duration of training, attrition rate, and hours of follow-up instruction. However, it is clear that this adjustment cannot take account of the fact that subjects in the TM groups practiced their technique more than twice as much as did those in the comparison groups.

Equally important, it should be remembered that TM is not just a method of relaxed concentration: the complete TM package includes a religious (or quasireligious) rationale. After all, the program is explicitly intended to promote a greater sense of happiness and well-being. Practitioners are informed that TM is the entryway into a new "age of enlightenment" characterized by personal fulfillment, community harmony, and peace. And they are specifically given the expectation that the disciplined practice of TM will lead to self-actualization and the attainment of higher stages of consciousness. It would be surprising if these kinds of expectations, especially in the context of the commitment of practitioners to the TM program and the social support provided by other TM practitioners, did not lead to reductions in trait anxiety and increases in self-actualization, especially when measured by self-reports. And it is not yet known whether the other techniques, practiced as long as TM and embedded in the same sort of culture, expectations, and beliefs that surround TM, might not show the same effects. Again, although Eppley et al. (1989) appear to demonstrate that TM reduces anxiety and Alexander et al. (1991) appear to demonstrate that TM increases self-actualization and feelings of well-being, the literature does not provide the kinds of controlled comparisons that are necessary to scientifically evaluate the specific effects of the TM program.

Concluding Comment

In undertaking even its limited review of the literature on TM (limited to a focus on those effects on human performance that have received the most extensive study), the committee was mindful of the fact that it was evaluating a psychological technique that is also an inherent part of a system of religious beliefs. It should be clear that TM is, for all intents and purposes, a form of religion. It has its origins in Hinduism, a religious tradition which arose on the Indian subcontinent, worships a divine trinity of Brahma, Vishnu, and Shiva as well as a number of other deities, emphasizes religious duty or dharma, and adheres to scriptures such as the Rig-Veda, the Upanishads, and the Bhagavad-Gita. TM, as practiced by the followers of the Maharishi Mahesh Yogi, is somewhat secularized, based in a Vedic "science of creative intelligence" and requiring no belief in divine beings as such. However, much of its vocabulary, including references to cosmic and unity consciousness and to higher states of being, is essentially religious in nature. Maharishi himself is referred to as "His Holiness" in official TM literature. In some respects, TM is to Hinduism what Unitarian Universalism is to Christianity.

The committee attempted to approach TM as a strictly secular practice, analogous to conventional therapeutic techniques such as biofeedback or progressive relaxation, but in the final analysis any attempt to isolate TM from the context of its surrounding structure of religious beliefs may be a serious distortion.

RESTRICTED ENVIRONMENTAL STIMULATION (REST)

REST refers to a set of techniques aimed at reducing the level of environmental stimulation to a practicable minimum. The acronym was coined by Suedfeld in 1980, who recommended it as a replacement for sensory deprivation—a term that had gained currency in the 1950s due in large measure to the work of Donald Hebb and his colleagues at McGill University (Shurley, 1992; Zubek, 1969). Suedfeld's suggested change in nomenclature, which was rapidly and widely adopted by other investigators in the area, made sense for several reasons. Chief among these is that modern REST techniques seek to drastically reduce or restrict environmental stimulation, and the McGill group's studies had relied on procedures that typically, and ironically, produced high levels of monotonous stimulation. As noted by Adams (1990), the earlier studies entailed neither silence nor darkness—defining characteristics of contemporary REST research—but rather brightly lit rooms, into which was piped low to moderate levels of unvarying white noise. Subjects were confined to these quarters for a protracted period (several days being the norm), during which time they lay on a bed while wearing a translucent mask over their eyes (to prevent the perception of clear, meaningful visual patterns) and cardboard cuffs or gloves on their hands (to reduce tactile stimulation).

Unsurprisingly, the psychological impact of these methods was inimical: hallucinations, stress reactions, and signs of thought disorder were common among participants in the McGill project (see Solomon et al., 1961). Subsequent studies, however, suggested that these outcomes may have been produced, at least in part, by expectations derived from the demand characteristics of the sensory deprivation situation (M. Barabasz and Barabasz, 1987; Suedfeld 1969). In any event, more recent research involving restricted—rather than monotonous—stimulation has frequently failed to replicate the negative effects reported earlier. To the contrary, this research has revealed that most people find restricted environmental stimulation to be an interesting, pleasant, and relaxing experience and that REST techniques may aid in the treatment of a broad spectrum of clinical disorders, particularly those related to stress or addictive behaviors (see Suedfeld and Borrie, 1993; Suedfeld and Kristeller, 1982). This suggests that REST, far from being a laboratory model of psychosis, may be used to enhance human performance in a number of domains.

In current use, REST typically involves two different procedures. In chamber REST, participants sit or lie on a bed in a completely dark and soundproofed room; a chemical toilet is provided for the subject's comfort and convenience, and both food and water are available on an as-needed basis. In flotation REST, participants are immersed in a quiet, dark tank of water warmed to body temperature and saturated with Epsom salts. (For hygienic reasons, people who participate in a "wet float" procedure are required to shower before as well as after they float, and the tank water is continuously circulated and purified. To simplify matters, some investigators prefer the "dry float" method, whereby subjects lie on a plastic liner that separates them from the water.) The typical chamber session lasts 24 hours, the typical tank session lasts 60 minutes. In either situation, hallucinations, stress reactions, or other adverse effects are rare, unless subjects are given to expect them.

Whether in a chamber or in a tank, the principal application of REST has been as an adjunctive treatment in medically or psychologically oriented therapy, especially for habit control and stress management. Evidence from several studies (reviewed by Suedfeld, 1990) suggests that compared to controls (selected from waiting lists for REST), 24 hours of chamber REST (regardless of whether or not it was accompanied by persuasive messages) both decreased the amount of smoking and increased the rate of abstinence as assessed 6 to 24 months after the single-session treatment. Similarly, 5 hours of chamber REST, during which snake-phobic patients were presented with photographic slides depicting snakes, was demonstrated to decrease behavioral avoidance of an actual, live snake more than did presentation of the same slides without REST (Suedfeld and Hare, 1977). Other clinical or health-related issues to which REST has been brought to bear include alcohol intake (Cooper et al., 1988), essential hypertension (Turner et al., 1987), and rheumatoid pain (Mereday et al., 1990).

In comparison with the body of research concerning the clinical and health applications of restricted stimulation, the literature on REST and the enhancement of human performance is much smaller and less well developed. For the purposes of this section, two aspects of this literature are of chief concern: effects of REST on memory and cognitive tasks and on psychomotor or athletic skills.

In an early experiment related to the effects of restricted stimulation on memory, problem solving, and other cognitive processes, Grissom (1966) read subjects a one-page passage from Tolstoy's *War and Peace* shortly after they had entered a chamber REST environment. Retention of the passage (scored in terms of verbatim recall) was assessed both immediately (as the subjects knew it would be) and either 8, 16, 20, or 24 hours later (which came as a surprise). During the intervening period, subjects either went about their normal daily affairs or they remained in the chamber (i.e., control versus REST conditions). The subjects who had stayed in the chamber forgot significantly less of what they had recalled initially than those who had left the chamber (as measured by the signed difference between immediate and delayed recall performance). The advantage of REST over control conditions was graded, in that it was strongest after 24 hours and weakest after 8.

Technically speaking, Grissom's results could be—and, indeed, have been (Suedfeld, 1980)—interpreted as evidence that REST enhances memory performance. It should be recognized, however, that these results are neither surprising nor do they imply anything special about REST. According to classic interference theory, the introduction of an "altered stimulating condition" (McGeogh and Irion, 1952) between the occasions of information acquisition and delayed retention testing decreases retroactive interference and thereby increases memory performance. This is just what Grissom found, as did Jenkins and Dallenbach (1924) long ago, in a study in which natural sleep served as the altered stimulating condition and as did Parker et al. (1981), in a more recent study involving acute alcoholic intoxication.

A potentially more interesting and informative approach to understanding the cognitive effects of REST concerns the idea that under restricted environmental circumstances patterns of thought become more flexible and inwardly focused. This idea derives from basic research indicating that REST reduces a person's resistance to counter-attitudinal information (Suedfeld, 1980) and provides the rationale for clinical interventions aimed at "unfreezing" the rigid structure of thoughts, emotions, motivations, and behaviors that support addictive habits, such as smoking (Suedfeld and Borrie, 1993). If this is indeed so, one might expect REST to promote problem solving, creativity, or other forms of "higher" cognitive functions. However, empirical investigations of this issue have yielded results that appear to be inconsistent, even contradictory.

On one side are studies showing that REST typically impairs the performance of cognitive tasks (e.g., verbal fluency or divergent thinking) that are "complex" in that they "require the solver to combine dimensions flexibly and to use unfamiliar procedures (frequently in combination); allow for a number of possible methods of reaching a solution; and have an open-ended or vague definition of the goal point" (Suedfeld et al., 1983:729). On the other side is a study by Suedfeld et al. 1987 (see also Metcalfe and Suedfeld, 1990) in which seven psychology professors each spent six, 90-minute sessions sitting alone in their office and six, 1-hour sessions in a wet-REST environment. During the office sessions and for 30 minutes after each float, subjects dictated ideas related to their research into a tape recorder. The recordings generated from each session were transcribed and returned to the subjects approximately 3 months after their final session. Subjects were asked to identify distinct "idea units" in their transcripts; indicate whether a given idea was novel or whether it was one they had pondered prior to the study; and rate the quality and creativity of each distinct thought. The ideas generated shortly after REST sessions were rated as being more novel and more creative than those developed during the office sessions. Along with this finding was a somewhat contrary subjective result: five of the seven subjects believed that REST either had no effect or a deleterious influence on the creativity of their ideas.

Although the authors interpreted these results as evidence for an enhancement of scientific creativity through REST, they were cognizant of an obvious methodological shortcoming, namely, that the novelty or creativity of a given idea was assessed by the subjects themselves. Whether the subjects' own ratings would square with those made by a disinterested third-party expert is an important—but regrettably unanswerable—question. For argument's sake, assume that those results are real and not simply a reflection of subjective bias or expectation effects (an assumption that is strengthened by the subjective reactions of the professors). How, then, does one reconcile the negative influence of REST on the performance of complex problem solving or reasoning tasks with its evidently positive effects on creativity?

One possible explanation of the contradictory findings relates to whether or not subjects are constrained to channel their cognitive resources on problems or ideas that are not of their own choosing. Although the deep sense of relaxation most people experience during REST (especially of the flotation variety) is partly attributable to pleasant somatic sensations (warmth, weightlessness, etc.), it is also due to the pleasant psychological realization that solitude has its own rewards. For as long as the REST session lasts, there are no telephones to answer, no errands to run, no outside demands to deal with. A person is thus free to focus inward and to devote attention to issues and problems of personal significance. Under such circumstances, the requirement to perform a standardized, research-oriented task of reasoning or problem solving (e.g., "unscramble the anagram ACHENEN" or "list as many words as possible that begin with K") is apt to be regarded by a subject as an intrusion rather than a challenge, with poor performance being the predictable outcome. Just how real or remote this possibility is remains to be seen through future studies of the relationship of REST and cognition.

Keyed by case studies and anecdotal reports (e.g., Hutchinson, 1984; Stanley et al., 1987), a number of REST researchers have recently begun to explore the second aspect of performance enhancement we are considering, psychomotor or athletic skills. In the first controlled study of this subject, Lee and Hewitt (1987) randomly assigned 36 female gymnasts (ranging in skill level from novice to intermediate) to one of three conditions: visual imagery practiced in a floatation tank, visual imagery practiced while on a mat, or a no-treatment control. Subjects in either the REST or mat conditions participated in six, 40-minute sessions held once a week. During each session, the subjects listened to a tape containing both relaxation suggestions and guided imagery instructions for visualizing various gymnastic routines. Every subject later participated in three state gymnastic meets, where her performance was scored by meet judges who did not know the condition assignments. Performance scores averaged across these three meets, and the subject's responses to a checklist of physical symptoms or complaints administered at the conclusion of the study, served as the dependent measures. The results showed that subjects given the imagery-plus-REST treatment attained a significantly higher performance score (regardless of their skill level) than either their control- or mat-condition counterparts, and they also reported marginally fewer physical complaints (provided they were intermediate rather than novice gymnasts).

In a conceptually related study, McAleney et al. (1991) examined the effects of REST-plus-imagery on the competitive performance of expert intercollegiate tennis players. Twenty varsity tennis players (at a Pac-10 university) mentally practiced a variety of shot-making skills (suggested to them through audio tape) either while seated in a well-lit room or while floating in a REST tank. Six, 50-minute treatments (REST-plus-imagery or imagery alone) were administered over the course of 3 weeks. At the end of the period, every participant played against a competitor who had been matched for ability by the team's coaches at a tournament prior to the experiment. Videotapes of the (posttreatment) matches were analyzed by blind raters and scored with respect to first-service performance (aces, services in play, or faults); key shots (winners, forced errors, or unforced errors); and the number of points won during the first 50 points of the match. Of the various dependent measures so derived, only one—the number of first-service winners—revealed a statistically significant advantage of REST-plus-imagery over imagery-alone conditions.

Two studies have to date been reported that deal with another form of athletic performance, basketball. In one of these studies (Suedfeld and Bruno, 1990), 30 university students (either occasional or novice basketball players) attempted 20 free throws one day before and one day after a single, 60-minute session. During the session they listened to a tape recording guiding them through multisensory (e.g., visual, tactile, proprioceptive) imagery of basketball foul shooting while floating in a REST tank, while reclining in a comfortable lounge chair, or while seated in a large, egg-shaped "alpha chair" designed to induce relaxation and improve concentration. Subjects practiced shooting free throws in their mind's eye. As one might expect, there were no appreciable differences among conditions in pretreatment shot-making success. On posttreatment, however, REST subjects made significantly more baskets (mean of 57%) than did subjects who had sat in either the alpha chair or in the more conventional recliner (means of 36% and 32%, respectively).

In the second study, Wagaman et al. (1991) asked 22 varsity basketball players to imagine themselves shooting, passing, and dribbling with precision in six separate sessions, spread over a 5-week interval. Every subject completed these sessions in either a lighted office or a flotation REST tank and subsequently participated in five regularly scheduled intercollegiate contests. Performance during these games was assessed by means of both an objective composite score (indexing the difference between, say, points scored and passes completed versus travelling violations and personal fouls) and coaches' subjective ratings.[9] In comparison with the control subjects, REST subjects achieved a significantly higher composite score, and were rated by their coaches as being better in terms of passing and shooting, but not in terms of dribbling, defense, or all-around ability.

In each of the four studies just noted, REST was always applied in tandem with imagery training. Consequently, as Suedfeld et al. (1993:153) have commented, these studies cannot answer the key question of whether REST "merely potentiates the effects of imagery, interacts synergistically with it, or is itself responsible for all or most of the effect." To address this question, Suedfeld et al. (1993) conducted an experiment in which they independently varied flotation REST and an imagery training and relaxation script as techniques for improving accuracy among 40 novice, intermediate, and expert dart players. Results indicated that a single, 1-hour session of REST by itself, and REST combined with the imagery/relaxation script, were equally effective in enhancing performance: shots on target increased by about 12 percent from pre- to posttreatment, irrespective of skill level. In contrast, the script alone and a no-treatment control condition produced no significant change in test-retest measures. Similar results have recently been reported by A. Barabasz et al. (1993) in their study of 24 students enrolled in a rifle marksmanship training course. The students were randomly assigned to one of two treatments: either 50 minutes of dry-float REST or an equal period of hypnotically suggested relaxation. (Neither the REST nor the relaxation subjects had been given any form of guided imagery training.) The REST subjects outperformed the relaxation subjects in a subsequent test of rifle-shot accuracy, as scored by ROTC instructors (who were blind to the experimental condition).

Considered collectively, the research to date provides suggestive evidence that REST—either alone or in combination with guided imagery/relaxation training—may enhance the performance of a variety of athletic or sporting skills. This evidence, however, cannot be construed as compelling, for several reasons. At present, the research consists of only six published papers (three of which appeared in nonrefereed journals), each reporting a single study involving a modest sample size. Moreover, in studies entailing multiple measures of performance (McAleney et al., 1991; Wagaman et al., 1991), it is not uncommon to find positive effects with certain measures and no effects with others. Whether such a mixture of outcomes reflects theoretically important and empirically principled dissociations among various performance indices, differences in measurement sensitivity, or merely the occurrence of type-I errors[10] is a difficult but important issue that remains to be resolved (see below).

Given these considerations, we believe that what is needed now is not just more research on the performance enhancing effects of REST but also better research—integrated, tightly reasoned investigations, organized in multi-experiment reports. Such investigations will need to address a long list of issues, none of which is news to researchers already active in the area, but which might appeal to the editors and reviewers of high-profile journals and attract new researchers to the field. For example, how long do the performance-enhancing effects of REST last? Are these effects unique to dry and wet flotation, or can they also be elicited through chamber REST?[11] What aspects of athletic performance are most amenable to improvement through REST?

One hypothesis, advanced by Suedfeld et al. (1993:153), is that skills that "require relatively low arousal and a full measure of control over a complex coordinated movement" are more apt to benefit from REST that are "activities that overwhelmingly emphasize brief bursts of speed or strength, or quick changes in motion or attention in response to the acts of other competitors." Although the implications of this idea need to be worked out and explored, the hypothesis does provide a plausible explanation for at least some of the mixed results reported, such as the observation of McAleney et al. (1991) that REST-plus-imagery improved first-service accuracy but did not effect either key shot success or points won—measures of performance that are more reflective of reaction. Finally, and most critically from a theoretical standpoint, how and why does REST enhance skilled performance? Do REST-related enhancements signify nothing more than expectancy or placebo effects? (The fact that Suedfeld and Bruno [1990] observed no intergroup differences in subjects' expectations of improvement that were solicited before treatment suggests otherwise.) Alternatively, is it the case that REST "potentiates internally generated imaginal activity (subjects' spontaneous imagining) and that such activity can be reactivated, at will, sometime after the REST experience despite the intrusion of normal levels of stimulation," as A. Barabasz et al. (1993:871) contend? Or might the key lie not in the reactivation of imaginal activity, but rather in the realization of profound levels of relaxation that were previously attainable only in the restricted sensory environment (see Suedfeld et al., 1993). Answers to these kinds of questions are essential if the promise of REST as a technique for enhancing human performance is to be turned into established fact.

SLEEP LEARNING

Sleep is universally recognized as an altered state of consciousness. Especially in some stages of sleep, an individual appears unresponsive to exogenous stimuli (unless they are very intense); at the same time, he or she may experience dreams, nightmares, and other endogenous mental events (although they are usually quickly forgotten upon awakening). The committee's first report, *Enhancing Human Performance* (Druckman and Swets, 1988), raised the possibility that sleepers, while appearing oblivious to environmental events, may nonetheless be able to process environmental events to some degree and retain them in memory after awakening. For example, a study of World War I military recruits by Thurstone seemed to indicate that learning of Morse code was facilitated by presenting lessons at night, when the soldiers were presumably asleep, as well as during regular daytime classes (Simon and Emmons, 1955). Reports of successful sleep learning also filtered out of the former Soviet Union and countries of Eastern Europe during the Cold War. Yet, most formal studies of sleep learning have yielded negative results, and most instances of positive findings were either anecdotal in nature or marred by the absence of proper controls or inadequate psychophysiological monitoring of sleep (for reviews, see Aarons, 1977; Eich, 1990).

Sleep learning has remained an open question for two reasons. First, a series of dramatic experiments by Evans and his associates (reviewed by Evans, 1990), appeared to show that some subjects could respond discriminatively to hypnosis-like suggestions for motor activity while remaining asleep, show an amnesia for these responses on awakening, and continue to respond on subsequent nights without further administration of the suggestions. These suggestion-induced changes in behavior qualify as learning. Second, recent studies of the amnesic syndrome and other disorders of memory support a distinction between explicit memory, or conscious recollection, and implicit memory, in which task performance is affected by past events even though subjects do not remember them (for reviews, see Schacter, 1987, 1992). If brain-injured and anesthetized patients can show evidence of implicit memory, it seems plausible that sleeping subjects might also do so.

The studies of sleep suggestion were performed by Evans and his associates (Evans et al., 1969, 1970; Perry et al., 1978). In the earlier studies (Evans et al., 1969, 1970), sleeping subjects received suggestions during the stage of sleep known as REM (rapid eye movement) that they would scratch their noses when they heard the word "*itch*" and adjust their pillows when they heard the word "*pillow*". Testing in the same or subsequent sleep stages revealed that subjects gave appropriate responses to between 14 and 20 percent of the cue words. Positive responses persisted, to at least some degree, over five subsequent nights without any repetition of the suggestion—and, for a subgroup of subjects who could be retested, some 5 months later as well. When interviewed after waking, however, the subjects had no awareness that they had received such cues or responded to them. Because such responses require perception of the cue, and their carryover to subsequent sleep stages and nights requires memory, this study makes a prima facie case for the acquisition and retention of memories during sleep, memories that are expressed implicitly, in response to the cue, rather than explicitly as conscious recollections of experience. Unfortunately, this study was beset by a number of flaws (for a detailed critique, see Wood, 1989). There was no control group to provide baseline information on nose-scratching and pillow-adjusting, and these behaviors were evaluated by a judge who was aware of the suggestions that the subjects had received. Perhaps most important, however, the investigators failed to follow conventional procedures for sleep staging. According to standardized criteria, stage REM is indicated by three criteria: high-frequency, low-amplitude beta activity in the electroencephalogram (EEG), with no low-frequency, high amplitude alpha activity (the latter indicative of cognitive arousal); rapid eye movements (REM) in the electrooculogram (EOG); and absence of submentalis muscle tone in the electromyogram (EMG). Evans et al. recorded only EEG and EOG, which makes it extremely difficult to discriminate stage REM sleep from waking. This last point is crucial, because motor activity is incompatible with stage REM: in other words, a subject who is in stage REM cannot physically respond to instructions for motor activity such as scratching one's nose and adjusting one's pillow. In recognition of this fact, Evans et al. referred to "Stage 1" sleep with and without REM. But the fact remains that on the psychophysiological evidence, the subjects who responded to the sleep suggestion might well have been at least partially awake. If so, then the studies of sleep suggestion do not count as evidence for sleep learning after all.

In an attempt to correct these problems, Perry et al. (1978) attempted a replication of the earlier study by Evans et al. (1969, 1970), but with tighter controls. A within-subjects control presented subjects with cues, like leg and blanket, for which no suggestions had been given, but to which appropriate responses were recorded; moreover, all responses were recorded on video tape (by means of an infrared camera), and evaluated by judges who were blind to the suggestions that had been given. Unfortunately, Perry et al. (1978) did not consider EMG criteria in the staging of sleep. In the final analysis, however, there proved to be no difference in response rate to critical and control cues. Although some degree of nose-scratching and pillow-adjusting was observed in response to suggestions, the levels of these activities did not differ from leg-moving and blanket-pulling. Thus, regardless of questions about the appropriateness of the stage of sleep and whether the subjects might have been at least partially awake during the tests, there was no evidence of differential responsiveness to the cues, and thus no evidence of implicit perception or memory during sleep.

In light of these findings, Wood and his colleagues (Wood et al., 1992) conducted the first formal comparison of explicit and implicit memory for information presented during sleep. In one test, subjects received presentations, during either stage REM or stage 2 (early non-REM sleep) of paired associates consisting of a homophone (e.g., hare, hair) and a context word (e.g., tortoise). In the other test, the paired associates consisted of a word and its category label (e.g., metal-gold). In each case, subjects received approximately five presentations of the list. The stage of sleep was measured by standard criteria, including EMG as well as EEG and EOG, and presentation of the list was interrupted as soon as the subject showed any signs of arousal (e.g., the appearance of alpha activity in the record). A control group heard the same lists while lying awake in a darkened room. Ten minutes after presentation of each list, the subjects were awakened (if they were sleeping). Those in the normal waking state showed clear priming effects, in that they were more likely to spell previously presented homophones in accordance with the context word (see Eich, 1984) and to generate category instances that had been presented earlier (see Kihlstrom, 1980). However, those who had slept during the stimulus presentations showed no evidence of priming.

Given the problems in the studies by Evans et al. (1969, 1970), and the negative results of Wood et al. (1992), it is difficult to be sanguine about the possibility of learning during sleep and retaining even implicit memories in a subsequent waking state. However, it is possible that the sleep-staging criteria employed by Wood et al. (1992) were too strict. That is, some evidence of sleep learning might be obtained in experiments that allow some level of cortical arousal in the subjects—conditions that approximate Thurstone's early study of Morse code. Subjects who are partially aroused during stimulus presentations might well show implicit memory for such events, in the absence of explicit memory. Wood (1989) has characterized this as "quasi sleep learning," because the person is aroused to some degree while encoding the information. This proposal is consistent with the suggestion made in Druckman and Swets (1988) that individuals might profit from "dynamic sleep-learning procedures" in which presentations are timed to coincide with periods when sleepers are relatively aroused (see Eich, 1990). Finally, even without cortical arousal, it is possible that some forms of implicit memory, such as repetition priming, might be preserved even when input takes place while a person is unambiguously asleep. The study by Wood et al. (1992) appears to rule out semantic priming, based on associative or conceptual relationships between the items presented during sleep. But it does not rule out repetition priming, or other forms of implicit memory that are mediated by presemantic, perceptual representations of stimulus input.

Although some knowledge might be acquired by means of quasi-sleep learning and expressed implicitly if not explicitly in subsequent waking life, any such effects might be offset by two costs. First, there is no reason to believe that sleep learning, even if it is possible, is anywhere near as efficient as learning in the normal waking state. Sleeping subjects, and those who are on the margins of wakefulness, may be unable to perform the elaborative and organizational activity necessary for good learning. However, to the extent that material is encoded at all during those "twilight" states, the principle of encoding specificity in memory might operate so as to make such material especially accessible when the person is sleep-deprived or exhausted. Second, quasi sleep learning effectively deprives a subject of sleep, so acquiring information during sleep may produce detrimental effects on performance the next day. However, dynamic sleep-learning procedures may make it possible to present information without arousing a person from the deepest, most restorative stages of sleep. For the present, the possibility of sleep learning, expressed in implicit memory during states of wakefulness, or in a state-dependent fashion in states of sleepiness, deserves further investigation. But any discussion of the benefits of sleep learning should include a comparative evaluation of the costs to effective and efficient performance in the normal waking state.

CONCLUSIONS

Consciousness may be altered by increasing a person's awareness of the surrounding world, decreasing that awareness, or changing the contents of that awareness. Thus, hypnotized subjects may believe that the world is as it is suggested by the hypnotist; a sleeper appears oblivious to events in the surrounding environment; restricted environmental stimulation interrupts the normal flow of sensory-motor activity; and transcendental meditation may induce a state of alert but content-free "pure consciousness." Claims have been made for the performance-enhancing qualities of each of these states, but a critical review of the available literature indicates that most of these claims are unsupported by scientific data. That is, either the results have been negative, or positive results have been contaminated by the lack of certain critical controls.

To the extent that performance is impaired by subjective feelings of pain and fatigue, hypnosis can enhance performance by reducing a subject's awareness of these potentially demoralizing conditions. This possibility is limited by the role of hypnotizability in moderating the effects of hypnotic suggestion: not everyone is hypnotizable enough to experience this effect. However, even individuals who are not hypnotizable may receive some benefit from the placebo component in hypnotic analgesia or from training in nonhypnotic stress inoculation.

By and large, direct hypnotic suggestions for enhanced performance have no effect on muscular strength and endurance, sensory thresholds, learning, and memory retrieval. Hypnotized subjects may *believe* that they are doing better, and this belief may have positive motivational properties, but the subjective experience of performance enhancement appears to be illusory.

Transcendental meditation (TM) has been offered as a means of enhancing performance, chiefly by reducing the deleterious effects of stress. Although TM has generated a voluminous body of research, the available studies suffer from a variety of methodological flaws that preclude firm conclusions. For example, it is not clear whether the positive effects observed in TM are due to the specific effects of the unique features of TM or to the frequency and discipline with which TM is practiced.

Restricted environmental stimulation (REST) has been offered as a technique for enhancing human performance, but most of the evidence supporting this proposal is based on the proven therapeutic effects of REST in controlling habit behaviors. There is some anecdotal evidence of the performance-enhancing effects of REST, and a few formal studies, but not enough for firm conclusions about the effects, if any, and their underlying mechanisms.

Although sleep learning is ineffective when measured in terms of an individual's ability to consciously remember material presented during sleep, the committee's last report raised the possibility that sleep learning could be expressed as implicit memory, in the absence of explicit recollection: more recent evidence indicates that this is not the case. Some degree of quasi sleep learning may be possible, but if so it is both likely to be inefficient and to have detrimental effects on a person's subsequent waking performance.

NOTES

[1]Although a variety of slightly different terms can be used to characterize an individual's "hypnotizability," we use the terms "hypnotizable" and "insusceptible" to characterize those who can and cannot be hypnotized.

[2]Hypnosis might share features in common with some of the other effects. It has been suggested that acupuncture is just a peculiarly Chinese form of hypnosis, or that hypnotic analgesia is just a placebo. If this were so, we would expect that response to acupuncture, or placebo, would be a function of hypnotizability. But they are not. The dissociation between hypnosis and acupuncture, or between hypnosis and placebo, the former mediated by hypnotizability but the latter not, shows that hypnosis is different from acupuncture or placebo.

[3]This study used a variant on the London-Fuhrer paradigm (discussed below); for a detailed secondary analysis, see Hilgard and Hilgard (1975, 1983); for a substantial replication, see Spanos et al. (1989).

[4]This research is independent of the literature, reviewed above, on the effects of hypnotically suggested time-distortion on memory.

[5]There is no evidence that a subject in a state of age regression to childhood loses access to his or her adult knowledge and abilities (O'Connell et al. 1970; Orne, 1951; Perry and Walsh, 1978).

[6]Hypnosis is clearly established as a potentially efficacious treatment modality in medicine and psychotherapy (American Medical Association, 1958), particularly for the relief of pain, but the general consensus within the field is that hypnotically refreshed memory is inherently unreliable (American Medical Association, 1985).

[7]The TM-Sidhi program, an extension of conventional TM technique that is available to highly experienced practitioners, is held to permit individuals to enhance sensory thresholds, perceive hidden objects, achieve direct awareness of past and future, become invisible, and levitate; for the adept, it also enhances feelings of inner peace, friendliness, and compassion. This brief review focuses entirely on standard TM and does not address the claims of the TM-Sidhi program.

[8]Similarly, the rationale for the TM-Sidhi program makes use of concepts in quantum mechanics.

[9]The coaches did not know the experimental conditions of the players.

[10]This occurs when an hypothesis of no difference between a treatment and a control condition is *rejected* when in fact it is true. (A type-II error, on the other hand, occurs when an hypothesis of no difference is *accepted* when in fact it is false.)

[11]In this regard, it merits mentioning that the positive finding noted above for REST as an effective method of smoking cessation was true for chamber—but not flotation (see Suedfeld, 1990).

PART V

New Directions

Chapters 10 and 11 present findings from two relatively new fields in the area of human performance. In Chapter 10 we consider socially induced affect: it has been the subject of many experimental studies, but its implications for performance have not been developed. Some of these implications are discussed in the chapter. As a part of the more general question of the relationship between affect and performance, socially induced affect has special relevance for performing the kinds of cooperative learning and team training tasks discussed in Chapters 5 and 7.

Thought suppression is a mental-control strategy that has been discussed in the clinical literature for over a century. However, only recently have its implications been subjected to the scrutiny of laboratory research. Chapter 11 considers those implications, both for research and performance.

10

Socially Induced Affect

Socially induced affect refers to an emotional experience in one person that is induced by someone else's affect, that person's observable emotions or feelings. This definition implies two parties—a person directly showing affect (the model) and a person observing the model and experiencing emotion as a consequence of the affect of the model. For example, a soldier's distress due to the loss of a loved one induces feelings of distress in his or her team unit members.[1] In this case, the soldier is the model and the team members are the observers.

The transfer of feelings from model to observer is incidental in the sense that it is caused not by an intended action of a person, but only by the presence of the other.[2] Identified originally by researchers working on problems of social facilitation (e.g., Zajonc, 1965), this transmission of affect from one person to another does not depend on the relationship that may exist between them; it occurs between strangers as well as between friends. Results from a large number of experiments document the phenomenon of socially induced affect.[3]

Socially induced affect has long been an important topic in psychology. (For historical accounts see Gladstein, 1984; Deutsch and Madle, 1975; Wispé, 1986; for extended discussions see Gladstein, 1983; Goldstein and Michaels, 1985; Hatfield et al., 1992; Hoffman, 1977; Stotland 1969.) Interest continues today in clinical, developmental, and social psychology (Demos, 1984; Gladstein, 1984; Hatfield et al., 1992). It has been used to explain processes in social learning (Bandura, 1971), helping behavior (Batson and Coke, 1983), the avoidance of people in distress (Berger, 1962), the patient-therapist relation (Freud, 1921/1957), and crowd behavior (Le Bon,

251

1920/1982). Since affective experience plays an important role in human behavior and performance, it is not surprising that socially induced affect is suggested in such a wide range of social phenomena.

In considering the effects of socially induced affect on performance, however, several points should be kept in mind. First, if an affective state alters performance, than the effects of socially induced affect should be similar to those of direct affect (based on one's own experiences and feelings) with the same characteristics, such as intensity or length of feeling. In these instances, socially induced affect is simply one of several methods that could be used to induce the desired affective state. To the extent that socially induced affect is different than directly induced affect—for example, if it is easier to use in some circumstances or its effects are more subtle—it may provide a unique way to influence performance.[4] Second, in any given situation, there are ways to enhance performance other than by inducing affect. The method used should be the one that produces change in the most efficient, cost-effective, and reliable way. Only by comparing the effects of alternative methods can this judgment be made. Third, when considering the influence of socially induced affect on performance, it should be noted that the meaning of "performance" depends on context: What is the goal of the activity? If the goal is to train technicians, the performance of interest may be average improvement in the speed and accuracy with which each person performs his or her tasks after training. If the goal of an Army unit is to overcome a series of obstacles, performance would be judged at the team level: How well did the team do? Performance is enhanced when the chances of reaching the intended goal are improved. We discuss issues of performance following a review of what is known to date about socially induced affect.

In this chapter, we first summarize what is known about socially induced affect from research. We then discuss alternative mechanisms that may explain the phenomenon, including the role of cognition, classical conditioning, and mimicry. We also consider several basic issues unresolved by the research completed to date, such as the role of culture and the difference between socially induced affect and direct affect. The major section on performance presents examples of the possible role played by socially induced affect in seven applied settings. These examples are intended to suggest fruitful areas for further research as well as offer implications for performance.

CONCORDANT AND DISCORDANT AFFECT

A typical experiment on socially induced affect takes the following form. On entering a laboratory, the subject meets another person who has also agreed to participate in the experiment. The experimenter tells both people that she is studying physiological changes that occur when a person experiences various types of physical stimuli. The two people draw lots to determine who will experience the stimuli and who will serve as a "control" subject. The control subject (observer) is told that his physiological changes will be assessed while the other person experiences the stimuli. Often, when the other subject plunges his hand into cold water and winces with pain, the observer twinges with pain, and when the other subject smiles with pleasure in response to an unknown stimulus, the observer expresses a more positive mood. When these reactions occur, the subject has experienced socially induced affect—that is, feelings caused by the observable feelings of another person.

Experiments of this type have demonstrated both concordant and discordant affect (Heider, 1958). Concordant induction is the transmission of affect in the same direction—either positive or negative—as in the experiment described above. Discordant induction is the transmission of the opposite affect: for example, when a performer's achievement produces envy in an observer or when a disliked person's failure produces happiness in the observer.[5] Four possibilities are then defined by the direction of the model's affect (positive or negative) and the observer's affect (positive or negative).[6] Our reviews of the research on socially induced affect is organized in terms of the framework of these four possibilities (after Heider, 1958).

A representative sampling of the many studies that have addressed the question of whether affect can be socially induced is shown in Table 10-1. Each study appears in the cell for which it provides evidence.[7] For example, the study of Haviland and Lelwica (1987) appears in the model-positive, observer-positive cell since it provides evidence for positive concordant induction. The study by Berger (1962) appears in both the model-negative, observer-positive and model negative, observer-negative cells since it provides evidence for both discordant and concordant induction.

For experiments that use physiological arousal (electrodermal response) as the dependent measure, the direction of observers' responses cannot be established unless another measure (e.g., self-report) is used at the same time; thus, studies that use only arousal are included as evidence for both discordant and concordant induction. Because of this approach, the number of studies in the discordant cells is higher than it would be if concordant induction were considered the default or usual response and a more specific burden of proof were required to demonstrate discordant induction. If the studies based on physiological arousal are removed from the two discordant cells in Table 10-1, the empirical support for the existence of discordant induction diminishes substantially, although it does not disappear. Discordant induction appears to exist, but much more research is needed to determine under what conditions. Although there is evidence for all four types of induction, by far the largest amount of evidence is in the negative-negative cell. It is clear that observing a

TABLE 10-1   Studies on Occurrence of Socially Induced Affect

Model Positive	Model Negative
Observer Positive Englis et al.,1982 (EDR, HR,[a] face,[c] EMG) Haviland and Lelwica, 1987 (face) Hsee et al., 1990 (face, self) Krebs, 1975 (EDR, HR, vas) Stotland, 1969 (EDR, self,vas)[b] Zillmann and Cantor, 1977 (self, face[c])	**Observer Positive** Berger, 1962 (EDR) Bramel et al., 1968 (self[a]) Craig (1968) (EDR) Craig and Weinstein, 1965 (EDR) Craig and Wood, 1969 (EDR, self[c]) Englis et al., 1982 (EDR, HR,[a] face,[c] EMG) Hygge and Ohman, 1976a (EDR) Hygge and Ohman, 1976b (EDR) King and Heller, 1984 (self[a]) Krebs, 1975 (EDR, HR, vas) Marks and Hammen, 1982 (self) Zillmann and Cantor, 1977 (self, face[c])
Observer Negative Aderman and Unterberger, 1977 (modeling, self) Bramel et al., 1968 (self[a]) Englis et al., 1982 (EDR, HR,[a] face,[c] EMG) King and Heller, 1984 (self[a]) Krebs, 1975 (EDR, HR, vas) Zillmann and Cantor, 1977 (self, face[c])	**Observer Negative** Berger, 1962 (EDR) Boswell and Murray, 1981 (self) Coyne, 1976 (self) Craig, 1968 (EDR) Craig and Lowery, 1969 (EDR, self[d]) Craig and Weinstein, 1965 (EDR) Craig and Wood, 1969 (EDR, self[c]) Eisenberg et al., 1988 (self, EMG) Englis et al., 1982 (EDR, HR,[a] face,[c] EMG) Gotlib and Robinson, 1982 (face, self[c]) Gurtman et al., 1990 (self) Hammen and Peters, 1978 (self) Haviland and Lelwica, 1987 (face) Howes and Hokanson, 1979 (self[c]) Hsee et al., 1990 (face, self) Hygge, 1978 (EDR, self) Hygge and Ohman, 1976a (EDR) Hygge and Ohman, 1976b (EDR) Krebs, 1975 (EDR, HR, vas) Marks and Hammen, 1982 (self) McNiel et al., 1987 (face,[c] self[c]) Miller et al., 1959 (monkeys) Mirsky et al., 1958 (monkeys) Paddock and Nowicki, 1986 (self) Sagi and Hoffman, 1976 (cry) Simner, 1971 (cry) Stephens et al., 1987 (self[c]) Stotland, 1969 (EDR, self, vas[b]) Strack and Coyne, 1983 (self) Vaughan and Lanzetta, 1980 (EDR, EMG) Vaughn and Lanzetta, 1981 (EDR, EMG) Winer et al., 1981 (self) Zillmann and Cantor, 1977 (self, face[c])

NOTES: Studies using only arousal as a dependent measure are placed in both observer-positive and observer-negative cells. Methods of measurement are in parentheses:

cry: babies' cries; **EDR:** electrodermal response; **EMG:** electromyograph of facial efference; **face:** facial efference, visually coded; **HR:** heart rate; **modeling:** observer imitation of performer; **monkey:** monkey's displays of distress or learned response to distress; **self:** self-reported feeling; **vas:** vasoconstriction

[a] Differences in described direction, but not statistically significant.
[b] Stotland's "imagine-him" and "imagine-self" conditions combined.
[c] Measured, but null results reported.
[d] Differences in described direction, but no significance test reported.

person's negative affect generates arousal and negative affect in an observer, but there is evidence for each type of induction.

Much of the work establishing that affect in one individual can arouse emotion in another was done in the area of social learning (Bandura, 1971). In social learning theory, a central concern is how the affective response of a model to an object influences the conditioning of a response to that object of a person observing the model. Thirty years ago, Berger (1962) provided evidence that observers physiologically respond when watching models experience pain in a learning situation. He labeled the observer's affective reaction to the model's emotional response vicarious instigation. Berger's article fostered an abundance of research (see Green and Osborne, 1985, for a review). Berger (1962) noted that in investigations of such vicarious conditioning or reinforcement, researchers took it for granted that the unconditioned response of an observer is the same as the emotion experienced by the model who is engaged in a learning task (see also Lindahl, 1977).

The basic paradigm for much of this work was established in Berger's (1962) seminal paper. He compared the electrodermal responses of participants who watched a model that they either believed was experiencing electrical shock or did not believe was experiencing electrical shock. His finding that someone who is observing another person in distress displays electrodermal responses has been replicated a number of times (e.g., Craig, 1968; Craig and Lowery, 1969; Hygge and Ohman, 1976a, 1976b). Electrodermal responses in observers are found not only when the model experiences pain (Craig and Wood, 1969; Vaughan and Lanzetta, 1980, 1981), but also failure (Craig and Weinstein, 1965), reward (Krebs, 1975), and pleasure (Stotland, 1969). Krebs (1975) also found changes in the heart rate of those watching a model experience positive and negative emotions. Although most investigators have used *physiological* measures of observers' responses, studies using *self-reports*, *facial expressions*, or both have also found evidence for both concordant and discordant socially induced affect (Aderman and Unterberger, 1977; Coyne, 1976; Gotlib and Robinson, 1982, Hsee et al., 1990; Hygge, 1978; Marks and Hammen, 1982). Children, too, have been found to experience emotions when watching another person experience emotion (Eisenberg et al., 1988; Zillmann and Cantor, 1977), and there is some evidence that affect can be socially induced in infants (Haviland and Lelwica, 1987).

A number of methods have been used in studies investigating aspects of socially induced affect. Even though each method has weaknesses, each has been successfully used to assess such affect. The outcomes across different dependent measures suggest that socially induced affect is not a phenomenon tied to a specific method. Supportive results are obtained even when direct effects of a model's situation and physical movement are controlled. Although it cannot be fully determined whether observers in many of these studies were experiencing concordant or discordant induction, the investigations have combined physiological and self-report measures that provide data indicating that much of the emotional arousal is concordant with a model's emotional state.

There is only a small amount of research that specifically examined discordant induction, but a few studies using *self-report measures* have demonstrated it. Interestingly, there appears to be more evidence of discordant induction—when a model experiences positive affect and the observers experienced negative affect—than when the model experiences negative affect (and the observers experience positive affect). Are people more likely to experience or report feeling negative in response to another's positive affect than they are to experience or report feeling positive in response to another's negative affect? More studies of discordant induction would be helpful in better understanding its dynamics. In particular, studies that use facial efference as measured by electromyographs as a dependent measure would be useful: this approach might allow experimenters to obtain direct information on the valence of the observer's reaction and would thus add to the current evidence for discordant induced affect.

It is critical to note that the socially induced affect may not be all of the emotion that an observer feels. Inasmuch as an observer's situation is necessarily different from a model's, a perfect match in emotion cannot be expected. Berger (1962) described a vicariously instigated emotion as the prelude to the observer's own emotional state: the socially induced sadness experienced in response to seeing a friend weep, for example, may lead to a feeling of concern in the observer not felt by the friend. Finally, other affect-inducing circumstances may be occurring simultaneously with a model's emotional response. That there are physiological or experiential differences between individuals does not exclude the possibility that affect in an observer is, at least partially, socially induced.

POSSIBLE MECHANISMS

To understand how socially induced affect influences human performance, one must consider how one person's emotions can induce emotion in another. Little systematic work has directly examined the mechanisms by which affect is socially induced. In the past, conditioning and cognitive explanations of empathic responses have been popular (Allport, 1924; Bandura, 1969; Heider, 1958; Stotland, 1969). More recently, mechanisms that focus on mimicry have been proposed for these phenomena (Hatfield et al., 1992; Vaughan and Lanzetta, 1980, 1981).

Cognition

Several explanations have put forth the finding that people become emotionally aroused when observing another person experience emotion. In reviewing those explanations, the critical issue is not whether cognition can cause emotional arousal, but rather the role it plays in the social induction of affect.

Appraisal of Consequences for One's Well-Being

The appraisal of a situation as having consequences for one's well-being is a primary source of emotional arousal (Lazarus, 1982, 1984). Thus, one way emotion can be socially induced is if a model's situation or actions indicate a potential change in the observer's well-being. For example, Allport (1924) claimed instigation of fear in another was due to direct fear of the situation. Certainly fear of a performer's situation or stimulus can induce emotional arousal in an observer; fear and anxiety may well be experienced when one comes upon another person getting mugged. Concordant induction would be explained by a model and an observer appraising the situation in the same way (McCosh, 1880); discordant induction would occur if the observer and the model appraised the situation in different ways. (For findings that show that different cognitive appraisals can lead to different emotions see Roseman, 1984; Smith and Ellsworth, 1985). Other examples of self-relevant instigation of affect in an observer include times when one person's anger induces another to be afraid of what the person will do or when one person is afraid because another's fear suggests a danger in their shared environment. In these cases, the implications for an observer's immediate well-being provide a fairly straightforward explanation for how one person's affect elicited affect in another. When another's emotion signals an actual or potential change in one's well-being, emotion is likely to be induced.

One interesting aspect of socially induced affect, however, is that it is sometimes generated in a person who does not appraise the situation as being relevant to his or her well-being. This type of induction is not explainable from the theoretical view that emotions are aroused only when the situation is appraised as being relevant for personal well-being (Lazarus, 1982, 1984; Lazarus and Smith, 1988). Examples of situations in which immediate self-interests are not at stake include the positive feelings associated with being around a happy person, a mother's distress when seeing her daughter's sadness at failing at an athletic completion, a child's pleasure in watching another child being teased to the point of tears, and a person's unhappiness at seeing a disliked coworker experiencing joy.

Several studies strongly suggest that socially induced affect cannot be solely explained by appraisals of implications for well-being. Affect can be socially induced in an observer even when the model is a stranger to the observer and when the observer knows that he or she is not going to experience the same treatment. In studies in which observers are assured that they will not experience the negative stimulus, they still show socially induced affect (Hygge and Ohman, 1976a; Vaughan and Lanzetta, 1980, 1981; see also Craig and Lowery, 1969). An even more mundane example is the affect induced by a person's reading a novel or watching a play or movie.

Imagining Oneself in Another's Shoes

Bandura (1969) and Stotland (1969) postulated that imagining oneself in another's situation or in similar situations is the reason one responds emotionally when watching another individual experience emotion. Bandura (1969) and Stotland (1969) seemed to propose a strong version of this argument—that imagination is the sole way affect is socially induced. However, the evidence suggests that a weak version of the argument is more probable—imagination is one mechanism.

Stotland (1969) tested his assumption that empathy (concordant affect) is the result of a cognitive or symbolic process involving an observer imagining him- or herself in the model's situation or imagining how the model must be feeling. Subjects who imagined how the model was feeling, or how they would feel in the situation, responded differently to different model or performer states. His most consistent finding was that there were no differences in the physiological responses of observers among conditions during which they viewed the model ostensibly experience pleasure, neutral feelings, or pain when subjects were instructed simply to watch the model's movements. Because this "watch-him" condition was taken as a noncognitive control, the null results in combination with the differences found while subjects were using their imagination was taken to mean that cognition is the mechanism responsible for vicarious instigation. This conclusion may not be the best one, however. The instructions given to subjects in the "watch-him" condition may have objectified the model. In the "watch-him" condition, the instructions made the model an object of scrutiny; this observational mind-set may have distanced him from the observer and lessened any response (Hoffman, 1977). Furthermore, the model had his back to the observers, so that any noncognitive mechanism that relies on facial expression could not have operated. A lack of response to the model's affect under this condition does not rule out a noncognitive mechanism.

If Stotland's view is taken to mean that certain activities or perceptual attitudes can eliminate socially induced affect, his findings are supportive. His results are then limited to the finding that imagining oneself in an affective situation leads to physiological changes and self-reported emotion congruent with the situation. This suggests only that imagining oneself in the situation of a model may be sufficient to generate the changes found in vicarious-instigation research, not that imagining oneself in the situation is necessary for affect to be socially induced.

Cognitive Consistency

Using ideas in Gestalt psychology, the notion that inconsistency or imbalance among cognition is aversive has played an important role in social psychology for decades (Abelson, 1983; Festinger, 1957; Harary, 1983; Heider, 1946, 1958; Zajonc, 1968, 1983). In trying to explain socially induced affect, cognitive consistency theories provide a means by which the effects of the relationship between a model and an observer can be understood as an essential variable in the occurrence of both concordant and discordant cases of the phenomenon. Heider (1958) argued that the preference for balanced cognitive states was a reason for a person who likes another to experience affect concordant with the other's affect and for a person who dislikes another to experience affect discordant with the other's affect.

How might different consistency theories claim affect is socially induced? First, a model and a model's affect may form a cognitive unit; for the situation to be balanced, the observer must have similar sentiments about each of the two elements in the unit (see Heider, 1958; Zajonc, 1968). If Paul feels positive about Maria, and Maria is experiencing positive affect, then Paul must feel positive about Maria's feelings for the situation to be balanced. Similarly, if Paul feels negative about Maria, and Maria is experiencing positive affect, then Paul must feel negative about Maria's feeling for the situation to be balanced. Whatever Paul is feeling about Maria's affect may be thought of as the part of Paul's overall emotional state that is socially induced. The mechanism involves the preference for consistency; an observer generates a positive or negative feeling about the perceived situation in order to maintain balance.

A second way in which cognitive consistency theories explain socially induced affect is in relation to "ought" (Heider, 1958) or the requirements of justice. People like to believe that what occurs is just (Lerner, 1980). Good people should be rewarded (including experiencing positive emotions), and bad people should be punished (including experiencing negative emotions). The notion of preference for "justice" has been the reasoning behind the few studies that have explicitly examined discordant induction (Aderman and Unterberger, 1977; Bramel et al., 1968; Zillmann and Cantor, 1977). If an observer believes the model to be a good person or to have committed a good act, then the model's happiness should be pleasant to the observer—it is a balanced situation. Similarly, if an observer believes the model to be a bad person or to have committed a bad act, then the model's happiness will be unpleasant to the observer—it is an imbalanced situation.

The "justice" explanation relies on the inherent affective consequence of states of (in)balance or (in)consistency. However, one need not postulate the justice motive or the external "ought" to consider cognitive consistency as a mechanism for socially induced affect. There is also no need for an observer to form an affective link between him- or herself and the model's affect as is implied by the unit formation process. In consistency theories, any cognitive imbalance is aversive and motivates change; furthermore, the resolution of imbalance is pleasant (Festinger, 1957; Heider, 1946, 1958). Thus, for example, when another person about whom one is negative feels good it causes imbalance, which is aversive. Similarly, when a positive other feels bad, the imbalance generates negative affect. Since both the existence and the restoration of balance is understood to be pleasant, the mere perception of a balanced or imbalanced relation between a model and his or her affect is enough to cause either positive or negative feelings in the observer.

The advantage of this proposed mechanism is that it explains both discordant and concordant induction and indicates how the relationship between an observer and a model would influence the type of induction. Furthermore, balance is a cognitive mechanism that does not rely on appraisals of well-being for the generation of affect. The pleasantness of balance and the unpleasantness of imbalance are simply attributes of the cognitive system. For example, an observer does not need to realize that it is good for his or her enemy to fail; just the juxtapositions of the cognition of "enemy" and "enemy's feeling negative" is enough to cause at least some level of positive affect.

Although cognitive consistency has appeal as an explanatory mechanism for socially induced affect, it is by no means time to abandon all the other discussed mechanisms. First, the consistency drive is only one of many that may cause affective reactions (Abelson, 1983; Zajonc, 1968): the social induction of affect is much too pervasive and reliable a phenomenon to consider it to be dependent on what can be a weak mechanism. In addition, this mechanism can only account for positive or negative changes in an observer's emotional state; anything more complex would no doubt require more cognitive work. Nonetheless, cognitive consistency theories explain how some degree of positive or negative affect is generated in an observer and how the relationship between an observer and a model might influence what is induced.

Classical Conditioning

A simple way by which the affect of others might induce a person's affect is through classical conditioning (Hoffman, 1990). If the emotional behaviors of others are frequently followed by affectively congruent emotional consequences for the observer—such as the pairing of others' smiling with gifts or kind words—the emotional expressions of others should become conditioned stimuli capable of eliciting congruent emotional reactions in observers (Allport, 1924; Bandura, 1965).

Englis et al. (1982) also propose that classical conditioning may be responsible for discordant responses. They give the example of a sadistic mother's smile signaling punishment for a child; repeated association of this display of pleasure with the incongruent outcome of punishment might lead to the acquisition of a discordant emotional response to the mother's smile. Their experiments found differences in the facial expressions of observers watching a model experience emotion that depended on whether the observers' rewards and shocks had been symmetrical with the model's smiles and grimaces or had been asymmetrical to the model's expression. These data provide some support for the notion that classical conditioning can alter the pattern of an observer's facial movements produced when a model is either pained or happy. Specifically, if a person's expressions have been predictive of an observer's outcome, the observer's own facial response to the other's expressions is then associated with that contingency.

Although Englis et al. (1982) limit their discussion and data to the instance when a specific individual's display, such as a mother's smile, is paired with incongruent outcomes, such as punishment, the conditioning mechanism might have broader implications. For example, people may learn that expressions of pleasure by disliked others are coupled with aversive outcomes; thus, positive expressions by any disliked person might induce negative affect. Classical conditioning provides a plausible mechanism for how discordant affect might be induced and how such induction might be related to the social relation between the model and the observer. Again, more research will surely yield new insights about this mechanism.

Mimicry

One obvious mechanism of social induction is mimicry of a model (Hatfield et al., 1992; Vaughan and Lanzetta, 1980, 1981). This section reviews the evidence for mimicry, with an emphasis on facial expressions.

Imitation of expressions is a phylogenetically ancient and basic form of intraspecies communication found in many vertebrate species (Brothers, 1990). McDougall (1908) held that a model's pain display is an unconditioned stimulus for mimicry. If mimicry is such a basic phenomenon, then the cognitive resources necessary for mimicry may be minimal. Of course, mimicry may occur as a result of the imaginal processes discussed above; in these cases the mechanisms may work together to create socially induced affect. It is also possible, however, that cognitive representations are not needed to match the movements of another; simply perceiving another's expression may be enough. Thus, mimicry may provide a mechanism for induction that is both noncognitive and does not rely on implications for well-being.

In the small amount of research on motor mimicry, there is support for the notion that people imitate others. Berger and Hadley (1975) examined whether muscle activity in an observer tends to parallel muscle use in a model. They recorded activity in the arms and lips of observers (using electromyographs (EMG)) who were watching videotapes of arm wrestling and stuttering. They found greater EMG activity in the observers' muscles that corresponded to the muscles being used by the models than in the muscles that did not correspond to the muscles being used by the models.

Evidence for facial mimicry is found in Dimberg's (1982, 1988) studies of facial reactions to facial expressions. He reports that 8-second presentations of slides of posed angry and happy faces elicited facial EMG responses in subjects consistent with the posed expression. Specifically, zygomatic activity (muscle used to pull cheeks back, as in a smile) was higher when subjects viewed a happy versus an angry face, and corrugator activity (muscle used to wrinkle the brows) was elevated when subjects viewed an angry face, and it was decreased when subjects viewed a happy face.

Mimicry of nonstatic faces has been demonstrated in several studies. Vaughan and Lanzetta (1980, 1981) report that a model's facial display of pain instigates congruent facial activation in an observer. Mimicry of positive expressions has been found by Bush et al. (1989), who tested facial reactions of individuals watching a videotaped comedy routine. Subjects saw two target comedy routines, one of which had smiling faces dubbed into the presentation during soundtrack laughter. Half the subjects had been told to inhibit their facial expressions. The half whose expressions were spontaneous displayed greater zygomatic and orbicularis oculi activity (narrows eyes, as when smiling, but also evident in pain grimace—see Englis et al., 1982) during the dubbed segments than during the segments without smiling faces.

There are a number of studies suggesting that mimicry is a mechanism by which affect might be socially induced. Support for the idea that mimicry can lead to affective resonance is found in the psychoanalytic literature (for a review, see Basch, 1983). In addition, because their data suggest that the instigated facial response of a observer is time locked with the model's expression, Vaughan and Lanzetta (1980) consider mimicry a likely mechanism for vicarious instigation, since a mimetic response should occur simultaneously with a model's response. A cognitive strategy such as retrieval of congruent imagery would take longer to initiate and subside.

Research suggests that facial mimicry plays a role in the generation of affect. Although other types of mimicry may relate to socially induced affect, most investigations of mimicry have concentrated on the face, and the best evidence currently available is about the role of the face (see Hatfield et al., 1992).

How might mimicry lead to socially induced affect? The observer's physical imitation of the model may lead to changes in the emotion of the observer. James (1890/1950) suggested that facial action leads to emotion, rather than emotion leading to facial action. Although this hypothesis is by no means universally accepted, the data tend to support the notion that facial efference can both initiate and modulate emotional experience (for a review, see Adelmann and Zajonc, 1989). Understanding of facial feedback is limited, however: more knowledge of the mechanisms, power, and moderating conditions of facial feedback is needed. Basic questions such as the frequency with which facial action alters affective state need to be addressed before one can understand the role of facial mimicry in socially induced affect.

Evidence that facial action might play a central role in socially induced affect is given by Vaughan and Lanzetta (1981). When they showed to undergraduate observers a videotape of a model displaying periodic pain expressions, they found that observers who were instructed to pose an expression of pain while the model was expressing pain experienced greater changes in skin conductance and heart rates than both observers instructed to inhibit their facial actions and those given no instructions regarding facial action. These data suggest that facial efference similar to that of a model increases the induction of emotion in an observer.

An example of spontaneous mimicry leading to socially induced affect is given by Bush et al. (1989), who evaluated amusement in relation to mimicry of smiling behavior. As described above, they showed videotapes of comedy routines, with smiling faces dubbed into one performance during soundtrack laughter and not into the other. Half the subjects had been told to inhibit their facial activity. Those in the spontaneous condition reported greater amusement during the routine with the dubs than during the nondubbed routine; furthermore, those in the spontaneous condition reported greater amusement during the dubbed routine than those told to inhibit their expressions. These findings support the perspective that mimicry of others' facial expressions can produce affective responses.

In considering its relation to performance, mimicry may combine with cognitive processes to influence choices. The issue is one of interpreting another person's expressions. The attribution of intentions on the basis of nonverbal behavior is a topic that has received considerable attention in the literature (e.g., Ekman and Friesen, 1969; Druckman and Bjork, 1991:Ch.9). As we discuss below, mimicry may be diagnostic of another's interest, attention, or liking for a model. It may also be a source of information used by observers during their "calculations" about responses or strategies.

Basic Issues

At present, investigations of socially induced affect have focused on proving that it occurs and some of the mechanism by which it may occur. Few studies have evaluated the amount of influence that socially induced affect has in people's overall or specific emotional experiences. Until there is better understanding of the frequency with which socially induced affect occurs and how strong it is when it does occur, it will be difficult to know the amount of influence it has in real-life situations. The efficacy with which each of the mechanisms described above induces affect needs to be evaluated and compared with each other and with methods of inducing direct affect. Key characteristics that should be evaluated include intensity of induced affect, duration of change in affect, and individuals' awareness of the changes in affect and their sources.

Also unexamined are factors that might moderate socially induced affect. Affect may be more or less likely to be socially induced in various situations or in different people. Buck (1984), for example, has found that people differ in their ability to send and receive nonverbal information. Some people's emotions may be more visible or "readable" to others; these individuals may tend to induce affect in others more often or more strongly. Those who pick up on nonverbal emotional cues may be more readily, more frequently, or more potently influenced by the emotions of others.

One potential moderating variable—the relationship between model and observer—has received both theoretical (James, 1890/1950; Heider, 1958) and empirical attention. Krebs (1975) found that subjects who believed they were similar to the model reported feeling worse and were more aroused while waiting for the model to receive a punishment than those who believed they were dissimilar. Zillmann and Cantor (1977) found that in conditions in which children reported liking the protagonist of a stimulus film, they also reported feelings similar to his (see also Miller, 1987).

Finally, cultural differences may influence socially induced affect. For example, the mimicry mechanism for socially induced affect may be more prevalent in cultures with norms for relatively more facial movement associated with emotion than in cultures with norms for relatively less movement (see Mesquita and Frijda, 1992). In "collectivist" cultures, the situation of a member of one's group may be perceived as being more directly relevant—perhaps even truly self-relevant—to the individual than in "individualistic" cultures (see Markus and Kitayama, 1991). There are, of course, other possible cultural influences on socially induced affect and it is important to keep in mind that all the mechanisms discussed in the preceding section above may function differently in different cultural settings. Those mechanisms can provide a basis for theoretically guided research on socially induced affect. One direction would be to design experiments that can distinguish among alternative interpretations or theories for observed effects. Another direction would be to compare effects obtained in different types of situations and cultures. The results could address issues of the extent to which interpretations of socially induced affect are situational or culture-specific.

The next section explores some potential applications or functions of socially induced affect. One should be reminded that others' emotions are only one source of affect; a sadist who happily smiles while hurting his or her victim is not likely to induce positive affect in the victim! Research needs to evaluate the relative strength of socially induced affect in various situations and to explain other routes to socially induced affect that may complement or counter the effects of mimicry.

AFFECT AND PERFORMANCE

As noted above, affect socially induced in individuals may influence their performance in the same ways that direct affect does. We first summarize general findings on the effects of affect on performance in several domains. We then explore areas in which socially induced affect may have a more unique role.

Several studies have found that mood influences performance of certain tasks. Slife and Weaver (1992) report that subjects put in a negative affective state were less skillful than other subjects in such metacognitive tasks as predicting their answers to math problems and rating their performances after attempting to answer the problems, but no differences in actual task performance were reported. Wolff and Gregory (1991) examined specific areas in which negative affect might influence performance. They found no differences in performance on verbal tests between those put in a temporary dysphoric mood and control subjects. They did find a significant decrement in performance by the dysphoric subjects in such visual-motor subtests as block design and object assembly. These losses may have been due to dysphoria's causing motor slowing or interference with perceptual organization. Radenhausen and Anker (1988) examined reasoning performance in depressed and elated subjects. They found a marginally significant difference in solving syllogisms, with those in negative moods doing worse. No differences in perceptual performance was found. Saavedra and Earley (1991) induced positive or negative affective states in subjects and examined the effect on a problem solving task. They report that subjects in the positive affect condition outperformed those in the negative affect condition. In addition, subjects in the positive affect condition were more likely to stay with their goal and task choice in a second round.

These results suggest that various types of skills are influenced by affect, a notable exception being math performance. It appears that, in general, more negative affect causes decrements in performance, and more positive affect facilitates performance. Note that for the most part, the skills examined in these studies are cognitive in nature. There is virtually no evidence on whether affect influences physical performance. It seems plausible that positive or negative affect could reduce reaction time or the performance of complex motor behaviors, for example, by distracting a performer. Clearly, before the effects of socially induced affect on performance can be established, a better understanding of the general effects of affect on cognitive and motor performance is needed.

There are two notable differences between socially induced and direct affect. First, socially induced affect is likely to play a larger role in interpersonal or social situations. Because socially induced affect might be a natural occurrence in social situations—such as when a small group is attempting to complete a task or when individuals are being trained—possible influences of socially induced affect on performance in these types of situations should be considered. Second, socially induced affect may be more diffuse and less tied to the appraisal of a situation than is direct affect. Socially induced affect may be more likely than direct affect to be mistakenly attributed to an aspect of the situation other than the people in it. Affect caused by appraising some aspect of the environment as having implications for one's own well-being has a source already connected to it. Affect induced socially by one of the mechanisms other than appraisal (classical conditioning, cognitive consistency, and mimicry) may not be tied to a specific object and thus may be more easily misassociated with some salient element of the situation. In a similar vein, Schwarz et al. (1991) reported that when people know the causes of their affective state, they are less likely to use it as information in reacting to their environment (e.g., in evaluating an argument). Keeping these factors in mind, we turn to specific ways in which socially induced affect might influence performance.

Results obtained from studies on a number of topics have implications for the relationship between socially induced affect and performance. Although support for a relationship is usually indirect, the evidence identifies seven areas of performance likely to be influenced by socially induced affect: performance of flight cockpit crews; attention; teaching and influencing; negotiating; panic behavior in groups; helping behavior; and group cohesion. Further research will be needed to distinguish specific effects of socially induced affect from other elements in the situation that may contribute to the observed performance, but the review does suggest possible socially induced affect of applications.

Flight Crew Performance

A recent study by Chidester et al. (1990) compared flight crews with two different types of leaders. One type of crew was led by a captain who displayed a positive emotional style characterized by frequent smiles, an optimistic outlook, and a sensitivity to other's feelings. Members of those crews also showed positive attitudes as they went about their work. Another type of crew was led by a captain whose expressive style was negative. He or she frowned, complained a lot, was irritable, and evinced a pessimistic attitude. Members of those crews, like their captains, appeared negative in interpersonal relations with their colleagues. The two crews differed in other ways. Members of the "negative" crew made more errors in performing their mission than members of the "positive" crew: they missed discovering indications of hydraulic loss, they flew at airspeeds above or below those required for the aircraft's configuration, and they made improper landings or missed an approach.

The differences in performance between the two types of crews may have been due to the differences between the captains in the way they communicated to their crew members. Just as positive feelings can energize a performer, negative feelings can distract him or her. However, other differences between the captains, correlated with expressive styles, may also have contributed to crew performances: for example, the positive-expressive captains may have delegated tasks more effectively, adopted different standards for evaluating workload, or had higher achievement motivation than the negative-expressive captains. But the direction of causation may have been reversed: negative captains may have been reacting to inept crews while the positive captains may have been responding to efficient crews. Common sense suggests that the effects were reciprocal, with influences from captain to crew and from crew to captain. Without data from more detailed research it is difficult to eliminate these plausible rival hypotheses for the findings.

The Chidester et al. (1990) study, while suggestive, illustrates problems of design that prevent attributing crew performance specifically to socially induced affect. Proper controls for other factors were not instituted: for example, crew members' affect may have been a result of the types of relationships formed between them and their captains. In this way, the study is similar to those summarized in the rest of this section. While clearly relevant, the studies are primarily explorative in the sense of providing bases for better designed experiments that can isolate effects produced by socially induced affect. Such experiments would control for factors correlated with a leader's expressed affect and also assess whether the expressed affect (positive or negative) is transmitted to group members (concordant or discordant) whose performance is evaluated. These kinds of experiments can be designed for each of the topics discussed below.

Attention

There may be motivational differences between direct and socially induced affect. For example, negative affect caused by a person's appraising a situation as detrimental to his or her well-being may be more likely to carry with it suggestions for specific action. This situation may be detrimental to performance in that the tendency for the action motivated by the appraisal and affect may interfere with the performance of the person's task. But for a person experiencing socially induced negative affect, because the person may be less aware of the cause (which is not as self-generated), it may precipitate a search for a cause; the negative affect may be used as information that there is trouble in the environment. (These differences may be less important in the case of positive affect, as there is less motivation associated with positive states.) For example, a person watching a radar screen for possible enemy incursions may be somewhat distracted if he or she is angry at being selected for this duty. A second person sitting next to the first, angry, person may be more distracted, however, if she or he is experiencing negative affect socially induced from the first person. The second person may have to exert effort to both deal with the negative affect and to discover the cause of the negative affect. That person, who is experiencing socially induced affect, might suffer a greater decrement in performance—responding as quickly as possible to signs of danger from the screen—than the first person.

Mimicry, discussed above as a mechanism for transmitted affect, may also have value as a diagnostic clue to another's interest or attention. Bush et al. (1986) found that supporters of President Reagan spontaneously mimicked his expressions more than did nonsupporters. This finding suggests that liking is indicated by mimicry. Less clear is the mechanism for this relationship. If mimicry indicates the amount of attention paid to the liked or disliked model, then it may be diagnostic of the extent to which observers are involved or interested in the model. An instructor could, for example, monitor the mimetic facial actions of his or her students: indications that they are not longer mimicking might signal that the time has come to review or clarify the material.

Teaching and Influencing

Better performance in teaching and influencing means changing knowledge or attitudes among students or an audience. There are several ways in which socially induced affect might contribute to such an outcome. In general, to the extent that the affective component of the message is integral to it, speakers more able to communicate that component are more effective. For example, an easily mimicked speaker may be better able than a less easily mimicked speaker to make the audience feel what he or she is feeling about the topic. Beyond that, however, socially induced affect in students or an audience can influence the teaching and persuasion processes in two ways: it may change how the observers respond to the message in ways that make learning or persuasion more or less likely; or it may be misattributed to or associated with various components of the situation, which influences the degree of persuasion or learning experienced.

A socially induced affective state might influence the way in which an audience responds to a persuasive message; for a review, see Schwarz et al. (1991). A speaker may induce either positive or negative affect in the audience. Positive moods have been found to increase persuasion (Janis et al. 1965). The reason for this appears to be that people in a positive mood pay less attention to the message, or do not engage in the effort to carefully consider the message; people in negative or neutral moods more systematically process the content of the message, and are thus more likely to detect flaws in it than are those in positive moods (Bless et al., 1990; Kuykendall and Keating, 1990; Mackie and Worth, 1989; Schwarz et al., 1991; Worth and Mackie, 1987). Thus, if simple persuasion is desired, inducing a positive mood in an audience would be beneficial. However, if the arguments in favor of the speaker's case are strong, it might be preferable to induce more negative moods, so that the audience carefully processes the information. Attitude change that results from careful processing is found to be more stable than attitude change in the absence of such processing (Petty and Cacioppo, 1986). In learning situations in which the goal is to increase students' thinking about the content of the message, positive moods may be detrimental.

Socially induced affect might also have an effect through misattribution to some component of a communication. One component is the speaker. For example, liking for a source might be increased if socially induced positive affect is associated with the source. A speaker who smiles a lot might create positive affect among the audience through people's mimicry of him or her. The audience might then associate this increase in positive affect with the source and thus like the speaker more.

This liking for the source could influence persuasion. People tend to be more persuaded by people they like (e.g., Roskos-Ewoldsen and Fazio, 1992). There is evidence, however, that the effect of liking for a speaker is limited. The physical attractiveness of a speaker, which increases liking for a speaker, influences acceptance of emotionally toned messages, but not of rationally toned messages (Pallak et al., 1983). Similarity of source to the target— also a cause of liking—increases persuasion (Dembroski et al., 1978), but primarily when the topic is a matter of subjective preference rather than objective reality (Goethals and Nelson, 1973). Thus, positive affect induced in an audience may increase the degree to which people are persuaded when the arguments are based on emotion or the topic is not a matter of objective reality.

In terms of enhancing performance, this approach would seem best when nonobjective factors may increase performance. For example, there may be a limited number of objective reasons why an individual should follow a code of conduct. A speaker who is liked may be more likely to persuade individuals to follow the code than one who is disliked. This could be valuable in an academic situation, for example, in which cheating is detrimental to the goals of the institution and group, but may not be clearly disadvantageous for an individual. A liked speaker may also be more effective under conditions of uncertainty, when facts are not readily available. When there are too few facts to support the preferability of any specific action (e.g., does the group head north or south to get around an obstacle?), a liked leader may be able to persuade his or her subordinates to take the action.

A second component with which socially induced affect might be associated is the topic of the communication. Through socially induced affect, a speaker may be able to influence the observers' attitudes toward specific topics. For example, if an instructor frowns during the discussion of a particular topic, the students may mimic the action and thus experience more negative affect. One consequence of this may be unintended "learning." For example, if an instructor is describing a new safety procedure to some trainees, the instructor may (unknowingly) frown during the presentation because he or she does not enjoy or approve of the procedure. The induction of this negative affect in the students may cause them to dislike the procedure and may cause them to be less persuaded that it is a good procedure. Unintended teaching and learning may not be all bad, however. The obvious case is a teacher who expresses a positive attitude toward a topic perhaps originally considered negative by a pupil. Concordant affect has been assumed in these examples. The effects may be reversed if discordant affect is induced. For example, if discordant affect occurs when a teacher is talking enthusiastically about a topic, the topic may become associated with negative affect for the students. If, as predicted by the classical conditioning and cognitive consistency mechanisms, discordant affect is induced when an observer dislikes the model, then a disliked teacher may consistently induce the opposite emotions in his or her pupils. This is an example of why it is important to be aware of variables that moderate or interact with socially induced affect.

Negotiating

There is a large research literature on the social-psychological aspects of negotiation and related forms of social interaction (e.g., Druckman, 1977; Pruitt, 1981; Pruitt and Rubin, 1985). Many of the studies deal with the "self-aggravating aspects of negotiations that are relatively independent of the substantive questions involved and that can impede or facilitate negotiations on any issue" (Frank, 1968:192). These aspects consist primarily of the emotional reactions of negotiators to their opponents' offers and proposals. Negative feelings may be the result of the competitive situation, a dislike for the opponent, or the realization that compromise will be needed if an agreement is to be attained. They can also be induced socially by the expressions of one's opposite number. Although we know much less about this source of affect in negotiation than other sources, there is reason to believe that it may have a strong influence on bargaining behavior, particularly when negotiation is viewed as an "expression game" (Goffman, 1969).

Goffman's expression-game metaphor is discussed by him in the context of strategic interaction. Emphasizing the nonverbal exchanges in negotiation, the expression game consists of alternating moves and countermoves, with negotiators' both managing the impressions they send and processing information they receive. Focusing on interaction processes, expression games are "assessment contests" designed to conceal or convey information; they illustrate the diagnostic value of nonverbal behavior in terms of clues to unarticulated intentions. The "clues" are the essence of the game, not merely factors that influence other forms of behavior (Druckman et al., 1982). Thus, an opponent's expressions are a source of information about his or her intentions, including the judgment that he or she is telling the truth (see the chapter on detecting deception in Druckman and Bjork, 1991). With regard to socially induced affect, inferences about another's intentions may be based on the feelings engendered in oneself by the other's expressions. When negative affect or anxious feelings are induced, a negotiator may be quick to conclude that the opponent is concealing information vital to obtaining an agreement.

A negotiator's feelings can move the process either toward or away from agreement. Research by Carnevale and Isen (1986) showed that when positive affect was induced, few contentious tactics were used, and joint benefits were improved. The positive affect served to offset the competitive feelings aroused by the bargaining task. However, although a positive opponent may be more liked than a negative opponent, the positive feelings may not translate into agreements. Johnson (1971b) found that when a scripted opponent acted in a warm manner toward the negotiating subject, the latter person liked the opponent more but did not reach a better agreement than when faced with a "cold" scripted opponent. The warm opponent served to reinforce the negotiator's feelings about the superiority of his or her positions. The induced good feelings were apparently attributed to the opponent's judgment about his or her position leading, perhaps, to a false estimate of the probability of agreement.

Findings obtained in another study by Johnson (1971a) suggest that a strategy consisting of alternating between negative (acting cold) and positive (acting warm) affect may be effective. Negotiators compromised more and evinced a larger change in attitudes when faced with a scripted opponent who alternated between showing anger and warmth than when faced with opponents who were either angry or warm throughout the interactions.

This finding suggests an advantage in "fine-tuning" one's expressions. Another way to do this is by creating expectations for toughness (showing anger) early and a willingness to compromise (conveying warmth) later in the process. A pattern in the other direction—going from relatively soft to tough postures—has been shown to produce impasses (Druckman and Bonoma, 1976). Of particular interest here is the effect of induced feelings on bargaining behavior. Although based only on a few studies, the finding coincides with effects obtained in many studies for alternative concession strategies (e.g., Druckman and Harris, 1990). Still to be determined, however, is whether the observed effect of the other's behavior is due primarily to expressions or to bargaining moves. Both are sources of information about intentions. Both are bases for the emotional experience during negotiation. A more precise rendering of the specific role played by socially induced affect in negotiation awaits further research.

Panic Behavior in Groups

Panic is a state that is detrimental to the performance of any task, particularly a group task under potentially dangerous conditions when order is essential to performance. Panic often occurs in group situations, and socially induced affect may well play a role in its occurrence. The affective states of members of a group appear to be related to the likelihood of panic and to survival in a crisis. Panic increases under perception of personal threat (Klein, 1976). Sako and Misumi (1982) found that the perceived possibility of escape from electric shock in a bottle-neck situation was associated with actual escape; the more people thought they would escape, the more they did. Kugihara et al. (1980) found that increased aggression and competition among members of a group decrease the percentage of members of a group that escape a panic situation. Overall, then, if negative affect—fear—can be prevented from being passed from one person to another, or if positive affect can be induced in the members of a group, then performance—sustained organization or order and greater survival—in panic situations should be improved.

Research on mass hysteria (e.g., outbreaks of psychogenic physical symptoms in a group) suggests that relationships among people is an important determinant of who experiences the hysterical symptoms. An individual is more likely to exhibit symptoms if a friend experiences symptoms (Small et al., 1991; Stahl and Lebedun, 1974; Wong et al., 1982). Like the finding on panic in a group, this finding suggests that the emotional state of one's friends is likely to have a strong influence on one's own emotional state. Within a large group, it may be pockets of friends that panic first. One way to mitigate panic might be to strengthen social ties between leaders trained not to panic and the members of their groups.

Helping Behavior

There is a fair amount of research that indicates that empathy can cause helping (Batson and Shaw, 1991). When one feels what another in distress is feeling, one may be more likely to help that person, although this may occur simply to alleviate one's own distress. On any group task in which members may possess different levels of skills, a factor that encourages one to help another may facilitate success. If liking another person increases socially induced affect, members of groups that like each other may be more likely to help one another. Another way to increase socially induced affect in groups—and potentially mutual helping—would be to use classical conditioning. A group member who has learned that the emotions of a fellow group member have implications for his or her own well-being may be more likely to experience socially induced affect and to help the fellow group member.

Group Cohesion

Socially induced affect can increase a group's cohesion. A particular member's positive affect may produce good feelings in other members. Those induced positive feelings may serve to increase one's liking for other group members. Such increased liking contributes to enhanced cohesion (Braaten, 1991). Moreover, empathy and group cohesion have been shown to be related (Roark and Sharah, 1989).

A number of studies have found that cohesiveness is associated with efficacy and success (Jaffe and Nebenzahl, 1990; Spink, 1990; Williams and Widmeyer, 1991), but some do not (Keyton and Springston, 1990). In a review of 40 years of research, Mudrack (1989) concluded that the effect of group cohesiveness on performance is not clear, and although Evans and Dion (1991) found in a meta-analysis of studies testing the effects of cohesiveness on group performance that the relation appears both stable and positive, they caution against generalizing these findings to real work groups. One problem is the variety of definitions of cohesiveness. To understand how socially induced affect might influence group performance, research needs to establish what components of cohesiveness are influenced by socially induced affect, and what effect these components have on group performance.

The effect of cohesion on group performance depends on the goals in the situation. Zaccaro and Lowe (1988) found that interpersonal cohesiveness, defined as satisfactory relationships with other members of the group, *inhibited* optimal productivity on an additive group task by causing task-interfering interactions among group members. However, when groups performed a disjunctive task—determining together what items would be needed to survive in the subarctic after a plane crash—such cohesiveness was associated with better performance (Zaccaro and McCoy, 1988). Thus, it may be best to induce positive affect only in groups whose tasks require cooperation and communication and to not induce positive affect or, even in some instances, to induce negative affect for groups performing simple additive tasks. The lack of positive affect, or the induced negative affect, would reduce interpersonal cohesion and interfere with communication among the group's members.

One possible benefit of positive feelings for a group is suggested by work done by Horwitz (1954). He had members of a sorority work together to solve jigsaw puzzles. Some of the puzzles were interrupted by the experimenter. When interrupted, the women were asked to vote on whether to continue the task. At the end of the series of tasks, participants were asked individually to list the puzzles on which they had worked. Horwitz found greater memory for interrupted tasks—known as the Zeigarnik effect—for puzzles on which the individual had not wanted to continue, as long as the group had voted to continue that puzzle. This suggests that the individual had taken on the group's goals: motivation was conveyed from the group to the individual. This socially induced motivation may promote individual performances within a group by increasing motivation for the group's goals in the individual. Similarly, in a longitudinal study of 54 work groups in several private and public organizations, such as engineering project groups and product assembly groups, Greene (1989) found that group acceptance of goals increased productivity.

CONCLUSIONS

There is evidence for the transmission of affect from one person to another. The evidence is stronger for the induction of the same affect (concordant socially induced affect) than for the induction of an opposite affect (discordant socially induced affect). When positive feelings are induced, it is more likely that a message will be accepted. Negative feelings lead to less acceptance of the communication due, perhaps, to a more critical evaluation of the message. The strength of socially induced affect, whether positive or negative, may depend on similarity and liking for the source, as well as cultural factors. Less is known about possible explanations for why it occurs. Plausible mechanisms involve cognition, conditioning, and mimicry. Perhaps all these processes are involved: for example, the initial induction may be due to conditioning or mimicry while its later effect on performance is due to cognitive appraisal processes.

A number of interesting implications for performance arise from the research to date:

•   Mimicry of another's facial expressions can facilitate persuasion or learning. It facilitates persuasion to the extent that it indicates liking for the source of a message; it facilitates learning to the extent that it indicates attention to and interest in the communication.

• Negative or anxious feelings conveyed by sources of deception may lead an observer to be suspicious of his or her intentions.

• Bargainers who alternate between negative and positive affect or who express negative affect in the early phases of negotiation and positive affect in the later phases may elicit more compromise from their opponents than bargainers who express either positive or negative affect throughout the negotiation.

• Better response to panic situations may occur in a group when a leader conveys positive affect, especially in a cohesive group.

• By increasing one's liking for a group, socially induced affect may enhance member motivation to perform, in terms of contributing to its goals.

Fewer implications can be drawn from research for the effects of socially induced affect on physical performance or motor skills. Nor has the research clearly distinguished between effects produced by direct and socially induced affect.

Both the basic exploration of socially induced affect and questions about its role in performance continue to raise interesting research issues. These types of questions are related. Greater understanding of the basic processes of socially induced affect can yield insights into the way it operates in real-world settings, especially in relation to performance. Examining how socially induced affect influences performance will, in turn, suggest ideas about the mechanisms responsible for the phenomenon.

NOTES

[1]We use the concept of "induction" rather than "contagion" for several reasons. First, induction refers to an action caused by something else (e.g., the ipecac induced vomiting); contagion implies that something has been transferred from one individual to another (e.g., a contagious virus). Second, with regard to affect, induction indicates that a model's emotion caused emotion in an observer; contagion suggests that a model's emotions were transferred to the observer. Third, the term induction better describes the general phenomenon of interest, as when affect expressed by one person causes affect in another person. Fourth, it does not imply that an observer's response must be identical to that of the performer: thus socially induced affect includes the possibility that an observer's affect is opposite that expressed by the model (discordant affect).

[2]Our definition of socially induced affect does not include situation's in which a person's extra-emotional behavior changes the emotions of another person. For example, if an officer tells a subordinate that he or she failed at a particular task, and the subordinate feels a negative emotion as a result of this evaluation, the subordinate's emotions have been influenced by an exchange of information. However, the subordinate's emotions were not influenced by the officer's emotions or their direct behavioral manifestations (e.g., facial expression). Therefore, work examining the effect of an evaluation on a person's self-esteem or motivation, for example, is not directly relevant to the present discussion. What would be relevant to socially induced affect, as defined in this chapter, is an understanding of how the emotions that accom-

pany the officer's message influence the subordinate's emotional reactions, and how these, in turn, might influence future performance.

[3]The phenomenon could also be referred to as socially induced emotion. The literature is not consistent in its use of the terms "emotion" and "affect," which leads to some confusion in measurement. If self-reports are used, the phenomenon being measured is emotion; if facial expressions and other observable physical responses are used, affect is being measured. Physiological measures, used in many experiments, may indicate either emotion or affect. To the extent that they correlate with a person's reported feelings, they indicate emotion. To the extent that they indicate arousal and are manifest in observable expression they reflect affect. The problem consists of distinguishing between whether emotion or affect is indicated by a measure. Although we try to maintain the distinction between affect and emotion noted above, in reporting on the research we use the term the investigators use.

[4]Of course, this does not mean that socially induced affect would always be superior to directly induced affect. If it is simpler to induce the desired state directly, and there are not apparent advantages in inducing affect through social means, then direct, nonsocial induction would be preferred.

[5]A "pure" discordant affect would occur when an entirely uninvolved detached observer experienced the opposite feeling of the performer: for example, a person watching someone on the news. Demonstrations of such effects depend on achieving proper controls for the effects of relationship (of the model and the observer) on the experience of affect. Such controls have not been completely achieved in the experiments completed to date and future experimentation should attempt to achieve insulation of an observer from a relationship with the model.

[6]A more complex instance is the induction of a different emotion of the same "valence" (direction), such as when a model's anger causes fear or sadness in the observer. This instance illustrates an induction of similar valence (concordant) but a different "flavor" of that affect (discordant emotion). Although this is an interesting case for future research, it is not treated in this chapter.

[7]Our definition of affect as observable emotion does not perfectly match the term as used in some of the research reviewed. For studies that use observers' self-reports as the dependent measure, the phenomenon being measured is emotion, not affect, in our terms, since it is not externally observed or measured.

11

Thought Suppression

People often try to control their thoughts in the hope that they will therefore be able to control their emotions, behaviors, or performances. It is clear from everyday life that the control of mental activity meets with some success: people can sometimes concentrate or study at will; they can sometimes eliminate bothersome worries from mind; they can sometimes relax, sometimes get aroused, sometimes get in a better mood; they may even seem to reduce their thoughts of food during a diet or of cigarettes while trying to quit smoking. And people who are grieving over a loss sometimes conclude that their eventual recovery was the result of putting the loss out of mind. Within a certain range of everyday uses, then, people can exercise some mental control. But in terms of the overall topic of enhancing human performance, the key issues for this chapter are research and theory on why people suppress thoughts, how effective thought suppression may be, what later consequences may result from it, and what alternatives exist that may be more effective in the pursuit of freedom from unwanted thoughts.

The form of thought suppression considered in this chapter is the intentional avoidance of a thought or category of thoughts: for example, "I don't want to think about food" or "I won't think about my ex-husband." This kind of suppression is distinguished from thought suppression that occurs in the service of intentional attention to something else. Wegner and Schneider (1989) distinguished between primary and auxiliary suppression: when one suppresses a thought simply to avoid that thought, they termed it primary thought suppression; when one suppresses a thought in order to focus on something else, it is auxiliary thought suppression. This chapter is about primary thought suppression.[1]

Primary thought suppression is, in some sense, more troublesome than auxiliary thought suppression. Rather than having a handy replacement thought, in primary thought suppression one has no obvious "next thing to think." One simply wants to escape a current thought, without a particular idea or activity to replace it.

MOTIVATION

One easy way to find out why people might suppress thoughts is to look over the titles of self-help books in any bookstore. Such books tout themselves as aids to the satisfaction of a variety of self-improvement desires, among them helping to produce freedom from worry, fear, depression, addiction, overweight, anger, low self-esteem, obsession, victimization, bad relationships, thoughts about traumatic life events, secrets of the past, stress, failure at work, and so on (see Starker, 1989). Quite aside from whether reading these books is useful in any way, the topics of the books present a catalog of issues for which people are seeking help, and thought suppression is a form of self-help, a strategy that is so simple and direct that one doesn't need to visit either a psychologist or a bookstore.

In general, it appears that thought suppression may be chosen as a self-help strategy when people are attempting to avoid painful emotions (e.g., fear, depression, anxiety), to control unwanted actions that the thoughts suggest (e.g., eating during a diet, smoking, suicide), to prevent the communication of secret or undesirable thoughts (e.g., victimization, inappropriate sexual desires or relationships), to prevent thoughts that may cause ineffective performance (e.g., failure, worry, low self-esteem), or to stop thoughts that are themselves abhorrent and appear to be occurring too often (e.g., death of a family member, hurting a child). Studies of the unwanted thoughts of both normal individuals and those diagnosed as having clinically significant obsessions indicate that people have a wide range of reasons to wish their thoughts away (Edwards and Dickerson, 1987; Rachman and de Silva, 1978; Rachman and Hodgson, 1980; Salkovskis and Harrison, 1984). Although some people prefer to use thought suppression more than do others, everyone seems to engage in suppression from time to time (Wegner and Zanakos, in press).

Thought suppression is often chosen as a mental control strategy in performance contexts. There are a variety of thoughts and actions that one might not want to experience when performance is at issue. For example, one might want to suppress thoughts of a previous bad performance or of a flaw in one's technique—such as raising one's shoulder in swinging a golf club—that is not desirable for performance. Like the desire not to hook the golf shot, the desire to avoid any performance flaw can be a compelling motive for suppression in a variety of performance settings.

Thought suppression strategies have also been recommended as forms of professional help. The idea that people can stop thoughts at will, and should be encouraged to do so, has been present in the psychological literature at least since the late nineteenth century (see Rosen and Orenstein, 1976). Thought stopping was introduced as a psychotherapeutic regimen in the contemporary literature by Wolpe and Lazarus (1966). Although there are a number of variations on the technique, in general a therapist recommends that a client suffering from some unwanted thought practice stopping it (usually first with the therapist, then later alone). In some variations, a client may be encouraged to say "stop" aloud, or even make a noise, move abruptly, or self-administer a mildly painful stimulus each time the thought recurs. In some cases, a therapist proposes that the client replaces the thought with some specific distractor. The technique of thought stopping is now widely recommended as a potentially effective treatment for several psychological symptoms (e.g., Ross, 1984; Seligman, 1990; Stauffer and Petee, 1988).

Thought suppression, then, is both a self-help technique and a strategy that is recommended by psychotherapists. Thought suppression is something people may attempt whenever they encounter circumstances in which they desire self-control—whenever there is a schism between what they might naturally say, do, or feel and what they would prefer to say, do, or feel.

EFFECTIVENESS

When one is motivated to suppress a thought, can it be done? The answer to this question depends on how successful one wants the suppression to be. If one is asking for total victory, then the answer is a clear no.

Overall, studies of thought-stopping techniques have indicated the likely ineffectiveness of suppression for some time. Clinical reports that thought stopping can be effective in individual cases are balanced by others that report it is ineffective, and such case research is difficult to evaluate or summarize. More controlled clinical studies that compare thought stopping to other therapeutic strategies—such as desensitization or relaxation, or even to no strategy at all—sometimes show positive results (Arrick et al., 1981), but more frequently the results are negative (Neziroglu and Neuman, 1990; Stern, 1978; Stern et al., 1973; Teasdale and Rezin, 1978). Summaries of the literature have repeatedly concluded that the technique remains unproven despite considerable research (Reed, 1985; Tryon, 1979). In sum, thought suppression as a therapeutic regimen for people suffering from naturally occurring unwanted thoughts does not appear to provide relief from those thoughts.

When a person attempts to suppress a thought under instructions to do so in a laboratory experiment, in turn, various measures indicate that the thought is still very much in mind. An early observation of the difficulty of suppression in the laboratory was made by Wegner et al. (1987), who asked subjects to try not to think of a white bear as the subjects reported their thoughts aloud. Although subjects regularly voiced a plan to distract themselves, and did report intervals of successful absorption in other things, they were incapable of sustaining suppression for very long. The typical participant expressed a replacement thought only to the end of a sentence, paragraph, or some other pause in the flow, and then abruptly signalled the occurrence of a thought about a white bear. On average, this happened more than once a minute in a 5-minute period. This effect has been replicated in several investigations (Clark et al., 1991; Lavy and van den Hout, 1990; Wegner et al., 1991; Wenzlaff et al., 1991).

People show similar vexations in their oral and written reports when they try to suppress thoughts that are more involving and relevant than a white bear. People cannot easily suppress thoughts of depressing events when they are asked to do so (Conway et al., 1991; Roemer and Borkovec, in press; Wenzlaff et al., 1988); they show similar difficulty in suppressing thoughts of exciting or arousing topics (Roemer and Borkovec, in press; Wegner et al., 1990), and they also express difficulty in stopping thoughts of people when instructed to do so (Wegner and Gold, 1993). By the simple measure of conscious reports of thought recurrence, then, thought suppression does not work.

Somewhat more surreptitious measures suggest similar conclusions. Psychophysiological evidence suggests the difficulty of thought suppression without any reporting requirement at all. For example, when subjects are asked to suppress thoughts that are exciting (say, of sex), they show skin conductance level (SCL) reactivity rivaling the strength of reactions that occur when they are asked explicitly to entertain those thoughts (Wegner et al., 1990). Other studies have also called on subjects to inhibit thinking about an exciting thought (using different kinds of instructions or situational pressures) and similarly observed increased SCL in comparison with subjects given no special instructions (Cohen et al., 1956; Martin, 1964; Koriat et al., 1972; and Pennebaker and Chew, 1985).

The continued influence of suppressed thoughts can also be discerned with the use of measures of cognitive accessibility—the ease with which the thought influences cognitive processing (see Higgins and King, 1981). Wegner and Erber (1992) examined the accessibility of suppressed thoughts by imposing cognitive loads on subjects who were attempting suppression during cognitive tasks. In one experiment, subjects made associations to word prompts as they tried to suppress thinking about a target word (e.g., house) or tried to concentrate on that word. Under the load imposed by time pressure to make fast associations, subjects gave the target word in response to target-related prompts (e.g., home) more often during suppression than during concentration. In a second experiment, Wegner and Erber used the Stroop color-word interference paradigm to measure accessibility. In this experiment, reaction times for naming colors of words under conditions of cognitive load were found to be longer when subjects had been asked to suppress thinking of the word than they were without load or when subjects had been asked to concentrate on the word (see also Wegner et al., in press).

The results of these investigations support the idea that thought suppression prompts the creation of an automatic cognitive process that searches for the suppression target. It does seem that during thought suppression some part of a person's mind is ironically tuned to the very thought she or he wishes to stop. This research suggests that this part-of-the-minds phenomenon indeed makes one more sensitive to that thought—at least while intentional attempts to distract oneself from the thought are undermined by concurrent activities. In fact, that corner of the mind makes a person more sensitive in the act of suppression than when one is intentionally concentrating on that thought.

Further indications of the potential ineffectiveness of thought suppression can be found in research on directed forgetting. To some degree, the suppression of thoughts is related to forgetting: it is much easier to keep a thought from consciousness, after all, if that thought can be completely erased from memory. This was an early observation of Freud (e.g., 1915/ 1957), one that suggests that a key measure of successful suppression would be the occurrence of forgetting.

In studies of intentional forgetting (see reviews by Anderson and Bjork, in press; R. A. Bjork, 1989), subjects are given material to learn and are asked at some point to forget it. The results of this research indicate that the recall of to-be-forgotten information is indeed impaired in comparison with information that is to be remembered. People are less able to volunteer those items they have been instructed to forget than the ones they have been asked to remember. It is possible, of course, that subjects in such experiments are reluctant to recall the information just because they are trying to humor the experimenter and go along with the request to forget. But a more subtle measure of memory suggests another indication of forgetting, one that is less susceptible to intentional contrivance: items that are to be forgotten don't seem to get in the way of later attempts to remember other things. As a rule, the standard finding in memory studies is that the presentation of one set of items to be remembered will interfere with a subject's ability to recall a subsequent set of items. This interference is not as likely to occur if subjects have been directed to forget the first set (R. A. Bjork, 1970; Geiselman et al., 1983).

This finding does not mean that the to-be-forgotten information is gone, however, because there are a variety of signs that it still has important effects. One key finding is that the recognition of to-be-forgotten information remains at about the same level as corresponding to-be-remembered information (e.g.,

Elms et al., 1970; Geiselman et al., 1983). In other words, when a memory test involves asking subjects to recognize whether specific items are ones that appeared in the initial memory list (rather than asking for free recall of the items), the subjects are as prone to recognize the items they tried to forget as those they tried to remember. Similarly, indirect tests of memory that examine the influence of items without specifically asking subjects to recall the items—such as word-fragment, stem completion, or perceptual identification tests—also show effects of exposure to the to-be-forgotten items that are about the same as to-be-remembered items (Basden et al., in press; E. L. Bjork et al., 1990; Paller, 1990). Finally, recall of the to-be-forgotten items can be reinstated fully by their being presented again as to-be-remembered items (Geiselman and Bagheri, 1985).

These findings and others suggest it is reasonable to say that directed forgetting produces retrieval inhibition. Intentional access to the to-be-forgotten items through free recall is inhibited, but the items remain at full strength as far as their storage in memory. Considered together, the studies of thought suppression and directed forgetting suggest an interesting possibility. It may be that environmental cues to suppressed thoughts or the to-be-forgotten items play a particularly important role in returning those items to conscious attention. The studies of thought suppression effectiveness generally show that the suppressed thoughts return automatically in response to relevant cues—as when, for example, people were cued to think the unwanted thought by the presentation of associated words or by the presentation of the thoughts themselves (Wegner and Erber, 1992; Wegner et al., in press). These findings are comparable to the findings of research on directed forgetting that indicate that the recognition of to-be-forgotten items is unimpaired.

Taken together, the studies suggest that the success of thought suppression may depend on the absence of environmental cues to the thought. A person may be able to keep a thought from mind, or to inhibit the retrieval of a memory, as long as the person is not reminded of the target by cues in the environment.

Although research on this possibility is incomplete, this suggestion makes sense in view of the finding that distractions from unwanted thoughts or emotions can sometimes be quite successful (e.g., Nolen-Hoeksema, 1993). In terms of directed forgetting, it is also known that the presentation of new information to be remembered aids in inhibiting the recall of items that are to be forgotten (Gelfand and Bjork, 1985). It is possible that when circumstances allow a person to be isolated from cues to unwanted thoughts or inhibited memories, the person can achieve some minimal level of freedom from those thoughts or memories. To the extent that one can become immersed in absorbing activities that have no relevance to suppressed thoughts or memories, one may escape those thoughts for a time. If there are replacements for old information that allows one to successfully update memories, a person may not suffer from the undesired retrieval of old items. But there are many sources of reminders, sometimes very subtle, that can bring suppressed thoughts back very quickly, and sensitivity to those reminders will remain for some time following suppression (Wegner and Erber, 1992).

The evidence currently available indicates that thought suppression can be difficult, even in the short run. When there are compelling replacements for an unwanted thought, as in the case of new information that is presented during intentional forgetting, a person may be able to avoid an unwanted thought, perhaps indefinitely. If no new information is available, however—or even worse, if reminders of the thought are presented—a person will succumb to the thought very easily. Having once tried not to think of something, a person becomes a pawn to subsequent circumstances, perhaps able to avoid the thought but sensitive to it's recall if environmental cues are presented.

CONSEQUENCES

It seems difficult to stop oneself from unintentional recall after having tried thought suppression (Rachman and de Silva, 1978). The thought returns to mind in such sharp bursts when one is reminded of it that one may well find oneself trying to suppress it again. Still, there are times when it is possible to relax suppression and let one's mind do what it will. It appears there are moments when it is even possible to return to formerly suppressed thoughts and think about them on purpose. What happens then?

Thought Rebound

Some laboratory research indicates that thinking about a topic that was once suppressed can become unusually preoccupying. This rebound of a suppressed thought was initially observed among subjects who had been asked to suppress the thought of a white bear (Wegner et al., 1987). The subjects individually thought aloud for 5 minutes and rang a bell if the thought of a white bear came to mind during suppression. As noted above, the subjects typically rang the bell and mentioned the thought of a white bear occasionally during this time. When the subjects were next asked to think about a white bear for a similar interval, they produced more mentions and more bell rings than did subjects who had simply been thinking of a white bear from the start.

The rebound effect has been observed several times for bell rings and mentions during a think-aloud period (Wegner et al., 1987; Wegner et al., 1991). It has also been observed when individuals write their ongoing thoughts and make check marks on paper for thought occurrences (Wenzlaff et al., 1991). These experiments have typically contrasted thought frequencies that occur when subjects are asked to think about something with those that occur when subjects are asked to think about something following a period of suppressing that thought. The rebound has also been observed among individuals who were asked to think about anything (not just the suppressed thought) following suppression (Clark et al., 1991). The effect is not always a strong one; it has not been observed at significant levels in studies attempting to replicate it with reduced sample sizes (Merkelbach et al., 1991).

The rebound effect appears to occur because of a certain "stickiness" of suppressed thoughts that is brought about by what people do during suppression. Typically, suppression brings to mind many items other than the suppressed thought. The person turns from one distracter to another, and another, as each fails to keep the unwanted thought away. The critical feature of such unfocused self-distraction is that it creates associations between the unwanted thought and all the various distracters. If one has focused in turn on a doorknob, the weather, and an intransigent fingernail as distracters from the thought of a white bear, for instance, these items are now likely to be reminders of a white bear, at least more so than the person did before the suppression. This means that many of the person's current contents of mind become linked to the unwanted thought during suppression. These items can then serve as cues to remind the person of the thought when the thought is invited—so to yield the observed rebound effect.

One test of this explanation of the rebound was offered by Wegner et al. (1987). This study called for some subjects to use a "focused" self-distraction strategy for suppression. Subjects were asked to try not to think of a white bear, but to think of a red Volkswagen in case they did. This instruction was intended to help subjects avoid using their current thoughts and context as distracters and was expected to produce an attenuation of the rebound effect. And in fact, this outcome was observed for bell rings and think-aloud mentions: the results showed a rebound effect only among those subjects for whom no special strategy was suggested. Presumably, subjects given the red VW as a distracting focus were later unlikely to think about red VWs very much during their opportunity to express the unwanted thought and so escaped the unusual level of contextual reminding that underlies the rebound.

If unfocused self-distraction operates by forging connections between environmental features and the unwanted thought, then the continuity of context between suppression and later expression would seem to be a key condition for the rebound effect. This possibility was tested when Wegner et al. (1991) asked subjects to suppress or express thoughts of white bears in the context of a slide show featuring either classroom scenes or shots of household appliances. Subjects who next expressed white bear thoughts in a different slide-show context showed no evidence of rebound. However, when these same subjects were invited again to express white bear thoughts with the initial slide-show context reinstated, the rebound appeared. Those who had initially suppressed the thought later experienced a rebound of preoccupation with it—but only when they were once again exposed to the slide show during which the suppression had taken place.

These findings indicate that the context of suppression plays a critical role in the rebound effect. Items on a person's mind become bonded to the unwanted thought during suppression, such that later reinstatements of context that bring back those items may have the effect of reintroducing the unwanted thought. Wenzlaff et al. (1991) followed up this idea to investigate the role of thought suppression in the bonding of thought and mood. They noted that a variety of research programs had examined, with mixed success, the possibility that thoughts experienced while a person is in a particular mood state might be more easily retrieved when that mood was experienced anew (e.g., Bower and Mayer, 1985). Research of this kind had not investigated suppressed thoughts, though, focusing instead only on thoughts that were given attention during a mood state. If suppression links the suppressed thought to context, then suppression of a thought during a mood state should link the thought to the mood such that the later reactivation of one would lead to the reinstatement of the other.

In one experiment, Wenzlaff et al. (1991) induced subjects by music to experience either a positive or negative mood and asked them to report their thoughts in writing while trying to think or not to think about a white bear. Later, all subjects were asked to think about a white bear and write their thoughts during a second mood induction (using different but equally moody music). These thought reports indicated that subjects who experienced similar moods during the periods of thought suppression and expression displayed a particularly strong rebound of the suppressed thought during the expression opportunity. Those who were led to experience different moods during initial suppression and later expression showed lessened evidence of a rebound effect.

A second experiment by Wenzlaff et al. (1991) tested the complementary connection—whether thought bonded to mood during suppression could later reinstate that mood. Initially, subjects who were in music-induced positive, negative, or neutral moods were asked to think or not to think about a white bear. Later, all subjects were asked to think about a white bear for a period, after which they reported their moods. The mood reports showed that subjects who had initially tried to suppress white bear thoughts experienced a reinstatement of the mood state that existed during the initial period of suppression. Those who first expressed white bear thoughts showed no evidence of such reinstatement.

These findings suggest that suppression may create a bond between a thought and the cognitive and emotional context in which the thought is suppressed. The contextualization of suppressed thoughts might be widely responsible for difficulties of self-control.

This finding has an interesting possible application in attempts to overcome additions. The contextualization process could link suppressed thoughts of tobacco, alcohol, or drugs, for instance, with the mental states that accompany withdrawal from these substances—and so build up strong linkages between our cravings and thoughts of the craved items. In suppressing a thought, a person may unwittingly play a role in making that thought more difficult to dispel in future instances. This idea suggests that one strategy for overcoming addictions is to try to quit in an unfamiliar setting.

Currently, however, behavior therapists usually suggest that self-control strategies should be conducted at home because these circumstances will allow adequate generalization of training. Learning that occurs at home presumably will enhance the performance of the learned activity (of not smoking, not drinking, etc.) in the home. However, there is little supporting evidence for the superiority of this approach: the research typically indicates that residential treatment and quitting at home are about equally effective (Cohen et al., 1989; Miller and Hester, 1986; Polich et al., 1981). It may be that quitting bad habits in residential treatment facilities offers some advantage because the distracters found at the facility will no longer be present to act as reminders when the person returns home and that this counteracts the generalization benefits that accrue from home treatment.

Emotion Dishabituation

The thought-rebound effect has not yet been observed with emotional thoughts. Roemer and Borkovec (in press), for instance, found no evidence of a postsuppression rebound for depressing, anxious, or even neutral thoughts. Kelly and Kahn (in press) reported no rebound effect for thoughts that subjects had identified as having some trouble avoiding, although these researchers did find a rebound following suppression of white bear thoughts. Wegner and Gold (1993), in turn, specifically examined the postsuppression rebound effects for comparable emotional and unemotional thoughts. The target thought for some subjects in this study was a still-desired past relationship, a "hot flame"; the target thought for others was a no-longer-desired past relationship, a "cold flame." A rebound of thoughts about the old flame was observed in two experiments for the relatively unemotional thought of the "cold flame," while this effect was not observed in either experiment for the relatively more emotional thought of the "hot flame." Although it is too early to draw a firm conclusion from this research, it suggests that the rebound of unwanted thoughts following suppression might be limited to thoughts that are not strongly emotional in tone.

Perhaps the reason that emotional thoughts do not seem to rebound is that the emotional reactions they promote are themselves heightened by prior suppression, and people therefore subtly suppress the thought even as it rebounds. In the old flame study, for example, Wegner and Gold (1993) tested the effect of suppression on psychophysiological reactivity to thoughts of an old flame. Subjects in the two experiments were asked to think about an old flame, and an initial finding was that those who thought about a hot flame showed higher skin conductance level (SCL) than those who focused on a cold flame. Subjects were then instructed either not to think about their old flame or to perform a comparison task (not thinking about the Statue of Liberty or thinking about the old flame). In a final period, subjects in both experiments were asked again to think about the old flame. Subjects who had previously suppressed the thought of a hot flame showed elevated SCL; those who had not suppressed the thought showed lowered SCLs; those focusing on a cold flame showed no such effect of suppression. These results suggest that trying not to think about a still-desired relationship may prolong emotional responsiveness to thoughts of the relationship (see also Wegner and Zanakos, in press).

Cioffi and Holloway (1993) found a parallel effect that thought suppression can also increase sensations of pain after the painful stimulus is removed. In a study of cold pressor pain, subjects were asked to submerge one hand in a circulating icewater bath as they tried either to focus on the pain, to suppress thoughts of the pain, or to distract themselves from the pain by focusing on an image. During the cold pressor task, subjects suppressing the pain showed higher SCL than those in the other conditions. When the cold pressor was stopped, subjects who had tried to suppress thoughts of the pain showed slower recovery from the experience in their self-reports of pain than the other subjects. And when all subjects were later given ambiguous somatic stimulation (an innocuous vibration on the back of the neck), those who had previously suppressed the pain rated the stimulation as more unpleasant than did those in the other groups. Suppression of pain thoughts, like the suppression of emotional thoughts, appears to magnify subsequent responses.

Research on postsuppression effects suggests that there are effects of attempts at thought suppression that presist even after its simple ineffectiveness is discovered. When people attempt thought suppression despite its ineffectiveness, they may often provoke ironic consequences—effects that are precisely the opposite of those they are attempting. Trying not to think about something can, at least in some circumstances, increase one's later preoccupation with that thought. And trying not to think about something of emotional significance may undermine the usual tendency to habituate to that thought and so prolong the emotion. By trying to suppress unwanted worries, moods, or self-defeating thoughts, people may in effect be increasing the emotional power of the very worries, moods, or thoughts they are trying to suppress.

The sensitivity that thought suppression produces could be a complicating factor in a variety of psychological problems. It has been noted by several researchers, for instance, that people suffering from even mild depression exhibit automaticity in their depressive thinking (Bargh and Tota, 1988; Gotlib and McCann, 1984; Wenzlaff, 1993). In other words, depressed people are so sensitive to depressive thoughts that such thoughts are easily brought to mind even when they are devoting the larger share of their attention to other things. This is precisely the kind of sensitivity that is promoted by thought suppression, and the observation that such problematic sensitivity accompanies depression raises the possibility that depressed people may be unwittingly involved in creating their own difficulties—by trying to suppress them. Perhaps the sensitivity to sad thoughts that occurs with depression is not as much a symptom of depression as it is a symptom of the person's attempt to suppress unwanted depressing thoughts. Ironically and lamentably, the fight against sad thoughts may actually strengthen them (Wenzlaff et al., 1988).

People with other psychological problems also show automatic access to thoughts related to the problem. Individuals reporting phobias, for instance, show evidence of unusual sensitivity to their phobias in the Stroop color-word paradigm (Watts et al., 1986). It is possible that the strong motive to avoid not only the phobic object or situation, but also thoughts of it, could prompt attempts at thought suppression. The resulting high levels of thought accessibility experienced by these people, then, may actually be caused in part by their attempts at thought suppression. Chronic levels of automatic activation could be produced by the mental control strategies that people use in their attempts to overcome unwanted thoughts of spiders, snakes, public speaking, or a variety of other phobia targets. More generally, the stresses that introduce mental load at many points in life may have the result of turning people's struggle against unwanted, seemingly automatic mental states into an invitation for these states to be overwhelming.

ALTERNATIVES

The research we have reviewed on the negative effects of thought suppression suggests that anything that can keep people from suppressing thoughts would be useful as a way of avoiding the effects that suppression can promote. But people are often quite tied to their strategy of suppression, and so alternatives are not readily accepted.

The most straightforward general alternative to suppression is exactly its reverse—concentration on an unwanted thought. This solution has been recommended by many different kinds of psychologists, using quite varied language, beginning most clearly with Sigmund Freud. Freud (1914/1958) suggested that people should talk about their emotional or traumatic experiences as a means of reducing long-term emotional disturbance, and this proposal was meant in part as a way to avoid suppression of thoughts. Although Freud and others also said that there was something useful about the expression or unleashing of emotion all by itself—the production of a "catharsis"—this observation has not been well-substantiated by the experimental literature (e.g., Geen and Quanty, 1977; see also Zillmann, 1993).

Still, other research suggests that the expression of emotion does have its uses. Rachman (1980) has argued that the processing of emotion requires time and attention and that prevention of this activity by suppression spurs continued emotion. Similarly, Foa and Kozak (1986) suggest that corrective information about emotional reactions may not be appreciated in the rush to suppress or avoid emotional thoughts and that a return to these ideas is critical for recovery from emotional pain. These theorists emphasize the therapeutic effects of exposure to the emotional thoughts per se, and there is much evidence that exposure is indeed helpful. Pennebaker and O'Heeron (1984) found, for example, that spouses who discussed the death of their loved ones with friends and family were less likely to later dwell on the deaths. The question of interest, then, is whether randomly assigning people to talk about emotional events with others would have the effect of reducing suppression and rumination about these events.

The research of Pennebaker (1990) on this topic is particularly instructive. He has conducted a series of studies that examine the psychological and health effects of communicating about traumatic events, on the theory that people usually inhibit such disclosure and suppress thoughts about the events and that this produces rumination, chronic physiological activation, and health deterioration. In a demonstration of what happens when this tendency is reversed, Pennebaker and Beall (1986) asked people to spend four consecutive evenings writing about past traumatic events. Those subjects who were asked not only to tell the facts of the events, but also to describe their emotions—and who did indeed achieve high levels of disclosure—showed improvements in their physical health in comparison with other subjects who did not take part in such disclosure. This phenomenon has been observed in other studies showing not only these health effects (e.g., Pennebaker et al., 1990), but also improvements in immune function (Pennebaker et al., 1988).

Pennebaker (1993) reports that following a traumatic or disastrous event that affects many people (e.g., an earthquake, volcanic eruption, or presidential assassination), the initial reaction of most people is to talk about it. Thus, during the early phases of response to such a stress, people show remarkable psychological resilience and a relatively low level of stress-induced illness. Within a few weeks, however, the topic becomes less timely, and there is a progressive tendency to avoid the public hashing and rehashing of the event. At this point people begin to find that ruminations about the event builds up to more distressing levels. Apparently, with the inhibition of talk about the event comes the suppression of thoughts about the event and then the negative consequences of suppression. The implication of Pennebaker's research is that psychological and health responses even to disasters could be improved by interventions that encourage people to talk about the events for longer than usually occurs.

In the case of anxieties or phobias, research also indicates that a reversal of suppression is often helpful. Therapeutic regimens that involve asking a client to accept graded increments in exposure to a feared stimulus have become recognized as highly effective in the treatment of phobic reactions (Barlow, 1988). Even more intense exposure strategies (sometimes called "flooding" or "implosion") can be useful in certain circumstances, although they are more aversive and can prompt clients to drop out of therapy (Barlow, 1988). When people are goaded or even forced into thinking about things that they normally suppress, much of the built-up power of those things to produce emotion is dissipated. This process is not easy. If one has a phobia about heights and has been avoiding heights of all kinds and thoughts about heights for many years, a proposal to begin taking rides in glass elevators is not likely to be easily accepted. The habit of suppressing thoughts of heights is an old habit and will also have accumulated massive power through inflating the emotional reaction to the thought.

Becoming exposed to an unwanted thought may therefore have to take place in the same way one becomes exposed to any other unpleasant reality—little by little, with help and lots of complaining. A person may approach a cold lake, for example, by sticking in one foot, yelling, running away, chattering to companions about how cold it is, rubbing and clapping her or his arms, waiting for the sun to come out, deciding just to "wade," going back in up to the ankles, admonishing those nearby not to splash, taking a few steps further, realizing one looks silly half wet, seeing others take the dive, and then, finally, ducking under. Even then one may need to duck a few more times in order to get used to it. The process of coming to grips with unwanted thoughts is a similar slow process, seldom a sheer act of will.

A proposal to think about an unwanted thought is consistent with current practice in clinical approaches to excessive worry. Borkovec's program of research on worry (e.g., Roemer and Borkovec, 1993) indicates that the reversal of suppression may be effective in such cases. In a provocative study on this problem, Borkovec et al. (1983) asked people who had indicated that they were chronic worriers to arrange for a half-hour worry period every day. Then, when the people found themselves worrying outside this time, they were not to suppress the worry, but instead were to make a special point of focusing on it in the worry period. During the worry period, they were to do nothing but worry. Over the course of a 4-week treatment program, these people showed improvement in comparison with another group of worriers who were left untreated: they worried less all day, and they sometimes found that they had nothing to do in the worry period.

The reversal of suppression is also a common part of therapy for obsessive-compulsive disorder. About 25 percent of individuals who are diagnosed with obsessive compulsive disorder suffer primarily from obsessions (recurrent, intrusive thoughts); the remainder may have such thoughts but also suffer from compulsions (the performance of rituals, or recurrent actions). The therapy of choice for those with compulsions is called "exposure with response prevention" and has evolved from the initial techniques suggested by Meyer (1966). In this approach, a person who has become involved in too-frequent hand washing in response to worries about contamination, for example, might be encouraged to get his or her hands dirty on purpose and then urged to avoid washing them for an extended period of time. The person's access to soap and water might even be limited for a time.

This approach, which is very effective with many kinds of compulsive activities (Barlow, 1988), reverses suppression. It makes a person think about the unwanted thought—in this case, contamination—and at the same time prevents the usual ritual the person uses to dispel the thought—washing. This approach doesn't have a clear analog in the case of obsession, however, as there is no action to prevent. Thought suppression per se is probably what the obsessive person is doing, and it is difficult for a therapist to prevent it. Eventually, however, it may be that the most successful therapies aimed at the obsessive facet of obsessive-compulsive disorders will also focus on the reversal of suppression.

On balance, the reversal of thought suppression is untried and highly experimental for other psychological or performance problems, and there is very little evidence at this point to recommend or discourage it. In the struggle against unwanted thoughts of food, for example, the idea that suppression should be stopped appears to indicate that dieting itself should be stopped. Although there is evidence that dieting can sometimes cause more harm than good and could be halted in many cases with good effect (Herman and Polivy, 1993), it is not clear whether asking people to think about food might have therapeutic effects—in the sense that they might become less obsessed with it. Evidence indicates that if people are asked to focus on thoughts of food as an aid to self-control, it is particularly useful for them to focus on the nonfood aspects of the food thoughts: for example, "Don't those marshmallows look like clouds?" (Mischel and Baker, 1975).

Asking depressed individuals to focus on their negative thoughts and feelings is similarly untested as a form of therapy. Coyne (1989) has made some initial suggestions in this regard, and there are some studies indicating that therapies that encourage depressed people to confront their negative thoughts may be useful (Beck and Strong, 1982; Feldman et al., 1982). However, many therapists may be very reluctant to something that seems to make depressed individuals feel worse, even if improved psychological health is the likely long-term result. Like the depressed individuals themselves, therapists may succumb to the client's motive to suppress thoughts and so prolong the problem; the desire to suppress thoughts can be just as powerful for onlookers as it is for participants. And it is not yet known whether thwarting suppression is the best strategy for various psychological problems.

There are also important issues of timing that have yet to be addressed in research on thought suppression. Suppression may be a useful technique just when circumstances make unwanted thoughts most insistent—say, at the height of an unpleasant experience. But turning to focus on the thoughts may be more effective once the most intense and difficult circumstances are over. Research on the relative effectiveness of avoidance and nonavoidance as coping strategies is consistent with this possibility (Mullen and Suls, 1982; Suls and Fletcher, 1985). This research indicates that an avoidance strategy is linked to more effective coping just after a stressful event, but that a nonavoidance strategy is associated with more effective coping as time goes on and the event recedes into the past.

CONCLUSIONS

Research on thought suppression is relatively new to psychology, and large portions of this research have been conducted primarily in the laboratory of one investigator. The conclusions we offer must be understood with these observations in mind. This chapter is intended more to alert readers to the recent emergence of a potentially useful perspective on mental control than to summarize a mature body of research that leads to strong conclusions. Yet, we believe there are enough preliminary indications to suggest that thought suppression may be a problematic strategy of mental control.

Although thought suppression or intentional forgetting may be effective when compelling distractions are available, cues or circumstances that would prompt the recurrence of the thought become especially powerful when a thought has been suppressed. Suppressed thoughts are more easily cued by the environment than they might have been had one never suppressed them, and once-suppressed thoughts that one later thinks about on purpose become stronger than they were before. Suppressing thoughts of emotional topics may not lead to the same magnitude of recurrence as suppression of thoughts of items or actions, it may increase the strength of the emotion attached to that topic. Psychotherapies that depend on suppression—such as thought stopping—are as yet unproven.

Alternatives to thought suppression exist that are likely to be more effective. In cases of anxiety-producing or obsessive thoughts, successful avoidance of the unwanted thought may occur when one faces the thought and even concentrates on it. Encouraging people to talk about their unwanted thoughts enhances their ability to cope with the events. It is not known whether this strategy is useful in all cases, and there are important exceptions. For example, encouraging depressed people to dwell on their problems is a technique that has not received enough research attention to allow any evaluation. In the cases of unwanted thoughts about fears or traumas or worries, however, the approach of confronting them may be more beneficial than the approach of trying to suppress them.

It should be emphasized that the present research on thought suppression does not support a blanket recommendation that people should never try to suppress thoughts. Rather, the available evidence suggests that an attempt not to think about an unwanted thought is likely to fail if it is the only strategy a person adopts for dealing with that thought.

NOTE

[1]There are many interesting issues involved in the study of auxiliary thought suppression, such as the subtle yet important need for suppression when one's habitual way of thinking about something gets in the way of new and improved thoughts. When one tries to drive a car with an odd arrangement of controls, for example, one must suppress the proclivity to respond to the old configuration. Or, when plans change, one must set aside thinking about the old plan and attempt to adapt to a new plan. Even in the everyday case of putting off a project or a concern until later, one engages in a kind of thought suppression. Several lines of research by experimental psychologists have examined the way in which people suppress thoughts in order to focus on a new thought (e.g., R. A. Bjork and Landauer, 1979; Gernsbacher and Faust, 1991; Tipper et al., 1991); but these are all cases of what we term auxilary thought suppression.

EPILOGUE

Institutional Impediments to Effective Training

The role of organizational values, attitudes, and structures in enhancing or impeding individual and team performance was not on the committee's agenda, nor were the committee members chosen for their expertise in that domain. Similarly, neither of the two previous books of the committee dealt with this topic. Yet, after almost a decade of work on issues of performance, we are struck by the key role of the organizational context in which performance occurs.

This epilogue is a product of the individual and collective experiences of committee members, past and present, during more than two dozen site visits. What we have encountered repeatedly during such site visits is most curious: an openness to changes that might improve individual or team performance coupled with institutional and organizational reasons why those changes cannot be implemented. We have gotten this message—to a greater or lesser extent—from people in a wide range of military, commercial, governmental, and educational settings.

In short, what has become apparent to us is that specifying the techniques and innovations that do and do not have the potential to enhance individual and team performance is only part of the battle. Without an organizational culture that fosters the changes needed to implement those innovations, proposals for change, however credible their source or convincing the evidence, will have little effect. This fact, however, is hardly news to most trainers and other practitioners. The purpose of this epilogue is to take the next step, that is, to specify some of the institutional attitudes and constraints that, in the committee's experience, appear to be the principal organizational impediments to improving human performance.

THE PERCEIVED VALUE OF TRAINING

The assessment of techniques and innovations that might enhance training has been a continuing theme during the life of the committee. Based on its analysis of existing research, the committee has suggested certain innovations and argued against certain existing practices. In general, individuals responsible for training in various real-world settings have responded positively— even enthusiastically—to the committee's recommendations. They have frequently argued, however, that it would really not be feasible, given the institutional realities of their particular job setting, to change existing training programs in ways that would implement those recommendations.

One argument is that the resources necessary to make the changes are not available. Training and retraining programs are not usually high among an organization's priorities, which translates into little and often inadequate funds, time, and personnel being assigned to the training mission. In part, the low priority assigned to training is based on financial considerations that are intrinsic to the nature of training: however fruitful training programs might be from a cost-benefit standpoint, the costs are immediate and the benefits are long term. Whenever the short-term bottom line is the primary concern of individuals responsible for management decisions, allocating resources to create or upgrade training or retraining programs will not be an appealing strategy. Such programs not only require expenditures, they also result in the temporary loss of production of the employees being trained or retrained. ("Training is a slice out of your profits," said one company official.) The benefits of such programs may also reflect well not on current management personnel, but, rather, on their successors (which runs counter to the principle, as a member of the Los Angeles Police Department put it, that one should only do enough so that "the bridge falls down when the next mayor is in office").

In addition to such financial considerations, however, training often seems not to be valued in absolute terms. Training programs and the people involved in those programs frequently have less than exalted positions or status in an organization. Such programs (particularly retraining programs) are frequently viewed as a necessary—or even unnecessary—evil. Retraining, refresher, and counseling programs, rather than being viewed as a normal part of improving ongoing job performance in a difficult profession, are viewed as remedial or disciplinary measures. It is little wonder, then, that such programs are frequently viewed by employees as punishment—as a sign that "you screwed up." In times of budgetary crises, such attitudes toward the value of training can add to the reasons that funds for training are among the first to be cut.

During recent years, for example, when being a police officer has become an ever more difficult, dangerous, and complicated job, funds to recruit and train officers have been cut in many communities. Excelling as a police officer requires a variety of motor, procedural, and interpersonal skills, and even, occasionally, that the wisdom of Solomon be executed in a second or two. Yet, in California, the basic course of training for a police officer can satisfy statewide requirements with as few as 560 hours of training. In contrast, cosmetologists in the state of California are required to undergo 1,600 hours of training simply to qualify for the state examination. In the city of Los Angeles in 1991, when no additional funds could be found for training, almost $15 million was found to pay the costs of lawsuits against the police for excessive use of force and unlawful shootings. During 1992 those costs rose to nearly $20 million. In 1993, as a consequence of a number of changes, one of which was a greater emphasis on and resources devoted to training, such costs to the city were dropped to less than $11 million. How much of the $9 million savings should be attributed to improved training, and how much to other factors (such as changes in police procedures and more effective work by the city attorney's office) is difficult to say, but it is worth noting that those savings dwarf the total funds allocated by the city of Los Angeles to training, per se.

The needs that drive training programs and determine their content often have little to do with such fundamental considerations as what skills are most necessary, complex, called on most frequently in the real-world environment, or most likely to be forgotten. Rather, administrative decisions as to how training time and resources are spent are often guided by regulations and fear of lawsuits. At the Nuclear Training Center in Connecticut, for example, the single consideration that is probably most influential in determining the content of training programs is the anticipated nature of upcoming certification testing by examiners from the Nuclear Regulatory Commission.

The way fear of lawsuits can influence the allocation of training resources is illustrated by an example cited by training personnel at the Los Angeles Police Academy. When two officers, out of a total of over 8,000 officers, shot dogs under circumstances where the justification for doing so was questionable, the immediate reaction was to propose that *all* officers should receive training on when shooting a dog is, or is not, justified. The proposal was eventually scrapped. The point is not that such training is without value, but, rather, that such an administrative reaction was guided by considerations other than a reasoned analysis of the best use of limited time and resources. Another example in the police world that illustrates that anticipated job demands are not the principal guide to training is the following: whereas 50 percent of police calls involve "dispute management," that is, intervening in conflicts and arguments between individuals, less than 1 percent of training time, until recently, had been devoted to dispute-management training.

In general, training programs are often not as effective as they might be because training is not highly valued. The converse, of course, is true as well: training programs are not highly valued because they are seldom as effective as they might be. Thus, a type of "catch 22" impedes progress.

SELECTION VERSUS TRAINING

One reason training programs are not as effective as they might be is a prevailing tendency to attribute differences in performance among individuals not to differences in level of training, experience, or practice, but, rather, to differences in innate ability. For whatever combination of reasons, the role of aptitude is overestimated and the role of practice, experience, and effort is underestimated in performance. (See Ericsson et al. [1993] for a recent example of the type of research findings that suggest that practice, not innate ability, is typically the larger factor in determining performance.)

The belief that the ability to perform well on a given task is a function of whether a person possesses the relevant talent or "gift" has a number of negative effects on organizations and individuals. First of all, it engenders a type of helpless attitude; people hope that they or the others they hire or work with have the "gift," so to speak, and they think there is nothing much to do if they do not. To the extent that an overemphasis on innate ability as a determinant of performance is a societal belief, it can function as a self-fulfilling prophecy: an early bad experience or poor performance—in a mathematics course, for example—can lead a person to think that he or she has no potential in that domain, which then, in turn, influences the path that the person follows. People avoid educational or job contexts that might give them the experience and training to succeed in domains where they have categorized themselves as without talent; conversely, they seek out contexts and roles that exercise talents they think they might have, which then fosters the development of those abilities. Stereotypes as to what innate abilities the members of different racial or ethnic groups tend to have and not have can also function in a self-fulfilling fashion.

At an organizational level, the innate-ability fallacy leads to an emphasis on selection rather than training. Resources are spent on trying to find individuals who possess an innate talent or characteristic of some type rather than on creating programs of training and experience that can improve performance in a given job context. Assessment instruments designed to give self-insight or insight into others are extraordinarily popular in a variety of real-world settings, even though credible evidence is lacking that such instruments actually enhance the selection of careers by individuals or the selection of individuals by organizations. The use of such instruments was examined in the committee's last report. The committee concluded that the widespread use of such instruments was based on considerations such as face validity and personal testimonials, rather than on solid evidence attesting to their effectiveness. For example, in the case of the Myers Briggs Type Indicator (Myers and McCaulley, 1985), which is probably the most popular of such assessment instruments, the committee was unable to find research evidence sufficient to justify its widespread use in career counseling (see Druckman and Bjork, 1991:Ch. 5).

MISUNDERSTOOD ASPECTS OF TRAINING

Errors

A generalization that emerges strongly from this report (see Chapters 3 and 4) and from the committee's last report (particularly Chapters 3 and 4) is that training procedures should introduce desirable difficulties for the learner. *Performance* during training is an unreliable indicator of the extent to which the *learning* that is the goal of training has been achieved. Conditions that yield a high rate of correct responses during training can fail to support performance in the posttraining environment; conversely, conditions that appear to slow or impede performance during training can enhance the subsequent real-world performance that is the target of the training.

Training regimens need to introduce the difficulties, unpredictability, and variability expected to be present in the posttraining setting. Manipulations of training that amount to crutches that prop up performance artificially—such as massing practice on a given subtask or keeping the conditions of practice constant and, hence, predictable—not only impede learning, but can also lead to illusions of comprehension or competence. Trainees who perform well under artificially easy training conditions can gain a false confidence in the extent to which critical knowledge and skills have actually been acquired. Introducing certain types of difficulty during training is "desirable," therefore, not only to enhance the learning process but also to educate the learner's subjective experience—that is, to provide real feedback to the learner as to the level of knowledge or skill that has, or has not, been achieved.

The foregoing conclusions suggest that quite dramatic changes are necessary in many existing training programs in a variety of institutions. In the committee's experience, training programs are usually designed to optimize performance *during* training. In part, that is so because individuals responsible for training act on the reasonable, if fallacious, assumption that there is a one-to-one correspondence between the conditions that enhance performance during training and the conditions that enhance the long-term learning that enhances performance on the job. Errors made during training are generally not viewed as opportunities for learning, but, rather, as evidence of a less-than-optimal training program. Thus, the role of errors and mistakes during training is poorly understood.

More important, however, is that the *meaning* of errors is misunderstood. The tendency to attribute differences in performance to differences in innate ability means that errors are to be avoided. To the extent that errors and mistakes are not viewed as a necessary aspect of an effective training program, but as evidence of questionable aptitude or ability—by both trainers and trainees—they are to be avoided. Certain mottos that seem common in Army training environments—such as "We do it right the first time" or "We don't practice mistakes"—seem to reflect such a mistaken view of the role and meaning of errors.

It would be misleading, however, to imply that such attitudes pervade all Army training. A striking counterexample is provided by the National Training Center in California, where units are brought in from around the United States to engage a so-called opposing force (OPFOR) regiment in a series of tank and infantry battles. The OPFOR, a highly trained and practiced regiment stationed at the Training Center, is nearly unbeatable on its home turf—1,000 square miles of harsh, uninhabited desert and mountains. The typical visiting unit is defeated decisively in the initial exercises, but it becomes much more competitive as training proceeds. Every misstep is analyzed in a unique after-action review that follows each engagement and permits communication across all levels of command. The basic idea is that there is more to be learned from defeat than from victory and that such learning is better accomplished in simulated battle than in actual combat.

Tests

Like errors, the role of tests as a component of training is commonly misunderstood. As highlighted in the committee's first report (see Druckman and Swets, 1988:Ch. 4), there is abundant evidence that tests are learning events. Information that is recalled and procedures that are carried out become more accessible to learners than they would have been without tests. And tests can increase the effectiveness of subsequent study opportunities, partly by providing feedback to the learner as to the information or procedures that are in need of further study. The importance of testing as a pedagogical device is supported not only by controlled experimentation in laboratory settings, but also by studies of educational environments. (See, e.g., the summary in the *New York Times* by Fiske [1990], which reports the results of the Harvard Assessment Seminar on those aspects of the college environment that do and do not enrich learning.)

The optimal use of tests as a component of training programs is often impeded by a focus on tests as assessment devices. Ideally, there should be a clear distinction between testing that is embedded within training as a pedagogical tool and testing that is administered at the end of training as an assessment tool. That distinction is typically blurred in actual training programs: as a consequence, trainees are afraid to volunteer answers that might be wrong or to speak up when they are confused or uncertain, and instructors are hesitant to use tests that might induce instructive errors (in part because they themselves may be assessed in terms of the scores of their trainees). Errors or uncertainties committed or admitted by a trainee become—formally or informally—part of that trainee's record. In certain highly monitored training programs, such as operator training in the nuclear power industry, there are even regulations requiring that certain types of errors and failures made by trainees during the training process must be reported to the appropriate regulatory agency. Management personnel in some such settings are even vulnerable to being charged with "negligent retention" of a given trainee on the basis of that trainee's performance during the training process.

One part of the problem, once again, is the tendency to attribute performance differences across individuals, however localized and temporary those differences may be, to differences in innate ability. As an overall generalization, trainers and trainees alike are too distressed by errors and mistakes—and too encouraged by successes and rapid improvement. Examples abound of trainees who appeared to perform perfectly at the end of training but who could not perform adequately months later in the posttraining environment, especially if the posttraining conditions differed from those of the training situation. (The fact that medical students, at the time of graduation, could remember only about 10 percent of the basic-science material they had presumably mastered during the first 2 years of medical school was one of the factors that led Harvard Medical School to move away from the traditional model of medical school education.) And errors during training may preclude rather than portend errors in the posttraining environment. In fact, constructing the conditions of training so as to avoid or minimize errors may simply defer those errors to a time and place where they matter much more.

Measures of Effectiveness

It almost goes without saying that the appropriate measure of a program of training or instruction is the extent to which that program facilitates posttraining performance. That is, the goal of training is to "transfer" that traiing in positive ways to the real-world settings in which the trainee will work. For a variety of reasons, however, measures of posttraining job performance are frequently missing or of questionable validity. And when appropriate measures exist, there may be no feedback loop: that is, there may be no administrative machinery in place that provides information to training personnel as to the actual performance of their trainees months or years after training.

If measures of the long-term consequences of a given training program tend not to be available to the people responsible for training, what do they use to evaluate different methods of training? The answer is that they tend to use one or both of two unreliable measures that have the potential to be very misleading: the performance of trainees during the training process and the evaluation of a given training program by the trainees themselves. As noted above, performance *during* training is a poor guide to choosing those conditions of training that maximize posttraining performance. Constructing the conditions of training so as to yield the maximum rates of correct performance during training will tend to result in a training program that stresses such undesirable characteristics as massed practice on subtasks, fixing the conditions of practice, and providing solutions and answers rather than providing opportunities for those solutions and answers to be generated by trainees themselves (see Druckman and Bjork, 1991:Ch. 3).

Trainees' ratings of their own happiness or satisfaction with a given training program are an equally unreliable basis for the design of training programs. Such ratings, frequently referred to as "happy sheets" or "smile sheets," are subject to the illusions of comprehension and competence noted above, illusions that may well be fostered by the types of manipulations that enhance performance during training, but fail to support posttraining performance. And the types of desirable difficulties that enhance learning, in part by exercising those processes likely to be demanded in the posttraining environment, are unlikely to be well received by trainees, almost by the very nature of such manipulations.

Most trainers may uncritically assume that trainee happiness and performance during training are appropriate criteria against which to evaluate training. But even trainers who understand that such criteria are faulty still face a problem in attempting to introduce innovations in training of the type the committee has recommended—because they themselves may well be evaluated in terms of the performance of their trainees during training or in terms of the happy sheets filled out by trainees. To really optimize training requires that supervisory personnel, not just the individuals who have the day-to-day responsibility for training, understand the practical implications of the committee's conclusions and recommendations on training.

Finally, when well-defined measures of the long-term consequences of training do not exist, training personnel lack a way to demonstrate the product of any special efforts and innovations on their part. It is demoralizing to believe that if you do a good job no one will know. Had Jaime Escalante (of *Stand and Deliver* fame) been teaching a standard honors course in calculus at Garfield High School in east Los Angeles, rather than an advanced-placement course, he might well have labored in vain—or possibly, been fired—because only students in the advanced-placement courses take a nationwide end-of-year test. That test provides not only a measure of student achievement, but also a measure, if an imperfect one, of instructor effectiveness. Without the undeniable achievements of his mostly minority students on the advanced-placement test, Escalante's unconventional teaching techniques might well have been viewed as simply eccentric and probably ill-advised.

TRAINERS AND ORGANIZATIONS

The extent to which a trainer can maximize his or her effectiveness as a teacher—or will even try to do so—depends heavily on the organizational attitudes and structures that characterize the work environment. To optimize training there needs to be communication—between instructors, across administrative levels, and between former trainees and current training personnel. And there needs to be cooperation rather than competition: that is, there need to be mechanisms to share knowledge, solutions, and innovations that appear promising on the basis of posttraining results. In actual practice, however, such communication and cooperation is frequently impeded by the attitude that the ability to teach is an innate talent, not a skill to be learned, and by administrative structures that isolate instructors or put them in competition with each other.

Teaching as a Skill

Teaching is a complex skill. To be a maximally effective instructor is itself a continuing and demanding learning process. Staying current with respect to the knowledge and skills that are to be taught is one necessary aspect of the learning process, of course, but doing only that much is far from sufficient. One needs also to work toward mastering the craft of instruction, which is a multifaceted and life-long process. To be most effective, an instructor needs to stay abreast of advances in high technology tools for training—such as computer-assisted devices of one kind or another, needs to stay current with respect to research findings that have significant implications for training methodologies, and needs to explore systematically the relative effectiveness of alternative technologies and techniques in the particular training context. Beyond those aspects of the process, there are important things to learn about one's self as a teacher, about the overall mission of one's institution or organization, and about one's students or trainees. There are many styles of teaching, for example, and it may take some time and effort for a person to determine which of those styles is most personally effective and comfortable. The most effective style may also differ as a function of the age, background, and goals of one's trainees. Finally, understanding how the knowledge and skills to be taught "fit in," so to speak, from an organizational standpoint—in terms of the demands one's trainees can be expected to face or in terms of other training those trainees are receiving or will receive—is also an important, and continuing, process.

Management personnel, and instructors themselves for that matter, are prone to view teaching not as a craft to be learned, but, rather, as a gift bestowed on certain individuals. The potential negative consequences of such an attitude are considerable. To the extent that an individual instructor views the ability to teach as an innate talent, criticism of his or her teaching, however constructive and specific, will tend to be either rejected as a kind of personal attack or accepted as evidence of limited potential, for example. One will be disinclined to seek advice and feedback, and to explore alternative techniques and methods.

At an implicit or explicit level, the notion that the ability to teach well is an innate talent is remarkably prevalent. Even in university settings, teaching tends not to be viewed as a skill to be learned. At lunch and elsewhere, professors talk to each other about research, politics, sports, the weather, and the stock market, among other things, but rarely, if ever, about teaching strategies and techniques. It is as though talking about such matters is off limits—possibly because one is at risk of implying that a colleague has failings as a teacher or that one has an elevated opinion of one's own "gifts" as a teacher.

From a management standpoint as well, the attitude that teaching is mostly or entirely an innate talent has negative consequences. One such consequence is a decreased likelihood of support for programs to upgrade and refine the skills of training personnel. The notion that the ability to teach well is a gift creates instead a tendency to simply hope that individuals selected as trainers have the "right stuff" in the first place. Another consequence of the failure to view teaching itself as a difficult skill is the tendency of organizations to recruit experts in a given domain to be instructors in that domain—without regard to their credentials or experience as teachers.

Expertise in a given domain hardly disqualifies one as a teacher, of course, but experts may not only lack experience and knowledge of those teaching principles that transcend particular domains, but may also lack an understanding of their own skill or be unable to adopt the perspective of a novice. A high level of expertise in golf, or writing computer code, or preparing tax forms, for example, is no guarantee that one can effectively teach those skills. Someone who grew up on skis may be less able to explain to a beginner how to turn, or stop, or get up again than a less expert person who learned to ski as an adult. At a very high level of expertise and practice, many aspects of complicated skills become automatic, which can make them unavailable to conscious analysis without special effort. One reason that teaching one's own children to drive an automobile is alternately frustrating, humorous, and terrifying is that so many aspects of skills as experienced drivers have become automatic over the years. When asked about the appropriate timing and sequencing of the shifter, clutch, and gas pedal in a standard-transmission car, for example, a person is often reduced to trying to observe what he or she does when shifting, which, typically, alters and disrupts the process.

In sum, being an effective instructor in a given domain goes beyond having expertise in that domain. It seems quite obvious that being good at something is not the same thing as being an effective teacher of that something—after all, it is common for elite musicians and athletes to have teachers and coaches who are not themselves elite performers—but that perception persists. Such a perception may explain, for example, why the manuals accompanying personal-computer software and hardware are frequently so frustrating and ineffective as instructional tools. It seems plausible that the writers of such manuals have frequently been selected primarily on the basis of their intimate knowledge of a given product—an engineer or computer technician, perhaps, who played a significant role in designing or refining that product—without regard to their skills, or lack thereof, as a writer or instructor or their skill in adopting the perspective of a learner.

Administrative Structures

Another contributor to nonoptimal training is organizational structures that act to isolate instructors. If it is true, as has been argued by a number of influential writers—particularly W. Edwards Deming—that the behavior of individuals within an organization is more heavily determined by that organization's structure than by characteristics of those individuals, then many instructors, unfortunately, are working in settings where they will never achieve their potential as teachers. In corporate, military, and educational settings, instructors can find themselves denied the types of communication and cooperation necessary to optimize the training for which they are responsible.

A number of historical and institutional factors may contribute to the isolation of teachers and trainers within organizations. One such factor is an assembly-line mentality toward training. Students or trainees are viewed as needing to be "fitted" with skills and knowledge that will later be demanded of them. Given that view, it may seem optimal to subdivide training into a number of nonoverlapping and narrowly defined programs or classes, the goal being to achieve a kind of mass-production efficiency. Trainees or students can be sent to different training programs or classes, as necessary, where it is an instructor's job to attach to those trainees skills or knowledge of some type. Over time, however, such a structure will frequently not only act to isolate instructors, but may also put them in competition with each other. A given class or training program becomes the province of an instructor or staff of instructors, who then come to view their primary goal as being more highly rated by supervisors and trainees than are other instructors, a goal that is not commensurate with optimizing the long-term effectiveness of training.

Whatever the factors that act to isolate instructors within organizations, the effect of that isolation is to prevent or slow the rate of desirable changes and innovations within training programs. Instructors need the opportunity to learn from each other, and individuals in key management positions need to view themselves as partners with instructors in the training enterprise. In fact, some of the innovations required to optimize the total training mission of an institution—introducing technological tools to enhance training, for example, or changing how individual training programs are interleaved and interrelated—can only be accomplished at the management level. Administrators, who possess the power and, unfortunately, often the inclination to stop innovation, also frequently possess the power to foster and implement desirable changes.

CONCLUDING COMMENTS

Having focused on certain impediments to effective training, and having attempted to illustrate those impediments, we have perhaps painted an excessively gloomy picture of what the committee encountered during its many site visits. Were it the goal of this chapter to provide examples of real-world training environments that are exemplary in one or more respects, that would not be difficult to do. We were impressed, in fact, by the potential for innovation, communication, and cooperation we saw illustrated across the range of military, commercial, educational, governmental, and sports settings we visited. In short, although it became clear to the committee that the impediments to effective training we have identified in this chapter are commonplace in real-world environments, it also became clear that they need not exist.

A final point that merits comment is that the impediments to effective training summarized in this chapter are not entirely independent of each other. The counterproductive attitudes, values, and structures that impede training arise, to a greater or lesser extent, from a common root: a misunderstanding of the characteristics and potential of humans as learners. The body of research on the cognitive and social processes that underlie the learning and performance of individuals and teams has grown to the point that it is a far better guide to training than is intuition or standard practice. In an era of global competition and information superhighways, when the survival value of being able to learn and change is greater than ever before, it is critical to draw on that resource to enhance training.

References

CHAPTER 1

Dennett, D.C.
1991 *Consciousness Explained.* Boston: Little, Brown.
Druckman, D., and R.A. Bjork, eds.
1991 *In the Mind's Eye: Enhancing Human Performance.* Committee on Techniques for the Enhancement of Human Performance, National Research Council. Washington, D.C.: National Academy Press.
Druckman, D., and J.A. Swets, eds.
1988 *Enhancing Human Performance: Issues, Theories, and Techniques.* Committee on Techniques for the Enhancement of Human Performance, National Research Council. Washington, D.C.: National Academy Press.
Goldstein, I.L.
1993 *Training in Organizations: Needs Assessment, Development, and Evaluation.* Pacific Grove, Calif: Brooks-Cole.

CHAPTER 2

Druckman, D., and R.A. Bjork, eds.
1991 *In the Mind's Eye: Enhancing Human Performance.* Committee on Techniques for the Enhancement of Human Performance, National Research Council. Washington, D.C.: National Academy Press.
Druckman, D., and J.A. Swets, eds.
1988 *Enhancing Human Performance: Issues, Theories, and Techniques.* Committee on Techniques for the Enhancement of Human Performance, National Research Council. Washington, D.C.: National Academy Press.
Orasanu, J., and E. Salas
1993 Team decision making in complex environments. In G. Klein, J. Orasanu, and R. Calderwood, eds., *Decision Making in Action: Models and Methods.* Norwood, N.J.: Ablex Publishing Co.

CHAPTER 3

Ackerman, P.L.
   1988   Determinants of individual differences during skill acquisition: Cognitive abilities
          and information processing. *Journal of Experimental Psychology: General* 117:288-
          318.
Anderson, J.R.
   1976   *Language, Memory, and Thought.* Hillsdale, N.J.: Lawrence Erlbaum.
   1983   *The Architecture of Cognition.* Cambridge, Mass.: Harvard University Press.
   1993   *Rules of the Mind.* Hillsdale, N.J.: Lawrence Erlbaum.
Anderson, J.R., F.G. Conrad, and A.T. Corbett
   1989   Skill acquisition and the LISP tutor. *Cognitive Science* 13:467-506.
Andrews, D.H.
   1988   Relationships among simulators, training devices, and learning: A behavioral view.
          Educational Technology January:48-54.
Bailey, J.S., R.G. Hughes, and W.E. Jones
   1980   Application of Backward Chaining to Air-to-Surface Weapons Delivery Training.
          AFHRL-TR-79-63, AD-A085 610. Operations Training Division, Air Force Human
          Resources Laboratory, Williams Air Force Base, Ariz.
Battig, W.F.
   1956   Transfer from verbal pretraining to motor performance as a function of motor task
          complexity. *Journal of Experimental Psychology* 51:371-378.
   1979   The flexibility of human memory. Pp. 23-44 in L.S. Cermak and F.I.M. Craik, eds.,
          Levels of Processing in Human Memory. Hillsdale, N.J.: Lawrence Erlbaum.
Biederman, I., and M. Shiffrar
   1987   Sexing day-old chicks: A case study and expert systems analysis of a difficult
          perceptual learning task. *Journal of Experimental Psychology: Learning, Memory
          and Cognition* 13:640-645.
Bilodeau, E.A., and I.M. Bilodeau
   1961   Motor-skills learning. *Annual Review of Psychology* 12:243-280.
Bjork, R.A., and A. Richardson-Klavehn
   1989   On the puzzling relationship between environment context and human memory. In
          C. Izawa, ed., *Current Issues in Cognitive Processes: The Tulane Flowerree Sympo-
          sium on Cognition.* Hillsdale, N.J.: Lawrence Erlbaum.
Bovair, S., D.E. Kieras, and P.G. Polson
   1990   The acquisition and performance of text-editing skill: A cognitive complexity analysis.
          Human Computer Interaction 5:1-48.
Bower, G.H., and T.R. Trabasso
   1964   Concept identification. Pp. 32-94 in R.C. Atkinson, ed., *Studies in Mathematical
          Psychology.* Stanford, Calif.: Stanford University Press.
Brown, J.S., A. Collins, and P. Duguid
   1988   Situated Cognition and the Culture of Learning. 1988 Tech Report No. IRL88-
          0008, Institute for Research on Learning, Palo Alto, Calif.
Bugelski, B.R., and T.C. Cadwallader
   1956   A reappraisal of the transfer and retroaction surface. *Journal of Experimental Psy-
          chology* 52:360-366.
Carnahan, H., and T.D. Lee
   1989   Training for transfer of a movement timing skill. *Journal of Motor Behavior* 21:48-
          59.
Caro, P.W., W.E. Corley, W.D. Spears, and A.S. Blaiwes
   1984   Training Effectiveness Evaluation and Utilization Demonstration of a Low Cost
          Cockpit Procedures Trainer. Report No. NAVTRAEQUIPCEN 78-C-001301. Seville
          Training Systems, Pensacola, Fla.

Carson, L.M., and R.L. Wiegand
  1979   Motor schema formation and retention in young children: A test of Schmidt's schema theory. _Journal of Motor Behavior_ 11:247-251.
Catrambone, R., and K.J. Holyoak
  1989   Overcoming contextual limitations on problem-solving transfer. _Journal of Experimental Psychology: Learning, Memory, and Cognition_ 15:1147-1156.
Charney, D.H., and L.M. Reder
  1987   Initial skill learning: An analysis of how elaborations facilitate the three components. In P. Morris, ed., _Modelling Cognition_. Chichester, England: John Wiley & Sons.
Cheng, P.W.
  1985   Restructuring versus automaticity: Alternative accounts of skill acquisition. _Psychological Review_ 92:414-423.
Chipman, S.F., J.W. Segal, and R. Glaser, eds.
  1985   Thinking and learning skills. _Research and Open Questions_, Vol. 2. Hillsdale, N.J.: Lawrence Erlbaum.
Christina, R.W., and D.M. Corcos
  1988   _Coaches Guide to Teaching Sport Skills_. Champaign, Ill.: Human Kinetics Publishers.
Cognition and Technology Group at Vanderbilt
  1990   Anchored instruction and its relationship to situated cognition. _Educational Research_ 19:2-10.
Cormier, S.M.
  1984   Transfer of Training: An Interpretive Review. Technical Report 608. U.S. Army Research Institute, Alexandria, Va.
  1987   The Structural Processes Underlying Transfer of Training. Transfer of Learning, Contemporary Research and Applications. U.S. Army Research Institute, Alexandria, Va.
Cox, J.A., R.D. Wood, Jr., L.M. Boren, and H.W. Thorpe
  1965   Functional and Appearance Fidelity of Training Devices for Fixed Procedures Tasks. HUMRRO Technical Report 65-4. Human Resources Research Office, Alexandria, Va.
Crawford, A.M., and K.S. Crawford
  1978   Simulation of operational equipment with a computer-based instructional system: A low cost-training technology. _Human Factors_ 20:215-224.
Druckman, D., and R.A. Bjork, eds.
  1991   _In the Mind's Eye: Enhancing Human Performance_. Committee on Techniques for the Enhancement of Human Performance, National Research Coucnil. Washington, D.C.: National Academy Press.
Fernandez, A., and A.M. Glenberg
  1985   Changing environmental context does not reliably affect memory. _Memory and Cognition_ 13:333-345.
Fisk, A.D., M.D. Lee, and W.A. Rogers
  1991   Recombination of automatic processing components: The effects of transfer, reversal, and conflict situations. _Human Factors_ 33:267-280.
Gagne, R.M.
  1954   Training devices and simulators: Some research issues. _American Psychologist_ 9:95-107.
Gibson, J.J.
  1979   _The Ecological Approach to Visual Perception_. Boston: Houghton Mifflin.
Gick, M.L., and K.J. Holyoak
  1983   Schema induction and analogical transfer. _Cognitive Psychology_ 15:1-38.

Godden, D.R., and A.D. Baddeley
1975   Context-dependent memory in two natural environments: On land and underwater. *British Journal of Psychology* 66:325-331.

Goldstein, M., and C.H. Rittenhouse
1954   Knowledge of results in the acquisition and transfer of a gunnery skill. *Journal of Experimental Psychology* 48:187-196.

Gray, W.D., and J.M. Orasanu
1987   Transfer of cognitive skills. In S.M. Cormier and J.D. Hagman, eds., *Transfer of Learning: Contemporary Research and Applications.* New York: Academic Press.

Greeno, J.G.
1989   Situations, mental models, and generative knowledge. In D. Klahr and K. Kotovsky, eds., *Complex Information Processing: The Impact of Herbert A. Simon.* Hillsdale, N.J.: Lawrence Erlbaum.

Greeno, J.G., D.R. Smith, and J.L. Moore
1993   Transfer of situated learning. Pp. 99-167 in D.K. Detterman and R.J. Sternberg, eds., *Transfer on Trial: Intelligence, Cognition, and Instruction.* Norwood, N.J.: Ablex.

Grimsley, D.L.
1969   Acquisition, Retention and Retraining: The Effects of High and Low Fidelity in Training Devices. HUMRRO Technical Report 69-1. Human Resources Research Organization, Alexandria, Va.

Hayes, J.R., and H.S. Simon
1977   Psychological differences among problem isomorphs. In N. Castellan, Jr., D. Pisoni, and G. Potts, eds., *Cognitive Theory,* Vol. 2. Hillsdale, N.J.: Lawrence Erlbaum.

Hendrickson, G., and W.H. Schroeder
1941   Transfer of training in learning to hit a submerged target. *Journal of Educational Psychology* 32:205-213.

Holding, D.H.
1976   An approximate transfer surface. *Journal of Motor Behavior* 8:1-9.

Holyoak, K.J.
1984   Analogical thinking and human intelligence. Pp. 199-230 in R.J. Sternberg, ed., *Advances in the Psychology of Human Intelligence,* Vol. 2. Hillsdale, N.J.: Lawrence Erlbaum.

Ince, F., R.C. Williges, and S.N. Roscoe
1975   Aircraft simulator motion and order of merit of flight attitude and steering guidance displays. *Human Factors* 17:388-400.

Independent Commission on the Los Angeles Police Department
1991   *Report of the Independent Commission on the Los Angeles Police Department.* Los Angeles, Calif.: Independent Commission on the Los Angeles Police Department.

Johnson, P.
1984   The acquisition of skill. Pp. 215-240 in M.M. Smyth and A.M. Wing, eds., *The Psychology of Human Movement.* London, England: Academic Press.

Johnson, S.L.
1981   Effect of training device on retention and transfer of a procedural task. *Human Factors* 23:257-272.

Judd, C.H.
1908   The relation of special training to general intelligence. *Educational Review* 36: 28-42.

Katona, G.
1940   *Organizing and Memorizing.* New York: Columbia University Press.

Kausler, D.H.
1974   *Psychology of Verbal Learning and Memory.* New York: Academic Press.

Kerr, R., and B. Booth
   1978   Specific and varied practice of a motor skill. *Perceptual and Motor Skills* 46:395-401.
Kessler, C.M.
   1988   Transfer of Programming Skills in Novice LISP Learners. Doctoral dissertation, Department of Psychology, Carnegie-Mellon University, Pittsburgh.
Klahr, D., and S.M. Carver
   1988   Cognitive objectives in a LOGO debugging curriculum: Instruction, learning, and transfer. *Cognitive Psychology* 20:362-404.
Knerr, C.M., J.E. Morrison, R.J. Mumaw, D.J. Stein, P.J. Sticha, R.G. Hoffman, D.M. Buede, and D.M. Holding
   1987   Simulation-Based Research in Part-Task Training. AF HRL-TR-86-12, AD-B107 293. Air Force Human Resources Laboratory, Brooks Air Force Base, Tex.
Langley, D.J., and H.N. Zelaznik
   1984   The acquisition of time properties associated with a sequential motor skill. *Journal of Motor Behavior* 16:275-301.
Lave, J.
   1988   *Cognition and Practice: Mind, Mathematics, and Culture in Everyday Life.* Cambridge, England: Cambridge University Press.
Lave, J., and E. Wenger
   1991   *Situated Learning: Legitimate Peripheral Participation.* Cambridge, England: Cambridge University Press.
Levine, M.
   1966   Hypothesis behavior by humans during discrimination learning. *Journal of Experimental Psychology* 71:331-338.
Lintern, G.
   1991   An informational perspective on skill transfer in human-machine systems. *Human Factors* 33:251-266.
Lintern, G., and S.N. Roscoe
   1980   Adaptive perceptual-motor training. In S.N. Roscoe, ed., *Aviation Psychology.* Ames: Iowa State University Press.
Logan, G.D.
   1988   Toward an instance theory of automatization. *Psychological Review* 95:492-527.
Logan, G.D., and S.T. Klapp
   1992   Automatizing alphabet arithmetic: I. Is extended practice necessary to produce automaticity? *Journal of Experimental Psychology: Learning, Memory and Cognition* 17:179-195.
MacKay, D.G.
   1982   The problems of flexibility, fluency, and speed/accuracy trade-off in skilled behavior. *Psychological Review* 89:483-506.
Mane, A., J.A. Adams, and E. Donchin
   1989   Adaptive and part-whole training in the acquisition of a complex perceptual-motor skill. The Learning Strategies Program: An Examination of the Strategies in Skill Acquisition. *Acta Psychologica* 71(Special Issue):179-196.
Mayer, R.E., and J.G. Greeno
   1972   Structural differences between learning outcomes produced by different instructional methods. *Journal of Educational Psychology* 63:165-173.
McGeoch G.O., and A.L. Irion
   1952   *The Psychology of Human Learning*, 2d ed. New York: Longmans.
McKendree, J.E., and J.R. Anderson
   1987   Frequency and practice effects on the composition of knowledge in LISP evaluation. In J.M. Carroll, ed., *Cognitive Aspects of Human-Computer Interaction.* Cambridge, Mass.: MIT Press.

Miller, R.B.
    1953   Handbook on Training and Training Equipment Design. Report No. 53-136. Wright
            Air Development Center, Wright-Patterson Air Force Base, Ohio.
    1954   Psychological Considerations in the Design of Training Equipment. Report No.
            WADC-TR-54-563, AD 71202. Wright Air Development Center, Wright-Patterson
            Air Force Base, Ohio.
Moore, J.L., and J.G. Greeno
    1991   Implicit understanding of functions in quantitative reasoning. In *Proceedings of the
            Thirteenth Annual Conference of the Cognitive Science Society*. Hillsdale, N.J.:
            Lawrence Erlbaum.
Naylor, J.C.
    1962   Parameters Affecting the Relative Efficiency of Part and Whole Practice Methods:
            A Review of the Literature. NAVTRADEVCEN 950-1, AD-275 921. U.S. Naval
            Training Device Center, Port Washington, N.Y.
Newell, K.M.
    1985   Skill learning. Pp. 203-226 in D.H. Holding, ed., *Human Skills*. Chichester, En-
            gland: John Wiley & Sons.
Novick, L.R., and K.J. Holyoak
    1991   Mathematical problem solving by analogy. *Journal of Experimental Psychology:
            Learning, Memory and Cognition* 17:398-415.
Osgood, C.E.
    1949   The similarity paradox in human learning: A resolution. *Psychological Review*
            56:132-143.
Patrick, J.
    1992   *Training: Research and Practice*. San Diego, Calif.: Academic Press.
Polson, P., and D.E. Kieras
    1985   A quantitative model of learning and performance of text editing knowledge. In L.
            Bormann and B. Curtis, eds., *Proceedings of CHI '85 Human Factors in Computing
            Systems Conference*. New York: Association for Computing Machinery.
Prophet, W.W., and H.A. Boyd
    1970   Device-Task Fidelity and Transfer of Training: Aircraft Cockpit Procedures Train-
            ing. Technical Report 70-10. Human Resources Research Organization, Alexan-
            dria, Va.
Reder, L.M., D.H. Charney, and K.I. Morgan
    1986   The role of elaborations in learning a skill from an instructional text. *Memory and
            Cognition* 14:64-78.
Restle, F.
    1962   The selection of strategies in cue learning. *Psychological Review* 69:329-343.
Robinson, E.J.
    1927   The "similarity" factor in retroaction. *American Journal of Psychology* 30:297-312.
Ross, B.H.
    1989   Distinguishing types of superficial similarities: Effects on the access and use of
            earlier problems. *Journal of Experimental Psychology: Learning, Memory, and
            Cognition* 15:456-468.
Salas, E., T.L. Dickinson, S.A. Converse, and S.I. Tannenbaum
    1993   Toward an understanding of team performance and training. In R. W. Swezey and
            E. Salas, eds., *Teams: Their Training and Performance*. Norwood, N.J.: Ablex.
Salmoni, A.W., R.A. Schmidt, and C.B. Walter
    1984   Knowledge of results and motor learning. A review and critical reappraisal. *Psy-
            chological Bulletin* 95(3):355-386.
Salvendy, G., and J. Pilitsis
    1980   The development and validation of an analytical training program for medical sutur-
            ing. *Human Factors* 22:753-770.

Sandberg, J., and B. Wielinga
1992 Situated cognition: A paradigm shift? *Journal of Artificial Intelligence in Education* 3:129-138
Schmidt, R.A.
1975 A schema theory of discrete motor skill learning. *Psychological Review* 82:225-260.
1988 *Motor Control and Learning: A Behavioral Emphasis.* Champaign, Ill.: Human Kinetics Publishers.
1991 *Motor Learning and Performance.* Champaign, Ill.: Human Kinetics.
Schmidt, R.A., and D.E. Young
1987 Transfer of movement control in motor skill learning. Pp. 47-49 in S.M. Cormier and J.D. Hagman, eds., *Transfer of Learning.* Orlando, Fla.: Academic Press.
Schneider, W., and R.M. Shiffrin
1977 Controlled and automatic human information processing: I. Detection, search and attention. *Psychological Review* 84:1-66.
Segal, J.W., S.F. Chipman, and R. Glaser, eds.
1985 Thinking and learning skills. *Relating Instruction to Research,* Vol. 1. Hillsdale, N.J.: Lawrence Erlbaum.
Shapiro, D.C., and R.A. Schmidt
1982 The schema theory: Recent evidence and developmental implications. Pp. 113-150 in J.A.S. Kelso and J.E. Clark, eds., *The Development of Movement Control and Coordination.* New York: John Wiley & Sons.
Shea, J.B., and R. Morgan
1979 Contextual interference effects on the acquisition, retention, and transfer of a motor skill. *Journal of Experimental Psychology: Human Learning and Memory* 5:179-187.
Shea, J.B., and S.T. Zimny
1983 Context effects in memory and learning movement information. Pp. 345-366 in R.A. Magill, ed., *Memory and Control of Action.* Amsterdam, The Netherlands: North-Holland.
Simon, H.A.
1980 Problem solving and education. Pp. 81-92 in D.T. Tuma and F. Reif, eds., *Problem Solving and Education.* Hillsdale, N.J.: Lawrence Erlbaum.
Singley, M.K.
1986 Developing Models of Skill Acquisition in the Context of Intelligent Tutoring Systems. Doctoral dissertation, Department of Psychology, Carnegie-Mellon University, Pittsburgh.
Singley, M.K., and J.R. Anderson
1989 *The Transfer of Cognitive Skill.* Cambridge, Mass.: Harvard University Press.
Smith, E.
1990 Content and process specificity in the effects of prior experiences. Pp. 1-59 in R.K. Srull and R.S. Wyer, Jr. eds., *Advances in Social Cogntion,* Vol. III. Hillsdale, N.J.: Lawrence Erlbaum.
Smith, E.R., N.R. Branscombe, and C. Bormann
1988 Generality of the effects of practice on social judgment tasks. *Journal of Personality and Social Psychology* 43:385-395.
Smith, S.M.
1979 Remembering in and out of context. *Journal of Experimental Psychology: Human Learning and Memory* 5:460-471.
1988 Environmental context-dependent memory. Pp. 13-34 in D.M. Thomson and G.M. Davies, eds., *Memory in Context: Context in Memory.* New York: John Wiley & Sons.

Smith, S.M., and E. Vela
 1986 Outshining: The Relative Effectiveness of Cues. Paper presented at the annual meeting of the Psychonomic Society, New Orleans, La.

Stucky, S.U.
 In Situated cognition: A strong hypothesis. In F.L. Engel, D.G. Boushuis, T. Bosser,
 press and G. Adewalk, eds., *Cognitive Modeling and Interactive Environments*. Proceedings of the NATO ARW.

Thorndike, E.L., and R.S. Woodworth
 1901 The influence of improvement in one mental function upon the efficiency of other functions. *Psychological Review* 8:247-261.

Trabasso, T.R., and G.H. Bower
 1966 Presolution dimensional shifts in concept identification: A test of the sampling with replacement axiom in all-or-none models. *Journal of Mathematical Psychology* 3:163-173.

Trollip, S.R.
 1979 The evaluation of a complex computer-based flight procedures trainer. *Human Factors* 21:47-54.

Tulving, E., and D.M. Thomson
 1973 Encoding specificity and retrieval processes in episodic memory. *Psychological Review* 80:352-373.

Valverde, H.H.
 1973 A review of flight simulator transfer-of-training studies. *Human Factors* 15:510-523.

Van Rossum, J.H.A.
 1990 Schmidt's schemotheory: The empirical base of the variability of practice hypothesis. A critical analysis. *Human Movement Science* 9:387-435.

Vela, E.
 1989 Environmental Context Dependent Memory: A Meta-Analytic Review. Paper presented at the annual meeting of the Psychonomic Society, Atlanta.

Vera, A.H., and H.A. Simon
 1993 Situated action: A symbolic interpretation. *Cognitive Science* 17:7-48.

Wheaton, G.R., A.M. Rose, P.W. Fingerman, A.L. Korotkin, and D.H. Holding
 1976 Evaluation of the Effectiveness of Training Devices: Literature Review and Preliminary Model. Research Memorandum 76-6. U.S. Army Research Institute, Alexandria, Va.

Whitehead, A.N.
 1929 *The Aims of Education*. New York: MacMillan.

Wiering, G.
 1992 A Diamond in the Rough: The National Training Center. Army Research, Development and Acquisition Bulletin, March-April:18-21.

Wightman, D.C.
 1983 Part-Task Training Strategies in Simulated Carrier Landing Final Approach Training. NAVTRAEQUIPCEN IH-347. Naval Training Equipment Center, Orlando, Fla.

Wightman, D.C., and G. Lintern
 1985 Part-task training for tracking and manual control. *Human Factors* 27:267-283.

CHAPTER 4

Asch, S.E.
 1969 A reformulation of the problem of associations. *American Psychologist* 24:92-102.

Baddeley, A.D., and D.J.A. Longman
  1978   The influence of length and frequency of training session on the rate of learning to type. *Ergonomics* 21:627-635.
Bahrick, H.P.
  1979   Maintenance of knowledge: Questions about memory we forgot to ask. *Journal of Experimental Psychology: General* 108:296-308.
Begg, I., S. Duft, P. Lalonde, R. Melnick, and J. Sanvito
  1989   Memory predictions are based on ease of processing. *Journal of Memory and Language* 28:610-632.
Bjork, R.A.
  1994   Memory and metamemory considerations in the training of human beings. In J. Metcalfe and A. Shimamura, eds., *Metamemory: Knowing about Knowing.* Cambridge, Mass.: MIT Press.
Blake, M.
  1973   Prediction of recognition when recall fails: Exploring the feeling-of-knowing phenomenon. *Journal of Verbal Learning and Verbal Behavior* 12:311-319.
Bowers, K.S., and E. Hilgard
  1988   Some complexities in understanding memory. Pp. 3-18 in H.M. Pettinati, ed., *Hypnosis and Memory.* New York: Guilford Press.
Brewer, W.F.
  1988   Memory for randomly sampled autobiographical events. Pp. 21-90 in U. Neisser and E. Winograd, eds., *Remembering Reconsidered: Ecological and Traditional Approaches to the Study of Memory.* New York: Cambridge University Press.
Brown, A.L., and D.R. Murphy
  1989   Cryptomnesia: Delineating inadvertent plagiarism. *Journal of Experimental Psychology: Learning, Memory and Cognition* 15:432-442.
Bruner, J.S., and L. Postman
  1949   Perception, cognition, and personality. *Journal of Personality* 18:14-31.
Catalano, J.F., and B.M. Kleiner
  1984   Distant transfer in coincident timing as a function of variability of practice. *Perceptual and Motor Skills* 58:851-856.
Crawford, H.J., and S.N. Allen
  1983   Enhanced visual memory during hypnosis as mediated by hypnotic responsiveness and cognitive strategies. *Journal of Experimental Psychology: General* 112:662-685.
Dawes, R.M.
  1990   The potential nonfalsity of the false consensus effect. Pp. 179-199 in R.M. Hogarth, ed., *Insights in Decision Making. A Tribute to Hillel J. Einhorn.* Chicago: University of Chicago Press.
Druckman, D., and R.A. Bjork, eds.
  1991   *In the Mind's Eye: Enhancing Human Performance.* Committee on Techniques for the Enhancement of Human Performance, National Research Council. Washington, D.C.: National Academy Press.
Drum, P.A., R.C. Calfee, and L.K. Cook
  1981   The effects of surface structure variables on performance in reading comprehension tests. *Reading Research Quarterly* 164:486-514.
Dunlosky, J., and T.O. Nelson
  1992   Importance of the kind of cue for judgments of learning JOLs and the delayed-JOL effect. *Memory and Cognition* 204:374-380.
Dywan, J., and K.S. Bowers
  1983   The use of hypnosis to enhance recall. *Science* 222:184-185.
Epstein, W., A.M. Glenberg, and M.M. Bradley
  1984   Coactivation and comprehension: Contribution of text variables to the illusion of knowing. *Memory and Cognition* 12:355-360.

Fischhoff, B.
  1975   Hindsight is not equal to foresight: The effects of outcome knowledge on judgment under uncertainty. *Journal of Experimental Psychology: Human Perception and Performance* 1:288-299.
Fischhoff, B., P. Slovic, and S. Lichenstein
  1977   Knowing with certainty: The appropriateness of extreme confidence. *Journal of Experimental Psychology: Human Perception and Performance* 3:552-564.
Gilovich, T.
  1981   Seeing the past in the present: The effect of associations to familiar events on judgments and decisions. *Journal of Personality and Social Psychology* 5:797-808.
  1990   Differential construal and the false consensus effect. *Journal of Personality and Social Psychology* 59:623-634.
Glenberg, A.M., and W. Epstein
  1985   Calibration of comprehension. *Journal of Experimental Psychology: Learning, Memory and Cognition* 11:702-718.
  1987   Inexpert calibration of comprehension. *Memory and Cognition* 151:84-93.
Glenberg, A.M., A.C. Wilkinson, and W. Epstein
  1982   The illusion of knowing: Failure in the self-assessment of comprehension. *Memory and Cognition* 10:597-602.
Glenberg, A.M., T. Sanocki, W. Epstein, and C. Morris
  1987   Enhancing calibration of comprehension. *Journal of Experimental Psychology: General* 116:119-136.
Goranson, R.E.
  1976   A paradox in educational communication. Pp. 63-76 in I. Kusyszyn, ed., *Teaching and Learning Process Seminars*, Vol.1. Toronto, Ont.: York University Press.
Griffin, D.W., and L. Ross
  1991   Subjective construal, social inference, and human misunderstanding. Pp. 319-359 in M. Zanna, ed., *Advances in Experimental Social Psychology*, Vol. 24. New York: Academic Press.
Hall, H.G., E. Domingues, and R. Cavazos
  1992   The Effects of Contextual Interference on Extra Batting Practice. Unpublished paper, Department of Psychology, California Polytechnic State University, San Luis Obispo.
Hart, J.T.
  1967   Memory and the memory-monitoring process. *Journal of Verbal Learning and Verbal Behavior* 6:685-691.
Hasher, L., M.S. Attig, and J.W. Alba
  1981   I knew it all along: or, did I? *Journal of Verbal Learning and Verbal Behavior* 20:86-96.
Heider, F.
  1958   *The Psychology of Interpersonal Relationships*. New York: Wiley.
Higgins, E.T.
  1989   Knowledge accessibility and activation: Subjectivity and suffering from unconscious sources. Pp. 75-123 in J.S. Uleman and J.A. Bargh, eds., *Unintended Thought*. New York: Guilford Press.
Jacoby, L.L., and M. Dallas
  1981   On the relationship between autobiographical memory and perceptual learning. *Journal of Experimental Psychology: General* 3:306-340.
Jacoby, L.L., and C.M. Kelley
  1987   Unconscious influences of memory for a prior event. *Personality and Social Psychology Bulletin* 13:314-336.

Jacoby, L.L., and K. Whitehouse
  1989   An illusion of memory: False recognition influenced by unconscious perception. *Journal of Experimental Psychology: General* 118:126-135.
Jacoby, L.L., L.G. Allan, J.C. Collins, and L.K. Larwill
  1988   Memory influences subjective experience: Noise judgments. *Journal of Experimental Psychology: Learning, Memory and Cognition* 14:240-247.
James, K.
  1986   Priming and social categorization factors: Impact on awareness of emergency situations. *Personality and Social Psychology Bulletin* 12:462-467.
Johnson, M.K.
  1988   Discriminating the origin of information. In T.F. Oltmanns and B.A. Maher, eds., *Delusional Beliefs: Interdisciplinary Perspectives*. New York: Wiley.
Johnson, M.K., M.A. Foley, A.G. Suengas, and C.L. Raye
  1988   Phenomenal characteristics of memories for perceived and imagined autobiographical events. *Journal of Experimental Psychology: General* 117:371-376.
Johnston, W.A., V.J. Dark, and L.L. Jacoby
  1985   Perceptual fluency and recognition judgments. *Journal of Experimental Psychology: Learning, Memory and Cognition* 11:3-11.
Jones, E.E., L. Rock, K.G. Shaver, G.R. Goethals, and L.M. Ward
  1968   Pattern of performance and ability attribution: An unexpected primacy effect. *Journal of Personality and Social Psychology* 10:317-340.
Kelley, C.M., and D.S. Lindsay
  1993   Remembering mistaken for knowing: Ease of retrieval as a basis for confidence in answers to general knowledge questions. *Journal of Memory and Language* 32:1-24.
Kerr, R., and B. Booth
  1978   Specific and varied practice of a motor skill. *Perceptual and Motor Skills* 46:395-401.
Laurence, J.R., and C. Perry
  1983   Hypnotically created memory among highly hypnotizable subjects. *Science* 222:523-524.
Loftus, E.F.
  1992   The Reality of Repressed Memories. Paper presented at the meeting of the American Psychological Association, Washington, D.C.
Nelson, T.O.
  1988   Predictive accuracy of the feeling of knowing across different criterion tasks and across different subject populations and individuals. In M.M. Gruneberg, P. Morris, and R.N. Sykes, eds., *Practical Aspects of Memory*, Vol. 2. New York: Wiley.
Nelson, T.O., and J. Dunlosky
  1991   When people's judgments of learning JOLs are extremely accurate at predicting subsequent recall: The "delayed-JOL effect." *Psychological Science* 2:267-270.
Nelson, T.O., and L. Narens
  1990   Metamemory: A theoretical framework and new findings. Pp. 125-141 in G. Bower, ed., *The Psychology of Learning and Motivation* Vol. 26. San Diego, Calif.: Academic Press.
Newton, L.
  1990   Overconfidence in the Communication of Intent: Heard and Unheard Melodies. Unpublished doctoral dissertation, Department of Psychology, Stanford University.
Olson, D.R.
  1986   The cognitive consequences of literacy. *Canadian Psychology* 27:109-121.

Piaget, J.
  1962   Comments on Vygotsky's critical remarks concerning the language and thought of
         the child and judgement and reasoning in the child. Attachment to L.S. Vygotsky
         Thought and Language. Cambridge, Mass.: MIT Press.
Piaget, J., and B. Inhelder
  1956   *The Child's Conception of Space.* London: Routledge and Kegan Paul.
Reder, L.M.
  1987   Strategy selection in question answering. *Cognitive Psychology* 19:90-138.
  1988   Strategic control of retrieval strategies. Pp. 227-259 in G. Bower, ed., *The Psychol-
         ogy of Learning and Motivation*, Vol. 22. San Diego, Calif.: Academic Press.
Reder, L.M., and F.E. Ritter
  1992   What determines initial feeling of knowing? Familiarity with question terms, not
         with the answer. *Journal of Experimental Psychology: Learning, Memory and
         Cognition* 18:435-451.
Reed, G.
  1974   *The Psychology of Anomalous Experience: A Cognitive Approach.* Boston, Mass.:
         Houghton Mifflin Co.
Richardson-Klavehn, A., and R.A. Bjork
  1988   Measures of memory. *Annual Review of Psychology* 39:475-543.
Roediger, H.L., and K.B. McDermott
  1993   Implicit memory in normal human subjects. In F. Boller and J. Gruffman, eds.,
         Handbook of Neuropsychology, Vol. 8. Amsterdam: Elsevier.
Ross, L.
  1977   The intuitive psychologist and his shortcomings: Distortions in the attribution pro-
         cess. Pp. 173-220 in L. Berkowitz, ed., *Advances in Experimental Social Psychol-
         ogy*, Vol. 10. New York: Academic Press.
Ross, L., D. Greene, and A. House
  1977   The "false consensus effect": An egocentric bias in social perception and attribution
         processes. *Journal of Experimental Social Psychology* 13:279-301.
Schmidt, R.A., and R.A. Bjork
  1992   New conceptualizations of practice: Common principles in three paradigms suggest
         new concepts for training. *Psychological Sciences* 3:207-217.
Schmidt, R.A., D.E. Young, S. Swinnen, and D.C. Shapiro
  1989   Summary knowledge of results for skill acquisition: Support for the guidance hy-
         pothesis. *Journal of Experimental Psychology: Learning, Memory and Cognition*
         15:352-359.
Schwartz, B.L., and J. Metcalfe
  1992   Cue familiarity but not target retrievability enhances feeling-of-knowing judgments.
         Journal of Experimental Psychology: Learning, Memory and Cognition 18:1074-
         1083.
Shea, J.B., and R.L. Morgan
  1979   Contextual interference effects on the acquisition, retention, and transfer of a motor
         skill. *Journal of Experimental Psychology: Human Learning and Memory* 5:179-
         187.
Smith, E.R., and M.A. Zarate
  1992   Exemplar-based model of social judgment. *Psychological Review* 991:3-21.
Spellman, B.A., and R.A. Bjork
  1992   When predictions create reality: Judgments of learning may alter what they are
         intended to assess. *Psychological Science* 3:315-316.
Srull, T.K., and R.S. Wyer
  1979   The role of category accessibility in the interpretation of information about persons:
         Some determinants and implications. *Journal of Personality and Social Psychology*
         37:1660-1672.

Warrington, E.K., and L. Weiskrantz
   1974   The effect of prior learning on subsequent retention in amnesic patients. *Neuropsychologia* 12:419-428.
Weaver, C.
   1990   Constraining factors in calibration of comprehension. *Journal of Experimental Psychology: Learning, Memory and Cognition* 16:214-222.
Whittlesea, B.W.A.
   1993   Illusions of familiarity. *Journal of Experimental Psychology: Learning, Memory and Cognition* 19:1235-1253.
Whittlesea, B.W.A., L.L. Jacoby, and K.A. Girard
   1990   Illusions of immediate memory: Evidence of an attributional basis for feelings of familiarity and perceptual quality. *Journal of Memory and Language* 29:716-732.
Wilson, T.D., and J.W. Schooler
   1991   Thinking too much: Introspection can reduce the quality of preferences and decisions. *Journal of Personality and Social Psychology* 60:181-192.
Wilson, T.D., D.S. Dunn, J.A. Bybee, D.B. Hyman, and J.A. Rotondo
   1984   Effects of analyzing reasons on attitude-behavior consistency. *Journal of Personality and Social Psychology* 47:5-16.
Witherspoon, D., and L.G. Allan
   1985   The effects of a prior presentation on temporal judgments in a perceptual identification task. *Memory and Cognition* 13:101-111.

CHAPTER 5

Aronson, E.
   1978   *The Jigsaw Classroom.* Beverly Hills, Calif.: Sage.
Astin, A.W.
   1985   *Achieving Educational Excellence.* San Francisco: Jossey-Bass.
Baker, L., and A.L. Brown
   1984   Metacognitive skills and reading. Pp. 353-394 in P.D. Pearson, eds., *Handbook of Reading Research.* New York: Longman.
Bandura, A.
   1971   *Psychological Modeling: Conflicting Theories.* Chicago: Aldine-Atherton.
Bansangue, M.
   1991   Achievement Effects of Collaborative Learning in Introductory Statistics: A Time Series Residual Analysis. Presentation at the joint annual meeting of the Mathematical Association of America and the American Mathematical Society, San Francisco.
Barnes, C.P.
   1980   Questions: The Untapped Resource. Paper presented at the annual meeting of the American Educational Research Association, Boston.
Berlyne, D.E.
   1960   *Conflict, Arousal, and Curiosity.* New York: McGraw-Hill.
Bloom, B.S.
   1956   Taxonomy of Educational Objectives: Handbook I. Cognitive Domain. New York: Longmans, Green.
Bossert, S.T.
   1988   Cooperative activities in the classroom. *Review of Research in Education* 15:225-252.
Brooks, J.E.
   1987   *An Instructor's Guide for Implementing Cooperative Learning in the Equipment*

Records and Parts Specialist Course. Army Research Institute Report No. 87-53. Alexandria, Va.: U.S. Army Research Institute.

Brooks, J.E., S.M. Cormier, J.D. Dressel, M. Glaser, B.W. Knerr, and R. Thoreson
1987   *Cooperative Learning: A New Approach for Training Equipment Records and Parts Specialists.* Technical Report No. 760. Alexandria, Va.: U.S. Army Research Institute.

Broome, B.J., and M. Chen
1992   Guidelines for computer-assisted group problem solving: Meeting the challenges of complex issues. *Small Group Research* 23(2):216-236.

Brown, A.L., and A.S. Palinscsar
1989   Guided cooperative learning and individual knowledge acquisition. Pp. 173-223 in L. Resnick, ed., *Knowing, Learning, and Instruction: Essays in Honor of Robert Glaser.* Hillsdale, N.J.: Lawrence Erlbaum.

Carpenter, J.L.
1986   The Effects of Competitive and Cooperative Learning Environments on Student Achievement and Attitudes in College Fencing Classes. Doctoral dissertation, University of Northern Colorado, Greeley.

Cooper, J., and R. Mueck
1990   Student involvement in learning: Cooperative learning and college instruction. *Journal on Excellence in College Teaching* 1:68-76.

Cooper, J., S. Prescott, L. Cook, L. Smith, R. Mueck, and J. Cuseo
1990   *Cooperative Learning and College Instruction: Effective Use of Student Learning Teams.* Long Beach: California State University Foundation.

Damon, W.
1984   Peer education: The untapped potential. *Journal of Applied Developmental Psychology* 5:331-343.

Dansereau, D.F.
1983   *Cooperative Learning: Impact on Acquisition of Knowledge and Skills.* Technical Report No. 586. Alexandria, Va.: U.S. Army Institute for Behavioral and Social Sciences.

1985   Learning strategy research. Pp. 209-239 in J.W. Segal, S. Chipman, and R. Glaser, eds., *Thinking and Learning Skills.* Vol. 1: *Relating Instruction to Research.* Hillsdale, N.J.: Lawrence Erlbaum.

1987   Transfer from cooperative to individual studying. *Journal of Reading* 30(7):614-619.

1988   Cooperative learning strategies. Pp. 103-120 in C.E. Weinstein, E.T. Goetz, and P.A. Alexander, eds., *Learning and Study Strategies: Issues in Assessment, Instruction, and Evaluation.* New York: Academic Press.

Davidson, N., ed.
1990   *Cooperative Learning in Mathematics: Handbook for Teachers.* New York: Addison-Wesley Publishing Co.

Deutsch, M.
1949   A theory of cooperation and competition. *Human Relations* 2:159-152.

1962   Cooperation and trust: Some theoretical notes. In M.R. Jones, ed., *Nebraska Symposium on Motivation.* Lincoln: University of Nebraska Press.

DeVries, D., and K. Edwards
1974   Student teams and learning games: Their effects on cross-race and cross-sex interaction. *Journal of Educational Psychology* 66(5):741-749.

Dimant, R.J., and D.J. Bearison
1991   Development of formal reasoning during successive peer interactions. *Developmental Psychology* 27(2):277-284.

Duin, A.H.
   1991   Computer-supported collaborative writing: The workplace and the writing class-
          room. *Journal of Business and Technical Communication* (5)2:123-150.
Fantuzzo, J.W., R.E. Riggio, S. Connelly, and L.A. Dimeff
   1989a Effects of reciprocal peer tutoring on academic achievement and psychological ad-
          justment: A component analysis. *Journal of Educational Psychology* 81:173-177.
Fantuzzo, J.W., L.A. Dimeff, and S.L. Fox
   1989b Reciprocal peer tutoring: A multimodal assessment of effectiveness with college
          students. *Teaching of Psychology* 16:133-135.
Fantuzzo, J.W., K. Polite, and N. Grayson
   1990   An evaluation of school-based reciprocal peer-tutoring across elementary school
          settings. *Journal of School Psychology* 28:309-324.
Fraser, S.C., A.L. Beaman, E. Diener, and R.T. Kelem
   1977   Two, three, or four heads are better than one: Modification of college performance
          by peer monitoring. *Journal of Educational Psychology* 69(2):101-108.
Frierson, H.T.
   1986   Two intervention methods: Effects on groups of predominantly black nursing stu-
          dents' board scores. *Journal of Research and Development in Education* 19(3):
          18-23.
Hagman, J.D., and J.F. Hayes
   1986   *Cooperative Learning: Effects of Task, Reward, and Group Size on Individual
          Achievement.* Army Research Institute Technical Report 704. Alexandria, Va.:
          U.S. Army Research Institute.
Hall, R.H., T.R. Rocklin, D.F. Dansereau, L.P. Skaggs, A.M. O'Donnell, J.G. Lambiotte, and
   M.D. Young
   1988   The role of individual differences in the cooperative learning of technical material.
          Journal of Educational Psychology 80(2):172-178.
Hall, J., and M. Williams
   1966   A comparison of decision-making performance in established and ad hoc groups.
          Journal of Personality and Social Psychology 3:214-222.
   1970   Group dynamics training and improved decision-making. *Journal of Applied Behav-
          ioral Science* 6:39-68.
Heller, P., R. Keith, and S. Anderson
   1992   Teaching problem solving through cooperative grouping. Part 1: group versus
          individual problem solving. *American Journal of Physics* 60(7):627-636.
Holubec, E., D.W. Johnson, and R.T. Johnson
   1993   Impact of cooperative learning on naval air-traffic controller training. *Journal of
          Social Psychology* 133:337-346.
Hungerland, J.E., J.E. Taylor, and M.F. Brennan
   1976   Utilization of Peer Instruction in Air Force Technical Training. Final Report 76-12,
          HumRRO, Air Force Office of Scientific Research, Bolling Air Force Base, Wash-
          ington, D.C.
Hwong, N., A. Caswell, D.W. Johnson, and R. Johnson
   1993   Effects of cooperative and individualistic learning structures on prospective elemen-
          tary teachers' music achievement and attitudes. *Journal of Social Psychology* 133:
          53-64.
Hythecker, V.I., T.R. Rocklin, D.F. Dansereau, J.G. Lambiotte, C.O. Larson, and A.M. O'Donnell
   1985   A computer-based learning strategy training module: Development and evaluation.
          Journal of Educational Computing Research 1(3):275-283.
Hythecker, V.I., D.F. Dansereau, and T.R. Rocklin
   1988   An analysis of the processes influencing the structured dyadic learning environment.
          Educational Psychologist 23(1):23-37.

Jacobs, G., and L.M. Icola
 1990 Disagreement Can Be Inviting: A Cooperative Learning Approach. Paper presented at the annual meeting of the American Educational Research Association, Boston.
Johnson, D.W., and R.T. Johnson
 1975 *Learning Together and Alone: Cooperation, Competition and Individualization.* Englewood Cliffs, N.J.: Prentice-Hall.
 1979 Conflict in the classroom: Controversy and learning. *Review of Educational Research* 49:51-70.
 1983 Social interdependence and perceived academic and personal support in the classroom. *Journal of Social Psychology* 120:77-82.
 1985a Classroom conflict: Controversy vs. debate in learning groups. *American Educational Research Journal* 22:237-256.
 1985b The internal dynamics of cooperative learning groups. Pp. 103-124 in R. Slavin, S. Sharan, S. Kagan, R.H. Lazarowitz, C. Webb, and R. Schmuck, eds., *Learning to Cooperate, Cooperating to Learn.* New York: Plenum.
 1987 Research shows the benefits of adult cooperation. *Educational Research* 45:27-30.
 1989 *Cooperation and Competition: Theory and Research.* Edina, Minn.: Interaction Book Company.
 1992a *Creative Controversy: Intellectual Challenge in the Classroom.* Edina, Minn.: Interaction Book Company.
 1992b Positive interdependence: Key to effective cooperation. In R. Hertz-Lazarowitz and N. Miller, eds., *Interaction in Cooperative Groups: The Theoretical Anatomy of Group Learning.* New York: Cambridge University Press.
Johnson, D.W., R.T. Johnson, L.A. Buckman, and T.S. Richards
 1985 The effects of prolonged implementation of cooperative learning on social support within the classroom. *Journal of Psychology* 119(5):405-411.
Johnson, D.W., R.T. Johnson, and E. Holubec
 1990 *Circles of Learning: Cooperation in the Classroom.* Edina, Minn.: Interaction Book Company.
Johnson, D.W., R.T. Johnson, W. Pierson, and V. Lyons
 1985 Controversy versus concurrence seeking in multi-grade and single-grade learning groups. *Journal of Research in Science Teaching* 22(9):835-848.
Johnson, D.W., R.T. Johnson, and K.A. Smith
 1986 Academic conflict among students: controversy and learning. In R. Feldman, ed., *Social Psychological Applications to Education.* Cambridge, England: Cambridge University Press.
 1991a *Active Learning: Cooperation in the College Classroom.* Edina, Minn.: Interaction Book Company.
 1991b Cooperative Learning: Increasing College Faculty Instructional Productivity. ASHE-ERIC Higher Education Report No. 4. School of Education and Human Development, George Washington University.
Johnson, D.W., R.T. Johnson, A. Ortiz, and M. Stanne
 1991 Impact of positive goal and resource interdependence on achievement, interaction, and attitutes. *Journal of General Psychology* 118:341-347.
Johnson, R.T., R. Bjorkland, and M. Krotee
 1983 The effects of cooperative, competitive, and individualistic student interaction patterns on achievement and attitudes on the golf skill of putting. *Research Quarterly for Exercise and Sport* 55:129-139.
Johnson, R.T., D.W. Johnson, and M.B. Stanne
 1986 Comparison of computer-assisted cooperative, competitive, and individualistic learning. *American Educational Research Journal* 23(3):382-392.

Johnson, R.T., D.W. Johnson, M.B. Stanne, A. Garibaldi
  1990   The impact of leader and member group processing on achievement in cooperative groups. *Journal of Social Psychology* 130:507-516.
Karp, D., and W. Yoels
  1987   The college classroom: Some observations on the meanings of student participation. *Sociology and Social Research* 60:421-439.
King, A.
  1990   Enhancing peer interaction and learning in the classroom through reciprocal questioning. *American Educational Research Journal* 27(4):664-687.
Knight, G.P., and E.M. Bohlmeyer
  1990   Cooperative learning and achievement: Methods for assessing causal mechanisms. Pp. 1-22 in S. Sharan, ed., *Cooperative Learning: Theory and Research*. New York: Praeger.
Kohn, A.
  1991   Group grading grubbing versus cooperative learning. *Educational Leadership* 5:83-87.
Lambiotte, J.G., D.F. Dansereau, A.M. O'Donnell, M.D. Young, L.P. Skaggs, R.H. Hall, and T.R. Rocklin
  1987   Manipulating cooperative scripts for teaching and learning. *Journal of Educational Psychology* 79:424-430.
Larson, C.O., and D.F. Dansereau
  1986   Cooperative learning in dyads. *Journal of Reading* 29(6):516-520.
Larson, C.O., D.F. Dansereau, E. Goetz, and M.D. Young
  1985a   Cognitive Style and Cooperative Learning: Transfer of Effects. Paper presented at the annual meeting, Southwest Educational Research Association, Austin, Texas.
Larson, C.O., D.F. Dansereau, V.I. Hythecker, A.M. O'Donnell, M. Young, J.G. Lambiotte, and T.R. Rocklin
  1986   Technical training: An application of a strategy for learning structural and functional information. *Contemporary Educational Psychology* 11(3):217-228.
Larson, C.O., D.F. Dansereau, A.M. O'Donnell, V.I. Hythecker, J.G. Lambiotte, and T.R. Rocklin
  1984   Verbal ability and cooperative learning: Transfer of effects. *Journal of Reading Behavior* 16(4):289-295.
  1985b   Effects of metacognitive and elaborative activity on cooperative learning and transfer. *Contemporary Educational Psychology* 10(4):342-348.
Lewin, K.
  1935   *A Dynamic Theory of Personality*. New York: McGraw-Hill.
  1948   *Resolving Social Conflicts*. New York: Harper.
Lewis, R.B.
  1991   Creative teaching and learning in a statics class. *Engineering Education* January-February:15-18.
Lowry, N., and D.W. Johnson
  1981   Effects of controversy on epistemic curiosity, achievement, and attitudes. *Journal of Social Psychology* 115:31-43.
Maier, N., and L. Hoffman
  1964   Financial incentives and group decision in motivating change. *Journal of Social Psychology* 64:369-378.
Marks, M.
  1991   *Cooperative Learning in Chemistry*. College Park, Md.: Center for Teaching Excellence.
McDonald, B.A., C.O. Larson, D.F. Dansereau, and J.E. Spurlin
  1985   Cooperative learning: Impact on knowledge acquisitions and skills. *Contemporary Educational Psychology* 10:369-377.

McDonnell, T.M.
  1990   Joining hands and smarts: Teaching manual legal research through collaborative learning groups. *Journal of Legal Education* 40(3):363-374.
Meloth, M.S., and P.D. Deering
  1992   Effects of two cooperative conditions on peer-group discussions, reading comprehension, and metacognition. *Contemporary Educational Psychology* 17:175-193.
Mesch, D., M. Lew, D.W. Johnson, and R.T. Johnson
  1986   Isolated teenagers, cooperative learning and the training of social skills. *Journal of Psychology* 120:323-334.
Mesch, D., D.W. Johnson, and R.T. Johnson
  1988   Impact of positive interdependence and academic group contingencies on achievement. *Journal of Social Psychology* 128(3):345-352.
Murray, F.B.
  1982   Teaching through social conflict. *Contemporary Educational Psychology* 7:257-271.
Nastasi, B.K., and D.H. Clements
  1991   Research on cooperative learning: Implications for practice. *School Psychology Review* 20(1):110-131.
Nemeth, C., and J. Wachtler
  1983   Creative problem solving as a result of majority vs. minority influence. *European Journal of Social Psychology* 13(1):45-55.
O'Donnell, A.M.
  1992   Scripted Cooperation: Cognitive and Affective Consequences of Explicit Incentives. Paper presented at the International Association for the Study of Cooperation in Education, Utrecht, Holland.
O'Donnell, A.M., and D.F. Dansereau
  1992   Scripted cooperation in student dyads: A method for analyzing and enhancing academic learning and performance. In N. Miller and R. Hertz-Lazarowitz, eds., *Interaction in Cooperative Groups: The Theoretical Anatomy of Group Learning.* Cambridge, England: Cambridge University Press.
O'Donnell, A.M., D.F. Dansereau, R.H. Hall, and T.R. Rocklin
  1987   Cognitive, social/affective, and metacognitive outcomes of scripted cooperative learning. *Journal of Educational Psychology* 79(4):421-437.
O'Malley, C., and E. Scanlon
  1990   Computer-supported collaborative learning: Problem solving and distance education. *Computers and Education* 15(1-3):127-136.
O'Neil, H.F., ed.
  1978   *Learning Strategies.* New York: Academic Press.
Palinscsar, A.S., and A.L. Brown
  1989   Classroom dialogue to promote self-regulated comprehension. Pp. 35-71 in J. Brophy, ed., *Teaching for Understanding and Self-Regulated Learning.* Greenwich, Conn.: JAI Press.
Palmer, J., and J.T. Johnson
  1989   Jigsaw in a college classroom: Effect on student achievement and impact on student evaluations of teacher performance. *Journal of Social Studies Research* 13(1): 34-37.
Patterson, M.E., D.F. Dansereau, and D. Newbern
  1992   Effects of communication aids and strategies on cooperative teaching. *Journal of Educational Psychology* 84(4):453-461.
Patterson, M.E., D.F. Dansereau, and D.A. Wiegmann
  1993   Receiving information during a cooperative episode: Effects of communication aids and verbal ability. *Learning and Individual Differences* 5(1):1-11.

Piaget, J.
   1926   *Language and Thought of the Child.* New York: Harcourt Brace.
Pressley, M., S. Symons, M.A. McDaniel, B.L. Snyder, and J.E. Turnure
   1988   Elaborative interrogation facilitates acquisition on confusing facts. *Journal of Educational Psychology* 80(3):268-278.
Reder, L.
   1980   The role of elaboration in the comprehension and retention of prose: A critical review. *Review of Educational Research* 49:5-53.
Rewey, K.L., D.F. Dansereau, S.M. Dees, L.P. Skaggs, and U. Pitre
   1992   Scripted cooperation and knowledge map supplements: Effects on the recall of biological and statistical information. *Journal of Experimental Education* 60(2):3-107.
Riggio, R.E., J.W. Fantuzzo, S. Connelly, and L.A. Dimeff
   1991   Reciprocal peer tutoring: A classroom strategy for promoting academic and social integration in undergraduate students. *Journal of Social Behavior and Personality* 6:387-396.
Rocklin, T.R., A.M. O'Donnell, D.F. Dansereau, J.G. Lambiotte, V.I. Hythecker, and C.O. Larson
   1985   Training learning strategies with computer-aided cooperative learning. *Computers and Education* 9(1):67-74.
Rosenshine, B., and C. Meister
   1991   Reciprocal Teaching: A Review of Nineteen Experimental Studies. Paper presented at the annual meeting of the American Educational Research Association, Chicago, Ill.
Ross, S.M., and F.J. DiVesta
   1976   Oral summary as a review strategy for enhancing recall of textual material. *Journal of Educational Psychology* 68:689-695.
Ross J., and D. Raphael
   1990   Communication and problem-solving achievement in cooperative learning groups. *Journal of Curriculum Studies* 22(2):149-164.
Salomon, G., and T. Globerson
   1989   When teams do not function the way they ought to. *International Journal of Educational Research* 13(1):89-98.
Segal, J.W., S. Chipman, and R. Glaser
   1985   *Thinking and Learning Skills*, Vol. 1: *Relating Instruction to Research.* Hillsdale, N.J.: Lawrence Erlbaum.
Sharan, S.
   1990   *Cooperative Learning: Theory and Research.* New York: Praeger.
Sharan, S., and C. Shachar
   1988   *Language and Learning in the Cooperative Classroom.* New York: Springer-Verlag.
Sherman, L.W.
   1986   Cooperative versus competitive educational psychology classrooms: A comparative study. *Teaching and Teacher Education* 2:283-295.
Shlechter, T.M.
   1988   *Effects of Small Group and Individual Computer-Based Instruction on Retention and on Training Lower Ability Soldiers.* Army Research Institute Technical Report No. ARI-RR 1497. Alexandria, Va.: U.S. Army Research Institute.
Slavin, R.E.
   1980   Cooperative learning. *Review of Educational Research* 50:315-342.
   1983   *Cooperative Learning.* New York: Longman.
   1985   An introduction to cooperative learning research. Pp. 177-210 in R. Slavin, S. Sharan, S. Kagan, R.H. Lazarowitz, C. Webb, and R. Schmuck, eds., *Learning to Cooperate, Cooperating to Learn.* New York: Plenum.

1987 Developmental and motivational perspectives on cooperative learning: A reconciliation. *Child Development* 58:1161-1167.

1990 *Cooperative Learning: Theory, Research, and Practice.* Englewood Cliffs, N.J.: Prentice-Hall.

1992 When and why does cooperative learning increase achievement? Theoretical and empirical perspectives. In R. Hertz-Lazarowitz and N. Miller, eds., *Interaction in Cooperative Groups: The Theoretical Anatomy of Group Learning.* New York: Cambridge University Press.

Smith, K., D.W. Johnson, and R. Johnson
1981 Can conflict be constructive? Controversy concurrence seeking in learning groups. *Journal of Educational Psychology* 73:651-633.

1984 Effects of controversy on learning in cooperative groups. *Journal of Social Psychology* 116:277-283.

Smith, K., R. Peterson, D.W. Johnson, and R. Johnson
1986 The effects of controversy and concurrence seeking on effective decision making. *Journal of Social Psychology* 126:237-248.

Stones, E.
1970 Students' attitudes to the size of teaching groups. *Educational Review* 21(2):98-108.

Swallow, J., M. Scardamalia, and W.P. Oliver
1988 Facilitating Thinking Skills Through Peer Interaction with Software Support. Paper presented at the annual meeting of the American Educational Research Association, New Orleans, La.

Tinto, V.
1975 Dropout from higher education: A theoretical synthesis of recent research. *Review of Educational Research* 45(1):89-125.

1987 *Leaving College: Rethinking the Causes and Cures of Student Attrition.* Chicago: University of Chicago Press.

Tjosvold, D.
1991 *The Conflict-Positive Organization.* Reading, Mass.: Addison-Wesley.

in *Learning to Manage Conflict: Getting People to Work Together Productively.*
press New York: Lexington Books.

Torrance, E.
1970 Influence on dyadic interaction on creative functioning. *Psychological Reports* 26:391-394.

1971 Stimulation, enjoyment and originality in dyadic creativity. *Journal of Educational Psychology* 62:45-48.

1973 Dyadic Interaction in Creative Thinking and Problem Solving. Paper presented at the annual meeting of the American Educational Research Association, New Orleans, La.

Totten, S., T. Sills, A. Digby, and P. Russ
1991 *Cooperative Learning.* New York: Garland Publishing, Inc.

Treisman, P.U.
1985 A Study of the Mathematics Performance of Black Students at the University of California, Berkeley. Doctoral dissertation, University of California, Berkeley.

Vasquez, B., D.W. Johnson, and R. Johnson
1993 Impact of cooperative learning on performance and retention of navy air-traffic controller trainees. *Journal of Social Psychology* 133:769-783.

Vygotsky, L.
1978 *Mind and Society.* Cambridge, Mass.: Harvard University Press.

Wales, C., and Stager, R.
1978 *The Guided-Design Approach.* Englewood Cliffs, N.J.: Educational Technology Publications.

Webb, N.M.
  1980   An analysis of group interaction and mathematical errors in heterogeneous ability groups. *British Journal of Educational Psychology* 50:266-276.
  1982   Peer interaction and learning in cooperative small groups. *Journal of Educational Psychology* 74(5):642-655.
  1985   Verbal interaction and learning in peer-directed groups. *Theory Into Practice* 24(1): 32-39.
  1989   Peer interaction and learning in small groups. *International Journal of Educational Research* 13(1):21-37.
  1992   Testing a theoretical model of student interaction and learning in small groups. In R. Hertz-Lazarowitz and N. Miller, eds., *Interaction in Cooperative Groups: The Theoretical Anatomy of Group Learning*. New York: Cambridge University Press.
Weinstein, C.E., E.T. Goetz, and P.A. Alexander, eds.
  1988   *Learning and Study Strategies: Issues in Assessment, Instruction, and Evaluation*. New York: Academic Press.
Wiegmann, D.A., D.F. Dansereau, and M.E. Patterson
  1992   Cooperative learning: Effects of role playing and ability on performance. *Journal of Experimental Education* 60(2):109-116.
Yager, S., D.W. Johnson, and R.T. Johnson
  1985   Oral discussion, group-to-individual transfer, and achievement in cooperative learning groups. *Journal of Educational Psychology* 77(1):60-66.

CHAPTER 6

Allport, G.W.
  1969   The historical background of modern social psychology. In G. Lindzey and E. Aronson, eds., *The Handbook of Social Psychology*, 2nd ed. Reading, Mass.: Addison-Wesley.
Anderson, P.H., and L. Lawton
  1992   A survey of methods used for evaluating student performance on business simulations. *Simulation & Gaming* 23:490-498.
Argyris, C., R. Putnam, and D.M. Smith
  1985   *Action Science*. San Francisco: Jossey-Bass.
Bassin, M.
  1988   Teamwork at General Foods: new and improved. *Personnel Journal* 67:62-70.
Berkowitz, L.
  1954   Group standards, cohesiveness, and productivity. *Human Relations* 7:505-519.
Boocock, S.S., and E.O. Schild, ed.
  1968   *Simulation Games in Learning*. Beverly Hills, Calif.: Sage Publications.
Bredemeier, M.E., and C.S. Greenblat
  1981   The educational effectiveness of simulation games: A synthesis of findings. *Simulation and Games* 12(3):307-332.
Brewer, M.B., and R.M. Kramer
  1985   The psychology of intergroup attitudes and behavior. *Annual Review of Psychology* 36:219-243.
Buller, P.F.
  1986   The team building-task performance relation: Some conceptual and methodological refinements. *Group and Organization Studies* 11:147-168.
Buller, P.F., and C.H. Bell Jr.
  1986   Effects of team building and goal setting on productivity: A field experiment. *Academy Of Management Journal* 29:305-328.

Campbell, D.T., and J.C. Stanley
   1963   *Experimental and Quasi-Experimental Designs for Research.* Chicago: Rand McNally.
Cherryholmes, C.
   1966   Some current research on effectiveness of educational simulations: Implications for alternative strategies. *American Behavioral Scientist* 10:4-7.
Chidester, T.R., and H.C. Foushee
   1988   Leader Personality and Crew Effectiveness: Factors Influencing Performance in Full-Mission Air Transport Simulation. Paper presented at the 66th Symposium of Aerospace Medical Panel on Human Behavior in High Stress Situations in Aerospace Ops, The Hague, Netherlands.
Crookall, D., and R.L. Oxford
   1990   *Simulation, Gaming, and Language Learning.* New York: Newbury House.
Dechant, K., and V.J. Marsick
   1992   How Groups Learn from Experience. Unpublished paper, Teacher's College, Columbia University.
Deep, S.D., B.M. Bass, and J.A. Vaughan
   1967   Some effects on business gaming of previous quasi-T group affiliations. *Journal of Applied Psychology* 51:426-431.
DeMeuse, K.P., and S.J. Liebowitz
   1981   An empirical analysis of team-building research. *Group and Organization Studies* 6:357-378.
Druckman, D.
   1968   Prenegotiation experience and dyadic conflict resolution in a bargaining situation. *Journal of Experimental Social Psychology* 4:367-383.
   1986   Stages, turning points, and crises: Negotiating military base-rights, Spain and the United States. *Journal of Conflict Resolution* 30:327-360.
   1994   Determinants of compromising behavior in negotiation: A meta-analysis. *Journal of Conflict Resolution.*
Druckman, D., and R.A. Bjork, eds.
   1991   *In the Mind's Eye: Enhancing Human Performance.* Committee on Techniques for the Enhancement of Human Performance, National Research Council. Washington, D.C.: National Academy Press.
Druckman, D. and J.A. Swets, eds.
   1988   *Enhancing Human Performance: Issues, Theories, and Techniques.* Committee on Techniques for the Enhancement of Human Performance, National Research Council. Washington, D.C.: National Academy Press.
Druckman, D., J. Husbands, and K. Johnston
   1991   Turning points in the INF negotiations. *Negotiation Journal* 7:55-67.
Dyer, W.G.
   1987   *Team Building: Issues and Alternatives,* 2nd ed. Reading, Mass.: Addison-Wesley.
Fletcher, J.
   1971   The effectiveness of simulation games as learning environments: A proposed program of research. *Simulation and Games* 2:473-488.
Francis, D., and D. Young
   1979   *Improving Work Groups: A Practical Manual for Team Building.* San Diego: University Associates.
Freeberg, N.E., and D.A. Rock
   1987   Development of a Small-Group Team Performance Taxonomy Based on Meta-Analysis. Final Report to Office of Naval Research. Educational Testing Service, Princeton, N.J.
French, W.D., and C.H. Bell
   1984   *Organizational Development: Behavioral Science Interventions for Organization Improvement,* 3rd ed. Englewood Cliffs, N.J.: Prentice-Hall.

Garsick, C.J.G.
   1988   Time and transition in work teams: Toward a new model of group development. *Academy of Management Journal* 31(1):9-41.
Gladstein, D.L.
   1984   Groups in context: A model of task group effectiveness. *Administrative Science Quarterly* 29:499-517.
Glenn, A.D., D. Gregg, and B. Tipple
   1982   Using role-play activities to teach problem solving: Three teaching strategies. *Simulation and Games* 13(2):199-209.
Glickman, A.S., S. Zimmer, R.C. Montero, P.J. Guerette, W.J. Campbell, B. Morgan, and E. Salas
   1987   The Evolution of Teamwork Skills: An Empirical Assessment with Implications for Training.   Technical Report 87-016.   Office of Naval Research, Human Factors Division, Orlando, Fla.
Goodman, P.S.
   1986   Impact of task and technology on group performance. In P.S. Goodman and Associates, eds., *Designing Effective Work Groups*. San Francisco: Jossey-Bass.
Gould, S.J., and N. Eldredge
   1977   Punctuated equilibria: The tempo and mode of evolution reconsidered. *Paleobiology* 3:115-151.
Greenblat, C.S.
   1975   Teaching with simulation games: A review of claims and evidence. In C.S. Greenblat and R.D. Duke, eds., *Gaming-Simulation: Rationale, Design, and Applications*. New York: Halsted Press.
Hackman, J.R.
   1976   Group influences on individuals. In M.D. Dunnette, ed., *Handbook of Industrial and Organizational Psychology*. Chicago: Rand McNally.
   1987   The design of work teams. In J. Lorsch, ed., *Handbook of Organizational Behavior*. New York: Prentice-Hall.
Hall, J.S., and W. Watson
   1971   The effects of a normative intervention on group decision-making performance. *Human Relations* 23:299-317.
Hall, E.R., and W.A. Rizzo
   1975   An assessment of U.S. Navy tactical training.   TAEG Report No. 18. Orlando, Fla: Training Analysis and Evaluation Group.
Hand, H.H., B.D. Estafen, and H.P. Sims
   1975   How effective is data survey and feedback as a technique of organization development? *Journal of Applied Behavioral Science* 11:333-347.
Hare, A.P.
   1992   *Groups, Teams, and Social Interaction: Theories and Applications*. New York: Praeger.
Harris, D.H., ed.
   1994   *Organizational Linkages: Understanding the Productivity Paradox*. Washington, D.C.: National Academy Press.
Hirokawa, R.Y.
   1983   Group communication and problem solving effectiveness: An investigation of group phases. *Human Communication Research* 9:291-305.
Hsu, T.
   1984   A further test of the group formation and its impacts in a simulated business environment. In D.M. Currie and J.W. Gentry, eds., *Developments in Business Simulation and Experiential Exercises*. Stillwater: Oklahoma State University Press.

Insko, C.A., R.L. Hoyle, G. Pinkley, G. Hong, and R.M. Slim
  1988   Individual-group discontinuity: The role of a consensus rule. *Journal of Experimental Social Psychology* 24:505-519.
Johnson, M., and T.M. Nelson
  1978   Game playing with juvenile delinquents. *Simulation and Games* 9:461-475.
Kahn, R.L.
  1991   Organizational theory. In V. Kremenyuk, ed., *International Negotiations: Analyses, Approaches, and Issues*. San Francisco: Jossey-Bass.
Klein, G., and M. Thordsen
  1989   Cognitive Processes of the Team Mind. Final Report to NASA-Ames Research Center. Klein Associates, Yellow Springs, Ohio.
Klein, G., C.E. Zsambok, M.M. Kyne, and D.W. Klinger
  1992   Advanced Team Decision Making: A Cognitive System for Developing Teampower. Report to the U.S. Army Research Institute. Klein Associates, Fairborn, Ohio.
Kremenyuk, V., ed.
  1991   *International Negotiations: Analyses, Approaches, and Issues*. San Francisco: Jossey-Bass.
LeVine, R.A., and Campbell, D.T.
  1972   *Ethnocentrism*. New York: Wiley.
Levinson, D.J.
  1986   A conception of adult development. *American Psychologist* 41:3-14.
London, M.
  1985   *Developing Managers*. San Francisco: Jossey-Bass.
Maier, N.R.F., and L.R. Hoffman
  1960   Quality of first and second solutions in group problem solving. *Journal of Applied Psychology* 44:278-283.
Maier, N.R.F., and R.A. Maier
  1957   An experimental test of the effects of "developmental" vs. "free" discussions on the quality of group decisions. *Journal of Applied Psychology* 41:320-323.
McGrath, J.E., G.C. Futoran, and J.R. Kelly
  1986   Complex Temporal Patterning in Interaction and Task Performance: A Report of Progress in a Program of Research on the Social Psychology of Time. Technical Report No. 86-1. Department of Psychology, University of Illinois.
McKenney, J.L., and W.R. Dill
  1966   Influences on learning in simulation games. *American Behavioral Science* 10:28-32.
Mead, G.H.
  1934   *Mind, Self, and Society*. Chicago: University of Chicago Press.
Messick D.M., and D.M. Mackie
  1989   Intergroup relations. *Annual Review of Psychology* 40:45-81.
Miesing, P., and J.F. Preble
  1985   Group processes and performance in a complex business simulation. *Small Group Behavior* 16:325-338.
Nisbett, R., and L. Ross
  1980   *Human Inference: Strategies and Shortcomings of Social Judgment*. Englewood Cliffs, N.J.: Prentice-Hall.
Norris, D.R., and R.E. Niebuhr
  1980   Group variables and gaming success. *Simulation and Games* 11:301-312.
Orasanu, J.
  1990   Shared Mental Models and Crew Performance. Laboratory, Cognitive Science. Technical Report #46, Princeton University.
Orasanu, J., and E. Salas
  1993   Team decision making in complex environments. In G. Klein, J. Orasanu, and R.

Calderwood, eds., *Decision Making in Action: Models and Methods*. Norwood, N.J.: Ablex Publishing Co.

Oswalt, I.
1993 Current applications, trends, and organizations in U.S. military simulation and gaming. *Simulation & Gaming* 24:153-189.

Pierfy, D.A.
1977 Comparative simulation game research, stumbling blocks and steppingstones. *Simulation and Games* 8:255-268.

Randel, J.M., B.A. Morris, C.D. Wetzel, and B.V. Whitehall
1992 The effectiveness of games for educational purposes: A review of recent research. *Simulation & Gaming* 23:261-276.

Resnick, L.B.
1991 Shared cognition: Thinking as social practice. In L.B. Resnick, J.M. Levine, and S.D. Teasley, eds., *Perspectives On Socially Shared Cognition*. Washington, D.C.: American Psychological Association.

Rizzo, W.A.
1980 Navy team training: Some critical issues. In S. Goldin and P. Thorndyke, eds., *Improving Team Performance: Proceedings of the Rand Team Performance Workshop*. Washington, D.C.: Office of Naval Research.

Schachter, S., N. Ellertson, D. McBride, and D. Gregory
1951 An experimental study of cohesiveness and productivity. *Human Relations* 4:229-239.

Schein, E.H.
1985 *Organizational Culture and Leadership*. San Francisco: Jossey-Bass.

Schild, E.O.
1968 The shaping of strategies. In S.S. Boocock and E.O. Schild, eds., *Simulation Games in Learning*. Beverly Hills, Calif.: Sage Publications.

Seashore, S.
1954 *Group Cohesiveness in the Industrial Work Group*. Institute for Social Research. Ann Arbor: University of Michigan.

Sherif, M., and C.W. Sherif
1956 *An Outline of Social Psychology*. New York: Harper and Row.

Shubik, M., and G.D. Brewer
1972 Models, Simulations, and Games: A Survey. Rand Report R-1060. The Rand Corporation, Santa Monica, Calif.

Stein, A.
1976 Conflict and cohesion: A review of the literature. *Journal of Conflict Resolution* 20:143-172.

Steiner, I.D.
1972 *Group Process and Productivity*. Orlando, Fla.: Academic Press.

Sundstrom, E., K.P. De Meuse, and D. Futrell
1990 Work teams: Applications and effectiveness. *American Psychologist* 45:120-133.

Tajfel, R.
1982 Social psychology of intergroup relations. *Annual Review of Psychology* 33:1-39.

Tannenbaum, S.I., R.L. Beard, and E. Salas
1992 *Team Building and its Influence on Team Effectiveness: An Examination of Conceptual and Empirical Developments*. Amsterdam: Elsevier.

Tuckman, B.W., and M. Jensen
1977 Stages of small-group development revisited. *Group and Organization Studies* 2:419-427.

Turner, J.C.
1987 *Rediscovering the Social Group: A Self-Categorization Theory*. New York: Basil Blackwell.

Van Sickle, R.
  1978 Designing simulation games to teach decision-making skills. *Simulation and Games* 9:413-425.
  1986 A quantitative review of research on instructional simulation gaming: A twenty-year perspective. *Theory and Research in Social Education* 14:245-264.
Vygotsky, L.S.
  1978 *Mind in Society*. Cambridge, Mass.: Harvard University Press.
Wegner, D.M.
  1986 Transactive memory: A contemporary analysis of the group mind. In B. Mullen and G.R. Goethals, eds., *Theories of Group Behavior*. New York: Springer-Verlag.
Wolf, F.M.
  1986 *Meta-Analysis: Quantitative Methods for Research Synthesis*. Sage University Paper Series on Quantitative Applications in the Social Sciences, Series no. 07-059. Beverly Hills, Calif.: Sage Publications.
Wolfe, J., D.D. Bowen, and C.R. Roberts
  1989 Team-building effects on company performance: A business game-based study. *Simulation and Games* 20:388-408.
Woodman, R.W., and J.J. Sherwood
  1980 The role of team development in organizational effectiveness: A critical review. *Psychological Bulletin* 88:166-186.

CHAPTER 7

Acheson, K.
  1964 The Effects of Feedback from Television Recordings and Three Types of Supervisory Treatment on Selected Teacher Behaviors. Doctoral dissertation, Stanford University. University Microfilms: Ann Arbor, Mich., No. 64-13542.
Archer-Kath, J., D.W. Johnson, and R.T. Johnson
  in   Individual versus group feedback in cooperative groups. *American Educational*
  press *Research Journal*.
Aronson, E., and M. O'Leary
  1982- The relative effectiveness of models and prompts on energy conservation: A field
  1983   experiment in a shower room. *Journal of Environmental Systems* 12:219-224.
Baldwin, T., and J. Ford
  1988 Transfer of training: A review and directions for future research. *Personality Psychology* 41:63-105.
Baldwin, T., and R. Magjurka
  1991 Organizational training and signals of importance: Effects of pre-training perceptions on intentions to transfer. *Human Resources Development* 21:25-36.
Baron, R., D. Moore, and G. Sanders
  1978 Distraction as a source of drive in social facilitation research. *Journal of Personality and Social Psychology* 36:816-824.
Baron, R., N. Kerr, and N. Miller
  1992 *Group Process, Group Decision, Group Action*. Pacific Grove, Calif.: Brooks/Cole.
Blake, R., and J. Mouton
  1962 Overevaluation of own group's product in intergroup competition. *Journal of Abnormal and Social Psychology* 64:237-238.
Blake, R., J. Mouton, and A. McCause
  1989 *Change by Design*. Reading, Mass.: Addison-Wesley.

Bond, C.
1982   Social facilitation: A self-presentational view. *Journal of Personality and Social Psychology* 42:1042-1050.

Bonoma, T., J. Tedeschi, and B. Helm
1974   Some effects of target cooperation and reciprocated promises on conflict resolution. *Sociometry* 37:251-261.

Borgida, E., and R. Nisbett
1977   The differential impact of abstract vs. concrete information decision. *Journal of Applied Social Psychology* 7:258-271.

Bowlby, J.
1969   *Attachment and Loss*, Vol. 1. London: Hogarth Press.
1973   *Attachment and Loss*, Vol. 2. London: Hogarth Press.
1980   *Attachment and Loss*, Vol. 3. New York: Basic Books.

Cannon-Bowers, J., E. Salas, and S. Converse
1990   Cognitive psychology and team training: Training shared mental models of complex systems. *Human Factors Society Bulletin* 33(12):1-4.

Cannon-Bowers, J., S. Tannebaum, and E. Salas
1991   Toward an integration of training theory and technique. *Human Factors* 33:281-292.

Cartwright, D., and A. Zander, eds.
1968   *Group Dynamics*. New York: Harper and Row.

Carver, C., and M. Scheier
1981   The self-attention-induced feedback loop and social facilitation. *Journal of Experimental Social Psychology* 175:545-568.

Cohen, D.
1990   What motivates trainees. *Training Development Journal* November 91-93.

Cohen, S., and L. Syme, eds.
1985   *Social Support and Health*. New York: Academic Press.

Cohen, S., and T. Willis
1985   Stress, social support, and the buffering hypothesis. *Psychological Bulletin* 98:310-357.

Coleman, J.
1961   *The Adolescent Society*. New York: Macmillan.

Connolly, T., L. Jessup, and J. Valacich
1990   Idea generation using a GDSS: Effects of anonymity and evaluative tone. *Management Science* 36:689-703.

Cook, T., and B. Frey
1978   The temporal persistence of experimentally induced attitude change: An evaluative review. In L. Berkowitz, ed., *Advances in Experimental Social Psychology*, Vol. 11. New York: Academic Press.

Cooper, G., M. White, and J. Lauber, eds.
1979   *Resource Management on the Flight Deck*. NASA Conference Publication 2120. Moffett Field, Calif.: NASA-Ames Research Center.

Cooper, L., D.W. Johnson, R.T. Johnson, and F. Wilderson
1980   The effects of cooperation, competition, and individualization on cross-ethnic, cross-sex, and cross-ability friendships. *Journal of Social Psychology* 111:243-252.

Crandall, J.
1982   Social interest, extreme response style, and implications for adjustment. *Journal of Research in Personality* 16:82-89.

Crombag, H.
  1966   Cooperation and competition in means-interdependent triads: A replication. *Journal of Personality and Social Psychology* 4(6):692-695.
Cutrona, C., and E. Troutman
  1986   Social support, infant temperament, and parenting self-efficacy. *Child Development* 57:1507-1518.
Deutsch, M.
  1949   An experimental study of the effects of cooperation and competition upon group processes. *Human Relations* 2:199-231.
  1962   Cooperation and trust: Some theoretical notes. Pp. 275-319 in M. Jones, ed., *Nebraska Symposium on Motivation.* Lincoln: University of Nebraska Press.
DeVries, D., and K. Edwards
  1973   Learning games and student teams: Their effects on classroom process. *American Educational Research Journal* 10:307-318.
Druckman, D., and R. Bjork, eds.
  1991   *In the Mind's Eye: Enhancing Human Performance.* Committee on Techniques for the Enhancement of Human Performance, National Research Council. Washington, D.C.: National Academy Press.
Druckman, D., R. Rozelle, and J. Baxter
  1982   *Nonverbal Communication: Survey, Theory, and Research.* Beverly Hills, Calif.: Sage Publications.
Dunnette, M., J. Campbell, and K. Jaastad
  1963   The effect of group participation on brainstorming effectiveness for two industrial samples. *Journal of Applied Psychology* 47:30-37.
Duval, S., and R. Wicklund
  1972   *A Theory of Objective Self-Awareness.* New York: Academic Press.
Eylon, B., and E. Reif
  1984   Effects of knowledge organization on task performance. *Cognition and Instruction* 1:5-44.
Fleming, R., and B. Sulzer-Azaroff
  1990   Peer Management: Effects on Staff Teaching Performance. Paper presented at the 15th Annual Convention for the Association of Behavior Analysis, Nashville.
Ford, J., M. Quinones, D. Sego, and J. Speer
  1991   Factors Affecting the Opportunity to Use Trained Skills on the Job. Paper presented at the 6th Annual Conference of Social Industrial Organizational Psychology, St. Louis.
Foushee, H.
  1984   Dyads and triads at 35,000 feet: Factors affecting group process and aircrew performance. *American Psychologist* 39(8):885-893.
Foushee, H., and K. Manos
  1981   Information transfer within the cockpit: Problems in intracockpit communication. In C. Billings and E. Cheaney, eds., *Information Transfer Problems in Aviation Systems.* TP-1875. Moffett Field, Calif.: NASA-Ames Research Center.
Foushee, H., J. Lauber, M. Baetge, and D. Acomb
  1986   *Crew Factors in Flight Operations: III. The Operational Significance of Exposure to Short-Haul Air Transport Operations.* NASA technical memorandum 88322. Moffett Field, Calif.: NASA-Ames Research Center.
Frank, M.
  1984   A Comparison Between an Individual and Group Goal Structure Contingency that Differed in the Behavioral Contingency and Performance-Outcome Components. Unpublished doctoral thesis, Department of Educational Psychology, University of Minnesota.

French, J.
    1951   Group productivity. Pp. 44-55 in H. Guetzkow, ed., *Groups, Leadership and Men.*
            Pittsburgh: Carnegie Press.
Fuller, F., R. Peck, O. Brown, S. Menaker, M. White, and D. Veldman
    1969   *Effects of Personalized Feedback during Teacher Preparation on Teacher Personal-
            ity and Teaching Behavior.* Austin: University of Texas.
Gabbert, B., D.W. Johnson, and R.T. Johnson
    1986   Cooperative learning, group-to-individual transfer, process gain and the acquisition
            of cognitive reasoning strategies. *Journal of Psychology* 120(3):265-278.
Geen, R.
    1976   Test anxiety, observation, and range of cue utilization. *British Journal of Social
            and Clinical Psychology* 15:253-259.
    1980   Test anxiety and cue utilization. Pp. 43-61 in I. Sarason, ed., *Test Anxiety: Theory,
            Research, and Applications.* Hillsdale, N.J.: Lawrence Erlbaum.
Gentner, D., and D. Gentner
    1983   Flowing waters or teeming crowds: Mental models of electricity. Pp. 99-129 in D.
            Gentner and A. Stevens, eds., *Mental Models.* Hillsdale, N.J.: Lawrence Erlbaum.
Goldman, S.
    1940   Personal manuscript. These papers are now part of the Smithsonian Collection and
            are quoted by C. Simons in "Supermarkets: How they grew." *The Smithsonian*
            1980:112.
Grossack, M.
    1953   Some effects of cooperation and competition upon small group behavior. *Journal of
            Abnormal and Social Psychology* 49:341-348.
Hagman, J., and J. Hayes
    1986   Cooperative learning: Effects of Task, Reward, and Group Size on Individual Achievement.
            Technical Report 704. Scientific Coordination Office, U.S. Army Research Institute
            for the Behavioral and Social Sciences, Boise, Idaho (ERIC Document Reproduction
            Service No. ED 278 720).
Hamill, R., T. Wilson, and R. Nisbett
    1980   Insensitivity to sample bias: Generalizing from a typical case. *Journal of Personal-
            ity and Social Psychology* 39:578-589.
Harkins, S., and R. Petty
    1982   The effects of task difficulty and task uniqueness on social loafing. *Journal of
            Personality and Social Psychology* 43:1214-1229.
Haynes, R.
    1986   The Relationship Between Adolescents' Body Image, Self-Esteem, Instrumental and
            Expressive Attitudes and Disturbed Eating Attitudes and Behaviors. Unpublished
            doctoral dissertation, Department of Psychology, New York University.
Hedges, L.V., and I. Olkin
    1985   *Statistical Methods for Meta-Analysis.* Orlando, Fla.: Academic Press.
Helmreich, R., and J. Wilhelm
    1989   When training boomerangs: Negative outcomes associated with cockpit resource
            management programs. Pp. 692-697 in R. Jenson, ed., *Proceedings of the Fifth
            Symposium on Aviation Psychology.* Columbus: Ohio State University.
Helmreich, R., J. Wilhelm, S. Gregorich, and T. Chidester
    1990   Preliminary results from the evaluation of cockpit resource management training:
            Performance ratings of flight crews. *Aviation, Space, Environmental Medicine* 61:576-
            579.
Hicks, W., and R. Klimoski
    1987   Entry into training programs and its effects on training outcomes: A field experi-
            ment. *Academy of Management Journal* 30:542-552.

Holubec, E., D.W. Johnson, and R.T. Johnson
in   Impact of cooperative learning on naval air-traffic controller training. *Journal of*
press   *Social Psychology.*

Hulten, B., and D. DeVries
1976   Team Competition and Group Practice: Effects on Student Achievement and Attitudes. Report #212 Center for Social Organization of Schools, Johns Hopkins University.

Hwong, N., A. Caswell, D.W. Johnson, and R.T. Johnson
in   Effects of cooperative and individualistic learning on prospective elementary teach-
press   ers' music achievement and attitudes. *Journal of Social Psychology.*

Ingham, A., G. Levinger, J. Graves, and V. Peckham
1974   The Ringelmann effect: Studies of group size and group performance. *Journal of*
Personality and Social Psychology 10:371-384.

James, N., and D.W. Johnson
1983   The relationship between attitudes toward social interdependence and psychological
health within three criminal populations. *Journal of Abnormal and Social Psychol-*
ogy 121:131-143.

James, S., and D.W. Johnson
1988   Social interdependence, psychological adjustment, orientation toward negative life
stress, and quality of second marriage. *Journal of Social Psychology* 128(3):287-
304.

Johnson, D.W.
1974   Communication and the inducement of cooperative behavior in conflicts: A critical
review. *Speech Monographs* 41:64-78.
1981   Student-student interaction: The neglected variable in education. *Educational Re-*
searcher 10:5-10.

Johnson, D.W., and R.T. Johnson
1974   Instructional goal structure: Cooperative, competitive, or individualistic. *Review of*
Educational Research 44:213-240.
1976   Students' perceptions of and preferences for cooperative and competitive learning
experiences. *Perceptual and Motor Skills* 42:989-990.
1979   Conflict in the classroom: Controversy and learning. *Review of Educational Re-*
search 49:51-70.
1981   Effects of cooperative and individualistic learning experiences on interethnic interaction. *Journal of Educational Psychology* 73:454-459.
1989   *Cooperation and Competition: Theory and Research.* Edina, Minn.: Interaction
Book Company.
1994   Team Versus Individual Training for Adults. Unpublished report, Cooperative Learning
Center, University of Minnesota.

Johnson, D.W., and F. Johnson
1994   *Joining Together: Group Theory and Group Skills,* 5th ed. Englewood Cliffs, N.J.:
Prentice-Hall.

Johnson, D.W., and A. Norem-Hebeisen
1977   Attitudes toward interdependence among persons and psychological health. *Psycho-*
logical Reports 40:43-50.

Johnson, D.W., R.T. Johnson, J. Johnson, and D. Anderson
1976   Effects of cooperative versus individualized instruction on student prosocial behavior, attitudes toward learning, and achievement. *Journal of Educational Psychology*
68:446-452.

Johnson, D.W., L. Skon, and R.T. Johnson
1980   Effects of cooperative, competitive, and individualistic conditions on children's problem-
solving performance. *American Educational Research Journal* 17(1):83-93.

Johnson, D.W., G. Maruyama, R.T. Johnson, D. Nelson, and L. Skon
1981   Effects of cooperative, competitive, and individualistic goal structures on achievement: A meta-analysis. *Psychological Bulletin* 89:47-62.

Johnson, D.W., A. Norem-Hebeisen, D. Anderson, and R.T. Johnson
1984   Predictors and concomitants of changes in drug use patterns among teenagers. *Journal of Social Psychology* 124:43-50.

Johnson, D.W., R.T. Johnson, L. Buckman, and P. Richards
1986a The effect of prolonged implementation of cooperative learning on social support within the classroom. *Journal of Psychology* 119:405-411.

Johnson, D.W., R.T. Johnson, and M. Krotee
1986b The relationship between social interdependence and psychological health within the 1980 United States Olympic ice hockey team. *Journal of Psychology* 120:279-292.

Johnson, D.W., R.T. Johnson, M. Stanne, and A. Garibaldi
1989   Impact of goal and resource interdependence on problem-solving success. *Journal of Social Psychology* 129:621-629.

1990   The impact of leader and member group processing on achievement in cooperative groups. *The Journal of Social Psychology* 130(4):507-516.

Johnson, D.W., R.T. Johnson, and E. Holubec
1991   *Cooperation in the Classroom.* Edina, Minn.: Interaction Book Company.

Johnson, R.T.
1976   The relationship between cooperation and inquiry in science classrooms. *Journal of Research in Science Teaching* 10:55-63.

Johnson, R.T., D.W. Johnson, and B. Bryant
1973   Cooperation and competition in the classroom. *Elementary School Journal* 74:172-181.

Johnson, R.T., F. Ryan, and H. Schroeder
1974   Inquiry and the development of positive attitudes. *Science Education* 58:51-56.

Johnson, R.T., R. Bjorkland, and M. Krotee
1983   The effects of cooperative, competitive, and individualistic student interaction patterns on achievement and attitudes on the golf skill of putting. *Research Quarterly* 55(2):129-134.

Johnson, R.T., D.W. Johnson, and M. Stanne
1985   The effects of cooperative, competitive, and individualistic goal structures on computer-assisted instruction. *Journal of Educational Psychology* 77:668-677.

1986   A comparison of computer-assisted cooperative, competitive, and individualistic learning. *American Educational Research Journal* 23:382-392.

Katz, D., and R. Kahn
1978   *The Social Psychology of Organizations,* 2nd ed. New York: Wiley.

Kerr, N., and S. Bruun
1981   Ringelmann revisited: Alternative explanations for the social loafing effect. *Personality and Social Psychology Bulletin* 7:224-231.

Kessler, R., and J. McLeod
1985   Social support and mental health in community samples. Pp. 219-240 in S. Cohen and S. Syme, eds., *Social Support and Health.* New York: Academic Press.

Kessler, R., R. Price, and C. Wortman
1985   Social facts in psychopathology: Stress, social support and coping processes. *Annual Review of Psychology* 36:531-572. Palo Alto, Calif.: Annual Reviews, Inc.

Kieras, D.
1988   What mental model should be taught: Choosing instructional content for complex engineering systems. Pp. 85-111 in J. Psotka, L. Massey, and S. Mutter, eds., *Intelligent Tutoring Systems: Lessons Learned.* Hillsdale, N.J.: Lawrence Erlbaum.

Kieras, D., and S. Bovair
  1984   The role of a mental model in learning to operate a device. *Cognitive Science* 8:255-273.
Kiesler, S., J. Siegel, and T. McGuire
  1984   Social psychological aspects of computer-mediated communication. *American Psychologist* 39(10):1123-1134.
Krauss, R. M., and M. Deutsch
  1966   Communication in interpersonal bargaining. *Journal of Personality and Social Psychology* 4:572-577.
LaRocco, J., S. House, and J. French
  1980   Social support, occupational stress, and health. *Journal of Health and Social Behavior* 21:202-218.
Lassiter, D., J. Vaughn, V. Smaltz, B. Morgan, and E. Salas
  1990   A Comparison of Two Types of Training Interventions on Team Communication Performance. Paper presented at the meeting of the Human Factors Society, Orlando, Fla.
Latane, B., K. Williams, and S. Harkins
  1979   Many hands make light the work: The causes and consequences of social loafing. *Journal of Personality and Social Psychology* 37:822-832.
Lew, M., D. Mesch, D.W. Johnson, and R.T. Johnson
  1986a Components of cooperative learning: Effects of collaborative skills and academic group contingencies on achievement and mainstreaming. *Contemporary Educational Psychology* 11:229-239.
  1986b Positive interdependence, academic and collaborative-skills group contingencies and isolated students. *American Educational Research Journal* 23:476-488.
Lewin, K.
  1943   *Forces Behind Food Habits and Methods of Change. The Problem of Changing Food Habits.* NRC Bulletin No. 108. Committee on Food Habits. Washington, D.C.: National Research Council.
Lockhead, J.
  1983   Beyond Emile: Misconceptions of Education in the Twenty-First Century. Paper presented at American Educational Research Association annual meeting, Montreal, Quebec.
Lorge, I., and H. Solomon
  1955   Two models of group behavior in the solution of eureka type problems. *Psychometrika* 20:139-148.
Marquart, D.J.
  1955   Group problem-solving. *Journal of Social Psychology* 41:103-113.
Martino, L., and D.W. Johnson
  1979   Cooperative and individualistic experiences among disabled and normal children. *Journal of Social Psychology* 107:177-183.
Marx, R., and R. Karren
  1990   The Effects of Relapse Prevention and Post-Training Followup on Time Management Behavior. Paper presented at the annual meeting of the Academic Management, San Francisco.
Mathieu, J., S. Tannenbaum, and E. Salas
  1990   A Casual Model of Individual and Situational Influences on Training Effectiveness Measures. Paper presented at the 5th annual conference on Social, Industrial, and Organizational Psychology, Miami.
McGrath, J., and D. Kravitz
  1982   Group research. In L. Porter and M. Rosenzweig, eds., *Annual Review of Psychology* 33:195-230. Palo Alto, Calif.: Annual Reviews, Inc.

McGuire, T., S. Kiesler, and J. Siegel
1987   Group and computer-mediated discussion effects in risk decision making. *Journal of Personality and Social Psychology* 52:917-930.

Mehrabian, A.
1971   *Silent Messages*. Belmont, Calif.: Wadsworth.

Mesch, D., M. Lew, D.W. Johnson, and R.T. Johnson
1986   Isolated teenagers, cooperative learning and the training of social skills. *Journal of Psychology* 120:323-334.

Mesch, D., D.W. Johnson, and R.T. Johnson
1988   Impact of positive interdependence and academic group contingencies on achievement. *Journal of Social Psychology* 128:345- 352.

Messick, D., and M. Brewer
1983   Solving social dilemmas: A review. In L. Wheeler and P. Shaver, eds., *Review of Personality and Social Psychology* 4:11-44. Newbury Park, Calif.: Sage Publications.

Miller, L., and L. Hamblin
1963   Interdependence, differential rewarding, and productivity. *American Sociological Review* 28:768-778.

Miller, N., and H. Harrington
1990   A situational identity perspective on cultural diversity and teamwork in the classroom. Pp. 39-75 in S. Sharon, ed., *Cooperative Learning: Theory and Application*. New York: Praeger.

Modrick, J.
1986   Team performance and training. Pp. 130-166 in J. Zeidner, ed., *Training and Human Factors in Systems Design Vol. 1: Human Productivity Enhancement*. New York: Praeger.

Moede, W.
1927   Die richtlinien der leistungs-psychologie. *Industrielle Psychotechnik* 4:193-207.

Morgan, B., and E. Salas
1988   A research agenda for team training and performance: Issues, alternatives, and solutions. *Proceedings of the Interservice/Industrial Training Systems Conference* 10:560-565.

Morse, K., M. Kysilka, and O. Davis
1970   Effects of Different Types of Supervisory Feedback on Teacher Candidates' Development of Refocusing Behaviors. Report Series No. 48, Austin Research and Development Center for Teacher Education, University of Texas.

Murray, F.
1983   Cognitive Benefits of Teaching on the Teacher. Paper presented at American Educational Research Association annual meeting, Montreal, Quebec.

Nel, E., R. Helmreich, and E. Aronson
1969   Opinion change in the advocate as a function of the persuasibility of its audience: A clarification of the meaning of dissonance. *Journal of Personality and Social Psychology* 12:117-124.

Nisbett, R.E., E. Borgida, R. Crandell, and H. Reed
1976   Popular induction: Information is not always informative. In J. Carrol and J. Payne, eds., *Cognition and Social Behavior*. Hillsdale, N.J.: Lawrence Erlbaum.

Norem-Hebeisen, A., and D.W. Johnson
1981   Relationships between cooperative, competitive, and individualistic attitudes and differentiated aspects of self-esteem. *Journal of Personality* 49:415-425.

O'Neil, H., E. Baker, and E. Kazlauskas
1992   Assessment of team performance. In R. Swezey and E. Salas, eds., *Teams: Their Training and Performance*. Norwood, N.J.: Ablex.

Orasanu, J., and E. Salas
1993 Team decision making in complex environments. In G. Klein, J. Orasanu, and R. Calderwood, eds., *Decision Making in Action: Models and Methods.* Norwood, N.J.: Ablex.

Orbell, J., R. Dawes, and A. van de Kragt
1988 Explaining discussion induced cooperation. *Journal of Personality and Social Psychology* 54:811-819.

Pentland, B.
1989 The Learning Curve and the Forgetting Curve: The Importance of Time and Timing in the Implementation of Technological Innovations. Paper presented at the 49th annual meeting of Academic Management, Washington, D.C.

Perry, P., and S. Downs
1985 Skills, strategies, and ways of learning. *Programmed Learning and Education Technology* 22:177-181.

Petty, R.
1977 A Cognitive Response Analysis of the Temporal Persistence of Attitude Changes Induced by Persuasive Communications. Unpublished doctoral dissertation, Department of Psychology, Ohio State University, Columbus.

Petty, R., S. Harkins, K. Williams, and B. Latane
1977 The effects of group size on cognitive effort and evaluation. *Personality and Social Psychology Bulletin* 3:575-578.

Putnam, J., J. Rynders, R.T. Johnson, and D.W. Johnson
1989 Collaborative skills instruction for promoting positive interactions between mentally handicapped and nonhandicapped children. *Exceptional Children* 55:550-557.

Qin, A.
1992 A Meta-Analysis of the Effectiveness of Achieving Higher Order Learning Tasks in Cooperative Learning Compared with Competitive Learning. Unpublished Ph.D. dissertation, Department of Educational Psychology, University of Minnesota.

Radke, M., and E. Caso
1948 Lecture and discussion-decision as methods of influencing food habits. *Journal of the American Dietetic Association* 24:23-41.

Radke, M., and D. Klisurich
1947 Experiments in changing food habits. Reported in K. Lewin, Group decision and social change. In E. Maccoby, T. Newcomb, and E. Hartley, eds., *Readings in Social Psychology.* New York: Henry Holt and Company.

Rogers, E., and F. Shoemaker
1977 *Communication of Innovations: A Cross-Cultural Approach.* New York: Free Press.

Rouillier, J., and I. Goldstein
1991 Determinants of the Climate for Transfer of Training. Paper presented at the Meetings of the Society of Industrial and Organizational Psychology, St. Louis, Mo.

Rowe, M.
1974 Wait-time and rewards as instructional variables. *Journal of Research on Science Teaching* 11:81-94.

Ruffell-Smith, H.
1979 A Simulator Study of the Interaction of Pilot Workload with Errors, Vigilance, and Decisions. NASA technical memorandum-78482. NASA-Ames Research Center: Moffett Field, Calif.

Sanna, L.
1992 Self-efficacy theory: Implication for social facilitation and social loafing. *Journal of Personality and Social Psychology* 62:774-786.

Sarason, I., and E. Potter
   1983   *Self-Monitoring: Cognitive Processes and Performance.* Seattle: University of Washington.
Sarason, I., H. Levine, R. Basham, and B. Sarason
   1983   Assessing social support: The social support questionnaire. *Journal of Personality and Social Psychology* 44:127-139.
Schachter, S.
   1959   *The Psychology of Affiliation.* Stanford, Calif.: Stanford University Press.
Seers, A., G. McGee, T. Serey, and G. Graen
   1983   The interaction of job stress and social support. *Academy of Management Journal* 26:273-284.
Short, J., E. Williams, and B. Christie
   1976   *The Social Psychology of Telecommunications.* London: Wiley.
Siegel, J., V. Dubrovsky, S. Kiesler, and T. McGuire
   1986   Group processes in computer-mediated communication. *Organizational Behavior and Human Decision Processes* 37:157-187.
Skon, L., D.W. Johnson, and R.T. Johnson
   1981   Cooperative peer interaction versus individual competition and individualistic efforts: Effects on the acquisition of cognitive reasoning strategies. *Journal of Educational Psychology* 73(1):83-92.
Smoke, W.H., and R.B. Zajonc
   1962   On the reliability of group judgments and decisions. In H. Criswell, H. Solomon, and P. Suppes, eds., *Mathematical Methods in Small Group Processes.* Stanford, Calif.: Stanford University Press.
Spurlin, J., D. Dansereau, C. Larson, and L. Brooks
   1984   Cooperative learning strategies in processing descriptive text: Effects of role and activity level of the learner. *Cognition and Instruction* 1(4):451-463.
Steiner, J.
   1967   Observing responses and uncertainty reduction. *Quarterly Journal of Experimental Psychology* 19:18-29.
Taylor, D.W.
   1954   Problem solving by groups. In *Proceedings XIV, International Congress of Psychology.* Amsterdam, The Netherlands: North Holland Publishing.
Taylor, S., and S. Thompson
   1982   Stalking the elusive "vividness" effect. *Psychological Review* 89:155-181.
Tjosvold, D.
   1990a   Cooperation and competition in restructuring an organization. *Canadian Journal of Administrative Sciences* 7:48-54.
   1990b   *Cooperation and Competition Theory: Antecedents, Interactions, and Consequences in 1,000 Incidents.* Burnaby, British Columbia: Simon Fraser University.
   1990c   Flight crew coordination to manage safety risks. *Group and Organizational Studies* 15:177-191.
   1990d   Making a technological innovation work: Collaboration to solve problems. *Human Relations* 43:1117-1131.
   1991   *Team Organization.* New York: John Wiley.
Tjosvold, D., and L. McNeely
   1988   Innovation through communication in an educational bureaucracy. *Communication Research* 15:568-581.
Trevino, L., R.H. Lengel, and R.L. Daft
   1987   Media symbolism, media richness, and media choice in organizations: A symbolic interactionist perspective. *Communication Research* 14:553-574.

Tuckman, B., K. McCall, and R. Hyman
  1969   The modification of teacher behavior: Effects of dissonance and coded feedback.
          American Educational Research Journal 6:607-619.
Turk, S., and I. Sarason
  1983   *Test Anxiety and Causal Attributions.* Seattle: University of Washington.
Vasquez, B., D.W. Johnson, and R.T. Johnson
  1993   Impact of cooperative learning on performance and retention of navy air-traffic
          controller trainees. *Journal of Social Psychology* 133:769-783.
Warring, D., D.W. Johnson, G. Maruyama, and R.T. Johnson
  1985   Impact of different types of cooperative learning on cross-ethnic and cross-sex rela-
          tionships. *Journal of Educational Psychology* 77:53-59.
Watson, G., and D.W. Johnson
  1972   *Social Psychology: Issues and Insights.* Philadelphia: Lippincott.
Webb, N.
  1982   Student interaction and learning in small groups. *Review of Educational Research*
          52:421-445.
Wheeler, R., and F. Ryan
  1973   Effects of cooperative and competitive classroom environments on the attitudes and
          achievement of elementary school students engaged in social studies inquiry activi-
          ties. *Journal of Educational Psychology* 65(3):402-407.
Williams, K.
  1981   The Effects of Group Cohesiveness on Social Loafing. Paper presented at the
          annual meeting of the Midwestern Psychological Association, Detroit.
Williams, K., S. Harkins, and B. Latane
  1981   Identifiability as a deterrent to social loafing: Two cheering experiments. *Journal
          of Personality and Social Psychology* 40:303-311.
Yager, S., D.W. Johnson, and R.T. Johnson
  1985   Oral discussion, group-to-individual transfer, and achievement in cooperative learn-
          ing groups. *Journal of Educational Psychology* 77:60-66.

CHAPTER 8

Abramson, L.Y., M.E.P. Seligman, and J.D. Teasdale
  1978   Learned helplessness in humans: Critique and reformulation. *Journal of Abnormal
          Psychology* 87:49-74.
Ames, C.
  1981   Competitive, cooperative and individualistic goal structures: The influence of indi-
          vidual and group performance factors on achievement attributions and affect. *American
          Educational Research Journal* 18:273-287.
  1984   Competitive, cooperative, and individualistic goal structures: A cognitive-motiva-
          tional analysis. Pp. 177-208 in R. Ames and C. Ames, eds., *Research on Motivation
          in Education: Vol 1. Student Motivation.* New York: Academic Press.
  1992   Achievement goals, motivational climate, and motivational processer. Pp. 161-176
          in G.C. Roberts, ed., *Motivation in Sport and Exercise.* Champaign, Ill.: Human
          Kinetics.
Anderson, J.G., and F.B. Evans
  1974   Causal models in educational research: Recursive models. *American Educational
          Research Journal* 11:29-39.
Bandura, A.
  1977   Self-efficacy: Toward a unifying theory of behavioral change. *Psychological Re-
          view* 84:191-215.

1982   Self-efficacy mechanism in human agency. *American Psychologist* 37:122-147.

1984   Recycling misconceptions of perceived self-efficacy. *Cognitive Therapy and Research* 8:231-255.

1986   *Social Foundations of Thought and Action: A Social Cognitive Theory.* Englewood Cliffs, N.J.: Prentice-Hall.

1988   Self-efficacy conception of anxiety. *Anxiety Research* 1:77-98.

1989   Human agency in social cognitive theory. *American Psychologist* 44:1175-1184.

1990   Perceived self-efficacy in the exercise of personal agency. *Journal of Applied Sport Psychology* 2:128-163.

Bandura, A., and N.E. Adams

1977   Analysis of self-efficacy theory of behavioral change. *Cognitive Therapy and Research* 1:287-308.

Bandura, A., and D. Cervone

1983   Self-evaluative and self-efficacy mechanisms governing the motivational effects of goal systems. *Journal of Personality and Social Psychology* 45:1017-1028.

Bandura, A., and D. Schunk

1981   Cultivating competence, self-efficacy, and intrinsic interest through proximal self-motivation. *Journal of Personality and Social Psychology* 41:586-598.

Bandura, A., and K.M. Simon

1977   The role of proximal intentions in self-regulation of refractory behavior. *Cognitive Therapy and Research* 1:177-193.

Bandura, A., N.E. Adams, and J. Beyer

1977   Cognitive processes mediating behavioral change. *Journal of Personality and Social Psychology* 35:125-139.

Bandura, A., L. Reese, and N.E. Adams

1982   Microanalysis of action and fear arousal as a function of differential levels of perceived self-efficacy. *Journal of Personality and Social Psychology* 43:5-21.

Baumeister, R.F.

1989   The optimal margin of illusion. *Journal of Social and Clinical Psychology* 8:176-189.

Betz, N.E., and G. Hackett

1981   The relationship of career-related self-efficacy expectations to perceived career options in college women and men. *Journal of Counseling Psychology* 23:399-410.

Biglan, A.

1987   A behavior-analytic critique of Bandura's self-efficacy theory. *Behavior Analyst* 10:1-15.

Biram, M., and G.T. Wilson

1981   Treatment of phobic disorders using cognitive and exposure methods: A self-efficacy analysis. *Journal of Counseling and Clinical Psychology* 49:886-899.

Bird, A.M., and J.M. Brame

1978   Self versus team attributions: A test of the "I'm OK, but the team's so-so" phenomenon. *Research Quarterly* 49:260-268.

Brockner, J.

1988   *Self-Esteem at Work: Research, Theory, and Practice.* Lexington, Mass.: Lexington Books.

Brody, E.B., B.D. Hatfield, and T.W. Spalding

1988   Generalization of self-efficacy to a continuum of stressors upon mastery of a high-risk sport skill. *Journal of Sport Psychology* 10:32 44.

Brown, I., Jr., and D.K. Inouye

1978   Learned helplessness through modeling: The role of perceived similarity in competence. *Journal of Personality and Social Psychology* 36:900-908.

Campbell, N.D., and G. Hackett
    1986   The effects of mathematics task performances on math self-efficacy and task inter-
           est. *Journal of Vocational Behavior* 28:149-162.
Carver, C.S., and M.F. Scheier
    1981   *Attention and Self-Regulation: A Control Theory Approach to Human Behavior.*
           New York: Springer-Verlag.
    1990   Origins and functions of positive and negative affect: A control-process view.
           Psychological Review 97:19-35.
Cervone, D., and P.K. Peake
    1986   Anchoring, efficacy, and action: The influence of judgmental heuristics on self-
           efficacy judgments and behavior. *Journal of Personality and Social Psychology*
           50:492-501.
Chase, M.A., C.D. Lirgg, and D.L. Feltz
    1993   Do Coaches Efficacy Expectations Predict Team Performance? Paper presented at
           North American Society for the Psychology of Sport and Physical Activity meeting,
           Brainerd, Minn.
Collins, J.
    1982   Self-Efficacy and Ability in Achievement Behavior. Paper presented at the meeting
           of the American Educational Research Association, New York.
Cook, T.D., and D.T. Campbell
    1979   *Quasi-Experimentation: Design and Analysis Issues for Field Settings.* Chicago:
           Rand McNally.
Corbin, C.B., D.R. Laurie, C. Gruger, and B. Smiley
    1984   Vicarious success experience as a factor influencing self-confidence, attitudes,
           and physical activity of adult women. *Journal of Teaching in Physical Education*
           4:17-23.
DiClemente, C.C.
    1981   Self-efficacy and smoking cessation maintenance: A preliminary report. *Cognitive*
           Therapy and Research 5:175-187.
Dowrick, P.W.
    1983   Self modelling. Pp. 105-124 in P.W. Dowrick and S.J. Biggs, eds., *Using Video:*
           Psychological and Social Applications. London: Wiley.
Dubbert, P.M., and G.T. Wilson
    1984   Goal-setting and spouse involvement in the treatment of obesity. *Behavior Re-*
           search and Therapy 22:227-242.
Duncan, O.D.
    1975   *Introduction to Structural Equation Models.* New York: Academic Press.
Dweck, C.S.
    1986   Motivational processes affecting learning. *American Psychologist* 41:1040-1048.
Dweck, C.S., and E.L. Leggett
    1988   A social-cognitive approach to motivation and personality. *Psychological Review*
           95:256-273.
Dzewaltowski, D.A.
    1989   Toward a model of exercise motivation. *Journal of Sport and Exercise Psychology*
           11:251-269.
Dzewaltowski, D.A., J.M. Noble, and J.M. Shaw
    1990   Physical activity participation: Social cognitive versus the theories of reasoned
           action and planned behavior. *Journal of Sport and Exercise Psychology* 12:388-
           405.
Earley, P.C.
    1993   East meets West meets Mideast: Further explorations of collectivistic and individu-
           alistic work groups. *Academy of Management Journal* 36:319-348.

Earley, P.C., and T.R. Lituchy
1991 Delineating goal and efficacy effects: A test of three models. *Journal of Applied Psychology* 76:81-98.

Eastman, C., and J.S. Marzillier
1984 Theoretical and methodological difficulties in Bandura's self-efficacy theory. *Cognitive Therapy and Research* 8:213-230.

Eden, D.
1990 *Pygmalion in Management*. Lexington, Mass.: Lexington Books.

Eden, D., and G. Ravid
1982 Pygmalion versus self-expectancy: Effects of instructor and self-expectancy on trainee performance. *Organizational Behavior and Human Performance* 30:351-364.

Eden, D., and A.B. Shani
1982 Pygmalion goes to boot camp: Expectancy, leadership, and trainee performance. *Journal of Applied Psychology* 67:194-199.

Elliott, E.S., and C.S. Dweck
1988 Goals: An approach to motivation and achievement. *Journal of Personality and Social Psychology* 54:5-12.

Erez, M.
1977 Feedback: A necessary condition for the goal setting-performance relationship. *Journal of Applied Psychology* 62:624-627.

Ericsson, K.A., R.T. Krampe, and C. Tesch-Romen
1993 The role of deliberate practice in the acquisition of expert performance. *Psychological Review* 100:363-406.

Evans, M.G.
1974 Extensions of a path-goal theory of motivation. *Journal of Applied Psychology* 59:172-178.

Feltz, D.L.
1982 Path analysis of the causal elements in Bandura's theory of self-efficacy and an anxiety-based model of avoidance behavior. *Journal of Personality and Social Psychology* 42:764-781.
1988a Gender differences in the causal elements of self-efficacy on a high-avoidance motor task. *Journal of Sport Psychology* 10:151-166.
1988b Self-confidence and sports performance. Pp. 423-456 in K.B. Pandolf, ed., *Exercise and Sport Sciences Reviews*. New York: MacMillan.

Feltz, D.L., and D.A. Mugno
1983 A replication of the path analysis of the causal elements in Bandura's theory of self-efficacy and the influence of autonomic perception. *Journal of Sport Psychology* 5:263-277.

Feltz, D.L., and C.A. Riessinger
1990 Effects of in vivo emotive imagery and performance feedback on self-efficacy and muscular endurance. *Journal of Sport and Exercise Psychology* 12:132-143.

Feltz, D.L., D.M. Landers, and U. Raeder
1979 Enhancing self-efficacy in high-avoidance motor tasks: A comparison of modeling techniques. *Journal of Sport Psychology* 74:884-891.

Feltz, D.L., A. Bandura, and C.D. Lirgg
1989 Perceived Collective Efficacy in Hockey. Paper presented at the American Psychological Association National Meeting, New Orleans.

Feltz, D.L., R. Neff, and M. Chase
1992 Effects of Early Success on Self-Efficacy and Persistence. Unpublished manuscript, Department of Physical Education and Exercise Science, Michigan State University, East Lansing.

Fennema, E.H., and J.A. Sherman
    1978   Sex-related differences in mathematics achievement and related factors: A further
            study. *Journal of Research in Mathematics Education* 9:189-203.
Festinger, L.
    1942   A theoretical interpretation of shifts in levels of aspiration. *Psychological Review*
            49:235-250.
    1954   A theory of social comparison processes. *Human Relations* 1:417-419.
Fishbein, M., and I. Ajzen
    1975   *Belief, Attitude, Intention, and Behavior: An Introduction to Theory and Research.*
            Reading, Mass.: Addison-Wesley.
Fitzsimmons, P.A., D.M. Landers, J.R. Thomas, and H. Vander Mars
    1991   Does self-efficacy predict performance in experienced weightlifters? *Research Quarterly
            for Exercise and Sport* 62:424-431.
Frank, J.D.
    1935   Individual differences in certain aspects of the level of aspiration. *American Jour-
            nal of Psychology* 47:119-128.
    1941   Recent studies of the level of aspiration. *Psychological Bulletin* 38:218-225.
Frese, M., and J. Sabini, eds.
    1985   *Goal Directed Behavior: The Concept of Action in Psychology.* Hillsdale, N.J.:
            Lawrence Erlbaum.
Fulk, J., and E.R. Wendler
    1982   Dimensionality of leader-subordinate interactions: A path-goal investigation. *Or-
            ganizational Behavior and Human Performance* 30:241-264.
Garland, H.
    1983   Influence and ability assigned goals and normative information on personal goals
            and performance: A challenge to the goal attainability assumption. *Journal of
            Applied Psychology* 68:20-30.
Garland, H., R. Weinberg, L. Bruya, and A. Jackson
    1988   Self-efficacy and endurance performance: A longitudinal field test of cognitive
            mediation theory. *Applied Psychology: An International Review* 37:381-394.
George, T.R., D.L. Feltz, and M.A. Chase
    1992   Effects of model similarity on self-efficacy and muscular endurance. *Journal of
            Sport and Exercise Psychology* 14:237-248.
Girodo, M., and D. Wood
    1979   Talking yourself out of pain: The importance of believing that you can. *Cognitive
            Therapy and Research* 3:23-33.
Gist, M.E.
    1989a   Effects of alternative training methods on self-efficacy and performance in computer
            software training. *Journal of Applied Psychology* 74:884-891.
    1989b   The influence of training method on self-efficacy and idea generation among man-
            agers. *Personnel Psychology* 42:787-805.
Gist, M.E., C. Schwoerer, and B. Rosen
    1989   Effects of alternative training methods on self-efficacy and performance in computer
            software training. *Journal of Applied Psychology* 74:884-891.
Gould, D., and M. Weiss
    1981   Effect of model similarity and model self-talk on self-efficacy in muscular endur-
            ance. *Journal of Sport Psychology* 3:17-29.
Griffin, N.S., and J.F. Keogh
    1982   A model for movement confidence. Pp. 213-236 in J.A.S. Kelso and J. Clark, eds.,
            The Development of Movement Control and Coordination. New York: Wiley.
Hackett, G.
    1985   The role of mathematics self-efficacy in the choice of math-related majors of

college women and men: A path analysis. *Journal of Counseling Psychology* 32:47-56.

Hackett, T.P., and N.H. Cassem
1974 Development of a quantitative rating scale to assess denial. *Journal of Psychosomatic Research* 18:93-100.

Halisch, F., and J. Kuhl, eds.
1987 *Motivation, Intention, and Volition.* New York: Springer-Verlag.

Harter, S.
1978 Effectance motivation reconsidered: Toward a developmental model. *Human Development* 21:34-64.
1981 The development of competence motivation in the master of cognitive and physical skills: Is there still a place for joy? Pp. 3-29 in G.C. Roberts and D.M. Landers, eds., *Psychology of Motor Behavior and Sport, 1980.* Champaign, Ill.: Human Kinetics.

Hattie, J.
1992 *Self-Concept.* Hillsdale, N.J.: Lawrence Erlbaum.

Horn, T.S.
1985 Coaches' feedback and changes in children's perceptions of their physical competence. *Journal of Educational Psychology* 77:174-186.

House, R.J., and T.R. Mitchell
1974 Path-goal theory of leadership. *Contemporary Business* (Fall), 3:81-98.

Jones, M.B.
1974 Regressing group on individual effectiveness. *Organizational Behavior and Human Performance* 11:426-451.

Jourden, F.J., A. Bandura, and J.T. Banfield
1991 The impact of conceptions of ability on self-regulatory factors and motor skill acquisition. *Journal of Sport and Exercise Psychology* 8:213-226.

Juneau, M., F. Rogers, A. Bandura, C.D. Taylor, and R.F. DeBusk
1986 Cognitive Processing of Treadmill Experiences and Self-Appraisal of Cardiac Capabilities. Unpublished manuscript, Department of Psychology, Stanford University.

Kanfer, F.H.
1990a Motivation and individual differences in learning: An integration of developmental differential, and cognitive perspectives. *Learning and Individual Differences* 2:219-237.
1990b Motivation theory and industrial/organizational psychology. Pp. 75-170 in M.S. Donnette and L. Hough, eds., *Handbook of Industrial and Organizational Psychology*, 2d ed., Vol. 1. Palo Alto, Calif.: Consulting Psychologists Press.

Kanfer, R., and P.L. Ackerman
1989 Motivation and cognitive abilities: An integrative/aptitude-treatment interaction approach to skill acquisition [monograph]. *Journal of Applied Psychology* 74:657-690.

Kaplan, R.M., C.J. Atkins, and S. Reinsch
1984 Specific efficacy expectations mediate exercise compliance in patients with COPD. *Health Psychology* 3:223-242.

Kavanagh, D., and S. Hausfeld
1986 Physical performance and self-efficacy under happy and sad moods. *Journal of Sport Psychology* 8:112-123.

Keinan, G.
1988 Training for dangerous task performance: The effects of expectations and feedback. *Journal of Applied Social Psychology* 18:255-273.

Kent, G.
1987 Self-efficacious control over reported physiological, cognitive, and behavioral symptoms of dental anxiety. *Behavior Research and Therapy* 25:341-347.

Kent, G., and R. Gibbons
  1987   Self-efficacy and the control of anxious cognitions. *Journal of Behavior Therapy and Experimental Psychiatry* 18:33-40.
Kerr, N.L.
  1989   Illusions of efficacy: The effects of group size on perceived efficacy in social dilemmas. *Journal of Experimental Social Psychology* 25:287-313.
Kirsch, I.
  1985   Self-efficacy and expectancy: Old wine with new labels. *Journal of Personality and Social Psychology* 49:824-830.
Kirschenbaum, D.S.
  1985   Proximity and specificity of planning: A position paper. *Cognitive Therapy and Research* 9:489-506.
Kirschenbaum, D.S., L.L. Humphrey, and S.D. Malett
  1981   Specificity of planning in adult self-control: An applied investigation. *Journal of Personality and Social Psychology* 40:941-950.
Kirschenbaum, D.S., S.D. Malett, L.L. Humphrey, and A.J. Tomarken
  1982   Specificity of planning and the maintenance of adult self-control: One-year follow-up of a study improvement program. *Behavior Therapy* 13:232-240.
Kuhl, J.
  1984   Volitional aspects of achievement motivation and learned helplessness: Toward a comprehensive theory of action control. Pp. 99-171 in B.A. Maher, ed., *Progress in Experimental Personality Research*, Vol. 13. New York: Academic Press.
  1992   A theory of self-regulation: Action versus state orientation, self-discrimination, and some applications. *Applied Psychology: An International Review* 41:97-129.
Latané, B., K.D. Williams, and S.G. Harksins
  1979   Many hands make light the work: The causes and consequences of social loafing. *Journal of Personality and Social Psychology* 37:823-832.
Lazarus, R.S.
  1979   Positive denial: The case of not facing reality. *Psychology Today* June:44-60.
Lee, C.
  1989   Theoretical weaknesses lead to practical problems: The example of self-efficacy theory. *Journal of Behavioral Therapy and Experimental Psychiatry* 20:115-123.
Lent, R.W., and G. Hackett
  1987   Career self-efficacy: Empirical status and future directions. *Journal of Vocational Behavior* 30:347-382.
Lewin, K., T. Dembo, L. Festinger, and P.S. Sears
  1944   Level of aspiration. In J.M. Hunt, ed., *Personality and the Behavior Disorders*. New York: Ronald Press.
Lewis, S.
  1974   A comparison of behavior therapy techniques in the reduction of fearful avoidance behavior. *Behavior Therapy* 5:648-655.
Lirgg, C.D.
  1991   Gender differences in self-confidence in physical activity: A meta-analysis of recent studies. *Journal of Sport and Exercise Psychology* 13:294-310.
Litt, M.D.
  1988   Self-efficacy and perceived control: Cognitive mediators of pain tolerance. *Journal of Personality and Social Psychology* 54:149-160.
Locke, E.A., and G.P. Latham
  1990   *A Theory of Goal Setting and Task Performance*. New York: Prentice-Hall.
Locke, E.A., E. Frederick, C. Lee, and P. Bobko
  1984   Effect of self-efficacy, goals, and task strategies on task performance. *Journal of Applied Psychology* 69:241-251.

Manderlink, G., and J.M. Harackiewicz
    1984   Proximal versus distal goal setting and intrinsic motivation. *Journal of Personality and Social Psychology* 47:918-928.
Manning, M.M., and T.L. Wright
    1983   Self-efficacy expectancies, outcome expectancies, and the persistence of pain control in childbirth. *Journal of Personality and Social Psychology* 45:421-431.
Markus, H., and Z. Kunda
    1986   Stability and malleability of the self-concept. *Journal of Personality and Social Psychology* 51:858-866.
Matsui, T.
    1987   Self-efficacy and perceived exerted effort as potential cues for success-failure attributions. *Surugadi University Studies* 1:89-98.
Matsui, T., and M.L. Onglatco
    1991   Instrumentality, expressiveness, and self-efficacy in career activities among Japanese working women. *Journal of Vocational Behavior* 39:241-250.
McAuley, E.
    1985   Modeling and self-efficacy: A test of Bandura's model. *Journal of Sport Psychology* 7:283-295.
    1990   Attributions, Affect, and Self-Efficacy: Predicting Exercise Behavior in Aging Adults. Paper presented at the meeting of the American Psychological Society, Dallas.
    1991   Efficacy and attributional determinants of affective reactions to exercise participation. *Journal of Sport and Exercise Psychology* 13:382-394.
    1992   Understanding exercise behavior: A self-efficacy perspective. Pp. 107-127 in G.C. Roberts, ed., *Motivation in Sport and Exercise*. Champaign, Ill.: Human Kinetics.
McAuley, E., and L.B. Jacobson
    1991   Self-efficacy and exercise participation in sedentary female exercise patterns. *American Journal of Health Promotion* 5:185-191.
Meyer, W.
    1982   Indirect communications about perceived ability estimates. *Journal of Educational Psychology* 74:888-897.
Nicholls, J.G.
    1984   Achievement motivation: Conceptions of ability, subjective experience, task choice and performance. *Psychological Review* 91:328-346.
O'Leary, A.
    1985   Self-efficacy and health. *Behavioral Research and Therapy* 23:437-451.
Ozer, E.M., and A. Bandura
    1990   Mechanisms governing empowerment effects: A self-efficacy analysis. *Journal of Personality and Social Psychology* 58:472-486.
Parker, L.E.
    1992   Working together: Perceived Self and Collective Efficacy at the Workplace. Unpublished manuscript, Institute for Social Research, University of Michigan, Ann Arbor.
Pervin, L.A.
    1989   *Goal Concepts in Personality and Social Psychology*. Hillsdale, N.J.: Lawrence Erlbaum.
Peterson, C., and L.M. Bossio
    1991   *Health and Optimism: New Research on the Relationship Between Positive Thinking and Physical Well-Being*. New York: The Free Press.
Rotter, J.B.
    1966   Generalized expectancies for internal versus external control of reinforcement. *Psychological Monographs* 80:(1, Whole No. 609).

Sanna, L.J.
    1992   Self-efficacy theory: Implication for social facilitation and social loafing. *Journal of Personality and Social Psychology* 62:774-786.

Scheier, M.F., and C.S. Carver
    1992   Effects of optimism on psychological and physical well-being: Theoretical overview and empirical update. *Cognitive Therapy and Research* 16:201-228.

Schunk, D.H.
    1981   Modeling and attributional effects on children's achievement: A self-efficacy analysis. *Journal of Educational Psychology* 73:93-105.
    1983a   Ability versus effort attributional feedback: Differential effects of self-efficacy and achievement. *Journal of Educational Psychology* 75:848-856.
    1983b   Goal difficulty and attainment information: Effects on children's achievement behaviors. *Human Learning* 2:107-117.
    1983c   Reward contingencies and the development of children's skills and self-efficacy. *Journal of Educational Psychology* 75:511-518.
    1984a   Enhancing self-efficacy and achievement through rewards and goals: Motivational and informational effects. *Journal of Educational Research* 78:29-34.
    1984b   Self-efficacy perspective on achievement behavior. *Educational Psychologist* 19:48-58.
    1985   Self-efficacy and classroom learning. *Psychology in the Schools* 22:208-223.

Schunk, D.H., and P.D. Cox
    1986   Strategy training feedback with learning disabled students. *Journal of Educational Psychology* 78:201-209.

Schunk, D.H., and T.P. Gunn
    1986   Self-efficacy and skill development: Influence of task strategies and attributions. *Journal of Educational Research* 79:238-244.

Schunk, D.H., and J.M. Rice
    1986   Extended attributional feedback: Sequence effects during remedial reading instruction. *Journal of Early Adolescence* 6:55-66.

Smith, R.E., F.L. Smoll, and B. Curtis
    1979   Coach effectiveness training: A cognitive-behavioral approach to enhancing relationship skills in youth sport coaches. *Journal of Sport Psychology* 1:59-75.

Spink, K.S.
    1990   Group cohesion and collective efficacy of volleyball teams. *Journal of Sport and Exercise Psychology* 12:301-311.

Strang, H.R., E.C. Lawrence, and P.C. Fowler
    1978   Effects of assigned goal level and knowledge of results on arithmetic computation: Laboratory study. *Journal of Applied Psychology* 63:446-450.

Stock, J., and D. Cervone
    1990   Proximal goal-setting and self-regulatory processes. *Cognitive Therapy and Research* 14:483-498.

Taylor, C.B., A. Bandura, C.K. Ewart, N.H. Miller, and R.F. DeBusk
    1985   Raising spouse's and patient's perception of his cardiac capabilities after clinically uncomplicated acute myocardial infarction. *American Journal of Cardiology* 55:635-638.

Taylor, S.E., and J.D. Brown
    1988   Illusion and well-being: A social psychological perspective on mental health. *Psychological Bulletin* 103:193-210.

Tubbs, M.E.
    1986   Goal setting: A meta-analytic examination of the empirical evidence. *Journal of Applied Psychology* 71:474-483.

Triandis, H.C.
    1977   *Interpersonal Behavior.* Belmont, Calif.: Brooks/Cole.

Vallerand, R.J.
  1983   The effects of differential amounts of positive verbal feedback on the intrinsic moti-
          vation of male hockey players. *Journal of Sport Psychology* 5:100-107.
Vealey, R.S.
  1986   Conceptualization of sport-confidence and competitive orientation: Preliminary in-
          vestigation and instrument development. *Journal of Sport Psychology* 8:221-246.
Weinberg, R.
  1985   Relationship between self-efficacy and cognitive strategies in enhancing endurance
          performance. *International Journal of Sport Psychology* 17:280-293.
  1992   Goal-setting and motor performance: A review and critique. Pp. 177-198 in G.C.
          Roberts, ed., *Motivation in Sport and Exercise.* Champaign, Ill.: Human Kinetics.
Weinberg, R., D. Gould, and A. Jackson
  1979   Expectations and performance: An empirical test of Bandura's self-efficacy theory.
          Journal of Sport Psychology 1:320-331.
Weinberg, R., M. Sinardi, and A. Jackson
  1982   Effect of bar height and modeling on anxiety, self-confidence and gymnastic perfor-
          mance. *International Gymnast* 2:11-13.
Wilkes, R.L., and J.J. Summers
  1984   Cognitions, mediating variables, and strength performance. *Journal of Sport Psy-
          chology* 6:351-359.
Wood, R.E., and A. Bandura
  1989   Impact of conceptions of ability on self-regulatory mechanisms and complex deci-
          sion-making. *Journal of Personality and Social Psychology* 56:407-415.
Wood, R.E., A.J. Mento, and E.A. Locke
  1987   Task complexity as a moderator of goal effects: A meta-analysis. *Journal of
          Applied Psychology* 72:416-425.
Wood, R.E., A. Bandura, and T. Bailey
  1990   Mechanisms governing performance in complex decision-making environments.
          Organizational Behavior and Human Decision Processes 46:181-201.
Yan Lan, L., and D.L. Gill
  1984   The relationships among self-efficacy, stress responses, and a cognitive feedback
          manipulation. *Journal of Sport Psychology* 6:227-238.
Yukl, G.A.
  1989   *Leadership in Organizations,* 2d ed. Englewood Cliffs, N.J.: Prentice-Hall.
Zander, A.
  1971   *Motives and Goals in Groups.* New York: Academic.
Zimmerman, B.J., and J. Ringle
  1981   Effects of model persistence and statements of confidence on children's self-effi-
          cacy and problem solving. *Journal of Educational Psychology* 73:485-493.
Zimmerman, B.J., A. Bandura, and M. Martinez-Pons
  1992   Self-motivation for academic attainment: The role of self-efficacy beliefs and per-
          sonal goal setting. *American Educational Research Journal* 29:663-676.

CHAPTER 9

Aarons, L.
  1977   Sleep-assisted instruction. *Psychological Bulletin* 83:1-40.
Adams, H.B.
  1990   The incredible history of REST technology. Pp. 11-28 in J.W. Turner and T.H.
          Fine, eds., *Restricted Environmental Stimulation: Research and Commentary.* To-
          ledo: Medical College of Ohio Press.

Alexander, C.N., and E.J. Langer, eds.
  1990   *Higher Stages of Human Development: Perspectives on Adult Growth.* New York: Oxford University Press.
Alexander, C.N., M.V. Rainforth, and P. Gelderloos
  1991   Transcendental Meditation, self-actualization, and psychological health: A conceptual overview and statistical meta-analysis. *Journal of Social Behavior and Personality* 6:189-247.
American Medical Association
  1958   Medical use of hypnosis. *Journal of the American Medical Association* 168:186-189.
  1985   Scientific status of refreshing recollection by the use of hypnosis. *Journal of the American Medical Association* 253:1918-1923.
As, A.
  1962   The recovery of forgotten language knowledge through hypnotic age regression: A case report. *American Journal of Clinical Hypnosis* 5:24-29.
Ault, R.L.
  1979   FBI guidelines for use of hypnosis. *International Journal of Clinical and Experimental Hypnosis* 27:449-451.
Banyai, E.I., and E.R. Hilgard
  1976   A comparison of active-alert hypnotic induction with traditional relaxation induction. *Journal of Abnormal Psychology* 85:218-224.
Barabasz, A., M. Barabasz, and J. Bauman
  1993   Restricted environmental stimulation technique improves human marksmanship. *Perceptual and Motor Skills* 76:867-873.
Barabasz, M., and A. Barabasz
  1987   Controlling experimental and situational demand variables in restricted environmental stimulation research. Pp. 110-121 in J.W. Turner and T.H. Fine, eds., *Second International Conference on Restricted Environmental Stimulation.* Toledo, Ohio: Iris Publications.
Barber, J., and D. Mayer
  1977   Evaluation of the efficacy and neural mechanism of a hypnotic analgesia procedure in experimental and clinical dental pain. *Pain* 4:41-48.
Barber, T.X.
  1969   *Hypnosis: A Scientific Approach.* New York: Van Nostrand Reinhold.
Barber, T.X., and D.S. Calverley
  1964a   Toward a theory of "hypnotic" behavior: An experimental study of "hypnotic time distortion." *Archives of General Psychiatry* 10:209-216.
  1964b   Toward a theory of "hypnotic" behavior: Enhancement of strength and endurance. *Canadian Journal of Psychology* 18:156-167.
Bergson, H.
  1886   [Unconscious simulation in the hypnotic state.] *Revue Philosophique* 22:525-531.
Bowers, K.S.
  1979   Time distortion and hypnotic ability: Underestimating the duration of hypnosis. *Journal of Abnormal Psychology* 88:435-439.
Bowers, K.S., and H.A. Brenneman
  1979   Hypnosis and the perception of time. *International Journal of Clinical and Experimental Hypnosis* 27:29-41.
Bowers, K.S., and T.M. Davidson
  1992   A neodissociative critique of Spanos's social-psychological model of hypnosis. Pp. 105-143 in S.J. Lynn and J.W. Rhue, eds., *Theories of Hypnosis: Current Models and Perspectives.* New York: Guilford.

Braid, J.
  1843   Neurypnology: Or the Rationale of Nervous Sleep Considered in Relation to Animal Magnetism. London: Churchill.
Bramwell, J.M.
  1903   *Hypnotism: Its History, Practice, and Theory.* London: Rider.
Charcot, J.M.
  1889   *Lectures on Diseases of the Nervous System.* London: New Sydenham Society.
Chaves, J.F.
  1989   Hypnotic control of clinical pain. Pp. 242-272 in N.P. Spanos and J.F. Chaves, eds., *Hypnosis: The Cognitive-Behavioral Perspective.* Buffalo, N.Y.: Prometheus.
Cooper, G.D., H.B. Adams, and J.C. Scott
  1988   Studies in REST: I. Restricted environmental stimulation therapy (REST) and reduced alcohol consumption. *Journal of Substance Abuse Treatment* 5:61-68.
Cooper, L.F., and M.H. Erickson
  1950   Time distortion in hypnosis II. *Bulletin of the Georgetown University Medical Center* 4:50-68.
  1954   *Time Distortion in Hypnosis.* Baltimore, Md.: Williams & Wilkins.
Cooper, L.F., and D.W. Rodgin
  1952   Time distortion in hypnosis and non-motor learning. *Science* 115:500-502.
Cooper, L.F., and C.E. Tuthill
  1952   Time distortion in hypnosis and motor learning. *Journal of Psychology* 34:67-76.
De Benedittis, G., A.A. Panerai, and M.A. Vallamira
  1989   Effects of hypnotic analgesia and hypnotizability on experimental ischemic pain. *International Journal of Clinical and Experimental Hypnosis* 37:55-69.
D'Eon, J.L.
  1989   Hypnosis in the control of labor pain. Pp. 273-296 in N.P. Spanos and J.F. Chaves, eds., *Hypnosis: The Cognitive-Behavioral Perspective.* Buffalo, N.Y.: Prometheus.
Dillbeck, M.C., and D.W. Orme-Johnson
  1987   Physiological differences between Transcendental Meditation and rest. *American Psychologist* 42:879-881.
Domangue, B.B., C.G. Margolis, D. Lieberman, and H. Kaji
  1985   Biochemical correlates of hypnoanalgesia in arthritic pain patients. *Journal of Clinical Psychiatry* 46:235-238.
Doob, L.W.
  1971   *The Patterning of Time.* New Haven: Yale University Press.
Druckman, D., and R.A. Bjork, eds.
  1991   *In the Mind's Eye.* Committee on Techniques for the Enhancement of Human Performance, National Research Council. Washington, D.C.: National Academy Press.
Druckman, D., and J.A. Swets, eds.
  1988   *Enhancing Human Performance.* Committee on Techniques for the Enhancement of Human Performance, National Research Council. Washington, D.C.: National Academy Press.
Dywan, J.
  1988   The imagery factor in hypnotic hypermnesia. *International Journal of Clinical and Experimental Hypnosis* 36:312-326.
Dywan, J., and K.S. Bowers
  1983   The use of hypnosis to enhance recall. *Science* 222:184-185.
Edmonston, W.E., and J.R. Erbeck
  1967   Hypnotic time distortion: A note. *American Journal of Clinical Hypnosis* 10:79-80.

Eich, E.
1984   Memory for unattended events: Remembering with and without awareness. *Memory and Cognition* 12:105-111.
1990   Learning during sleep. Pp. 88-108 in R.R. Bootzin, J.F. Kihlstrom, and D.L. Schacter, eds., *Sleep and Cognition*. Washington, D.C.: American Psychological Association.

Elliotson, J.
1843   *Numerous Cases of Surgical Operations Without Pain in the Mesmeric State*. London: Baliere.

Elton, D., G. Burrows, and G. Stanley
1980   Chronic pain and hypnosis. Pp. 269-289 in G.D. Burrows and L. Dennerstein, eds., *Handbook of Hypnosis and Psychosomatic Medicine*. Amsterdam, The Netherlands: Elsevier/North Holland.

Eppley, K.R., A. Abrams, and J. Shear
1989   Differential effects of relaxation techniques on trait anxiety: A meta-analysis. *Journal of Clinical Psychology* 45:957-974.

Erdelyi, M.H.
1988   Hypermnesia: The effect of hypnosis, fantasy, and concentration. Pp. 64-94 in H.M. Pettinati, ed., *Hypnosis and Memory*. New York: Guilford.

Esdaile, J.
1850   *Mesmerism in India, and Its Practical Application in Surgery and Medicine*. London: Longmans, Green, and Co.

Evans, F.J.
1990   Behavioral responses during sleep. Pp. 77-87 in R.R. Bootzin, J.F. Kihlstrom, and D.L. Schacter, eds., *Sleep and Cognition*. Washington, D.C.: American Psychological Association.

Evans, F.J., and M.T. Orne
1965   Motivation, performance, and hypnosis. *International Journal of Clinical and Experimental Hypnosis* 19:277-296.

Evans, F.J., L.A. Gustafson, D.N. O'Connell, M.T. Orne, and R.E. Shor
1969   Sleep-induced behavioral response: Relationship to susceptibility to hypnosis and laboratory sleep patterns. *Journal of Nervous and Mental Disease* 148:467-476.
1970   Verbally induced behavioral responses during sleep. *Journal of Nervous and Mental Disease* 15:171-187.

Eysenck, H.J.
1941   An experimental study of the improvement of mental and physical functions in the hypnotic state. *British Journal of Medical Psychology* 18:304-316.

Farthing, G.W.
1992   *The Psychology of Consciousness*. Englewood Cliffs, N.J.: Prentice-Hall.

Feltz, D., and D. Landers
1983   The effects of mental practice on motor skill learning and performance: A meta-analysis. *Journal of Sport Psychology* 5:25-57.

Fowler, W.L.
1961   Hypnosis and learning. *International Journal of Clinical and Experimental Hypnosis* 9:223-232.

Fraisse, P.
1984   Perception and estimation of time. *Annual Review of Psychology* 35:1-36.

Fromm, E.
1970   Age regression with unexpected reappearance of a repressed childhood language. *International Journal of Clinical and Experimental Hypnosis* 18:79-88.

Fromm, E., D.P. Brown, S.W. Hurt, J.Z. Oberlander, A.M. Boxer, and G. Pfeifer
1981   The phenomena and characteristics of self-hypnosis. *International Journal of Clinical and Experimental Hypnosis* 29:189-246.

Geiselman, R.E., R.P. Fisher, D.P. MacKinnnon, and H.L. Holland
  1985   Eyewitness memory enhancement in the police interview: Cognitive retrieval mne-
          monics versus hypnosis. *Journal of Applied Psychology* 70:401-412.
Gibbon, J., and L. Allan, eds.
  1984   Timing and time perception. *Annals of the New York Academy of Sciences*, Vol.
          423. New York: New York Academy of Sciences.
Glisky, M.L., D.J. Tataryn, B.A. Tobias, J.F. Kihlstrom, and K.M. McConkey
  1991   Absorption, openness to experience, and hypnotizability. *Journal of Personality
          and Social Psychology* 60:263-272.
Goldstein, A., and E.R. Hilgard
  1975   Failure of opiate antagonist naloxone to modify hypnotic analgesia. *Proceedings of
          the National Academy of Sciences USA* 72:2041-2043.
Graham, C., and H.W. Liebowitz
  1972   The effects of suggestions on visual acuity. *International Journal of Clinical and
          Experimental Hypnosis* 20:169-186.
Gray, W.H.
  1934   The effect of hypnosis on learning to spell. *Journal of Educational Psychology*
          25:471-473.
Green, D.M., and J.A. Swets
  1966   *Signal Detection Theory and Psychophysics.* New York: Wiley.
Greene, R.J., and J. Reyher
  1972   Pain tolerance in hypnotic analgesic and imagination states. *Journal of Abnormal
          Psychology* 79:29-38.
Grissom, R.J.
  1966   Facilitation of memory by experiential restriction after learning. *American Journal
          of Psychology* 79:613-617.
Gudjonsson, G.H.
  1984   A new scale of interrogative suggestibility. *Personality and Individual Differences*
          5:303-314.
Guerra, G., G. Guantieri, and F. Tagliaro
  1985   Hypnosis and plasmatic beta-endorphins. Pp. 259-266 in D. Waxman, P.C. Misra,
          M. Gibson, and M.A. Basker, eds., *Modern Trends in Hypnosis.* New York: Ple-
          num.
Hadfield, J.A.
  1924   *The Psychology of Power.* New York: Macmillan.
Hilgard, E.R.
  1965   *Hypnotic Susceptibility.* New York: Harcourt, Brace, and World.
  1977   *Divided Consciousness: Multiple Controls in Human Thought and Action.* New
          York: Wiley-Interscience.
  1986   *Divided Consciousness: Multiple Controls in Human Thought and Action*, rev. ed..
          New York: Wiley-Interscience.
Hilgard, E.R., and J.R. Hilgard
  1975   *Hypnosis in the Relief of Pain.* Los Altos, Calif.: Kaufman.
  1983   *Hypnosis in the Relief of Pain*, rev. ed. Los Altos, Calif.: Kaufman.
Hilgard, J.R., and S. LeBaron
  1984   *Hypnotherapy of Pain in Children with Cancer.* Los Altos, Calif.: Kaufman.
Hilgard, E.R., H. Macdonald, G.D. Marshall, and A.H. Morgan
  1974   The anticipation of pain and of pain control under hypnosis: Heart rate and blood
          pressure responses in the cold pressor test. *Journal of Abnormal Psychology* 83:561-
          568.
Hofling, C.K., B. Heyl, and D. Wright
  1971   The ratio of total recoverable memories to conscious memories in normal subjects.
          Comprehensive Psychiatry 12:371-379.

Holmes, D.S.
  1984   Meditation and somatic arousal reduction: A review of the experimental evidence. *American Psychologist* 39:1-10.
Hull, C.L.
  1932   *Hypnosis and Suggestibility: An Experimental Study.* New York: Appleton-Century-Crofts.
Hutchinson, M.
  1984   *The Book of Floating: Exploring the Private Sea.* New York: Morrow.
Jenkins, J.G., and K.M. Dallenbach
  1924   Oblivescence during sleep and waking. *American Journal of Psychology* 35:605-612.
Jevning, R., A.F. Wilson, W.R. Smith, and M.E. Morton
  1978   Redistribution of blood flow in acute hypermetabolic behavior. *American Journal of Physiology* 235:R89-R92.
Jevning, R., R.K. Wallace, and M. Beidebach
  1992   The physiology of meditation: A review. A wakeful hypometabolic integrated response. *Neuroscience and Biobehavioral Reviews* 16:415-424.
Johnson, L.S.
  1979   Self-hypnosis: Behavioral and phenomenological comparisons with heterohypnosis. *International Journal of Clinical and Experimetnal Hypnosis* 27:240-264.
  1981   Current research in self-hypnotic phenomenology: The Chicago paradigm. *International Journal of Clinical and Experimental Hypnosis* 29:247-258.
Johnson, L.S., and D.G. Weight
  1976   Self-hypnosis versus heterohypnosis: Experiential and behavioral comparisons. *Journal of Abnormal Psychology* 85:523-526.
Johnson, L.S., S.L. Dawson, J.L. Clark, and C. Sikorsky
  1983   Self-hypnosis versus hetero-hypnosis: Order effects and sex differences in behavioral and experiential impact. *International Journal of Clinical and Experimental Hypnosis* 31:139-154.
Johnson, M.K., and C.L. Raye
  1981   Reality monitoring. *Psychological Review* 88:67-85.
Johnson, R.F.Q.
  1976   Hypnotic time-distortion and the enhancement of learning: New data pertinent to the Krauss-Katzell-Krauss experiment. *American Journal of Clinical Hypnosis* 19:89-102.
Johnson, W.R.
  1961   Hypnosis and muscular performance. *Journal of Sports Medicine and Physical Fitness* 1:71-79.
Johnson, W.R., and G.F. Kramer
  1960   Effects of different types of hypnotic suggestions upon physical performance. *Research Quarterly* 31:469-473.
  1961   Effects of stereotyped nonhypnotic, hypnotic, and posthypnotic suggestions upon strength, power, and endurance. *Research Quarterly* 32:522-529.
Johnson, W.R., B.H. Massey, and G.F. Kramer
  1960   Effects of post-hypnotic suggestions on all-out effort of short duration. *Research Quarterly* 31:142-146.
Jones, B., and N.P. Spanos
  1982   Suggestions for altered auditory sensitivity, the negative subject effect and hypnotic susceptibility. *Journal of Personality and Social Psychology* 43:637-647.
Kihlstrom, J.F.
  1980   Posthypnotic amnesia for recently learned material: Interactions with "episodic" and "semantic" memory. *Cognitive Psychology* 12:227-251.

1984   Conscious, subconscious, unconscious: A cognitive perspective. Pp. 149-211 in K.S. Bowers and D. Meichenbaum, eds., *The Unconscious Reconsidered.* New York: Wiley.

Kihlstrom, J.F., and T.M. Barnhardt
1993   The self-regulation of memory, for better and for worse, with and without hypnosis. Pp. 88-125 in D.M. Wegner and J.W. Pennebaker, eds., *Handbook of Mental Control.* Englewood Cliffs, N.J.: Prentice-Hall.

Kihlstrom, J.F., and I.P. Hoyt
1988   Hypnosis and the psychology of delusions. Pp. 66-109 in T.F. Oltmanns and B.A. Maher, eds., *Delusional Beliefs.* New York: Wiley-Interscience.

1990   Repression, dissociation, and hypnosis. Pp. 181-208 in J.L. Singer, ed., *Repression and Dissociation: Implications for Personality Theory, Psychopathology, and Health.* Chicago: University of Chicago Press.

Knox, V.J., and K. Shum
1977   Reduction of cold pressor pain with acupuncture analgesia in high- and low-hypnotic subjects. *Journal of Abnormal Psychology* 86:639-643.

Knox, V.J., A.H. Morgan, and E.R. Hilgard
1974   Pain and suffering in ischemia: The paradox of hypnotically suggested anesthesia as contradicted by the reports from the "hidden observer." *Archives of General Psychiatry* 30:840-847.

Knox, V.J., K. Shum, and D.M. McLaughlin
1978   Hypnotic analgesia vs. acupuncture analgesia in high- and low-susceptible subjects. Pp. 101-108 in F.H. Frankel and H.S. Zamansky, eds., *Hypnosis at Its Bicentennial: Selected Papers.* New York: Plenum.

Knox, V.J., C.E. Handfield-Jones, and K. Shum
1979   Subject expectancy and the reduction of cold pressor pain with acupuncture and placebo acupuncture. *Psychosomatic Medicine* 41:477-486.

Knox, V.J., W.L. Gekoski, K. Shum, and D.M. McLaughlin
1981   Analgesia for experimentally induced pain: Multiple sessions of acupuncture compared to hypnosis in high- and low-susceptible subjects. *Journal of Abnormal Psychology* 90:28-34.

Krauss, H.K., R. Katzell, and R.J. Krauss
1974   Effect of hypnotic time-distortion upon free-recall learning. *Journal of Abnormal Psychology* 83:141-144.

Laurence, J.R., and C. Perry
1983   Hypnotically created memory among highly hypnotizable subjects. *Science* 222:523-524.

Lee, A.B., and J. Hewitt
1987   Using visual imagery in a flotation tank to improve gymnastic performance and reduce physical symptoms. *International Journal of Sport Psychology* 18:223-230.

Levitt, E.E., and J.P. Brady
1964   Muscular endurance under hypnosis and in the motivated waking state. *International Journal of Clinical and Experimental Hypnosis* 12:21-27.

Loftus, E.F.
1975   Leading questions and the eyewitness report. *Cognitive Psychology* 7:560-572.

Loftus, E.F., J. Schooler, and W.A. Wagenaar
1985   The fate of memory: Comment on McCloskey and Zaragoza. *Journal of Experimental Psychology: General* 114:375-380.

London, P., and M. Fuhrer
1961   Hypnosis, motivation, and performance. *Journal of Personality* 29:321-333.

London, P., M. Conant, and G.C. Davison
1966   More hypnosis in the unhypnotizable: Effects of hypnosis and exhortation on rote learning. *Journal of Personality* 34:71-79.

Loomis, E.A.
 1951   Space and time perception and distortion in hypnotic states. *Personality* 1:283-293.
Manzer, C.W.
 1934   The effect of verbal suggestion on output and variability of muscular work. *Psychological Clinic* 22:243-247.
McAleney, A. Barabasz, and M. Barabasz
 1991   Effects of flotation restricted environmental stimulation on intercollegiate tennis performance. *Perceptual and Motor Skills* 71:1023-1028.
McCloskey, M., and M. Zaragoza
 1985   Misleading postevent information and memory for events: Arguments and evidence against memory impairment hypotheses. *Journal of Experimental Psychology: General* 114:1-16.
McCrae, R.R., and P.T. Costa
 1985   Openness to experience. Pp. 145-172 in R. Hogan and W.H. Costa, eds., *Perspectives in Personality*, Vol. 1. Greenwich, Conn.: JAI Press.
McGeogh, J.A., and A.L. Irion
 1952   *The Psychology of Human Learning*, rev. ed. New York: Longmans.
McGlashan, T.H., F. J. Evans, and M. T. Orne
 1969   The nature of hypnotic analgesia and placebo response to experimental pain. *Psychosomatic Medicine* 31:227-246.
Mead, S., and E.F. Roush
 1949   A study of the effect of hypnotic suggestion on physiologic performance. *Archives of Physical Medicine* 30:700-705.
Mereday, C., C. Lehmann, and R. Borrie
 1990   Flotation for the management of rheumatoid arthritis. Pp. 255-259 in J.W. Turner and T.H. Fine, eds., *Restricted Environmental Stimulation: Research and Commentary*. Toledo: Medical College of Ohio Press.
Metcalfe, J.
 1990   Composite holographic associative recall model (CHARM) and blended memories in eyewitness testimony. *Journal of Experimental Psychology: General* 119:145-160.
Metcalfe, J., and P. Suedfeld
 1990   Enhancing the creativity of psychologists through flotation REST. Pp. 204-212 in J.W. Turner and T.H. Fine, eds., *Restricted Environmental Stimulation: Research and Commentary*. Toledo: Medical College of Ohio Press.
Miller, M.E., and K.S. Bowers
 1986   Hypnotic analgesia and stress inoculation in the reduction of pain. *Journal of Abnormal Psychology* 95:6-14.
 1993   Hypnotic analgesia: Dissociated experience or dissociated control? *Journal of Abnormal Psychology* 102:29-38.
Morgan, W.P.
 1980   Hypnosis and sports medicine. Pp. 359-375 in G.D. Burrows and L. Dennerstein, eds., *Handbook of Hypnosis and Psychosomatic Medicine*. Amsterdam, The Netherlands: Elsevier/North Holland.
Nash, M.R.
 1987   What, if anything, is regressed about hypnotic age regression? A review of the empirical literature. *Psychological Bulletin* 102:42-52.
Nicholson, N.C.
 1920   Notes on muscular work during hypnosis. *Bulletin of the Johns Hopkins Hospital* 31:89-91.
Nogrady, H., K.M. McConkey, and C. Perry
 1985   Enhancing visual memory: Trying hypnosis, trying imagination, trying again. *Journal of Abnormal Psychology* 94:195-204.

O'Connell, D.N., R.E. Shor, and M.T. Orne
   1970   Hypnotic age regression: An empirical and methodological analysis. *Journal of Abnormal Psychology Monograph* 76(3, Pt. 2):1-32.
Olness, K., H.J. Wain, and N.G. Lorenz
   1980   A pilot study of blood endorphin levels in children using self-hypnosis to control pain. *Journal of Developmental and Behavioral Pediatrics* 4:187-188.
Orme-Johnson, D.W.
   1973   Autonomic stability and Transcendental Meditation. *Psychosomatic Medicine* 35:341-349.
Orne, M.T.
   1951   The mechanisms of hypnotic age regression: An experimental study. *Journal of Abnormal and Social Psychology* 46:213-225.
   1959   The nature of hypnosis: Artifact and essence. *Journal of Abnormal and Social Psychology* 58:277-299.
   1962   On the social psychology of the psychological experiment: With special reference to demand characteristics and their implications. *American Psychologist* 17:776-783.
   1965   Psychological factors maximizing resistance to stress: With special reference to hypnosis. Pp. 286-328 in S.Z. Klausner, ed., *The Quest for Self-Control.* New York: Free Press.
   1966   Hypnosis, motivation, and compliance. *American Journal of Psychiatry* 122:721-726.
   1979   The use and misuse of hypnosis in court. *International Journal of Clinical and Experimental Hypnosis* 27:311-341.
Orne, M.T., and K.M. McConkey
   1981   Toward convergent inquiry into self-hypnosis. *International Journal of Clinical and Experimental Hypnosis* 29:313-323.
Orne, M.T., D.A. Soskis, D.F. Dinges, and E.C. Orne
   1984   Hypnotically induced testimony. Pp. 171-213 in G.L. Wells and E.F. Loftus, eds., *Eyewitness Testimony: Psychological Perspectives.* Cambridge, England: Cambridge University Press.
Orne, M.T., W.G. Whitehouse, D.F. Dinges, and E.C. Orne
   1988   Reconstructing memory through hypnosis: Forensic and clinical implications. Pp. 21-63 in H.M. Pettinati, ed., *Hypnosis and Memory.* New York: Guilford.
Ornstein, R.F.
   1969   *On the Experience of Time.* Hammondsworth, U.K.: Penguin.
Parker, P.D., and T.X. Barber
   1964   Hypnosis, task-motivating instructions, and learning performance. *Journal of Abnormal and Social Psychology* 69:499-504.
Parker, E.S., J.M. Morihisa, R.J. Wyatt, B.L. Schwartz, H. Weingartner, and R.C. Stillman
   1981   The alcohol facilitation of human memory: A dose response study. *Psychopharmacology* 74:88-92.
Pastore, R.E., and C.J. Scheirer
   1974   Signal detection theory: Considerations for general application. *Psychological Bulletin* 81:945-958.
Perry, C., and B. Walsh
   1978   Inconsistencies and anomalies of response as a defining characteristic of hypnosis. *Journal of Abnormal Psychology* 87:574-577.
Perry, C.W., F.J. Evans, D.N. O'Connell, E.C. Orne, and M.T. Orne
   1978   Behavioral response to verbal stimuli administered and tested during REM sleep: A further investigation. *Waking and Sleeping* 2:317-329.

Putnam, W.H.
    1979   Hypnosis and distortions in eyewitness memory. *International Journal of Clinical and Experimental Hypnosis* 27:437-448.

Reeves, J.L., W. H. Redd, F. K. Storm, and R.V. Minogawa
    1983   Hypnosis in the control of pain during hyperthermia treatment of cancer. Pp. 857-861 in J.J. Bonica, V. Lindblom, and A. Iggo, eds., *Advances in Pain Research and Therapy*, Vol. 5. New York: Raven.

Register, P.A., and J.F. Kihlstrom
    1987   Hypnotic effects on hypermnesia. *International Journal of Clinical and Experimental Hypnosis* 35:155-170.
    1988   Hypnosis and interrogative suggestibility. *Personality and Individual Differences* 9:549-558.

Reiser, M.
    1976   Hypnosis as an aid in criminal investigation. *Police Chief* 46:39-40.

Rieger, C.
    1884   *Der Hypnotismus.* Jena, Germany: Gustav Fischer.

Roche, S.M., and K.M. McConkey
    1990   Absorption: Nature, assessment, and correlates. *Journal of Personality and Social Psychology* 59:91-101.

Rosenhan, D., and P. London
    1963   Hypnosis in the unhypnotizable: A study in rote learning. *Journal of Experimental Psychology* 65:30-34.

Roush, E.S.
    1951   Strength and endurance in the waking and hypnotic state. *Journal of Applied Physiology* 3:404-410.

Ruch, J.C.
    1975   Self-hypnosis: The result of heterohypnosis or vice versa? *International Journal of Clinical and Experimental Hypnosis* 23:282-304.

St. Jean, R.
    1980   Hypnotic time distortion and learning: Another look. *Journal of Abnormal Psychology* 89:20-24.
    1989   Hypnosis and time perception. Pp. 175-186 in N.P. Spanos and J.F. Chaves, eds., *Hypnosis: The Cognitive-Behavioral Perspective.* Buffalo, N.Y.: Prometheus Press.

St. Jean, R., and C. MacLeod
    1983   Hypnosis, absorption, and time distortion. *Journal of Abnormal Psychology* 92:81-86.

St. Jean, R., and L. Robertson
    1986   Attentional versus absorptive processing in hypnotic time estimation. *Journal of Abnormal Psychology* 95:40-42.

St. Jean, R., C. MacLeod, W.C. Coe, and M.L. Howard
    1982   Amnesia and hypnotic time estimation. *International Journal of Clinical and Experimental Hypnosis* 30:127-137.

Sanders, G.S., and W.L. Simmons
    1983   Use of hypnosis to enhance eyewitness accuracy: Does it work? *Journal of Applied Psychology* 68:70-77.

Schacter, D.L.
    1987   Implicit memory: History and current status. *Journal of Experimental Psychology: Learning, Memory, and Cognition* 13:501-518.
    1992   Understanding implicit memory: A cognitive neuroscience approach. *American Psychologist* 47:559-569.

Scharf, B., and H.S. Zamansky
   1963   Reduction of word-recognition threshold under hypnosis. *Perceptual and Motor Skills* 17:499-510.
Scheflin, A.W., and J.L. Shapiro
   1989   *Trance on Trial.* New York: Guilford.
Schulman, R.E., and P. London
   1963   Hypnosis and verbal learning. *Journal of Abnormal and Social Psychology* 67:363-370.
Schwartz, W.S.
   1978   Time and context during hypnotic involvement. *International Journal of Clinical and Experimental Hypnosis* 26:307-316.
   1980   Hypnosis and episodic memory. *International Journal of Clinical and Experimental Hypnosis* 28:375-385.
Sears, A.B.
   1955   A comparison of hypnotic and waking learning of the International Morse Code. *Journal of Clinical and Experimental Hypnosis* 3:215-221.
Sheehan, E.P., H.V. Smith, and D.W. Forrest
   1982   A signal detection study of the effects of suggested improvement on the monocular visual acuity of myopes. *International Journal of Clinical and Experimental Hypnosis* 30:138-146.
Sheehan, P.W.
   1988a   Confidence, memory, and hypnosis. Pp. 95-127 in H.M. Pettinati, ed., *Hypnosis and Memory.* New York: Guilford.
   1988b   Memory distortion in hypnosis. *International Journal of Clinical and Experimental Hypnosis* 36:296-311.
Shor, R.E., and R.D. Easton
   1973   Preliminary report on research comparing self- and hetero-hypnosis. *American Journal of Clinical Hypnosis* 16:37-44.
Shurley, J.T.
   1992   Sensory deprivation and sensory isolation research, and political torture: A 35-year critical retrospective. Pp. 200-210 in A. Kales, C.M. Pierce, and M. Greenblatt, eds., *The Mosaic of Contemporary Psychiatry in Perspective.* New York: Springer-Verlag.
Simon, C.W., and W.H. Emmons
   1955   Learning during sleep? *Psychological Bulletin* 52:328-342.
Slotnick, R., and P. London
   1965   Influence of instructions on hypnotic and nonhypnotic performance. *Journal of Abnormal Psychology* 70:38-46.
Slotnick, R.S., R.M. Liebert, and E.R. Hilgard
   1965   The enhancement of muscular performance in hypnosis through exhortation and involving instructions. *Journal of Personality* 33:37-45.
Smith, H.V., D.W. Forrest, and E.P. Sheehan
   1983   Suggested improvement, music, and the visual acuity of myopes: A reply. *International Journal of Clinical and Experimental Hypnosis* 31:241-242.
Smith, M.C.
   1983   Hypnotic memory enhancement of witnesses: Does it work? *Psychological Bulletin* 94:387-407.
Solomon, R.L., P.E. Kubzansky, P.H. Leiderman, J. Mendelson, and D. Wexler, eds.
   1961   *Sensory Deprivation.* Cambridge, Mass.: Harvard University Press.
Spanos, N.P.
   1989   Experimental research on hypnotic analgesia. Pp. 206-240 in N.P. Spanos and J.F.

Chaves, eds., *Hypnosis: The Cognitive-Behavioral Perspective.* Buffalo, N.Y.: Prometheus.

Spanos, N.P., and J. Katsanis
1989   Effects of instructional set on attributions of nonvolition during hypnotic and nonhypnotic analgesia. *Journal of Personality and Social Psychology* 56:182-188.

Spanos, N.P., A.H. Perlini, and L.A. Robertson
1989   Hypnosis, suggestion, and placebo in the reduction of experimental pain. *Journal of Abnormal Psychology* 98:285-293.

Spiegel, D., and L.H. Albert
1983   Naloxone fails to reverse hypnotic alleviation of chronic pain. *Psychopharmacology* 81:140-143.

Stalnaker, J.M., and M.W. Richardson
1930   Time estimation in the hypnotic trance. *Journal of General Psychology* 4:362-366.

Stalnaker, J.M., and E.E. Riddle
1932   The effect of hypnosis on long-delayed recall. *Journal of General Psychology* 6:429-440.

Stanley, J., M. Mahoney, and C. Reppert
1987   REST and enhancement of sports performance. Pp. 168-183 in J.W. Turner and T.H. Fine, eds., *Second International Conference on Restricted Environmental Stimulation.* Toledo, Ohio: Iris Publications.

Sterling, K., and J.G. Miller
1940   The effect of hypnosis upon visual and auditory acuity. *American Journal of Psychology* 53:269-276.

Stern, J.A., M. Brown, A. Ulett, and I. Sletten
1977   A comparison of hypnosis, acupuncture, morphine, Valium, aspirin, and placebo in the management of experimentally induced pain. In W.E. Edmonston, ed., *Conceptual and Investigative Approaches to Hypnosis and Hypnotic Phenomena. Annals of the New York Academy of Sciences* 296:175-193.

Suedfeld, P.
1969   Changes in intellectual performance and in susceptibility to influence. Pp. 126-166 in J.P. Zubek, ed., *Sensory Deprivation: Fifteen Years of Research.* New York: Appleton-Century-Crofts.
1980   *Restricted Environmental Stimulation: Research and Clinical Applications.* New York: Wiley.
1990   Restricted environmental stimulation and smoking cessation: A 15-year progress report. *International Journal of the Addictions* 25:861-888.

Suedfeld, P., and R.A. Borrie
1993   Health and Clinical Applications of Restricted Environmental Stimulation Therapy (REST). Unpublished manuscript, Department of Psychology, University of British Columbia.

Suedfeld, P., and T. Bruno
1990   Flotation REST and imagery in the improvement of athletic performance. *Journal of Sport and Exercise Psychology* 12:82-85.

Suedfeld, P., and R.D. Hare
1977   Sensory deprivation in the treatment of snake phobia: Behavioral, self-report, and physiological effects. *Behavior Therapy* 8:240-250.

Suedfeld, P., and J.L. Kristeller
1982   Stimulus reduction as a technique in health psychology. *Health Psychology* 1:337-357.

Suedfeld, P., P.B. Landon, and E.J. Ballard
1983   Effects of reduced stimulation on divergent and convergent thinking. *Environment and Behavior* 15:727-738.

Suedfeld, P., J. Metcalfe, and S. Bluck
  1987   Enhancement of scientific creativity by flotation REST (Restricted Environmental Stimulation Technique). *Journal of Environmental Psychology* 7:219-231.
Suedfeld, P., D.E. Collier, and B.D.G. Hartnett
  1993   Enhancing perceptual-motor accuracy through flotation REST. *The Sport Psychologist* 7:151-159.
Sutcliffe, J.P.
  1960   "Credulous" and "sceptical" views of hypnotic phenomena: A review of certain evidence and methodology. *International Journal of Clinical and Experimental Hypnosis* 8:73-101.
  1961   "Credulous" and "skeptical" views of hypnotic phenomena: Experiments in esthesia, hallucination, and delusion. *Journal of Abnormal and Social Psychology* 62:189-200.
Tataryn, D.J.
  1992   Psychophysical and Signal-Detection Analyses of Hypnotic Anesthesia. Unpublished doctoral dissertation, Department of Psychology, University of Arizona.
Tebecis, A.K., and K.A. Provins
  1974   Accuracy of time estimation during hypnosis. *Perceptual and Motor Skills* 39:1123-1126.
Tellegen, A., and G. Atkinson
  1974   Openness to absorbing and self-altering experiences ("absorption"), a trait related to hypnotic susceptibility. *Journal of Abnormal Psychology* 83:268-277.
Timm, H.W.
  1981   The effect of forensic hypnosis techniques on eyewitness recall and recognition. *Journal of Police Science and Administration* 9:188-194.
True, R.M.
  1949   Experimental control in hypnotic age regression. *Science* 110:583.
Turk, D.C., D. Meichenbaum, and M. Genest
  1983   *Pain and Behavioral Medicine: A Cognitive Behavioral Perspective.* New York: Guilford.
Turner, J.A., and C.R. Chapman
  1982   Psychological interventions for chronic pain: A critical review. II. Operant conditioning, hypnosis, and cognitive-behavioral therapy. *Pain* 12:23-46.
Turner, J.W., T.H. Fine, A. McGrady, and J.T. Higgins
  1987   Effects of biobehaviorally assisted relaxation training on blood pressure and hormone levels and their variation in normotensives and essential hypertensives. Pp. 87-109 in J.W. Turner and T.H. Fine, eds., *Second International Conference on Restricted Environmental Stimulation.* Toledo, Ohio: Iris Publications.
Tversky, B., and M. Tuchin
  1989   A reconciliation of the evidence on eyewitness testimony: Comments on McCloskey and Zaragoza. *Journal of Experimental Psychology: General* 118:86-91.
Wadden, T.A., and C.H. Anderton
  1982   The clinical uses of hypnosis. *Psychological Bulletin* 91:215-243.
Wagaman, J.D., A. Barabasz, and M. Barabasz
  1991   Flotation REST and imagery in the improvement of collegiate basketball performance. *Perceptual and Motor Skills* 72:119-122.
Wagstaff, G.F.
  1983   Suggested improvement of visual acuity: A statistical reevaluation. *International Journal of Clinical and Experimental Hypnosis* 31:239-240.
Wagstaff, G.F., and M. Ovenden
  1979   Hypnotic time distortion and free-recall learning: An attempted replication. *Psychological Research* 40:291-298.

Wells, W.R.
   1947   Expectancy versus performance in hypnosis. *Journal of General Psychology* 35:99-
           119.
Whitehouse, W.G., D.F. Dinges, E.C. Orne, and M.T. Orne
   1991   Hypnotic hypermnesia: Enhanced memory accessibility or report bias? *Journal of
           Experimental Psychology: Learning, Memory, and Cognition* 97:289-295.
Williams, G.W.
   1929   The effect of hypnosis on muscular fatigue. *Journal of Abnormal and Social Psy-
           chology* 24:318-329.
   1930   A comparative study of voluntary and hypnotic catalepsy. *American Journal of
           Psychology* 42:83-95.
Wood, J.M.
   1989   Implicit and Explicit Memory for Verbal Stimuli Presented During Sleep. Unpub-
           lished doctoral dissertation, Department of Psychology, University of Arizona.
Wood, J.M., R.R. Bootzin, J.F. Kihlstrom, and D.L. Schacter
   1992   Implicit and explicit memory for verbal information presented during sleep. *Psy-
           chological Science* 3:236-239.
Young, P.C.
   1925   An experimental study of mental and physical functions in the normal and hypnotic
           states. *American Journal of Psychology* 36:214-232.
   1926   An experimental study of mental and physical functions in the normal and hypnotic
           states: Additional results. *American Journal of Psychology* 37:345-356.
Zamansky, H.S., B. Scharf, and R. Brightbill
   1964   The effect of expectancy for hypnosis on prehypnotic performance. *Journal of
           Personality* 32:236-248.
Zelig, M., and W.B. Beidelman
   1981   The investigative use of hypnosis: A word of caution. *International Journal of
           Clinical and Experimental Hypnosis* 29:401-412.
Zubek, J.P., ed.
   1969   *Sensory Deprivation: Fifteen Years of Research.* New York: Appleton-Century-
           Crofts.

CHAPTER 10

Abelson, R.P.
   1983   Whatever became of consistency theory? *Personality and Social Psychology Bulle-
           tin* 9:37-54.
Adelmann, P.K., and R.B. Zajonc
   1989   Facial efference and the experience of emotion. *Annual Review of Psychology*
           40:249-280.
Aderman, D., and G.L. Unterberger
   1977   Contrast empathy and observer modeling behavior. *Journal of Personality* 45:267-
           280.
Allport, F.H.
   1924   *Social Psychology.* Cambridge, Mass.: Riverside Press.
Bandura, A.
   1965   Vicarious processes: A case of no-trial learning. In L. Berkowitz, ed., *Advances in
           Experimental Social Psychology.* New York: Academic Press.
   1969   *Principles of Behavior Modification.* New York: Holt, Rinehart and Winston.
   1971   Vicarious- and self-reinforcement processes. In R. Glaser, ed., *The Nature of Rein-
           forcement.* New York: Academic Press.

Basch, M.F.
    1983   Empathic understanding: A review of the concept and some theoretical consider-
            ations. *Journal of the American Psychoanalytic Association* 31:101-126.
Batson, C.D., and J.S. Coke
    1983   Empathic motivation of helping behavior. Pp. 417-433 in J.T. Cacioppo and R.E.
            Petty, eds., *Social Psychophysiology: A Sourcebook*. New York: Guilford.
Batson, C.D., and L.L. Shaw
    1991   Evidence for altruism: Towards a pluralism of prosocial motives. *Psychological
            Inquiry* 2:107-122.
Berger, S.M.
    1962   Conditioning through vicarious instigation. *Psychological Review* 69:450-466.
Berger, S.M., and S.W. Hadley
    1975   Some effects of a model's performance on an observer's electromyographic activity.
            American Journal of Psychology 88:263-276.
Bless, H., G. Bohner, N. Schwarz, and F. Strack
    1990   Mood and persuasion: A cognitive response analysis. *Personality and Social Psy-
            chology Bulletin* 16:331-345
Boswell, P.C., and E.J. Murray
    1981   Depression, schizophrenia, and social attraction. *Journal of Consulting and Clinical
            Psychology* 9:641-647.
Braaten, L.J.
    1991   Group cohesion: A new multidimensional model. *Group* 15:39-55.
Bramel, D., B. Taub, and B. Blum
    1968   An observer's reaction to the suffering of his enemy. *Journal of Personality and
            Social Psychology* 8:384-392.
Brothers, L.
    1990   The Neural Basis of Primate Social Communication. Paper presented at the sympo-
            sium "Empathy in Infancy and Later Development" at a meeting of the American
            Association for the Advancement of Science, New Orleans, La.
Buck, R.
    1984   *The Communication of Emotion*. New York: Guilford.
Bush, L.K., G.J. McHugo, and J.T. Lanzetta
    1986   The effects of sex and prior attitude on emotional reactions to expressive displays of
            political leaders. *Psychophysiology* 23:427.
Bush, L.K., C.L. Barr, G.J. McHugo, and J.T. Lanzetta
    1989   The effects of facial control and facial mimicry on subjective reactions to comedy
            routines. *Motivation and Emotion* 13:31-52.
Carnevale, P.J., and A.M. Isen
    1986   The influence of positive affect and visual access on the discovery of integrative
            solutions in bilateral negotiation. *Organizational Behavior and Human Decision
            Processes* 37:1-13.
Chidester, T.R., B.G. Konki, H.C. Foushee, C.L. Dickinson, and S.V. Bowles
    1990   *Personality Factors in Flight Operations: Vol. 1. Leader Characteristics and Crew
            Performance in a Full-Mission Air Transport Simulation*. NASA Technical Memo-
            randum No. 102259. Moffett Field, Calif.: NASA-Ames Research Center.
Coyne, J.C.
    1976   Depression and the response of others. *Journal of Abnormal Psychology* 85:186-
            193.
Craig, K.D.
    1968   Physiological arousal as a function of imagined, vicarious, and direct stress experi-
            ences. *Journal of Abnormal Psychology* 3:513-520.

Craig, K.D., and H.J. Lowery
   1969   Heart-rate components of conditioned vicarious autonomic responses. *Journal of Personality and Social Psychology* 11:381-387.
Craig, K.D., and M.S. Weinstein
   1965   Conditioning vicarious affective arousal. *Psychological Reports* 17:955-963.
Craig, K.D., and K. Wood
   1969   Physiological differentiation of direct and vicarious affective arousal. *Canadian Journal of Behavioral Science* 1:89-105.
Dembroski, T.M., T.M. Lasater, and A. Ramirez
   1978   Communicator similarity, fear arousing communications, and compliance with health care recommendations. *Journal of Applied Social Psychology* 8:254-269.
Demos, V.
   1984   Empathy and affect: Reflections on infant experience. Pp. 9-35 in J. Lichtenberg, M. Bornstein, and D. Silver, eds., *Empathy II*. Hillsdale, N.J.: The Analytic Press.
Deutsch, F., and R.A. Madle
   1975   Empathy: Historic and current conceptualization, measurement, and a cognitive theoretical perspective. *Human Development* 18:267-287.
Dimberg, U.
   1982   Facial reactions to facial expressions. *Psychophysiology* 19:643-647.
   1988   Facial electromyography and the experience of emotion. *Journal of Psychophysiology* 2:277-282.
Druckman, D., ed.
   1977   *Negotiations: Social-Psychological Perspectives*. Beverly Hills, Calif.: Sage.
Druckman, D., and R.A. Bjork, eds.
   1991   *In the Mind's Eye: Enhancing Human Performance*. Committee on Techniques for the Enhancement of Human Performance, National Research Council. Washington, D.C.: National Academy Press.
Druckman, D., and T.V. Bonoma
   1976   Determinants of bargaining behavior in a bilateral monopoly situation II: Opponent's concession rate and similarity. *Behavioral Science* 21:252-262.
Druckman, D., and R. Harris
   1990   Alternative models of responsiveness in international negotiation. *Journal of Conflict Resolution* 34:234-251.
Druckman, D., R. Rozelle, and J. Baxter
   1982   *Nonverbal Communication: Survey, Research, and Theory*. Beverly Hills, Calif.: Sage Publications.
Eisenberg, N., R.A. Fabes, D. Bustamante, R.M. Mathy, P.A. Miller, and E. Lindholm
   1988   Differentiation of vicariously induced emotional reactions in children. *Developmental Psychology* 24:237-246.
Ekman, P., and W.V. Friesen
   1969   Nonverbal leakage and clues to deception. *Psychiatry* 32:88-106.
Englis, B.G., K.B. Vaughan, and J.T. Lanzetta
   1982   Conditioning of counter-empathetic emotional responses. *Journal of Experimental Social Psychology* 18:375-391.
Evans, C.R., and K.L. Dion
   1991   Group cohesion and performance: A meta-analysis. *Small Group Research* 22:175-186.
Festinger, L.
   1957   *A Theory of Cognitive Dissonance*. Evanston, Ill.: Row, Peterson, and Co.
Frank, J.
   1968   *Sanity and Survival: Psychological Aspects of War and Peace*. New York: Vantage Books.

Freud, S.
  1921/   Group psychology and the analysis of the ego. J. Strachey, trans. Pp. 169-209 in J.
  1957   Rickman, ed., *A General Selection from the Works of Sigmund Freud.* New York:
          Doubleday.
Gladstein, G.A.
  1983   Understanding empathy: Integrating counseling, developmental, and social psycho-
          logical perspectives. *Journal of Counseling Psychology* 30:467-482.
  1984   The historical roots of contemporary empathy research. *Journal of the History of
          the Behavioral Sciences* 20:38-59.
Goethals, G.R., and E.R. Nelson
  1973   Similarity in the influence process: The belief-value distinction. *Journal of Person-
          ality and Social Psychology* 25:117-122.
Goffman, E.
  1969   *Strategic Interaction.* Philadelphia: University of Pennsylvania Press.
Goldstein, A.P., and G.Y. Michaels
  1985   *Empathy: Development, Training, and Consequences.* Hillsdale, N.J.: Lawrence
          Erlbaum.
Gotlib, I.H., and L.A. Robinson
  1982   Responses to depressed individuals: Discrepancies between self-report and observer-
          rated behavior. *Journal of Abnormal Psychology* 91:231-240.
Green, G., and J.G. Osborne
  1985   Does vicarious instigation provide support for observational learning theories? A
          critical review. *Psychological Bulletin* 97:3-17.
Greene, C.N.
  1989   Cohesion and productivity in work groups. *Small Group Behavior* 20:70-86.
Gurtman, M.B., K.M. Martin, and N.M. Hintzman
  1990   Interpersonal reactions to displays of depression and anxiety. *Journal of Social and
          Clinical Psychology* 9:256-267.
Hammen, C.L., and S.D. Peters
  1978   Interpersonal consequences of depression: Responses to men and women enacting a
          depressed role. *Journal of Abnormal Psychology* 87:322-332.
Harary, F.
  1983   Consistency theory is alive and well. *Personality and Social Psychology Bulletin*
          9:60-64.
Hatfield, E., J.T. Cacioppo, and R. Rapson
  1992   Primitive emotional contagion. In M.S. Clark, ed., *Review of Personality and Social
          Psychology.* Newbury Park, Calif.: Sage Publications.
Haviland, J.M., and M. Lelwica
  1987   The induced affect response: 10-week-old infants' responses to three emotional
          expressions. *Developmental Psychology* 23:97-104.
Heider, F.
  1946   Attitudes and cognitive organization. *Journal of Psychology* 21:107-112.
  1958   *The Psychology of Interpersonal Relations.* New York: John Wiley.
Hoffman, M.L.
  1977   Empathy, its development and prosocial implications. *Nebraska Symposium on
          Motivation* 25:169-217.
  1981   Is altruism part of human nature? *Journal of Personality and Social Psychology*
          40:121-137.
  1990   Empathy and justice motivation. *Motivation and Emotion* 14:151-172.
Horwitz, M.
  1954   The recall of interrupted groups tasks: An experimental study of individual motiva-
          tion in relation to groups goals. *Human Relations* 7:3-38.

Howes, M.J., and J.E. Hokanson
1979 Conversational and social responses to depressive interpersonal behavior. *Journal of Abnormal Psychology* 96:341-344.

Hsee, C.K., E. Hatfield, and J.G. Carlson
1990 The effect of power on susceptibility to emotional contagion. *Cognition and Emotion* 4:327-340.

Hygge, S.
1978 The observer's acquaintance with the model's stimulus in vicarious classical conditioning. *Scandinavian Journal of Psychology* 19:231-239.

Hygge, S., and A. Ohman
1976a Conditioning of electrodermal responses through vicarious instigation and perceived threat to a performer. *Scandinavian Journal of Psychology* 17:65-72.
1976b The relation of vicarious to direct instigation and conditioning of electrodermal responses. *Scandinavian Journal of Psychology* 17:217-222.

Jaffe, E.D., and I.D. Nebenzahl
1990 Group interaction and business game performance. *Simulation & Gaming* 21:133-146.

James, W.
1890/ *The Principles of Psychology.* New York: Dover.
1950

Janis, I.L., D. Kaye, and P. Kirschner
1965 Facilitating effects of eating while reading on responsiveness to persuasive communications. *Journal of Personality and Social Psychology* 1:181-186.

Johnson, D.W.
1971a Effects of the order of expressing warmth and anger on the actor and the listener. *Journal of Counseling Psychology* 18:571-578.
1971b Effects of warmth of interaction, accuracy of understanding, and the proposal of compromises on listener's behavior. *Journal of Counseling Psychology* 18:207-216.

Keyton, J., and J. Springston
1990 Redefining cohesiveness in groups. *Small Group Research* 21:234-254.

King, D.A., and K. Heller
1984 Depression and the response of others: A re-evaluation. *Journal of Abnormal Psychology* 93:477-480.

Klein, A.L.
1976 Changes in leadership appraisal as a function of the stress of a simulated panic situation. *Journal of Personality and Social Psychology* 34:1143-1154.

Krebs, D.
1975 Empathy and altruism. *Journal of Personality and Social Psychology* 32:1134-1146.

Kugihara, N., J. Misumi, and S. Sato
1980 Experimental study of escape behavior in a simulated panic situation: I. *Japanese Journal of Experimental Social Psychology* 20:55-67.

Kuykendall, D., and J.P. Keating
1990 Mood and persuasion: Evidence for the differential influence of positive and negative states. *Psychology and Marketing* 7:1-9.

Lazarus, R.S.
1982 Thoughts on the relations between emotion and cognition. *American Psychologist* 37:1019-1024.
1984 On the primacy of cognition. *American Psychologist* 39:124-129.

Lazarus, R.S., and C.A. Smith
1988 Knowledge and appraisal in the cognition-emotion relationship. *Cognition and Emotion* 2:281-300.

Le Bon, G.
1920/ *The Crowd, A Study of the Popular Mind*, 2nd ed. Atlanta, Georgia: Cherokee
1982 Publishing.
Lerner, M.J.
1980 *The Belief in a Just World: A Fundamental Delusion*. New York: Plenum Press.
Lindahl, M.B.
1977 Emotion and cognition in vicarious instigation research. *Scandinavian Journal of Psychology* 18:85-91.
Mackie, D.M., and L.T. Worth
1989 Processing deficits and the mediation of positive affect in persuasion. *Journal of Personality and Social Psychology* 57:27-40.
Marks, T., and C.L. Hammen
1982 Interpersonal mood induction: Situational and individual determinants. *Motivation and Emotion* 6:387-399.
Markus, H.R., and S. Kitayama
1991 Culture and the self: Implications for cognition, emotion, and motivation. *Psychological Review* 98:224-253.
McCosh, J.
1880 *The Emotions*. New York: Charles Scribner's Sons.
McDougall, W.
1908 *An Introduction to Social Psychology*. Boston, Mass.: Luce.
McNiel, D.E., H.S. Arkowitz, and B.E. Pritchard
1987 The response of others to face-to-face interaction with depressed patients. *Journal of Abnormal Psychology* 96:341-344.
Mesquita, B., and N.H. Frijda
1992 Cultural variations in emotions: A review. *Psychological Bulletin* 112:179-204.
Miller, R.E., J.V. Murphy, and I.A. Mirsky
1959 Non-verbal communication of affect. *Journal of Clinical Psychology* 15:155-158.
Miller, R.S.
1987 Empathetic embarrassment: Situational and personal determinants of reactions to the embarrassment of another. *Journal of Personality and Social Psychology* 53:1061-1069.
Mirsky, I.A., R.E. Miller, and J.V. Murphy
1958 The communication of affect in rhesus monkeys: 1. An experimental method. *American Psychoanalytic Association Journal* 6:433-441.
Mudrack, P.E.
1989 Group cohesiveness and productivity: A closer look. *Human Relations* 42:771-785.
Paddock, J.R., and S. Nowicki, Jr.
1986 Paralanguage and the interpersonal impact of dysphoria: It's not what you say but how you say it. *Social Behavior and Personality* 14:29-44.
Pallak, S.R., E. Murroni, and J. Koch
1983 Communicator attractiveness and expertise, emotional versus rational appeals, and persuasion: A heuristic versus systematic processing interpretation. *Social Cognition* 2:122-141.
Petty, R.E., and J.T. Cacioppo
1986 *Communication and Persuasion*. New York: Springer-Verlag.
Pruitt, D.G.
1981 *Negotiation Behavior*. New York: Academic Press.
Pruitt, D.G., and J.Z. Rubin
1985 *Social Conflict: Escalation, Stalemate, and Settlement*. New York: Random House.
Radenhausen, R.A., and J.M. Anker
1988 Effects of depressed mood induction on reasoning performance. *Perceptual and Motor Skills* 66:855-860.

Roark, A.E., and H.S. Sharah
1989   Factors related to group cohesiveness. *Small Group Behavior* 20:62-69.
Roseman, I.J.
1984   Cognitive determinants of emotion: A structural theory. In P. Shaver, ed., *Review of Personality and Social Psychology, 5: Emotions, Relationships, and Health.* Beverly Hills, Calif.: Sage Publications.
Roskos-Ewoldsen, D. R., and R.H. Fazio
1992   The accessibility of source likability as a determinant of persuasion. *Personality and Social Psychology Bulletin* 18:19-25.
Saavedra, R., and P.C. Earley
1991   Choice of task and goal under conditions of general and specific affective inducement. *Motivation and Emotion* 15:45-65.
Sagi, A., and M.L. Hoffman
1976   Empathic distress in the newborn. *Developmental Psychology* 12:175-176.
Sako, H., and J. Misumi
1982   An experimental study of the effects of perceived likelihood of successful escape on escape behavior in a simulated panic situation. *Japanese Journal of Experimental Social Psychology* 21:141-148.
Schwarz, N., H. Bless, and G. Bohner
1991   Mood and persuasion: Affective states influence the processing of persuasive communications. *Advances in Experimental Social Psychology* 24:161-199.
Simner, M.L.
1971   Newborn's response to the cry of another infant. *Developmental Psychology* 5:136-150.
Slife, B.D., and C.A. Weaver
1992   Depression, cognitive skill, and metacognitive skill in problem solving. *Cognition and Emotion* 6:1-22.
Small, G.W., M.W. Propper, E.T. Randolph, and S. Eth
1991   Mass hysteria among student performers: Social relationship as a symptom predictor. *American Journal of Psychiatry* 148:1200-1205.
Smith, C.A., and P.C. Ellsworth
1985   Patterns of cognitive appraisal in emotion. *Journal of Personality and Social Psychology* 48:813-838.
Spink, K.S.
1990   Group cohesion and collective efficacy of volleyball teams. *Journal of Sport and Exercise Psychology* 12:301-311.
Stahl, S.M., and M. Lebedun
1974   Mystery gas: An analysis of mass hysteria. *Journal of Health and Social Behavior* 15:44-50.
Stephens, R.S., J.E. Hokanson, and R. Welker
1987   Responses to depressed interpersonal behavior: Mixed reactions in a helping role. *Journal of Personality and Social Psychology* 52:1274-1282.
Stotland, E.
1969   Exploratory investigations of empathy. In L. Berkowitz, ed., *Advances in Experimental Social Psychology*, Vol. 4. New York: Academic Press.
Strack, S., and J.C. Coyne
1983   Social confirmation of dysphoria: Shared and private reactions to depression. *Journal of Personality and Social Psychology* 44:798-806.
Vaughan, K.B., and J.T. Lanzetta
1980   Vicarious instigation and conditioning facial expressive and autonomic responses to a model's expressive display of pain. *Journal of Personality and Social Psychology* 38:909-923.

1981   The effect of modification of expressive displays on vicarious emotional arousal. *Journal of Experimental Social Psychology* 17:16-30.
Williams, J.M., and W.N. Widmeyer
1991   The cohesion-performance outcome relationship in a coacting sport. *Journal of Sport and Exercise Psychology* 13:364-371.
Winer, D.L, T.O. Bonner, P.H. Blaney, and E.J. Murray
1981   Depression and social attraction. *Motivation and Emotion* 5:153-166.
Wispé, L.
1986   The distinction between sympathy and empathy: To call forth a concept, a word is needed. *Journal of Personality and Social Psychology* 50:314-321.
Wolff, K.C., and R.J. Gregory
1991   The effects of a temporary dysphoric mood upon selected WAIS–R subtests. *Journal of Psychoeducational Assessment* 9:340-344.
Wong, S.W., B. Kwong, Y.K. Tam, and M.M. Tsaoi
1982   Psychological epidemic in Hong Kong: I. Epidemiological study. *Acta Psychiatrica Scandinavica* 65:421-436.
Worth, L.T., and D.M. Mackie
1987   Cognitive mediation of positive affect in persuasion. *Social Cognition* 5:76-94.
Zaccaro, S.J., and C. Lowe
1988   Cohesiveness and performance on an additive task: Evidence for multidimensionality. *Journal of Social Psychology* 128:547-558.
Zaccaro, S.J., and M.C. McCoy
1988   The effects of task and interpersonal cohesiveness on performance of a disjunctive group task. *Journal of Applied Social Psychology* 18:837-851.
Zajonc, R.B.
1965   Social facilitation. *Science* 149:269-274.
1968   Cognitive theories in social psychology. Pp. 319-411 in G. Lindzey and E. Aronson, eds., *The Handbook of Social Psychology*. Reading, Mass.: Addison-Wesley.
1983   Discussion of Abelson's talk on Cartwright's founders' day. *Personality and Social Psychology Bulletin* 9:55-59.
Zillmann, D., and J.R. Cantor
1977   Affective responses to the emotions of a protagonist. *Journal of Experimental Social Psychology* 13:155-165.

CHAPTER 11

Anderson, M.C., and R.A. Bjork
in   Mechanisms of inhibition in long-term memory: A new taxonomy. In D. Dagenbach
press   and T. Carr, eds., *Processes in Attention, Memory, and Language*. New York: Academic Press.
Arrick, M.C., J.R. Voss, and D.C. Rimm
1981   The relative efficacy of thought stopping and covert assertion. *Behavior Research and Therapy* 19:17-24.
Bargh, J.A., and M.E. Tota
1988   Context-dependent automatic processing in depression: Accessibility of automatic constructs with regard to self but not others. *Journal of Personality and Social Psychology* 54:925-939.
Barlow, D.
1988   *Anxiety and Its Disorders*. New York: Guilford Press.
Basden, B.H., D.R. Basden, and G.J. Gorgano
in   Directed forgetting in implicit and explicit memory tests: A comparison of meth-
press   ods. *Journal of Experimental Psychology: Learning, Memory, and Cognition*.

Beck, J.T., and S.R. Strong
1982 Stimulating therapeutic change with interpretations: A comparison of positive and negative connotation. *Journal of Counseling Psychology* 29:551-559.

Bjork, E.L., R.A. Bjork, and H.A. Kilpatrick
1990 Direct and Indirect Measures of Inhibition in Directed Forgetting. Paper presented at the meeting of the Psychonomic Society, New Orleans.

Bjork, R.A.
1970 Positive forgetting: The noninterference of items intentionally forgotten. *Journal of Verbal Learning and Verbal Behavior* 9:255-268.

1989 Retrieval inhibition as an adaptive mechanism in human memory. Pp. 309-330 in H.L. Roediger and F.I.M. Craik, eds., *Varieties of Memory and Consciousness: Essays in Honor of Endel Tulving*. Hillsdale, N.J.: Lawrence Erlbaum.

Bjork, R.A., and T.K. Landauer
1979 On keeping track of the present status of people and things. Pp. 52-60 in M.M. Gruneberg, P.E. Morris, and R.N. Sykes, eds., *Practical Aspects of Memory*. London: Academic Press.

Borkovec, T.D., L. Wilkinson, R. Folensbee, and C. Lerman
1983 Stimulus control applications to the treatment of worry. *Behaviour Research and Therapy* 21:247-251.

Bower, G.H., and J.D. Mayer
1985 Failure to replicate mood-dependent retrieval. *Bulletin of the Psychonomic Society* 23(1):39-42.

Cioffi, D., and J. Holloway
1993 The delayed costs of suppressed pain. *Journal of Personality and Social Psychology* 64:274-282.

Clark, D.M., S. Ball, and D. Pape
1991 An experimental investigation of thought suppression. *Behavior Research and Therapy* 29:253-257.

Cohen, S., E. Lichtenstein, J.O. Prochaska, J.S. Rossi, et al.
1989 Debunking myths about self-quitting: Evidence from 10 prospective studies of persons who attempt to quit smoking by themselves. *American Psychologist* 44:1355-1365.

Cohen, S.I., A.J. Silverman, and N.R. Burch
1956 A technique for the assessment of affect change. *Journal of Nervous and Mental Disease* 124:352-360.

Conway, M., A. Howell, and C. Giannopolous
1991 Dysphoria and thought suppression. *Cognitive Therapy and Research* 15:153-166.

Coyne, J.C.
1989 Employing therapeutic paradox in the treatment of depression. Pp. 163-183 in L.M. Ascher, ed., *Therapeutic Paradox*. New York: Guilford.

Edwards, S., and M. Dickerson
1987 Intrusive unwanted thoughts: A two-stage model of control. *British Journal of Medical Psychology* 60:317-328.

Elms, D.G., C. Adams, and H.L. Roediger
1970 Cued forgetting in short-term memory: Response selection. *Journal of Experimental Psychology* 86:103-107.

Feldman, D.A., S.R. Strong, and D.B. Danser
1982 A comparison of paradoxical and nonparadoxical interpretations and directives. *Journal of Counseling Psychology* 29:572-579.

Foa, E.B., and M.J. Kozak
1986 Emotional processing of fear: Exposure to corrective information. *Psychological Bulletin* 99:20-35.

Freud, S.
   1915/   Repression. In J. Strachey ed., *The Standard Edition of the* Complete Psychological
   1957   Works of Sigmund Freud 14:146-158. London: Hogarth.
   1914/   Remembering, repeating, and working-through. In J. Strachey, ed., *The Standard*
   1958   *Edition of the Complete Psychological Works of Sigmund Freud* 12:145-150. Lon-
           don: Hogarth.
Geen, R.G., and M.B. Quanty
   1977   The catharsis of aggression: An evaluation of a hypothesis. Pp. 1-37 in L. Berkowitz,
           ed., *Advances in Experimental Social Psychology*, Vol. 10. New York: Academic
           Press.
Geiselman, R.E., and B. Bagheri
   1985   Repetition effects in directed forgetting: Evidence for retrieval inhibition. *Memory*
           and Cognition 13:57-62.
Geiselman, R.E., R.A. Bjork, and D. Fishman
   1983   Disrupted retrieval in directed forgetting: A link with posthypnotic amnesia. *Jour-*
           nal of Experimental Psychology: General 112:58-72.
Gelfand, H., and R.A. Bjork
   1985   On the Locus of Retrieval Inhibition in Directed Forgetting. Paper presented at the
           meeting of the Psychonomic Society, Boston, Mass.
Gernsbacher, M.A., and M.E. Faust
   1991   The mechanism of suppression: A component of general comprehension skill. *Journal*
           of Experimental Psychology: Learning, Memory, and Cognition 17:245-262.
Gotlib, I.H., and C.D. McCann
   1984   Construct accessibility and depression: An examination of cognitive and affective
           factors. *Journal of Personality and Social Psychology* 47:427-439.
Herman, C.P., and J. Polivy
   1993   Mental control of eating: Excitatory and inhibitory food thoughts. Pp. 491-505 in
           D.M. Wegner and J.W. Pennebaker, eds., *Handbook of Mental Control*. Englewood
           Cliffs, N.J.: Prentice-Hall.
Higgins, E.T., and G. King
   1981   Accessibility of social constructs: Information-processing consequences of indi-
           vidual and contextual variability. Pp. 69-121 in N. Cantor and J.F. Kihlstrom, eds.,
           Personality, Cognition, and Social Interaction. Hillsdale, N.J.: Lawrence Erlbaum.
Kelly, A.E., and J.H. Kahn
   in   Effects of suppression of personal intrusive thoughts. *Journal of Personality and*
   press   *Social Psychology*.
Koriat, A., R. Melkman, J.A. Averill, and R.S. Lazarus
   1972   The self-control of emotional reactions to a stressful film. *Journal of Personality*
           40:601-619.
Lavy, E.H., and M.A. van den Hout
   1990   Thought suppression induces intrusions. *Behavioral Psychotherapy* 18:251-258.
Martin, B.
   1964   Expression and inhibition of sex motive arousal in college males. *Journal of Abnor-*
           mal and Social Psychology 68:307-312.
Meyer, V.
   1966   Modifications of expectations in cases with obsessional rituals. *Behavior Research*
           and Therapy 4:273-280.
Merkelbach, H., P. Muris, M.A. van den Hout, and P. de Jong
   1991   Rebound effects of thought suppression: Instruction-dependent? *Behavioral Psy-*
           chotherapy 19:225-238.
Miller, W.R., and R.K. Hester
   1986   Inpatient alcoholism treatment: Who benefits? *American Psychologist* 41:794-805.

Mischel, W., and N. Baker
    1975   Cognitive appraisals and transformations in delay behavior. *Journal of Personality and Social Psychology* 31:254-261.
Mullen, B., and J. Suls
    1982   The effectiveness of attention and rejection as coping styles: A meta-analysis of temporal differences. *Journal of Psychosomatic Research* 26:43-49.
Neziroglu, F., and J. Neuman
    1990   Three treatment approaches for obsessions. *Journal of Cognitive Psychotherapy* 4:377-392.
Nolen-Hoeksema, S.
    1993   Sex differences in control of depression. Pp. 306-324 in D.M. Wegner and J.W. Pennebaker, eds., *Handbook of Mental Control*. Englewood Cliffs, N.J.: Prentice-Hall.
Paller, K.A.
    1990   Recall and stem completion priming have different electrophysiological correlates and are modified differentially by directed forgetting. *Journal of Experimental Psychology: Learning, Memory, and Cognition* 16:1021-1032.
Pennebaker, J.W.
    1990   *Opening Up: The Healing Power of Confiding in Others*. New York: Morrow.
    1993   Social mechanisms of constraint. Pp. 200-219 in D.M. Wegner and J.W. Pennebaker, eds., *Handbook of Mental Control*. Englewood Cliffs, N.J.: Prentice-Hall.
Pennebaker, J.W., and S.K. Beall
    1986   Confronting a traumatic event: Toward an understanding of inhibition and disease. *Journal of Abnormal Psychology* 95:274-281.
Pennebaker, J.W., and C.H. Chew
    1985   Behavioral inhibition and electrodermal activity during deception. *Journal of Personality and Social Psychology* 49:1427-1433.
Pennebaker, J.W., and R. O'Heeron
    1984   Confiding in others and illness rates among spouses of suicide and accidental death victims. *Journal of Abnormal Psychology* 93:473-476.
Pennebaker, J.W., J.K. Kiecolt-Glaser, and R. Glaser
    1988   Disclosure of traumas and immune function: Health implications for psychotherapy. *Journal of Consulting and Clinical Psychology* 56:239-245.
Pennebaker, J.W., M. Colder, and L.K. Sharp
    1990   Accelerating the coping process. *Journal of Personality and Social Psychology* 58:528-537.
Polich, J.M., D.J. Armour, and H.B. Braiker
    1981   *The Course of Alcoholism*. New York: Wiley.
Rachman, S.
    1980   Emotional processing. *Behavior Research and Therapy* 18:51-60.
Rachman, S., and P. de Silva
    1978   Abnormal and normal obsessions. *Behavior Research and Therapy* 16:233-248.
Rachman, S.J., and R.J. Hodgson
    1980   *Obsessions and Compulsions*. Englewood Cliffs, N.J.: Prentice-Hall.
Reed, G.F.
    1985   *Obsessional Experience and Compulsive Behavior*. Orlando, Fla.: Academic Press.
Roemer, L., and T.D. Borkovec
    in   The effects of suppressing thoughts about emotional material. *Journal of Abnormal*
    press   *Psychology*.
    1993   Worry: Unwanted cognitive activity that controls unwanted somatic experience. Pp. 220-238 in D.M. Wegner and J.W. Pennebaker, eds., *Handbook of Mental Control*. Englewood Cliffs, N.J.: Prentice-Hall.

Rosen, G.M., and H. Orenstein
  1976 A historical note on thought stopping. *Journal of Consulting and Clinical Psychology* 44:1016-1017.
Ross, D.M.
  1984 Thought stopping: A coping strategy for impending feared events. *Issues in Comprehensive Pediatric Nursing* 7:83-89.
Salkovskis, P.M., and J. Harrison
  1984 Abnormal and normal obsessions: A replication. *Behavior Research and Therapy* 22:549-552.
Seligman, M.E.P.
  1990 *Learned Optimism: How to Change Your Mind and Your Life*. New York: Pocket Books.
Starker, S.
  1989 *Oracle at the Supermarket: The American Preoccupation with Self-Help Books*. New Brunswick, N.J.: Transactions.
Stauffer, C.L., and F. Petee
  1988 *Fly Without Fear*. New York: Dodd, Mead and Co.
Stern, R.S.
  1978 Obsessive thoughts: The problem of therapy. *British Journal of Psychiatry* 133:200-205.
Stern, R.S., M.S Lipsedge, and I.M. Marks
  1973 Obsessive ruminations: A controlled trial of thought-stopping technique. *Behavior Research and Therapy* 11:659-662.
Suls, J., and B. Fletcher
  1985 The relative efficacy of avoidant and nonavoidant coping strategies: A meta-analysis. *Health Psychology* 4:249-288.
Teasdale, J.D., and V. Rezin
  1978 Effects of thought stopping on thoughts, mood, and corrugator EMG in depressed patients. *Behavior Research and Therapy* 16:97-102.
Tipper, S.P., B. Weaver, S. Cameron, J.C. Brehaut, and J. Bastedo
  1991 Inhibitory mechanisms of attention in identification and localization tasks: Time course and disruption. *Journal of Experimental Psychology: Learning, Memory, and Cognition* 17:681-692.
Tryon, G.S.
  1979 A review and critique of thought stopping research. *Journal of Behavior Therapy and Experimental Psychiatry* 10:189-192.
Watts, F.N., F.P. McKenna, R. Sharrock, and L. Trezise
  1986 Colour-naming of phobia-related words. *British Journal of Psychology* 77:97-108.
Wegner, D.M., and R. Erber
  1992 The hyperaccessibility of suppressed thoughts. *Journal of Personality and Social Psychology* 63:903-912.
Wegner, D.M., and D.B. Gold
  1993 Fanning Old Flames: Arousing Romantic Obsession Through Thought Suppression. Unpublished manuscript, Department of Psychology, University of Virginia.
Wegner, D.M., and D.J. Schneider
  1989 Mental control: The war of the ghosts in the machine. Pp. 287-305 in J. Uleman and J. Bargh, eds., *Unintended Thought*. New York: Guilford Press.
Wegner, D.M., and S. Zanakos
  in   Chronic thought suppression. *Journal of Personality*.
  press
Wegner, D.M., D.J. Schneider, S. Carter, and T. White
  1987 Paradoxical effects of thought suppression. *Journal of Personality and Social Psychology* 53:5-13.

Wegner, D.M., J.W. Shortt, A.W. Blake, and M.S. Page
    1990   The suppression of exciting thoughts. *Journal of Personality and Social Psychology* 58:409-418.
Wegner, D.M., D.J. Schneider, B. Knutson, and S.R. McMahon
    1991   Polluting the stream of consciousness: The effect of thought suppression on the mind's environment. *Cognitive Therapy and Research* 15:141-152.
Wegner, D.M., J.D. Lane, and S. Dimitri
    in   The allure of secret relationships. *Journal of Personality and Social Psychology.*
    press
Wenzlaff, R.M.
    1993   The mental control of depression: Psychological obstacles to emotional wellbeing. Pp. 239-257 in D.M. Wegner and J.W. Pennebaker, eds., *Handbook of Mental Control.* Englewood Cliffs, N.J.: Prentice-Hall.
Wenzlaff, R.M., D.M. Wegner, and D. Roper
    1988   Depression and mental control: The resurgence of unwanted negative thoughts. *Journal of Personality and Social Psychology* 55:882-892.
Wenzlaff, R.M., D.M. Wegner, and S.B. Klein
    1991   The role of thought suppression in the bonding of thought and mood. *Journal of Personality and Social Psychology* 60:500-508.
Wolpe, J., and A.A. Lazarus
    1966   *Behavior Therapy Techniques.* New York: Pergamon Press.
Zillmann, D.
    1993   Mental control of angry aggression. Pp. 370-392 in D.M. Wegner and J.W. Pennebaker, eds., *Handbook of Mental Control.* Englewood Cliffs, N.J.: Prentice-Hall.

EPILOGUE

Druckman, D., and R. Bjork, eds.
    1991   *In the Mind's Eye: Enhancing Human Performance.* Committee on Techniques for the Enhancement of Human Performance, National Research Council. Washington, D.C.: National Academy Press.
Druckman, D., and J. Swets, eds.
    1988   *Enhancing Human Performance: Issues, Theories, and Techniques.* Committee on Techniques for the Enhancement of Human Performance, National Research Council. Washington, D.C.: National Academy Press.
Fiske, E.
    1990   How to learn in college: Little groups, many tests. *The New York Times* March 5:1.
Ericsson, K.A., R.T. Krampe, and C. Tesch-Romer
    1993   The role of deliberate practice in the acquisition of expert performance. *Psychological Review* 100:363-406.
Myers, I.B., and M.H. McCaulley
    1985   *Manual: A Guide to the Development and Use of the Myers-Briggs Type Indicator.* Palo Alto, Calif.: Consulting Psychologists Press.

APPENDICES

A

Committee Activities

In order to cover the variety of topics of its charge, the committee undertook many activities in addition to full committee meetings—including site visits to relevant field settings and laboratories, detailed briefings by experts, and reviews of relevant literature.

The committee met four times during 1991-1993, twice at the National Research Council facilities in Washington, D.C., once at the Beckman Center in Irvine, California, and once at the Army's National Training Center (NTC) at Fort Irwin, California. The NTC meeting included briefings, discussions, and demonstrations of training procedures used to prepare soldiers for combat missions. The meetings and site visits included presentations by the following experts:

James Banks, research psychologist, Army Research Institute, Presidio of Monterey Field Unit

Barbara Black, chief, Army Research Institute Field Unit, Fort Knox, Kentucky

John Seely Brown, Vice President for Advanced Research, Xerox, Palo Alto Research Center

Brigadier General William G. Carter, II, Commanding Officer, National Training Center

Neil Cosby, manager, Institute for Defense Analysis Simulation Center

Gerald C. Davison, professor of psychology, University of Southern California

Michael Drillings, research psychologist, Army Research Institute

James Greeno, research scientist, Xerox Palo Alto Research Center

Captain Grimsley, National Training Center

Jack Hiller, director, Training Systems Research Division, Army Research Institute

Nels Klyver, Los Angeles Police Academy

Major Milton Koger, research psychologist, Army Research Institute

George Lawton, research psychologist, Army Research Institute

Major Robert D. Leitzel, National Training Center

Staff Sergeant Marconi, Fort Knox, Kentucky

Colonel Pat O'Neal, National Training Center

Zita Simutos, director, Manpower and Personnel Research Division, Army Research Institute

Robert Sulzen, research psychologist, Army Research Institute

Most of the rest of the committee's work was carried out through subcommittees on specific topics. Our subcommittee organization tracks almost directly to the chapter organization of this report, and members wrote the drafts of chapters. In one case, the work of a subcommittee (team building and team training) resulted in two chapters.

The Effect of Context on Training

Lynne M. Reder and Roberta Klatzky constituted this subcommittee, and Gen. Paul F. Gorman (ret.) of Cardinal Point, Inc. provided advice. It carried out site visits to the Federal Aviation Administration Academy in Oklahoma (April 1992) and to Xerox Palo Alto Research Center in California (November 1992), where John Seely Brown and James Greeno briefed the subcommittee. Site visits were also made to the Los Angeles Police Academy (December 1992) and to the Institute for Defense Analysis, Alexandria, Virginia (April 1993).

Illusions of Comprehension

Larry L. Jacoby and Robert A. Bjork constituted this subcommittee, which was advised by Colleen M. Kelley, of Macalester College. The subcommittee visited the Institute of Defense Analysis in Alexandria, Virginia, in April, 1993.

Cooperative Learning

Donald F. Dansereau and David W. Johnson constituted this subcommittee. It carried out a site visit to the Federal Aviation Administration Academy in Oklahoma (April 1992).

Team Building and Team Training

David W. Johnson and Daniel Druckman constituted this subcommittee. It carried out site visits to the Federal Aviation Administration Academy in

Oklahoma (April 1992) and to the Sillin Nuclear Energy Center in Connecticut (October 1992). The subcommittee was briefed by Gary Shirts, president of Simulation Training Systems and David Crookall, editor of *Simulation & Gaming*. It also benefited from discussions with Nancy Dixon of George Washington University.

Self-Confidence and Performance

Deborah L. Feltz constituted this subcommittee. Research assistance was provided by Brenda A. Riemer of Michigan State University, and Bernard Weiner, professor of psychology at the University of California at Los Angeles provided advice.

Altered States of Consciousness

John F. Kihlstrom and Eric Eich constituted this subcommittee. It carried out site visits to Illusions Engineering in Westlake, California (June 1992 and October 1992), and to Fort Knox, Kentucky (April 1992). The subcommittee was briefed by Peter Suedfeld, professor of psychology at the University of British Columbia. Its review of the transcendental meditation literature was aided by material supplied by David Orme-Johnson and his colleagues at the Maharishi International University in Fairfield, Iowa.

Socially Induced Affect

Daniel Druckman and Robert B. Zajonc constituted this subcommittee, which benefited from consultant Daniel McIntosh of the University of Denver. Daniel McIntosh prepared a review paper for the subcommittee, "Enhancement of Performance Through Socially Induced Affect."

Mental-Control Strategies

Daniel M. Wegner, Eric Eich, and Robert A. Bjork constituted this subcommittee.

Organizational Cultures and Performance

Robert A. Bjork chaired this subcommittee with the collaboration of Daniel Druckman and David W. Johnson. It made a site visit to the Sillin Nuclear Energy Center in Connecticut (October 1992), where it was briefed by Michael Brown, Director of Nuclear Training, and a site visit to the Los Angeles Police Academy in California (December 1992) where it was briefed by Nels Klyver.

B

Biographical Sketches

In the interest of brevity, publications are not included in these sketches.

ROBERT A. BJORK is professor of psychology at the University of California, Los Angeles (UCLA). He earlier served as professor at the University of Michigan and has held visiting appointments at The Rockefeller University; the University of California, San Diego; Bell Laboratories; and Dartmouth College. His research interests focus on how information is encoded and accessed in human memory and on the implications of that research for training and instruction. He was awarded UCLA's Distinguished Teaching Award and has chaired the Committee on Intercollegiate Athletics at UCLA. He is a fellow of the Society of Experimental Psychological Association and the American Psychological Society. He is the appointed editor of *Psychological Review* (1995-2000) and served earlier as editor of *Memory and Cognition* (1981-1985). He holds a Ph.D. degree in mathematical psychology from Stanford University.

DONALD F. DANSEREAU is professor of psychology and research scientist at the Institute of Behavioral Research at Texas Christian University. His research interests in the area of applied cognition focus on techniques for improving communication, learning, and performance. His specific research topics include cooperative learning among peers and node-link maps as alternatives to standard texts, and he has served as principal investigator in 13 federally funded research projects. He is a recipient of the chancellor's Award for Research and Creativity at Texas Christian University. He holds a Ph.D. degree in psychology from Carnegie-Mellon University.

383

DANIEL DRUCKMAN is study director at the National Research Council and adjunct professor of conflict management at George Mason University. Previously, he held senior positions at Mathematica, Inc., and Booz, Allen, and Hamilton and was a research scholar at the International Institute of Applied Systems Analysis in Laxenburg, Austria. He has also been a consultant to the U.S. Foreign Service Institute, the U.S. Arms Control and Disarmament Agency, and the U.S. Institute of Peace. His research interests focus on factors that influence negotiating behavior, and on ways to improve the negotiation process through situation design and training. He currently serves on the editorial boards of the *Journal of Conflict Resolution*, the *Negotiation Journal*, and the *Journal of Applied Social Psychology* and is an associate editor of *Simulation & Gaming*. He holds a Ph.D. degree in social psychology from Northwestern University.

ERIC EICH is associate professor of psychology at the University of British Columbia. He previously served as director of the Behavioral Sciences Laboratory at the University of California, Irvine, and held a visiting appointment in the departments of psychology and anesthesiology at University of California, Los Angeles. His research centers on the state-dependent effects of drugs, emotions, and environments on learning and remembering and is supported by grants from the (U.S.) National Institute of Mental Health and the (Canadian) Natural Sciences and Engineering Research Council (NSERC). He is the recipient of an NSERC University Research Fellowship, a Killam Memorial Fellowship, and the Knox Master Teacher Award. He is a member of the American Psychological Society and currently serves on the editorial board of *Memory and Cognition*. He holds a Ph.D. degree in cognitive psychology from the University of Toronto.

DEBORAH L. FELTZ is professor and chair of physical education and exercise science at Michigan State University (MSU). Her research interests have centered on the interrelationships among self-confidence, anxiety, and sport performance. She has earned early career distinguished scholar awards from the American Alliance of Health, Physical Education, Recreation, and Dance and the North American Society for the Psychology of Sport and Physical Activity, and she has received a distinguished faculty award from MSU. She is a fellow of the American Academy of Kinesiology and Physical Education and the American Psychological Association. She served on the sport psychology advisory committee to the U.S. Olympic Committee (1989-1992) and currently serves on the editorial board of the *Journal of Sport and Exercise Psychology*. She holds a Ph.D. degree in sport psychology from Pennsylvania State University.

LARRY L. JACOBY is a professor of psychology at McMaster University. He earlier served as a professor at the University of Utah. His research interests focus on how information is stored and retrieved from human memory and on the distinction between automatic and consciously controlled processes. He currently serves on the editorial boards of the *Journal of Memory and Language* and the *Journal of Experimental Psychology: Learning, Memory and Cognition.* He holds a Ph.D. degree in memory from Southern Illinois University.

DAVID W. JOHNSON is professor of educational psychology at the University of Minnesota. His research interests focus on cooperation and competition, conflict resolution, team effectiveness, organizational change, experiential learning, relationships among diverse team members, and the implications of that research for training and instruction. He has received awards for outstanding research from the American Personnel and Guidance Association, the Society for the Psychological Study of Social Issues (Gordon Allport Award), the Association for Specialists in Group Work (Division of American Association for Counseling and Development), the American Society for Engineering Education, and the National Council for Social Studies. He has received the Award for Outstanding Contribution to American Education from the Minnesota Association for Supervision and Curriculum Development. He is a fellow of the American Psychological Association. He holds an Ed.D. degree in psychology from Columbia University.

JOHN F. KIHLSTROM is professor of psychology at the University of Arizona. He previously held positions at Harvard University and the University of Wisconsin and has held visiting appointments at Stanford University, the University of Michigan, and Macquarie University in Australia. His research interests focus on cognition in a personal and social context with a special emphasis on the relations between conscious and nonconscious mental life. In 1979, he received the American Psychological Association's Distinguished Scientific Award for an Early Career Contribution to Psychology; he has also received numerous awards for his contributions to hypnosis research. He is a fellow of the American Psychological Association and the American Psychological Society. He has chaired grant review panels at the National Institute of Mental Health and is editor-elect of *Psychological Science* (1994-1999). He holds a Ph.D. degree in personality and experimental psychopathology from the University of Pennsylvania.

ROBERTA L. KLATSKY is professor and head of the Department of Psychology at Carnegie-Mellon University. She was previously a professor at the University of California, Santa Barbara, and she has held visiting appointments at Stanford University and the Instituto Tecnologico y de

Estudios Superiores de Monterrey, Mexico. Her research is concerned with perception through touch and locomotion and with motor planning and performance. She has studied how people's abilities to perceive through non-visual modalities and plan action change with training. She has served as chair of the American Psychological Association's Committee on Scientific Awards, and she currently serves on the National Research Council's Committee on Human Factors and the governing board of the Psychonomic Society. She is a fellow of the American Psychological Association and the American Psychological Society. She holds a Ph.D. degree in cognitive psychology from Stanford University.

LYNNE M. REDER is a professor of psychology at Carnegie-Mellon University. Her research interests include developing a unified model of memory and understanding the use of strategies and metacognitive judgments for information retrieval, and she has also been concerned with developing instructional materials to maximize retention and retrieval. Reder has served on the editorial boards of *Memory and Cognition*, and *Journal of Experimental Psychology: Human, Learning and Memory*. She holds a Ph.D. degree in experimental psychology from the University of Michigan.

DANIEL M. WEGNER is professor of psychology at the University of Virginia. He earlier served as a professor at Trinity University in San Antonio, Texas, and has held a visiting appointment at the University of Texas at Austin. His research interests focus on the role of thought in the self-control of thought, emotion, and action. He currently serves on editorial boards for the *Journal of Personality and Social Psychology, Social Cognition,* and *Basic and Applied Social Psychology*. He holds a Ph.D. degree in social psychology from Michigan State University.

ROBERT B. ZAJONC is Charles Horton Cooley professor of psychology and director of the Institute for Social Research at the University of Michigan, Ann Arbor. He has held visiting professorships at the University of Amsterdam, Oxford University, Stanford University, and the Maison des Sciences de l'Homme in Paris. His research interests focus on the basic processes involved in social behavior and most recently with the interface between cognition and emotion. He is a recipient of the Distinguished Scientific Contribution Award of the American Psychological Association, and he is a fellow of the American Academy of Arts and Sciences. He currently serves as chair of the Executive Board of the Social Science Research Council. He holds a Ph.D. degree in social psychology from the University of Michigan and honorary degrees from the University of Louvain and the University of Warsaw.

Index

A

Abstract instruction, 11, 26, 33, 34, 36-39, 56
Accountability, 16, 141, 144, 156-157, 165, 166, 168
ACT (Adoptive Control of Thought) model, 28-29
Affective processes. *See* Mental and emotional states; Socially induced affect
Age regression, 226-227
Algorithmic transfer, 30-31, 37
Altered states of consciousness, 8, 17-19, 207-208, 246
    see also Hypnosis; Restricted environmental stimulation; Sleep learning; Transcendental meditation
Amnesia, 74-75
    posthypnotic, 209, 212
Analogical transfer, 29, 32, 43
    based on irrelevant or ambiguous detail, 61-62
Anchored instruction, 39
Anesthesia, hypnotic, 18, 210-214, 247
Animal magnetism, 209, 210
Anxiety
    and self-confidence, 17, 201-203
and socially induced affect, 275
and thought suppression and confrontation, 20, 278, 290, 293
and transcendental meditation, 18, 234-235
Apprenticeship, 33, 35, 39
Attention, and socially induced affect, 267-268
Attributional processes, 7, 68
    and self-confidence, 17, 179, 182, 191
    and team confidence, 185-186
Automatic processing, 48-49
Auxiliary thought suppression, 277, 293n

B

Bargaining. *See* Negotiation and bargaining
Basic skills and training, 35
Behavioral patterns
    modeling of in team training, 152
    and self-confidence, 180-181
Bodily expressions. *See* Facial expressions; Nonverbal expressions